Soft Matter

SRLT

NORTHWESTERN UNIVERSITY PRESS

Studies in Russian Literature and Theory

SERIES EDITORS

Caryl Emerson

Gary Saul Morson

William Mills Todd III

Andrew Wachtel

Justin Weir

Soft Matter

The Poetics of Weakness
in Late Soviet Socialism

Julia Vaingurt

NORTHWESTERN UNIVERSITY PRESS / EVANSTON, ILLINOIS

Northwestern University Press
www.nupress.northwestern.edu

Copyright © 2025 by Northwestern University. Published 2025 Northwestern
University Press. All rights reserved.

Printed in the United States of America

10 9 8 7 6 5 4 3 2 1

Library of Congress Cataloging-in-Publication Data

Names: Vaingurt, Julia, author.
Title: Soft matter : the poetics of weakness in late Soviet socialism / Julia Vaingurt.
Other titles: Studies in Russian literature and theory.
Description: Evanston, Illinois : Northwestern University Press, 2025. | Series:
    Studies in Russian literature and theory | Includes bibliographical references and
    index.
Identifiers: LCCN 2024032954 | ISBN 9780810148154 (paperback) | ISBN
    9780810148161 (cloth) | ISBN 9780810148178 (ebook)
Subjects: LCSH: Russian literature—20th century—History and
    criticism. | Masculinity—Russia—20th century. | Masculinity in literature.
Classification: LCC PG3022 .V35 2025 | DDC 891.73/4409353—dc23/
    eng/20241029
LC record available at https://lccn.loc.gov/2024032954

For Tom and Bella

Contents

Illustrations

Acknowledgments

This book would never have been possible had I not had the tremendous fortune of landing a position as a faculty member at the University of Illinois Chicago. The financial and intellectual support I have received over the years from this institution are immense and incalculable. I am especially grateful to UIC's Institute for the Humanities, whose fellowship gifted me with a year of writing and with the intellectually stimulating community of brilliant faculty fellows. It was a pleasure to meet regularly, workshop our projects, and discuss our writing progress with Mahrad Almotahari, Adam Goodman, Michael Jin, Laura Hostetler, and Atef Said. Special gratitude goes to Mark Canuel and Linda Vavra, at the time the institute's director and associate director, respectively, who were incredibly helpful and generous with their time and advice throughout my fellowship year. The School of Literatures, Cultural Studies and Linguistics, to which my department belongs, has been generously supporting our annual Workshop on Russian and Eurasian Modernisms, at which I was able to present and workshop portions of this book.

I have been truly fortunate in my colleagues, whom I look forward to seeing and speaking with every morning; whom I look up to and learn from daily. Inspiring conversationalists, perceptive critics, and all-around *warm* people, Matthew Kendall, Michał Paweł Markowski, Marina Mogilner, and Karen Underhill create an atmosphere of scholarly excitement, encouragement, and support. I benefited greatly from the agile mind and contagious intellectual energy of Michał Markowski; many of my ideas have been formed during our spirited analytical sparring. Michał, moreover, suggested the title for this book, for which I am grateful. Whenever I need to gauge the analytical rigor and clarity of my reasoning and make sure that my ideas do not go against historical fact or common sense, I try them out on my wonderful friend, the awe-inspiring scholar Marina Mogilner. Many other UIC colleagues and friends have been unstinting with their time, encouragement, and wisdom. In particular, I wish to acknowledge Elise Archias, Nina Dubin, Rachel Havrelock, Sigrid Luhr, Ellen McClure, Imke Meyer, Susanne Rott,

Margarita Saona, Heidi Schlipphacke (who read one of the chapters and offered crucial comments), Blake Stimson, and Alfred Thomas. Abigail Stahl, until recently assistant director of academic operations and graduate programs for the School of Literatures, Cultural Studies and Linguistics, helped me through all day-to-day logistics with kindness, responsiveness, and exemplary professional expertise.

In the course of writing this book, I have been continuously challenged, stimulated, and sustained by engaging conversations with, and probing questions from, past and present graduate students, many of whom are now professors themselves: Andrzej Brylak, Tetyana Dzyadevych, Hanna Gadbois, Andrei Gorkovoi, Agnieszka Jezyk, Sasha Lindskog, Nicoletta Rousseva, Raisa Shapiro, Charlie Smith, Anna Szawara, Brian Zdancewicz, and Vladislav Zemenkov. Special thanks to Nadezhda Gribkova, Konstantin Mitroshenkov, Polina Peremitina, Olga Seliazniova, and Anton Svynarenko, who became particularly active interlocutors and collaborators on this project and others. I am also grateful to John Stachelski, who, as an awardee of the LAS Undergraduate Research Initiative, traveled to Russian archives and produced research on Vonnegut's visits to Russia that had an invaluable impact on chapter 2 of this book.

Crucially, it is at UIC that I have built a long professional partnership and personal friendship with the amazing Colleen McQuillen. Colleen and I have worked side by side for thirteen years, and by now it is hard to think of an idea that has germinated in my brain without her influence. Colleen has read most of this book and offered critical feedback and emotional support. I trust her judgment and her friendship wholeheartedly.

I also owe a debt of gratitude for the astute observations and constructive opinions of many friends and colleagues. I have enjoyed the privilege of invigorating discussions on this book and many other topics with Polina Barskova, Maria Belodubrovskaia, Evgenii Bershtein, Eliot Borenstein, Edyta Bojanowska, Marijeta Bozovic, Julia Bekman Chadaga, Jinyi Chu, Katerina Clark, David Cooper, Jacob Emery, Lioudmila Fedorova, Leah Feldman, Elena Fratto, Elizabeth Geballe, Ilya Gerasimov, Nina Gourianova, Matthew Jesse Jackson, Ilya Kukulin, Susan McReynolds, John McKay, Ainsley Morse, William Nickell, Joanna Niżyńska, Serguei Oushakine, Sarah Phillips, Kevin Platt, John Randolph, Rebecca Reich, Kristin Romberg, Irina Sandomirskaja, Alexander Spektor, Valeria Sobol, William Mills Todd III, and Justin Weir. I must express my deepest appreciation to Caryl Emerson, Mieka Erley, Lilya Kaganovsky, Anna Katsnelson, and Mark Lipovetsky, who graciously read large or small parts of this manuscript at its various stages and made transformative suggestions.

I was privileged to present portions of this book to various academic audiences and to benefit greatly from the feedback they offered. In particular, I would like to acknowledge Matthias Schwartz and Dirk Uffelmann's conference "Socialism's Divergent Masculinities. Representations of Male Subjectivities in Soviet Constellations and Beyond" at Leibniz-Zentrum für Literatur- und Kulturforschung, Berlin, June 16–18, 2022.

I am indebted to Avram Brown, an editor extraordinaire, for his keen eye and perfect pitch. He has doubtless made me sound a bit better than I would otherwise sound, is attentive to exigencies of style, punctuation, and grammar that usually leave me cold, and always has my back.

I am deeply thankful to Gary Saul Morson and Faith Wilson Stein of Northwestern University Press for taking on and championing this project; to the press's copy editor Elizabeth Yellen, for making sure the book adheres to the press's style; and to my project editor Maia Rigas, for shepherding the book to the finishing stage. Abby Coykendall did a spectacular job on the index and offered a few exceedingly useful copyediting suggestions. Thanks are also due to the press's two anonymous reviewers, whose comments were judicious, generous, and very helpful. I am very grateful to Emilia Kabakov for giving me permission to place Ilya Kabakov's *The Rope of Life* (1985, catalog no. 7) on the cover. I would like to thank Harriet Murav and the editorial staff of *The Slavic Review*, where an earlier version of chapter 4 was published under the title "Low Spirits and Immoderate Meditations in Venedikt Erofeev's *Moskva-Petushki*" (*Slavic Review* 81, no. 1[Spring 2022]). Reprinted with permission.

I am enormously inspired by the formidable presence in my life of two incredible women: my daughter, Bella Vaingurt Berman, a constant source of my admiration, pride, and tenderness, and my mother, Rita Vaingurt Utschen, an unremitting generator of warmth, care, and feistiness. I dare to imagine that my father, Mikhail Vaingurt, had he been alive to read the book, would have been pleased with its arguments; I certainly held many imaginary conversations with him while writing it. My wonderful in-laws, Elaine and Richard Berman, have always supported me with affection, encouragement, and unflagging enthusiasm. Tom Berman, what a dream it is to go through life sharing strengths and weaknesses, joys and burdens with you—your love and companionship make it all possible.

Note on the Text

Bibliographical references follow a modified Library of Congress transliteration system. Elsewhere, names are given in their standard English form when one exists.

Soft Matter

Introduction

THERE IS NO attribution to Lao Tzu in the credits to An-
drei Tarkovsky's *Stalker* (1979), although the Chinese philosopher's dictum
that "weakness is great and strength is trifling" appears right around the film's
midpoint, where it concludes a prayer.[1] In a voice-over, the Stalker prays for
seemingly incongruous things: that he and his companions might succeed
in their arduous mission, and that they might "find belief in themselves and
become helpless like children." He then recites the following passage from
Lao Tzu verbatim:

> Слабость велика, сила ничтожна.
> Когда человек родится, он слаб и
> гибок; когда он умирает, он крепок
> и черств. Когда дерево произрастает,
> оно гибко и нежно, и когда оно сухо
> и жестко, оно умирает. Черствость и
> сила—спутники смерти. Гибкость и
> слабость выражают свежесть бытия.
> Поэтому, что отвердело, то не победит.

> Weakness is all, strength is insignificant.
> When a man is born, he is weak and
> yielding; when he dies, he is strong
> and hard. When a tree begins to grow,
> it is yielding and tender, and when it is dry
> and tough it dies. Hardness and
> strength are the concomitants of death. Pliancy and
> weakness express the freshness of existence.
> Therefore, that which has grown hard will not prevail.[2]

The passage ties the three above-stated objectives of the prayer into one
logical sequence, as meanwhile we see an object, perhaps a stone, fall into a

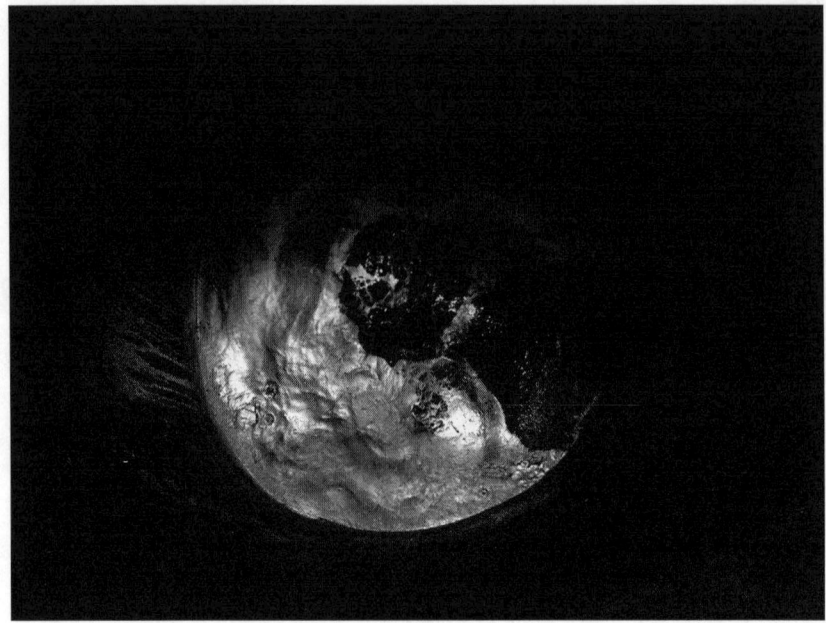

Fig. 1. Stone falling into a well during the Stalker's prayer. *Stalker*
(dir. Andrei Tarkovsky, 1979).

well and break the water's reflection of the moon into a pattern reminiscent of the yin-yang (fig. 1). And, as if to continue with this concealed allusion, the film jump-cuts to the Stalker squeezing himself through a hole in an abandoned wall, then proceeding to scale this wall in what Geoff Dyer describes as "teeth-bared concentration" (fig. 2).[3] Here the viewer may very well be reminded of a line from *Tao Te Ching* (*The Book of the Way and Its Virtue*): "There is nothing in the world more soft and weak than water, yet for attacking things that are hard and strong there is nothing that surpasses it; nothing can take its place."[4]

This episode strikes me as crucial for two reasons. First, it eloquently and unequivocally articulates the virtue and potency of weakness—the idea this book identifies as constitutive of a particular discourse in late Soviet culture. Second, via this idea, the film attempts an exit, however unobtrusively, from late Soviet insularity, establishing latent ties with classical Chinese philosophy;[5] with nineteenth-century Russian literature, as the above-cited Russian translation from *Tao Te Ching* first appears as an epigraph to Nikolai Leskov's "The Buffoon Pamphalon" ("Skomorokh Pamfalon," 1887);[6] and, via Leskov's story, with Origen of Alexandria and Byzantine hagiography;[7]

Fig. 2. The Stalker scaling the wall. *Stalker* (dir. Andrei Tarkovsky, 1979).

and, quite possibly, with Western postmodernism, which has developed its own philosophical and artistic praxes of "weak thought." (Gianni Vattimo's philosophy of weakening will be discussed below.) The Stalker's recitation of Lao Tzu's lines, then, does not just tell of the virtue of mutability and relationality but also practices it, establishing weak ties, both synchronic and diachronic, with the world that lies beyond the quotidian and knowable. From a condition of being in the world, weakness thereby becomes a mode of connecting with it.

Tarkovsky's film ends inconclusively. In the Zone, to which it is the Stalker's self-appointed job to escort wayfarers unscathed, there is a room that allegedly grants one's innermost desire. After the mission, the Stalker returns home distraught, bemoaning his perceived failure and the loneliness of his pursuits. His prayer, one might suppose, remains unanswered. And yet, the film does not quite give up on the weakness it has espoused, but rather ends with a scene of miracle. As the Stalker's daughter telekinetically moves a glass on a table until it falls without breaking, we hear the voice-over recitation of a poem. The voice appears to belong to the actress playing the child's mother (the incomparable Alisa Freindlich), but it seems to reach our ears as if emanating from and resonating through the child's consciousness. We register the movement and hear the thoughts of this lame and mute child. And so, after conceding that weakness might amount simply to a condition of tragic failure—the exhaustion of strength and prospects—the film nevertheless encourages the viewer with a sense of hope.

There is an air of exceptionality to the Stalker's strivings, tinged as they are with a sense of repeated failure and continuous exertion; his wife calls him "a holy fool," suggesting thereby his otherness and apartness. And yet, looking right into the camera as if to emphasize the point, the wife further declares: "Such is life, such are we" ("Takaia zhizn', takie my"). We get the sense that she is describing not just her and her husband's life but a particular social and aesthetic phenomenon. The point of this book is to elaborate this "Such is life, such are we." What does it mean to identify with a community on the basis of vulnerability and failed strivings? Whom does the wife address here as she looks right into the camera?

THE BENEFITS OF EXHAUSTION

Self-identification with weakness appears to be a particular property of many late Soviet fictional characters. These are persons who recognize their own weakness and "chicken-heartedness" (to use Venedikt Erofeev's term[8]) but, so far from suffering from it or attempting to overcome it, they cultivate it. In what follows, I will attempt to show that late Soviet underground narratives were constructed by emplotting characters' recognition and cultivation of their own various weaknesses. The weakness of protagonists, moreover, infectiously contaminated the very texture of writing itself; as a formal feature, weakness manifested itself in the abandonment of linear, logical, and authoritative narrative. *Soft Matter: The Poetics of Weakness in Late Soviet Socialism* examines how, in reflecting on and rejecting Cold War rhetorical strategies, Soviet artists sought new ways of approaching fiction, arriving at weakness as a crucial principle in the formation of both narrative and character.

More than a mere symptom of exhaustion after the cataclysms of the twentieth century, I contend, this pervasive weakness is indeed strategic: it is an aesthetic strategy and an ethical code allowing like-minded artists a feeling of recognition, kinship, and commonality. Weak characters in late Soviet fiction elicit a sense of affinity in artists of a particular milieu. As the photographer Dmitry Konrad reminisces about Andrei Bitov's novel *Pushkin House* (*Pushkinskii dom*, 1964–71), "The protagonist was close to me in his internal organization, a kind of indefiniteness, softness [*miagkost'*], if not to say spinelessness [*miagkotelost'*]."[9] In his notebooks, Erofeev recognizes the selfsame trait as a symptom of the prose of his generation, produced by "'milksops' [*khliupiki*], 'whiners' [*nytiki*], 'infantile youths,' 'star boys.' The piercing prose of questioning."[10]

The epithets given in quotation marks here derive from articles by critics, who borrowed them from the very writers they thus disparaged; for example, *nytiki* and *khliupiki* appear first in Aksenov's *Ticket to the Stars* (*Zvezdnyi bilet*, 1961). These are terms Aksenov's protagonist Dmitry Denisov uses at various times to describe himself and his circle of friends. They are never uttered out loud, and Denisov himself, being a stand-in for Aksenov, does not use them with any degree of approval.[11] However, they strike hostile critics as handy definitions for a new, and to them loathsome, linguistic register. The critics read the new language itself as a symptom of precisely that which these words purport to describe: a certain and unpardonable "cheekiness," "looseness," "gappiness" (*razviaznost'*, *razukhabistost'*)—in a word, a lack of solidity and cohesion.[12] But when Erofeev records them in his notebook, he reclaims them, evaluating them differently, rather positively, as a form of incisive "questioning."

In this questioning prose, characters appeared as if unmoored, restless, and aimless. As will be described in chapter 6, which focuses on Bitov, Soviet critics were alarmed by this drastic departure from socialist-realist conventions of characterization. Particularly disconcerting was that these newly wishy-washy and loose characters were *men*. (Soviet underground literary culture, just like official literary culture, of the 1960s and 1970s was heavily male dominated, a situation that began to change somewhat in the late 1970s, then drastically in the years of perestroika and glasnost, when women writers and, consequently, female protagonists began to enter Russian prose in great numbers.[13]) Describing the world of the Soviet intelligentsia of the 1960s, Petr Vail and Aleksandr Genis remark that "'our people' [*svoi*] always meant men, even if there were women among them"; thus when the critical consensus bemoaned the emergence of deficient characters, this specifically meant *weak men*.

These attacks on specific authors, texts, and characters formed part of the broader discussion, in late Soviet media, of the alleged crisis of masculinity. In their article "The Crisis of Masculinity in Late Soviet Discourse," Elena Zdravomyslova and Anna Temkina trace this alarm-raising to the demographer B. Urlanis, who in 1970 produced a series of articles in *Literaturnaia gazeta* arguing that men as hitherto known had become an endangered species.[14] In one such piece, titled "Save the Men!" ("Beregite muzhchin!"), Urlanis adduces a number of biological and historical factors to account for this sad state of affairs and proposes that the government and female partners consider men's dire diminishment and protect them from further degeneration.

Notably, the alleged crisis of masculinity was likewise a hot topic in Western scholarship and media already in the late 1960s, when, for example, American researchers took up such topics as the environmental and epochal factors behind a purported late nineteenth-century decline in American manliness: industrialization and urbanization; the bureaucratization and corporatization of the economy; women's emancipation; and the closure of the frontier.[15] This sudden scholarly interest in the nineteenth-century "crisis of masculinity" appeared in the atmosphere of the 1960s and 1970s feminist, civil, and gay rights movements, and signaled anxieties as to the ways in which these movements might challenge conventional norms of masculinity. It is perhaps not coincidental that, as will be discussed in chapter 1, the late 1970s saw American Slavists produce several studies of the "superfluous man" in Russian literature, seeking explanations for a lack of initiative, of outlets for agency, and finding them, at least in the Russian context, in historical and political circumstances.

Curiously, while Western scholarship began, in the late 1980s and 1990s, to doubt the usefulness of the notion of a "crisis" of masculinity in the West, it continues to be maintained that Russian men in the "era of stagnation" indeed experienced such a crisis. For example, Marko Dumančić's recent study, *Men Out of Focus: The Soviet Masculinity Crisis in the Long Sixties* (2021), sees the alleged crisis as symptomatic of Khrushchev's de-Stalinization practices. According to Dumančić, the appearance of complex, flawed, and rootless characters in late Soviet film was the result of a paradox: on the one hand, de-Stalinization meant questioning Stalinist ideals of masculinity; but on the other, the concomitant meandering and rootlessness bespoke anxiety over these changes, over the possible disadvantages they might bring.

Proponents of the "crisis of masculinity" paradigm tend to critique hegemonic Stalinist masculinity as complicit in state terror, and to read the postwar emergence of alternative patterns of masculinity as resulting from the bankruptcy of the Stalinist model. In this framing, however, some deficiency is typically ascribed to these postwar alternatives—which raises a key question: if the strong masculinity model results in the Gulag (and for that matter, the Holocaust), then why should we bemoan its weakening, and cling to it as something to be desired? My study departs from the "crisis of masculinity" paradigm and attempts to argue that—without romanticizing it or ignoring its pitfalls—weak masculinity does not have to mean masculinity in crisis. On the contrary, it offers its own benefits, and new venues for self-expression and identity formation.

Following Serguei Oushakine's pioneering conceptualization of masculinity in the context of Slavic studies, I approach Soviet masculinity as an essentially empty sign that encompasses a multitude of practices and derives its meaning from its placement within the structure of binary oppositions, and from its capacity for reiteration.[16] Weak masculinity thus constitutes a variant of this eminently variable concept. It simultaneously depends on and deconstructs the binary opposition of *masculine* and *feminine* (in which the former is associated with strength, the latter with weakness). Citing Lacan's theory of subjectivity—in which the subject emerges in the process of identifying with a prescribed position in the linguistic structure and its system of differences, and of concomitantly recognizing its own insufficiency and dependency on the Other—Oushakine critiques the "crisis of masculinity" discourse as reducing an essential state of being to a historically and geographically localized phenomenon: "This initial dividedness [*iskhodnaia razdelennost'*] . . . makes us suspicious of any scholarly attempt to see in the Other only reflections of a crisis of masculine identity—only one's own paranoid fantasies, called to compensate for one's phobias and inferiority complexes." Oushakine reminds us that, after all, any identity is built on some form of *lack*: "Insufficiency and inadequacy [*nedostatochnost' i nepolnotsennost'*] are the originary principles of any identity."[17] The chapters that follow analyze a tradition of writing in which, for one reason or another, this essential lack was embraced rather than disavowed. Most crucially, then, while the *weakening* examined here primarily affects male characters, in texts written by authors who identify as male, the book considers and conditionally advocates the salutary potential of weakness in general, and for all.

The structural and diegetic weakness of late Soviet texts can be interpreted, naturally, as an expression of the intellectual, moral, and physical exhaustion one experiences in a world where power is associated with superiority and violence; but often overlooked are artists' bold attempts to seek out potential *advantages* of this exhaustion. In his 1967 essay "The Literature of Exhaustion," John Barth puts it this way: "In an age of ultimacies and final solutions—at least *felt* ultimacies, in everything from weaponry to theology, the celebrated dehumanization of society, and the history of the novel—[novelists'] work in several ways reflects and deals with ultimacy, both technically and thematically."[18] In my view, Barth here addresses the ethics of embracing one's limits. In this regard, what appears as a crisis of hegemonic masculinity (of certainty in one's righteousness, willingness to use force, etc.) might in fact represent an attempt by artists to create texts that recognize their own constraints, resist certainty and totality, and model new subject positions on the basis of weakness and interpretation rather than power and knowledge.

Scholars who lament weak masculinity in the late Soviet context invariably connect these characters' lack of resolve with the tradition of "superfluous men" in Russian literature. My book attempts a correction, by proposing a unique view of the Russian postmodernists' relationship with their own cultural heritage. Here I advance two arguments. The first is that these writers creatively play with and examine, rather than merely adopt, Russian culture's native variants of weakness (kenosis, holy foolishness, and the nineteenth-century "superfluous man" trope). To be sure, there is much

9

in the position of their weak protagonists that hearkens back, for example, to Dostoevsky's Underground Man; but this shared code harbors a tendency to break through isolation and inertia, to transform weakness into a peculiar resilience. These characters, as well as the narratives themselves, do not just *appear* weak, nor can it simply be said that they *are* weak; rather, they *cultivate* and *perform* weakness. As the chapters of this book will demonstrate, in seeking an appropriate form for these performances, late Soviet writers often tap into and creatively reappropriate modernist and avant-garde experiments. The works analyzed here, then, deploy disparate elements—Russian cultural and philosophical tradition; homegrown and international modernist and avant-garde artistic practices; Soviet political and medical discourses; and American postmodern literature—to accomplish unique and powerful performances of weakness.

My second argument is that there indeed exists a separate literary tradition of "weak men" that goes back to the nineteenth-century classics but that has remained unnoticed in scholarship, upstaged by the superfluous man (*lishnii chelovek*), little man (*malen'kii chelovek*), and holy fool (*iurodivyi*) tropes. This alternative genealogical line, that of weak men, can be traced to the works of Nikolai Leskov and Lev Tolstoy; and, in the twentieth century, Andrei Platonov should perhaps likewise be considered from this standpoint. In contrast to the superior isolationism of holy fools, the solipsism and inertia of superfluous men, and the cog-in-the-machine victimhood of little men, weak men exhibit doubt and self-questioning *along with* an aptitude for concern for the other, openness to change, and mental flexibility. To escape the usual analysis of postwar weak men through the familiar prism of superfluity, in subsequent chapters I draw on Walter Benjamin's idea of "weak messianic power," Jack Halberstam's celebration of the queer art of failure, Giorgio Agamben's theory of impotentiality, Taoism's valorization of pliability and suppleness as preconditions for ecological relationality, and most importantly, Gianni Vattimo's philosophy of weakening.

THE THEORIZATION OF WEAK THOUGHT

According to the Italian philosopher Gianni Vattimo, the ethical choice of "weak thought"—thought that acknowledges its own limits and contingent nature—represents a response to the violence wrought by absolute metaphysical systems with pretensions to truth.[19] The ethics of weakness lies in the turn from metaphysics to hermeneutics, in the recognition that no claim to absolute knowledge will stand up to scrutiny. Such weak subjectivity might, in my view, offer an escape from the binary between the liberal concept of the "individual," a free and autonomous personality, and, on the other hand, the post-structuralist, postmodern concept of "subject," an entity that derives its substance from its participation in dominant discourses, fully defined by, enmeshed in, and imprisoned by them. The in-betweenness of weak subjects allows them to operate within a dominant discourse, and yet subscribe to it "weakly"—that is, tentatively and questioningly—and thus to extricate themselves at least somewhat from its influence.

Vattimo's philosophy of weakening represents a persistent defense, in post-postmodern times, of the postmodern "incredulity" toward and deconstruction of all grand narratives and irrevocable truths.[20] Vattimo believes that weakness—understood in terms of the questioning of universal propositions; acute attention and responsiveness to others around you; openness to conversation, flexibility, and situatedness—is the only actionable principle for progressive politics today. In his conclusion to the edited volume *Weakening Philosophy*, Vattimo examines and parries the idea that Nietzsche's critique of Western metaphysics and the destruction of previously extant moral codes must of necessity lead to the politics of force, and back to the natural state of "the war of all against all, where the 'weak perish' and only power is affirmed."[21] To support his case, he quotes Nietzsche's own argument that in the environment of uncertainty, those who thrive will be the "most moderate, those who have no need of extreme articles of faith, who not only concede but even love a good deal of contingency and nonsense."[22] Vattimo concludes that by this formulation, Nietzsche must have had in mind artists, who are most able to "experiment with a freedom derived." What would such experimentation entail?

In *Nihilism and Emancipation: Ethics, Politics, and Law* (2004), Vattimo revisits "weak thought," formulated twenty years prior,[23] in particular addressing the accusation that such weakness amounts to moral relativism and passivity, and attempting to draft a possible course of action, both artistic and political. Well aware of the absolutist and fundamentalist backlash against postmodern indeterminacy, Vattimo adduces two points: (1) historically, the concept of absolute truth came in for questioning because of the involvement of such truth in the catastrophes of the twentieth century, and to ignore this fact would be morally irresponsible; and (2) self-irony, and the questioning of one's social institutions, can serve as a precondition for transformative change, which is based on the willingness to consider and experiment with alternatives.[24] According to Vattimo, weak thought is the only viable alternative to the politics of force, as it builds truth on the basis of consensus, rather than forcing consensus on the basis of preordained truth. Weak thought stimulates a coming together. As Richard Rorty emphasizes in his foreword to *Nihilism and Emancipation*, the humility characteristic of Vattimian weak thought and weak being does not preclude action or transformation, but rather promotes them.[25] Despite the religious associations this word might evoke, "humility" is not meant to result in quietism or a life outside the realm of the social; to the contrary, it is a precondition for the work of building new coalitions. Vattimian weak thought, itself an intellectual product of the postmodern period, is a fitting framework to examine artistic attempts at weakening in late Soviet postmodernism. Despite their cultural isolation, I contend, late Soviet writers, especially those who created in underground conditions, were keenly aware of contemporaneous cultural processes abroad, and were eager to take part in them.

COLLECTIVE WEAKNESS

With the recent resurgence of a political left in the United States, many scholars have undertaken to reassess socialism as experienced in the Soviet Union. Russian historians and anthropologists have taken a particular interest in the relatively tranquil late Soviet period, with an eye toward explaining, along with the causes of state socialism's demise, such elements as made it attractive. Among the most notable attempts to define late Soviet subjectivity is Alexei Yurchak's *Everything Was Forever, Until It Was No More: The Last Soviet Generation* (2006). According to Yurchak, members of the last Soviet generation chose to live *vne* ("outside"), demarcating for themselves a nonpartisan space of freedom, in which it was possible to counterbalance a moderate, none-too-fanatical belief in socialism with a none-too-obsessive desire for the occasional black-market goods (both material and spiritual) from the capitalist West. In Yurchak's model, then, the average late Soviet young person, somewhat like the "weak subjects" I consider in this study, straddled the border between full acceptance and total rejection. And yet, this easygoing late Soviet subjectivity is quite different from the previous generation's *weak* subjectivity identified in my book. The former is predicated on what Yurchak calls an "acceptance of everything," an absence of discontent either with society or oneself, and of any political commitment whatsoever, whereas the latter still believes in the worthwhileness of ethical questioning—of oneself and one's social institutions.

I propose to read the discourse of weakness that arises in response, and resistance, to Cold War discourses of power, not as a mode of exiting the social space and practicing "politically incorrect" individualism, but as a mode of action—an active attempt, for instance, to resist the martial disposition regnant in a world divided into two hostile camps. In response to Cold War discourses of progress and expansion, of iron curtains and superpowers, various artists sought alternative rhetorical strategies through which one's relation to the world and the other could be reconceptualized.

Mark Lipovetsky's and Mikhail Epstein's seminal works on Russian postmodernism placed late Soviet fiction in the context of Western post-modernism, demonstrating similar preoccupations as a response to the epistemological crises and traumas wrought by a catastrophic twentieth century.[26] In my study, I build on this idea, but endeavor to add the consideration that Russian underground fiction not only responded to the vicissitudes of postmodernity but also quite purposefully sought to break with Soviet isolationism and alienation, and to promote a *shared* aesthetics.

For obvious reasons, most scholarship approaches Russian experimental and underground fiction as reactive, in form and content, to officially sanctioned narratives produced in the mode of socialist realism. Such a focus is perfectly justified, but my book attempts to expand the frame of reference, from socialist-realist doctrine to the international discursive practices of the post-1945 period, and to interpret correspondences between Russian writers and their Western counterparts in terms of a new solidarity. The artists examined in this book directed their resistance not only against the Soviet regime but against *worldwide* cultural processes that valorized heroics, endless action, and entertainment over introspection and ethical doubt.[27]

My project shares Ann Komaromi's interest in Soviet dissident writers' search for connection. She redefines the concept of autonomy to disassociate it from Western brands of individualism or sociopolitical indifference, and shows that Soviet dissident writers, often interpreted primarily as "dropouts" from the dominant discourse, in fact often sought to build new coalitions and effect change.[28] Taking Komaromi's cogent argument as a point of departure, I aim to contribute an analysis of weakness as a mode through which, to some key writers, this connectedness seemed attainable.[29]

WEAK PRESENTS

I began writing this book in 2014, when Putin's Russia first invaded Ukraine and took over Crimea. That year marked a new escalation of the tensions between Russia and the West, signaling a resurgence of the Cold War, or at the very least, of Cold War rhetoric in public discourse. I was inspired to investigate ways in which alternative rhetorical strategies might be used to resist the politics of force, to help pivot away from the pervasive atmosphere of confrontation. It is with this goal in mind that I turned to the late Soviet period, to explore how various authors, both in the United States and Soviet Union, produced a counterdiscourse. A product of its time, much like the official "thesis" of which it constituted an antithesis, this counterdiscourse of *strategic weakness* traveled across borders and united an international community of artists inclined to resist the divisiveness of the world.

As I was writing this book on weakness, the rhetoric of strength and entitlement gained momentum in the global political arena. The year 2014 saw the appearance of a particularly appalling manifestation of the politics of force: the slogan "Crimea is ours," which seemed to assert a categorical ownership, not only of Crimea but of truth itself. Eschewing self-doubt or questioning, it stood as a Kremlin-endorsed refutation of postmodernity. The rise of strongmen around the world seemed to follow the same rhetorical playbook: promises of a return to tradition; the restoration of stability, law, and order; exclusionary politics; raw masculinity; and the purposeful, tactical stoking of anger and resentment. In the name of law and order, violence, war, and political and socioeconomic instability are unleashed. In my own country, the rhetoric of strength was a favorite propagandistic tactic of former president Donald Trump, who consistently used it to incite violence. At the rally on January 6, 2021, that touched off the Capitol insurrection, Trump exhorted his followers at the top of his voice, "You'll never take back our country with weakness. You have to show strength and you have to be strong."[30] Shortly thereafter, aggrieved by the insufficient support they received from Trump after the insurrection, Proud Boy activists began calling him "extraordinarily weak" on social media, while Nicholas Fuentes, leader of the white-supremacist America First group, wrote on his Telegram channel that Mr. Trump's response to the Capitol insurrection was "very weak and flaccid."[31]

Similarly, since coming to power, Putin has projected the image of traditional hegemonic masculinity, using catchy idiomatic expressions to disavow weakness—for example, "Russia is getting up off its knees [*podnimaetsia s kolen*]"—and to signal revanche vis-à-vis the West.[32] As I was finishing the book, the political situation only became more dire. Putin's politics of force, aimed at restoring Russia's former imperial might, culminated in the catastrophic war on Ukraine and its people.

In this age of increasing authoritarianism around the world—of crises in democratic deliberation, the extreme polarization of political discourse, and the growing threat of violent insurrection—it is more topical than ever to investigate whether there exists a viable alternative to the ubiquitous politics of force, and specifically, whether this alternative lies in the embracing of *weakness* as an aesthetic, ethical, and ideological imperative. Political divisions, moreover, divert our attention from the looming ecological catastrophe that has us all under the same gun and that can only be addressed through cooperation and concerted efforts. We are well acquainted with the discourses of rights, demands, and above all, power, and with the fact that these discourses promote our separation and isolation, and help make victims of us. I therefore propose we explore the poetics of *weakness*, as it might offer us new tools and strategies for reaching ecological relationality, social solidarity, and political consensus.

The book encompasses a broad range of attitudes informed, even enabled, by *weakness*: how the subject relates to contemporary political and medical discourses; to the present world beyond Russia; to the literary past and the planetary future. Chapter 1 explores Russian literary and cultural tradition to propose a typology of weakness. Examining the extant categories of "superfluous man," "little man," and "holy fool," it outlines their degree of affinity or departure from the category of "weak man" to which this book is dedicated. Each subsequent chapter is devoted to a particular fictional mode of the cultivation of weak subjectivity in late Soviet fiction: gender subversion in chapter 2, queer holy foolishness in chapter 3, intemperance in chapter 4, madness in chapter 5, and such writing disorders as graphomania and writer's block in chapter 6.[33] The first two of these chapters address two key American models of male protagonist subject formation that gained currency in the Soviet cultural imagination: Ernest Hemingway's hypermasculinity and Kurt Vonnegut's antiheroism. The Russian counterculture abounded with Hemingway admirers who modeled their identities on the virile "Papa," but this study is concerned with the extraordinary popularity of Kurt Vonnegut's *Slaughterhouse 5* in the land of the Soviets. Specifically, it explores the Theater of the Soviet Army's staging of *Wanderings of Billy Pilgrim*, and Yuly Kim and Vladimir Dashkevich's remarkable one-act lyric opera, *Cinderella in the Concentration Camp*. Chapter 3 addresses the cult of Hemingway, and in particular, how Evgeny Kharitonov constructed subjectivity in opposition to this cult. The chapter also analyzes Kharitonov's creative reappropriation of a homegrown variant of weakness: holy foolishness. The fourth chapter, dedicated to Venedikt Erofeev's cult novel *Moscow–Petushki* (*Moskva–Petushki*, 1969–70; published in English as *Moscow to the End of the Line*), examines the relationship between late Soviet character formation and the Russian philosophical, religious, and cultural tradition, considering, in particular, how much Erofeev's weak subjectivity is indebted to this tradition, and how much it deviates from it. The fifth chapter discusses Sasha Sokolov's novel *A School for Fools* (*Shkola dlia durakov*, 1973) in the context of contemporaneous medical discourses that pathologized political dissidence as a mental disorder. And finally, the last chapter analyzes Andrei Bitov's creative struggles—his own writer's block and existence at loose ends, and that of his characters—as a response to the threat of nuclear annihilation, and as a sign of preoccupation with ecological and ontological finitude. Bitov's continuous questioning of how to live, write, and relate to the world under conditions of universally shared vulnerability is particularly relevant today.

In 2018, Hokkaido University's research magazine *Tackling Global Issues* dedicated an issue to the investigation of soft matter as the "material of the future." "Soft matter" as a concept in science was introduced in 1991 by the Nobel laureate physicist Pierre-Gilles de Gennes, who used this term to identify highly complex and dynamic substances whose behavior and patterns of change cannot be predicted from their molecular composition. Unlike hard materials, characterized by ordered structure, strong intermolecular interactions, and resistance to external stimuli, soft matter is highly responsive to and interactive with the environment. This intriguing degree of malleability (flexibility), reactivity, and indeterminacy is conditioned by two factors: these substances consist of aggregates of molecules that move collectively, and yet that are held together by "weak intermolecular interactions."[34] According to this Hokkaido University Global Campus report, we are both made of, and surrounded by, soft matter: our bodies are mostly soft matter; our natural world consists of myriad varieties of soft matter, such as sand, fog, and milk; and people have long produced such soft-matter substances as glass and concrete. But according to the writers of this report, it is the twenty-first century that will truly usher in the era of soft matter. Materials around us are becoming softer, lighter, and more flexible. Our eyes become accustomed to liquid crystal displays, and to lighter, more flexible contact lenses; soft components are used in automobiles and surgical instruments. Soft matter is not only more versatile; it is also more sustainable.

In the age of steel, there arose the human wish to steel oneself; surrounded by electronics, people merge with and morph into their devices, becoming cyborgian themselves. Could it be that softness, pliability, indeterminacy—the proverbial weakness of the characters and texts I explore in this book—might come into their own precisely in our twenty-first century, in this time of our great susceptibility to our environment, when we are called to evince flexibility before it and adapt ourselves to its needs? I titled this book *Soft Matter* because it examines the poetics of weakness, or softness, hoping that it might present an alternative to rhetorical and discursive mechanisms of force, and thus embody an inspiration for transformative change.

A Typology of Weakness:
Lacking Heroes in Literature and Film

THE SUPERFLUOUS MAN

In *Terror and Greatness*, Kevin Platt examines the codependence in Russian cultural memory of the two eponymous concepts. As he notes, despotic terror has repeatedly been justified in this milieu with reference to the notion that an enormous country like Russia requires a strong ruler, able to bring it together and direct its development with "a strong hand."[1] Russian history has certainly seen its share, and then some, of "strong hands." According to an attendant myth in the Russian cultural imagination, the authoritarian state goes (strong) hand in hand with the reactive impotence of its male citizens.

There exists a scholarly consensus, for example, that the emergence of the "superfluous man" in nineteenth-century Russian literature was predicated on a dearth of venues for action, agency, and self-expression in tsarist Russia. For my own part, I can observe that, upon hearing that I was writing a book on the poetics of late Soviet weakness, colleagues would often ask if my case studies might not constitute updates of the superfluous man. Indeed, "superfluous people" is the category through which late Soviet protagonists have usually been analyzed. For example, Marko Dumančić's reading of the "crisis of masculinity" in late Soviet culture sees a "return of the superfluous man":

> Although clearly distinct, the upheavals that followed both Russia's nineteenth-century industrialization and the West's 1950s economic boom generated fears that men could not rise to the challenge, disoriented as they were by seismic changes that were taking place. As a result, nineteenth-century Russia and the long sixties in twentieth-century Europe and the Soviet Union can both be viewed as times of "superfluous masculinity."[2]

Here I will attempt to delineate the distinction between "superfluous men" and my proposed category of "weak men."

17

There are several definitions of the superfluous man. The character is a bit of a misnomer. It originated with Turgenev's "The Diary of a Superfluous Man" ("Dnevnik lishnego cheloveka"), although Turgenev himself never used it to identify a particular type. Moreover, as the authors of *A History of Russian Literature* observe, Turgenev's Chukalturin, who identifies as "superfluous," "does not quite fit with the rest of the characters bearing the name of a superfluous man." The scholars elaborate on the discrepancy:

> Even though he does fight a duel and fails in love, socially and psychologically he has little in common with the stock character. It is unlikely that either of the original superfluous men—Onegin and Pechorin—would socialize with him, since he stands significantly below them on the social ladder. . . . Chukalturin seems superfluous mostly because he is dying of tuberculosis.[3]

As for how Turgenev himself conceptualized this type: Lydia Ginzburg pinpointed the quality of inner emptiness, a kind of "coldness," with which Turgenev endowed Rudin, whom one character describes as "cold as ice, and he knows it, although he pretends to be passionate."[4] According to Ginzburg, the superfluous man took shape in Turgenev's failed attempt to model a protagonist on Mikhail Bakunin, whom he wished to present as rather brilliant and devoted to "abstract aims" and principles, but from whom he subtracted the famed anarchist's characteristic energy: "Turgenev retained Bakunin's abstractness and hortatory fervor in his Rudin, but he deprived the character of force. The vast logical speculations of the young Bakunin were turned into the impotent introspection of the superfluous man."[5] Turgenev's own understanding of "superfluity," then, can range from the sensation of one's own extraneousness in the world to apathy, deflation, and a deficiency of feeling and inner vitality.

Perhaps the word itself is to blame for such an indefiniteness of meaning. The original Russian word rendered in English as "superfluous," *lishnii*, has two related but actually quite different connotations: "useless" and "unnecessary," or "extra" and "additional." This range of meanings imparted the term with a certain ambiguity, enabling scholars to understand "superfluous" in various ways and apply it to a variety of different characters.

Dumančić's reading of compromised masculinity rests on the definition of superfluity proposed by Jesse and Betty Clardy in *The Superfluous Man in Russian Letters*, citing which Dumančić summarizes:

> The superfluous man combined seemingly contradictory characteristics; some writers saw him as brave but apathetic, while for others he combined cowardice with high moral standards. Central to most expressions of male superfluity in the nineteenth century was the "hope that somewhere in the

universe there exists a beautiful truth that will give his life meaning and purpose, and that this will eliminate the vicious pain of feeling useless on this
earth."[6]

In discussing Onegin, Pechorin, Oblomov, and a slew of Turgenev's characters, the Clardys state: "All endure purposeless lives and are unable to find
meaning in human activity or even in life."[7] Their hardly enthusiastic evaluation of these characters clearly gravitates toward the meaning of *lishnii* as
"unnecessary" or "extraneous": "The heroes convey feelings of uselessness
and gradually regress until they succumb to early deaths. Egocentrics and
manic depressives, they would have been termed 'melancholiacs' in an earlier time. Their most notable characteristic, however, is their fear."[8]

According to the Clardys, this state of wretchedness is a direct conse-
quence of tsarist authoritarianism, "the hierarchical structure of a master-
slave relationship in Russian society."[9] Such an assessment follows the interpretation of literary superfluity offered by the nineteenth-century radical
critics, first and foremost, Nikolai Dobroliubov, who in his famous review
of Goncharov's *Oblomov*, titled "What Is Oblomovism?" ("Chto takoe
Oblomovshchina?," 1859), blames the political structure of Russian society
for the predicament of the idealistic, indolent, and day-dreamy Oblomov:
"The main thing here is not Oblomov, but Oblomovshchina. Perhaps
Oblomov would even have started work had he found an occupation to his
liking; but for that he would have had to develop under somewhat different
conditions."[10] Dobroliubov goes on to claim that Oblomov embodies a malaise afflicting well-nigh every protagonist of Russian literature:

> It was observed long ago that all the heroes in the finest Russian stories and
> novels suffer from their failure to see any purpose in life and their inability to
> find a decent occupation for themselves. As a consequence, they find all occu-
> pations tedious and repugnant, and in this they reveal an astonishing resem-
> blance to Oblomov. Indeed, open, for example, *Onegin, A Hero of Our Times,
> Who is To Blame?, Rudin,* "The Diary of a Superfluous Man," or *Hamlet from
> Shchigry County*—in every one of these you will find features identical with
> Oblomov's.[11]

Dobroliubov here pinpoints a new type of character, or rather a trend—that
of historically and politically conditioned superfluity: "The feature common
to all these men is that nothing in life is a vital necessity for them, a shrine in
their hearts, a religion, organically merged with their whole being, so that to
deprive them of it would mean depriving them of their lives."[12] Adopting Dobroliubov's idea that these characters are victims of their environment, the
Clardys nevertheless shift the focus. Whereas for Dobroliubov, superfluity

has to do with the environmentally conditioned inability to attach oneself to a meaningful cause, the Clardys rather emphasize passivity, the characters' *succumbing* to their stultifying milieu: "[Chekhov] has drawn a vivid picture of those individuals who have passively surrendered themselves to the destructive organisms of their environment."[13]

By contrast, in her study *Conformity's Children: An Approach to the Superfluous Man in Russian Literature*, Ellen Chances offers a more generous reading of this character. Relying in particular on *lishnii's* meaning of "additional, surplus," Chances defends superfluous characters as representatives of nonconformity and protest against an uninspiring, unjust life. This relatively positive evaluation of the character has precedent; in Dobroliubov's own time, it was proposed by none other than Aleksandr Herzen. In "The Superfluous and the Jaundiced" ("Lishnie liudi i zhelcheviki," 1860), Herzen attempts to stick up for superfluous men—a category he sees himself as belonging to, generation- and class-wise—in the face of slights on the part of Dobroliubov and other leaders of the journal *The Contemporary* (*Sovremennik*). In this piece, Herzen seeks in particular to distinguish his own generation of "superfluous men," who are conscious of their superfluity and desperate strivings for a better world, from the new generation of people like Chernyshevsky, for whom he coins the neologism *zhelcheviki* ("people filled with bile," "jaundiced"). The connotation is one of a practically physiological malaise, a state of choleric bitterness, uncontrollable and enfeebling. This new, contemporary type is just as superfluous as its predecessor, but lacking the self-awareness thereof: "gaping, unnerved lads who lose their heads before the toughness of practical work, and expect a gratuitous solution of their difficulties and answers to problems which they have never been able to state clearly."[14] In the end, however, Herzen makes a conciliatory gesture, defending both generations, the superfluous and the jaundiced, as alike signaling the need for, and harboring the seeds of, sociopolitical change; both are

> strange phenomena . . . whose very distortion points to latent forces, ill at ease and seeking something different. The *Raskolniki* and the Decembrists stand foremost among them, and they are followed by all the Westerners and Easterners, the Onegins and the Lenskys, the superfluous and the jaundiced. All of them, like Old Testament prophets, were at once a protest and a hope. By them Russia was exerting itself to escape from the Petrine period, or to digest it to her real body and her healthy flesh. These pathological formations called forth by the conditions of the life of the period invariably pass away when the conditions are changed, just as now superfluous men have already passed away; but it does not follow that they deserve judgment and condemnation, unless from their younger comrades in service.[15]

Continuing Herzen's line of thought, Chances defends superfluous men from the radical critics like Chernyshevsky and Dobroliubov, who called them "flabby, weak-willed liberals,"[16] and even from their own author-creators. According to Chances, these characters are bound to fail, not because of their own deficiency and passivity but because authors like Turgenev harbored ambivalent, conflicted attitudes toward nonconformity. On the one hand, such authors sympathized with their characters' attempts to exit the rut of conventional existence, but on the other, they could not imagine the refusal to submit to extant reality as resulting in anything but defeat.[17] In Chances's view, these characters are paragons of individualism, misunderstood and misused by their very creators—reared as these writers were in the confining milieu of the Russian intelligentsia. In particular, Chances adduces the "will to belong," which she seems to read as a particularly Russian, national trait, and owing to which these authors were simply more comfortable with conformity and social cohesion. In this interpretation, superfluity is profoundly idiosyncratic for Russian society; it is a sign of radical individualism and its failure to thrive in these particular geographic and historical circumstances.

Herzen read superfluity as presaging the advent of new social forces; but it follows from Chances's interpretation that one could scarcely build a movement or coalition on the basis of superfluity. Even in Herzen's reading, the concept is suffused with inertia and isolation. The superfluity of superfluous characters isolates them. By contrast, the *weakness* of *weak* characters, as the following chapters are meant to show, harbors a different sociopolitical potential.

Furthermore, though Dobroliubov and the Clardys evaluate superfluous men negatively, and Herzen and Chances more positively, for both camps, superfluity is not a choice but a condition. Whether we read superfluity as an a priori surrender and ineffectual idealism, or as failed protest, meaningful in its intentions but not its execution, either way, superfluity suggests an enforced state of being. No one *decides* to be superfluous. These characters do not *choose* superfluity out of some distaste for the idea of being, to the contrary, essential or needed. In this, they differ radically from the weak characters I propose to consider in this book, who choose and performatively enact weakness because they find the idea of strength morally or aesthetically bankrupt.

LITTLE MEN

However removed from society superfluous men might find themselves—misplaced as they are in this world that impedes their agency—they appear fundamentally dependent on and reactive to the power structures at hand.

Victimhood figures prominently even in the positive interpretations discussed above. "Superfluous men" share this condition of victimhood and dispossession with Russian literature's "little men." On the other hand, the deprivation experienced by men like Onegin, Pechorin, and Chatsky is spiritual or existential rather than material; it is hardly the same thing as the wretched state of the little man. The former are usually as Dobroliubov described them: idle aristocrats who yearn for a sphere of activity but are too languid to attain it (with the notable exception of Turgenev's Chulkaturin). Unlike the superfluous men, whose origins in romantic literature conditioned their romantic allure, little men were created in "physiological" sketches of the Natural School, which endeavored to portray urban locales and their inhabitants as they would be seen rather than imagined. These little men were usually poor and downtrodden clerks, limited in their means, abilities, and aspirations.

Fear and trepidation, which the Clardys ascribe to superfluous men, and Chances to their authors, are in fact defining characteristics of such "little men" as Gogol's Bashmachkin, Dostoevsky's Devushkin, and Chekhov's Belikov. Abused and humiliated by the surrounding world, these characters are overwrought by phobias, as enumerated by Mikhail Epstein: sociophobia, enochlophobia, agoraphobia, heterophobia.[18]

These little men wish primarily to be left alone. They also seem to sense that literary naturalism's privileging of *optics* threatens to fixate them in their unprepossessing outward appearance. According to A. A. Faustov and S. V. Savinkov, the defining objective of little men is to isolate themselves from everyone, to escape the gaze of the other.[19] It is their continuous self-perception as objects of the other's gaze, these authors suggest, that makes little men feel thinglike and inanimate. Seeking to be as inconspicuous as possible, they are inclined to make their living in occupations demanding little in the way of ingenuity or creativity: Bashmachkin and Devushkin are both copyists. Gogol makes the mechanicity of Bashmachkin's work part and parcel of his thingness. Dostoevsky's Devushkin recognizes himself in Bashmachkin but objects to this portrait as an objectification, and proposes that, to the contrary, a meager outer shell may hide a rich inner world of sense and sensation. This recognition and crisis of consciousness leads him to attempt to transform himself, from mere copyist to author, thus from an object of analysis to a subject of his own making. In particular, I would emphasize that the affronted Devushkin finds Gogol's Bashmachkin preposterous—"I—I mean, it is an ill-intentioned book, Varenka; it's simply unrealistic, because it couldn't be the case that such a clerk existed"[20]—even as, in virtually the same breath, he gives the impression that he believes Akaky Akakievich to be based directly on him. But there is a logic to this incongruity. It is precisely the absolute recognizability of the portrait that makes it so improbable: no one could be so utterly known.

Epstein suggests that the linguistic orientation of these characters—he includes here Chekhov's titular "man in a case," a provincial teacher of classical Greek—bespeaks their desire to escape from the world of external and material reality (which is spontaneous) into the world of signs (which is systematic and ordered).[21] If we apply the conceptual framework of Lacan, we can say that these little men's would-be solace in the orderliness of signs is foredoomed, as the encounter with language only brings them closer to the recognition of their alienation and lack. Just when they believe themselves ensconced in a system of formal relations that would give them a proper, stable place, they encounter a gaping hole, and are left with nothing but their sense of alienation.

It is not, then, just acquiescence, meekness, and fear that define little men. At the onslaught of the world, some indeed wish to retract further into their nullity, to become more thinglike or "play dead"; but others, to the contrary, aspire to magnify themselves, transform from objects of someone's description to the subject of their own making. Uniting them in their littleness is the fact that their self-perception (subjectivity) is entirely conditioned by a sense—we might say a paranoid sense, even if it seems understandable in sociopolitical terms—of the immensity of power, of the symbolic order that confines them. In the thrall of this power, they consistently orient themselves toward, and internalize, the other.[22]

HOLY FOOLS

Alienation likewise informs the subjectivity of still another variant of native deficiency, holy foolishness (*iurodstvo*), except that holy fools form their subjectivity via submission to the religious (Christian) rather than secular authority. In her study of the role of holy foolishness in the novels of Dostoevsky, Harriet Murav observes, "In the hagiography, the holy fool is seen as one who acts within the dominant theological framework of Russian Orthodoxy. . . . The hagiographer constructs the sanctity of the holy fool by means of [this] notion of conformity to a model."[23]

In imitation of Christ, holy fools conspicuously defy societal norms and rules of behavior, and practice extreme forms of asceticism. The basis of this is scriptural; in 1 Corinthians, Paul famously declares, "We are *fools for Christ's sake*, but ye are wise in Christ; we are weak, but ye are strong; ye are honorable, but we are despised." In Russian cultural tradition, it was customary to regard people with mental illnesses or exhibiting strange behavior as touched by God, following Paul: "For since in the wisdom of God the world through its wisdom did not know him, God was pleased through the foolishness of what was preached to save those who believe" (1 Corinthians 1:21). However, both in hagiographic texts and in nineteenth-century Russian literature, we mostly encounter holy fools who *feign* folly "for Christ's sake." A. M. Panchenko reads holy foolishness as a form of theatricality,[24] while Murav emphasizes that "the hagiographer understands the madness or foolishness of the saint to be a choice."[25]

In nineteenth-century Russian literature and art, the performative rejection of the ways of the world serves as a form of critique. Murav argues, for example, that "Dostoevsky, in the figure of the holy fool, seeks to deconstruct the predominantly scientific, Western, and secular categories by which Russian culture, in its turn toward modernity, found a new way of organizing itself."[26]

Unlike little men, whose alienation and exclusion are in no way a goal, but rather a matter of shame, holy fools *choose* outsiderhood, and the humiliation they court comes with a silver lining. Theirs is a model-based humility, intended to bring them sanctity rather than dishonor, growth rather than degradation. Holy fools wield a certain power. Dostoevsky's titular "idiot" Myshkin—who is not incidentally a *prince*—seeks to treat all with kindness and Christian love but finds it almost impossible to withhold a damning judgment, and other characters frequently perceive his goodness as condescending. Notably, when Myshkin attempts to spare General Ivolgin by indulging him in his lies, the latter, upon retrospective contemplation, finds this compassionate leniency more unbearable than the harshest recrimination and, crushed, dies of a heart attack.

Holy fools do not exhibit the haughty detachment of superfluous men; their performance is based rather on the affect of humility. Even so, theirs is a form of nonconformism and kenotic self-abnegation that, based as it is on renunciation of the world, presumes a superiority to it, and can result in the opposite of humility—hubris. While Christ's kenosis might be conceptualized as a genuine weakening—God's self-emptying and integration with lowly humanity, so as to save it—the holy fool's imitation of Christ may be interpreted oppositely, as something prideful. It is isolationist and ego boosting, rather than ego defying.

It is evident, then, that all three of these traditional types of deficient, conventionally "weak" characters, and the types of subjectivities they embody, feature an emphasis on (in some cases, even a striving for) isolation and outsiderhood. My contention in this study will be that, although the late Soviet discourse of weakness was certainly formulated in opposition to official and dominant discourses of strength and power, the weak subjectivity we find in underground fiction is *not* based in exceptionality. Late Soviet "weaklings" share their vulnerability with little men, their propensity for self-reflection with superfluous men, and their performativity with holy fools; but they should be regarded as a separate category, since they do not perceive themselves in isolation from the world. Even Erofeev's Venichka—among the characters under consideration, the one most inclined to seclusion—

insists on his distinction from Byronic heroes, on the incongruity between his own search for a sphere of intimacy and, on the other hand, some sense of being "above" the world. This is a key difference between weak characters and holy fools, even as the latter were the object of considerable interest in the Soviet artistic underground of the 1960s and 1970s.

STAGNATION

The exhaustion exhibited by late Soviet "weaklings" hardly separates them from Soviet society of the time; this period, after all, would eventually be dubbed that of "stagnation." It was Gorbachev who introduced the term at the 26th Party Congress in 1986 and listed its symptoms: "inertia; a congealing of forms and methods of management; declining dynamism in work; the growth of bureaucratization."[27] Ostensibly describing the country's economic situation, the term "stagnation" became especially associated with ideological and cultural decline, with the loss of ideals and a lack of initiative in all aspects of life. This view of late Soviet culture as steeped in fatigue and depletion, sluggishness and unproductivity, has recently been called into question by quite a few historians, who aim to show, by contrast, the complexity and richness of everyday life in the period—in particular, late Soviet achievements in politics, science and technology, and art.[28] And yet, it would be hard to deny the Soviet intelligentsia's own pervasive sense of material and ideological slump. Furthermore, if, per Lyotard, postmodernity is marked by "incredulity toward metanarratives," then the emptying out of ultimacies is the shared, global condition of the post-Holocaust, post-Gulag, post-Vietnam and Watergate, post-crushing of the Prague Spring generations. This feeling of intense disillusionment with received truths, and the ethics of *doubt* engendered by this feeling, is precisely where members of the Soviet intelligentsia could find common ground with their Western counterparts.[29] Being weak, and embracing this weakness, thus hardly means being superfluous, extraneous, or out of place in the late 1960s and 1970s; it is precisely being current, contemporary.

In the Soviet Union, the "Thaw"—all the political and cultural liberalizations that followed the death of Stalin (1953) and Khrushchev's denunciation of his "cult of personality" and abuses of power at the 20th Party Congress (1956)—inaugurated a period of hopefulness in the possibility of change, of building "socialism with a human face," of creating a cohesive, less violent and hierarchical, more egalitarian social body. By the latter half of the 1960s, after Khrushchev's removal from office (1964), the Siniavsky-Daniel trial (1966), and the suppression of the Prague Spring (1968), this hopefulness gave way to a renewed sense of pessimism and helplessness. While the ruling party resumed its politics of force (albeit without the mass terror of Stalinism) and discourse of power, many artists chose to accept their position of weakness as bearing a certain ethical and relational potential.

Strength became depleted in more senses than one: as an attribute, but also as a value. Now it was up to artists to explore whether weakness might be key to the well-lived life. Their dissent and departure from mainstream culture came not from some status as the only weak ones in a culture of strongmen—as said, they were hardly alone in their weakness—but from their *conscious acceptance* of weakness and reevaluation of it. In exploring weakness and its possible advantages, Soviet writers were certainly aware not only of Western experiments with antiheroic subjectivity but also of their own cultural heritage. In the process, they creatively played with and examined, rather than merely adopted, Russian literature and philosophy's native variants of weakness.

NINETEENTH-CENTURY PROTOTYPES OF THE WEAK MAN

Importantly, an attempt was made already in the nineteenth century to create a distinct category of "weak character," separate from the "superfluous man." In a polemic with Chernyshevsky about Turgenev's characters, Pavel Annenkov introduced—in an article titled "The Literary Type of the Weak Man. Apropos of Turgenev's story 'Asya'" ("Literaturnyi tip slabogo cheloveka. Po povodu turgenevskoi 'Asi,'" 1858)—the titular new type of the "weak" character, who is said to emerge in, and to befit, those historical periods that are relatively free of upheaval. According to Annenkov, tumultuous times produce heroic and unwavering personalities, but more stable periods give rise to people inclined to test their own beliefs, to probe the validity and ethics thereof. To Chernyshevsky, Turgenev's N. N. is a superfluous (and inept) man, but Annenkov launches a defense of such characters as, to the contrary, morally superior to those people he calls *tsel'nye*. The word *tsel'nyi* has numerous English equivalents, including, perhaps most apt in this case, "integral." Given its associations with *tselyi* ("whole," "complete"), and with *tsel'* ("aim"), it suggests *cohesion* around a *purpose*. The counterparts of these "integral" people must thus lack wholeness, completeness, cohesion. For Annenkov, then, weakness is bound up with incompleteness, with the state of being in shambles. (Faustov and Savinkov carefully trace the instances in which Turgenev's characters bemoan their own *rassypchatost'*, their "crumblingness" or inner disarray.[30]) But in Annenkov's view, this incompleteness and lack of solidity should be associated with thoughtfulness, with the questioning of accepted truths.

Per Annenkov, characters inclined to question their own rights and righteousness are not only more ethical than thoughtlessly determined and heroic characters, they are also less egotistical. In this, by the way, he diverges from Turgenev himself, who in his speech "Hamlet and Don Quixote" ("Gamlet i Don-Kikhot," 1860) offered his own typology of personalities, according to which Don Quixote's heroic attachment to an ideal is selfless, whereas Hamlet's propensity for analysis and introspection is egotistical:

> Analysis above all, and egoism—hence disbelief. [Hamlet] lives completely for himself; he is truly an egoist. . . . He is incessantly occupied with his own condition, not with his obligations. Doubting everything, Hamlet understandably does not spare even himself; his mind is too well-developed to be satisfied with what he finds within himself. He is conscious of his own weaknesses, but all self-consciousness makes for strength—thence proceeds his sarcasm, the opposite of Don Quixote's enthusiasm.[31]

Notably, Turgenev here identifies the paradox of weakness: that consciousness of it can constitute a strength.

In contrast to Turgenev, Annenkov believes that it is heroic characters, with their unwavering belief in their truth, who are egotistical, discounting as they do the rights and reasoning of others. Their "integrality" or "solidity" (*tsel'nost'*) is truly isolationist. Integral individuals think of themselves as complete entities, and this thought prevents them from imagining themselves as being a part of a larger whole. In Annenkov's reading, weak characters, by contrast, are hardly individualists. They are, indeed, "people-minded," *narodnye*—as witness, says Annenkov, the existence of such persons in the Masonic circle of Novikov, where education was understood not as the mere passive adoption of external truths but as a painstaking exploration of their applicability. It is these "weak" people, according to Annenkov, who, more than the "integral" heroes, represent their country and land, who represent civic-mindedness. The ostensible ineffectuals of the Novikov circle (and by extension, it is implied, the weaklings of the Russian intelligentsia in general) are only to be praised for bearing within themselves "the pledges of a moral education" and demonstrating, by their example, the "defects [that] prevent [one] from taking an active part in society."

> Let the "weak" man renounce the pleasure of feeling justified in many instances and merely enjoy the feeling of having renounced it; let him step down into the civic and social life of the masses to open up new channels and paths which will never be overgrown; for if they are well laid, the people will immediately surge out onto them; finally let him recognize the importance of his calling.[32]

Contrary to Chernyshevsky's accusations of passivity, Annenkov credits this weakness as a promise of change, a pledge to the future: "The circle of so-called 'weak' characters is the historical material out of which our present-day life [or 'the very life of modernity,' *samaia zhizn' sovremennosti*] is being created."[33]

Building on Annenkov's understanding of weakness, Faustov and Savinkov delineate the constitutive difference between the superfluous character and the weak character: the former can truly only perceive himself—for instance, Dostoevsky's Underground Man, who is unable to exit his own mind, suffering from inertia and self-isolation, is a superfluous character—while the weak character is aware of other human beings, and of the larger whole of which he is a part.

PIERRE BEZUKHOV AS THE PROTOTYPICAL
NINETEENTH-CENTURY WEAK CHARACTER

If we accept this definition of weakness, we might further point to Pierre Bezukhov, who is not typically associated with any of the three character types discussed above, as a quintessential example of this category. *War and Peace* (*Voina i mir*) constantly registers the weakness felt by various characters at various times—the weakness they feel in comparison to other, stronger, more confident, men, up to the tsar and Napoleon; the country at large; or vast forces like history or divine providence. But it is Pierre who is specifically described as a person of "weak character" on several occasions, including at the novel's outset: "He immediately recalled his promise to Prince Andrew not to go there [to Kuragin's]. Then, as happens to people of weak character, he desired so passionately once more to enjoy that dissipation he was accustomed to, that he decided to go."[34] Notably, Pierre's weakness is emphasized, but also pointedly dissociated from *physical* strength, which he possesses in spades. Bound up with a lack of self-control and self-confidence, Pierre's weakness is at first presented as a negative quality, one that makes him a victim of various high-society intrigues and scrapes. And yet it is precisely his inner dissonance that ultimately imbues him with self-reflection and the ability to self-correct; it is also this weakness that leads him, in the end, to take responsibility and disentangle himself from the deleterious influences of others. The next mention of Pierre's "weak character" comes in the context of his reassessment of his own motives, and the causes of his own failures.

> Pierre was one of those people who, in spite of an appearance of what is called weak character, do not seek a confidant in their troubles. He digested his sufferings alone. "It is all, all her fault," he said to himself; "but what of that?

> Why did I bind myself to her? Why did I say 'Je vous aime' to her, which was a lie, and worse than a lie? I am guilty and must endure."[35]

Tolstoy consistently shows Pierre's process of moral reflection as a split between trying to comfort himself with received truths and, on the other hand, sensing his own wrongness, which places him in a weak but ethical position. Notably, in *The Young Tolstoy* (*Molodoi Tolstoi*), Boris Eikhenbaum argues that Tolstoy's painstaking recording of his own weaknesses in his diaries, which recalls Pierre's self-inventorying cited above, does not constitute a mere abstract moral questioning, but rather a process of self-education— the formulation of a future program of behavior and action.[36]

For her part, Ginzburg connects Pierre's "weak will" with his profile as a character most change oriented and open to the world. "Pierre has certain organic qualities"—his "weak-willed gentleness [*miagkost'*, literally, and importantly, 'softness'] and goodness (a heightened capacity, that is, for pity and sympathy)," which shape his "organic, spontaneous reactions to the surrounding world, and [Tolstoy] has no doubt about [these qualities'] stability. They interact with the character's secondary sociohistorical attributes."[37] Pierre's particular combination of organic and sociohistorical attributes results in his eventually becoming a Decembrist. Lina Steiner likewise sees Pierre's character, including his weakness, as exemplary of growth: "Pierre's naivete, his weakness of will, his lack of self-control and occasional outbursts of temper all make him an ideal subject for a pedagogical novel, and that is indeed how Tolstoy envisioned Pierre's story."[38] We might also associate this pedagogical element with Pierre's brief but meaningful affiliation with the Masons, for whom the process of painstaking self-analysis, self-reflection, and self-correction was key to pedagogy, and for whom pedagogy was key to doing good in the world. According to Ginzburg, it was precisely under the influence of Masonry that Russian intellectual culture of the nineteenth century transformed from mere inquiry to *self*-inquiry, to the endeavor to understand one's purpose and course of future action;[39] it can be inferred from her analysis that she finds attentiveness to one's own weakness more *realistic*, more psychologically cogent, than confidence.[40] Tolstoy mocks the ritualistic and superficial aspects of Masonry in the novel, but nevertheless seems to sympathize with its underlying aims, and thus makes Masonry an important step in Pierre's attempt to combine self-questioning with consideration of the public good, and to find his place in the world.

Pierre's "softness" (*miagkost'*), his mental and emotional flexibility and responsiveness to others, ensures his ultimate fate as a comic character, in the classical Greek sense of showing resilience, surviving; in this, he is a counterpart to the tragic Prince Andrei Bolkonsky, whose steadfastness is bound up with his doom. Early in the book, Pierre subscribes to the Hegelian idea

29

of the extraordinary personality who drives forward the historical process, and he hopes to discover this extraordinariness in himself; but he comes to abandon this idea and perceive himself rather as part of a totality (and not a totality in himself), as seen in his vision of life as a liquid, vibrating globe and himself a tiny drop in it. This vision of life's fluidity fits well with the organic flexibility and softness of character that, through Pierre, are affirmed as qualities necessary for life; in this vision, incorporation and fluidity become generative principles of one's being in the world. Whereas Andrei's solidity, and his calcification in old ways, eventually lead to his demise, Pierre is supremely resilient, fitting into the world not despite, but because of, his weakness.

TOLSTOY AND LESKOV TURN TO LAO TZU

Tolstoy would on several occasions turn to the wisdom of Lao Tzu, finding in it much affinity with his own thinking. He was particularly drawn to the Chinese philosopher's dictum, cited at the outset of this book, that "weakness is great, strength is trifling." In an 1884 diary entry, Tolstoy recorded his Russian rendering of this passage from a French translation:

Из Лаоцы. Когда человек родится, он гибок и слаб; когда он колян и крепок—он умирает. Когда деревья родятся, они гибки и нежны. Когда они сухи и жестки, они умирают. Крепость и сила—спутники смерти. Гибкость и слабость—спутники жизни. Поэтому то, что сильно, то не побеждает. Когда дерево стало крепко, его срубают. То, что сильно и велико, то ничтожно; то, что гибко и слабо, то важно.[41]

From Lao Tzu: When a man is born, he is flexible and weak; when he is [kolyan] and tough, he dies. When trees are born, they are flexible and tender. When they are dry and tough, they die. Hardness and strength are the companions of death. Flexibility and weakness are the companions of life. Therefore, that which is strong, does not win. When a tree hardens, it is cut down. That which is strong and great is insignificant; that which is flexible and weak is important.

Tolstoy would revise his rendering of this passage several times. Later, in 1893–1894, he collaborated with E. I. Popov on a Russian translation of the *Tao Te Ching*, using the German and French versions of Viktor von Strauss and Stanislas Julien respectively;[42] this came out as a separate edition in 1910, with a foreword by Tolstoy. Here Tolstoy connects his Gospel-derived doctrine of nonresistance to evil to the Taoist concept Tolstoy renders in Russian as *nedelanie* ("nonaction").[43] As explained by Tolstoy, Lao Tzu's teaching espouses moving away from the life of the body—associated with the affirmation of one's ego—and toward the life of the spirit, associated with unity with others and the world: "Tao is achieved via the abstinence from everything personal and corporeal."[44] This might sound like a call for total detachment from the world, but in a letter to an anonymous correspondent published in 1907 in the *Stock Market News* (*Birzhevye vedomosti*), Tolstoy reformulates this thought into a call to be less self-oriented and more *other*-oriented: "Real life is that in which all former energy, all passion of existence is transferred outside of oneself, onto the service of that process of unity, harmony, and ever greater reasonableness between beings, in which universal life resides."[45] The explicit formulation of these ideas of nonaction and nonresistance to evil came later in Tolstoy's life, but their seeds are already evident in *War and Peace*. Napoleon's certainty of his right to power and conquest is presented as folly, while consciousness of the vulnerability of one's army—of the need to refrain as much as possible from action, so as to avoid casualties—is to Kutuzov's credit. And in Pierre Bezukhov, weakness—combining Annenkovian nonsolidity and Taoist softness and responsiveness—turns out not to isolate but to incorporate him into the world, into action and a life with others.

In 1887, in the course of revising his story "The Buffoon Pamphalon," which had been written a year earlier but barred by both the secular and ecclesiastical censorship, Nikolai Leskov gave it an epigraph: none other than Lao Tzu's words on the power of weakness.[46] That same year, Leskov wrote his very first letter to Tolstoy, expressing his affinity with the latter's worldview. Like Tolstoy, Leskov associated Lao Tzu's idea about weakness with the renunciation of one's ego, and with an understanding of spirituality, not as superficial piety, as ascetic-prideful detachment from the world, but as service and positive action in God's universe. In a letter to his son, for example, in the course of referencing Christian theology, he adduces the ideal of *softness* in a manner reminiscent of Lao Tzu: "Try to understand God according to St. Paul: clay does not argue with the Potter: He molds you into the vessel needed in His household at the moment. You want to be a cabinet vase, but in His household you are needed as a pot for cooking soup or taking out slop."[47] Leskov's controversial story is ostensibly based on the seventeenth-century hagiography of Theodoulos the Stylite, but as I. N. Mineeva observes, the author's approach to his source is polemical. Instead of validating Theodoulos's righteousness, Leskov focuses on his counterpart, the buffoon Cornelius. Theodoulos rejects earthly life and spends his days in solitary contemplation, but Cornelius, who does not think of himself as saintly, and spends his days in profane, impious pursuits, is always ready to offer a helping hand to anyone in need. In Leskov's story, the venerable stylite comes to realize that there is more divine presence in the buffoon's care for others than in his own devout asceticism. Clearly understanding Leskov's polemical (perhaps even heretical) stance, the religious censorship forbade publication. In his revised version, Leskov makes several concessions, changing names so as to seem less blasphemous, and the ending, so that the stylite is returned to his life of abstemious seclusion; but the epigraph he adds only highlights the story's original point.

As Mineeva also notes, Leskov alludes in this story to Origen of Alexandria and that theologian's idea of the world as a school for the education of the human being.[48] In this piece, then, holy foolishness, as a separation from the world, and the sanctification of oneself through kenosis and self-abasement, are counterposed to the righteousness of humble readiness to serve people. In this schema, self-abasement out of pride is a form of *strength* (asceticism, after all, requires great stamina), as opposed to the *weakness* of heeding the call of the other. In 1890, Tolstoy begins work on his own parody of a hagiographic text, "Father Sergius" ("Otets Sergii"), which dramatizes a message quite similar to that of Leskov. Prince Stepan Kasatsky is induced by extreme pride to become the monk and hermit Father Sergius. The greater the world's estimation of his sanctity, the further he finds himself from faith and the life of the spirit. Only when he stops aspiring to perfection, accepts his vulnerability, and leaves his hermitage does he approach true spiritual transcendence. He seeks the opportunity to learn about righteousness from Pashenka, an indigent woman whose utterly unremarkable life constitutes a failure in the eyes of the world, but who is selflessly dedicated to the service of her family. Notably, as a spiritual exemplar, Pashenka does not embody self-effacement or kenosis per se, but rather the acceptance of life's imperfection and the self's vulnerability as preconditions of relationality. Humility, if and only if combined with empathy and good deeds, is the model of weakness Tolstoy espouses.

WEAK THOUGHT AND OTHER FORMS OF WEAKNESS UNDER STALINISM

In the twentieth century, vulnerability, self-doubt, and melancholic longing become the characteristic affects of Andrei Platonov's prose. Beset by an uncertain and draining thoughtfulness,[49] his characters keep trying to "domesticate" the cold, impersonal new rhetoric of the Soviet system, taking abstractions from official newspeak and attempting to imbue them with concreteness, personal meaning, and intimacy. These are quintessentially weak characters; but it is precisely their doubt—their consciousness of the gap between grand aspirations and the contingencies of human or material existence—that act as predicates for an ethical and truly collective outlook.

In *Men without Women: Masculinity and Revolution in Russian Fiction, 1917–1929*, Eliot Borenstein examines how in *Chevengur* (1928) Platonov scrutinizes and experiments with his own formerly cherished beliefs that a communal utopia must by necessity be a brotherhood, in which the feminine, as the nexus of either social or natural weakness, is expunged. Borenstein cogently argues, however, that the novel demonstrates the ultimate unviability of the purely masculine, exclusionary comradeship: "The arrival of women heralds the end of the male utopia, and yet the decision to bring them to the city is nearly unanimous. The inclusion of women in Chevengur does not lead to an unqualified acceptance of femininity and sexuality, but is rather the acknowledgment that antifemale, antisexual ideologues are unable to come up with a viable alternative to biology and tradition."[50] Borenstein demonstrates how Platonov simultaneously espouses and negates the ideal of "the hyper-masculinized self-sufficiency."[51] Noteworthy in this context is Platonov's review of the theatrical production of *The Idiot* and his admiration for Prince Myshkin, whom, according to Borenstein, Platonov reproaches in only one aspect: "A lack of warriorlike masculinity: Myshkin has yet to rid himself of pity. He must still learn that such feelings should be channeled away from love of weakness into the struggle to transform this weakness into strength, into 'the construction of iron palaces of power on the swampy ripples of powerlessness.'"[52] It is this very pity, this persistent and unsuccessful struggle to transform one's weakness into strength, that all of Platonov's protagonists so memorably evince.

Furthermore, in a 1934 article titled "On the First Socialist Tragedy" ("O pervoi sotsialisticheskoi tragedii"), Platonov cautions against the belief that humanity can free itself entirely from nature and its fortuities. "With the right moment of force it is possible to overturn the world, but so much will be lost in the journey and in the travel time of the lever that in practical terms the victory will be useless."[53] Platonov's critique of the radical biopolitical project of the Soviet state foregrounds the latter's adherence to categorical reasoning, to which Platonov's texts counterpose a conceptualization of all matter, from people to machines to flowers, as alike in its desire for communism and its limited capacity to realize it. When in *Chevengur*, Chepurnyi acutely senses that "the burdock also longs for communism, and that weeds are live plants in a state of friendship," when Dvanov hears, in the ringing of bells, "anxiety, faith, and doubt," and Zakhar Pavlovich discerns independent life in "vulnerable machines,"[54] we might sense a mere anthropomorphizing; but as Jonathan Platt argues, it is in this empathetic consideration of the frailty and contingency of *everything* that sprouts of true communist solidarity can perhaps be found.[55]

In "Honest Jacobins: High Stalinism and the Socialist Subjectivity of Mikhail Lifshitz and Andrei Platonov," Pavel Khazanov draws a distinction between the earlier *Chevengur* (1928) and *The Foundation Pit* (*Kotlovan*, 1930), in which characters worry that their deficiencies make them unfit for the new socialist society, and the later *Happy Moscow* (*Shchastlivaia Moskva*, 1936), in which this self-reflection itself, and the understanding that the process of self-transformation is ever ongoing, incorporates them into the collective.

Khazanov sees Platonov's texts as foregrounding the "dialectical relationship between human utopian desires and their creative non-satiation."[56] He further argues, however, that Platonov's emphasis on the *soul* as an unceasing producer of unsatisfiable desires resonates with Andrei Zhdanov's 1934 call for writers to become "engineers of human souls," in that both shift the focus of their ostensibly Marxist milieu from material to metaphysical and spiritual transformation. The difference, per Khazanov, is that whereas Stalinist subjectivization of Soviet citizens turned "objective errors [into] manifestations of subjective, personal evil,"[57] Platonov, even as he shares Stalinism's prioritizing of feelings over matter, would rather reduce subjective difference on the basis of objective, and *common*, deficiency. For Platonov, the perpetual urge to remake oneself is a universal condition, uniting all humankind in a utopian socialist community; no one is excluded from deficiency and the desire to overcome it.

In Khazanov's reading of *Happy Moscow*, Platonov here pits two socialist subjectivities exhibiting two forms of weakness against each other. The first weakness is represented by the title character Moscow, whose debility is physical. Left disabled by an accident during her parachute training—an activity that metonymizes Soviet prowess and valor—she is unburdened by "the difficult effort of self-reflection necessary for becoming a true socialist"; her physical disability only underscores her service as an instrument, an object of societal transformation rather than its subject: "She happily writes herself into the Soviet project, whose official founding memory she symbolically shares, but at the cost of herself remaining a 'dead tool of salutary history.' . . . By the end of the text, the former daughter of the Revolution is both a literal and symbolic cripple, missing all the parts that had made her happy."[58] Her counterpart is Sartorius, whose weakness is rather his searing spirit of dissatisfaction and critique; this frailty, however, is precisely what makes him integral to the community, to socialist self-transformation.

In this interpretation, despite her gender, Moscow shares certain of the strengths and deficiencies characteristic of male heroes of Stalin-era fiction and cinema, as described by Lilya Kaganovsky in *How the Soviet Man Was Unmade: Cultural Fantasy and Male Subjectivity under Stalin* (2008). In this study, Kaganovsky tackles the paradox of the Stalinist model of masculinity: the contradictory valorization of hegemonic masculinity on the one hand, and on the other, the hierarchical, rigidly vertical power structure, in which no one was to be quite as strong and masculine as Stalin. As Kaganovsky shows, this tension resulted in the proliferation of literary and cinematic characters whose heroism and martial readiness had to go hand in hand with severe physical and psychic deficiencies. Kaganovsky reads this forcibly acquired inadequacy as a form of sacrifice to the masculinity whose hegemony could never be questioned.

In a way, Kaganovsky's argument reformulates the dynamic we have encountered in scholarship on nineteenth-century Russian culture: the unhealthy relationship between state power and the male citizens who dwell under it. Like superfluous men, socialist-realist characters are forced to feel deficient vis-à-vis the ideal constantly imposed on them, and toward which their progress is foreclosed. And yet, unlike superfluous men, they can derive a sense of satisfaction from offering their debility in service—to buttress the very ideal that cripples them. In this self-sacrifice, they seem closer to another model of nineteenth-century masculinity, the holy fool.

THE LATE SOVIET WEAK MAN
IN FILM AND MASS MEDIA

It is precisely this kind of strength in the guise of weakness that the poet and critic Igor Gulin identifies as an essential characteristic of Soviet masculinity, which was undergoing certain key transformations in the late 1960s:

> From birth, the Soviet man [*sovetskii muzhchina*] derived his strength from weakness. The collateral of his frail masculinity was the rejection of normal, sexualized masculinity for the sake of a lofty, sacrificial one. The sacrifice was made in history: in the great past or future. But by the 1970s, the past ceased to belong to him—it belonged to the fathers (the war) and grandfathers (the revolution)—while the future was disappearing right before his eyes. The future was not accepting any sacrifices, even if you wanted to offer one. This is how the heroically weak [*geroicheski slabyi*] Soviet man slowly disappears, remaining only as a figure of often comical ressentiment (as incarnate in Vysotsky). He becomes simply weak and pathetic.[59]

Explaining the stagnation era's pervasive nihilism and disorientation with reference to a *disappearance of the future* fits well with the "crisis of masculinity" paradigm discussed in the introduction. This assessment of late Soviet masculinity comes in an article by Gulin titled "If She Reproaches You, That Means She Loves You" ("Korit—znachit liubit"), which focuses on the feminine gaze in cinema of the stagnation period. Here Gulin suggests that the pessimism and exhaustion of the time, and the experience of mature socialism as a general senescence, led to the creation of films in which men are worn out and diminished. According to Gulin, Soviet films of the late 1960s evince an understanding of the Soviet order as a papered-over void. In particular, this cover-up is effected by the gaze of the other: "The point of all these movies is not that the [Soviet] order is bad, but that it is a pure game, a mirage. It is held together by the strong gaze of the other. And all it takes for disorientation [*rasteriannost'*] to set in is if that gaze slackens."[60] In this interpretation, the role of women in cinema of the 1970s is to be strong, not for any feminist, emancipatory purpose,[61] but so as to supply the orienting gaze in an atmosphere of pessimism and perplexity. This gaze takes the form of a "reproach" (*ukor*), but as Gulin perspicaciously observes, not just in the sense of remarking on men's insufficiency; this "reproach" also registers *recognition*, providing disoriented men with a sense of place, of belonging, which they have otherwise lost.

Gulin thus associates the late Soviet weak man with two affects, one presumably emanating from the man himself—resentment toward the former heroic forms of masculine weakness—and the other emanating toward him: the reproachful gaze registering disappointment with him. Both these feelings would fall under the category of low-intensity feelings, or what Sianne Ngai calls "ugly feelings." According to Ngai, such feelings are less powerful than classical political passions, but on the other hand, they are, in their ambiguity and illegibility, more conducive than passions to the fostering of ironic distance in a reader or viewer, and of sociopolitically useful interpretations and diagnoses.

> Whereas Hobbes and Aristotle have shown how the principle of mutual fear actively binds men into the contracts that support the political commonwealth, and how anger advances the redressing of perceived injustices through retaliation, it is difficult to imagine how either of these actions might be advanced by an affective state like, say, irritation. While one can be irritated without realizing it, or knowing exactly what one is irritated about, there can be nothing ambiguous about one's rage or terror, or about what one is terrified or enraged about. Yet the unsuitability of these weakly intentional feelings for forceful or unambiguous action is precisely what amplifies their power to diagnose situations, and situations marked by blocked or thwarted action in particular.[62]

The ambivalence and illegibility of these feelings, for example, might complicate the schema proposed by Gulin. Does Vysotsky, as the degraded endpoint of the old, heroic type of weak masculinity, appear as such in *The Meeting Place Cannot Be Changed* (*Mesto vstrechi izmenit' nel'zia*, 1979)? Does he perform this same role in Kira Muratova's *Korotkie vstrechi* (*Brief*

Encounters)? In both roles, Vysotsky plays a peripatetic, unsettled character; in both he appears unsuited for domestication, and he elicits various forms of reproach. While this combination of traits suggests agency and presence in the later *Meeting Place*, Kaganovsky interprets Vysotsky's character Maksim in *Brief Encounters* as an empty signifier, an absent masculinity, unreliable and fickle.[63] Kaganovsky reads Muratova's film as foreclosing the possibility of the male gaze, of directly identifying with a strong male lead. Vysotsky's character is weakened by the structure of looking: his lot is to be looked *at*—a situation he would just as soon *flee*.

But whereas Maksim attempts to escape the objectification and weakening that the gaze of the other would impose on him, the most popular films of the 1970s center on what Gulin would term *simply* weak, *unheroically* weak men—men who have internalized the reproach cast on them and structured their identity accordingly. Consider the phenomenon of the strangely charismatic Andrei Miagkov, whose very surname suggests the unmanly softness his most beloved characters evince. Think of *The Irony of Fate, or Enjoy your Bath!* (*Ironiia sud'by, ili S legkim parom!*, 1976) or *Office Romance* (*Sluzhebnyi roman*, 1977); how does one explain the advent of such a romantic lead? In both films, the reproachful gaze of various female characters eventually gives way to understanding and appreciation—and male *self*-reproach gives way to *self*-understanding—without Miagkov's characters ever needing to become more stereotypically manly.

The weak characters of late Soviet cinema arouse conflicting emotions. Miagkov's characters are bossed around by various females; they are childish and unsure of themselves. Their disorientation is literal. In *The Irony of Fate*, Zhenia gets drunk with his buddies and ends up in the wrong apartment, wrong neighborhood, wrong city, which in the end turns out to be exactly the right place for him to be. In *Office Romance*, Anatoly Novoseltsev is also quite literally misplaced, being the only male in an otherwise all-female department, unable to secure a much-needed promotion. However, when pitted against more conventional types of masculinity, both characters win by comparison. Ippolit, played by Yury Iakovlev, and Yury Samokhvalov, played by Oleg Basilashvili, are foils to Miagkov's heroes; they perform the role of stereotypically desirable masculinity. Radiating stability, ambition, and late Soviet prosperity and propriety, these characters consider themselves, and are considered by the women around them, perfect males, natural breadwinners. These characters seem to preexist any "crisis of masculinity," or to have bypassed it entirely. But, perhaps precisely because they have substituted self-reproach and questioning with the ready-made formulas of "correct" manliness, they are more susceptible to negative behavior than Miagkov's ever-uncertain, childishly unformed characters.

According to Natalia Lesskis, *The Irony of Fate* dramatizes a yearning for communication and intimacy unmediated by state or party, not pre-scribed by external socio-ideological dictates.[64] In the conversation between Ippolit and Miagkov's Zhenia, Ippolit accuses his interlocutor of unmoored-ness to any system of values: "For you there is nothing traditional, nothing lawful, nothing sacred. You are uncontrollable [*neupravliaemyi*]." To which Zhenia responds, "People like you are always right, about everything, be-cause you live properly, as expected, as prescribed. But that is your weak-ness. . . . It is impossible to shoehorn life into a verified scheme [*podognat' pod vyverenuiu skhemu*]."[65]

Curiously, this little manifesto is declared by a not-so-young man who still lives with his mother and is barely able to make do without her care, and whose life has, up to this moment, been predictable, familiar, and free of the necessity of personal choice, even in such "local" matters as interior decor. (After all, it was not just whole neighborhoods, streets, and apartment blocks in Moscow and Leningrad that looked identical; *inside* the apartments, too, everyone had the exact same furniture.) While Zhenia identifies the "weak-ness" belying Ippolit's self-assurance, Zhenia's own *focal* weakness signals a yearning for escape from conventionality and predictability. In a way, it matches what Jack Halberstam identifies as the "queer art of failure," a will-ingness to take uncharted roads and to get lost in them.[66] In *The Irony of Fate*, it is alcoholic intoxication that enables this lostness, that introduces the element of chance into the predictable sphere of existence; Lesskis compares this aspect of the film with the alcoholic rituals of Erofeev's *Moscow–Petushki* (to be discussed in chapter 4), arguing that the film marked the first attempt to bring Russian underground intelligentsia culture (embodied by Erofeev) out of its small, elite circle and into broader public view.[67] In going from text to film—to the Soviet equivalent of the American *It's a Wonderful Life*, no less, as *The Irony of Fate* was shown every New Year's Eve—this culture be-came universally Soviet. This reading suggests that audiences were ready to embrace characters like Miagkov's Zhenia and Anatoly Novoseltsev, despite the reproaches and derision they encounter in the diegetic space of films, and despite, or perhaps because of, their queering of Soviet masculinity.

Within the ethos of the 1970s intelligentsia, the complexity and un-predictability of weakness went hand in hand with the cult of kindness. As Mark Lipovetsky describes, "[This] was the period when 'kindness' was de-clared the highest value and utilized as a primary *aesthetic* criterion."[68] In this context, kindness seems to emerge as a sensation that arises in mor-ally ambivalent situations and performs the guiding role usually assigned to conventional morality. It is also associated with weakness of will. Kindness, especially when divorced from cultural prescriptions or moral codes, takes us into the realm of ethics, which Foucault defines as "the relation with your-self when you act."[69] In this view, unlike morality, which exists a priori and is coded in principles and rules, ethics relies on individual choice, on one's assessment of complicated, morally ambiguous situations. (How Foucauldian ethics bears on my theorization of weakness is described in note 36 of this chapter.)

One such *kind* character is Buzykin, the exhausted protagonist of *Autumn Marathon* (*Osennii marafon*, 1979; dir. Georgii Daneliia), played by Oleg Basilashvili. Besieged by the demands of his all-enduring wife and his impatient mistress to choose between them, Buzykin is perpetually unable to do so. The obstacle is not so much some desire to keep both—he actually seems to have little need or desire for either—but rather *kindness*, his inability to hurt either one with his choice. Situating him within the cultural discourses of the Soviet late 1970s, where kindness reigned supreme, Lipovetsky calls Buzykin an "unwilling trickster."[70] Analyzing this kindness—in particular, how their "trickster" methods of avoiding cruelty hardly aid the protagonists of sad comedies like *Autumn Marathon* in their relations with others—Lipovetsky adduces the opinion of two well-known Soviet film critics, the brother and sister Andrei Zorky and Neia Zorkaya, who see literary precedent for Buzykin's combination of culturedness and delicacy, compassion, and fear of harming others. He shares these traits, they argue, with many of the heroes of classic Russian literature—men who suffer in anguish but cannot change, and are too weak, in other words too *kind*, to deliver the cold, hard truth. As the Zorkys bemoan the consequences of this kindness:

> Andrey Bolkonsky could not honestly tell his wife Lise that he did not love her, and when she died, he mourned long and hard, hardly rejoicing in his newly found freedom. And Prince Lev Myshkin? Wasn't his weak-willed oscillation between Aglaya Epanchina and Nastasya Fillipovna duplicit? Wouldn't it have been more correct to put Aglaya in her place and to give NF a hint about her shameful past without ever intending to become engaged to her? Finally, why do Chekhov's heroes so often submit to people who are strong and crude, why do they suffer from the pressure of the self-confident and the know-it-all?[71]

Buzykin's attempts to not harm those around him are thus read as the latest in an unfortunate line of deficient behavior. Buzykin's kindness makes him a pitifully weak character whose kindheartedness only distresses "his" two women. He must therefore endure all the reproachful gazes coming to him, not least from the Zorkys. And yet, it's hard not to empathize with his (self-imposed) plight. As Adam Phillips and Barbara Taylor write in their book-length examination of kindness, this quality means "susceptibility to others, a capacity to identify with their pleasures and sufferings."[72] And it is precisely this susceptibility that makes Buzykin both pitiful and endearing, and pushes the viewer into an ethical quandary, as evident in the Zorkys' litany of unanswered questions.

SOTNIKOV, SHEPITKO, AND THE TRIUMPH OF WEAKNESS

But perhaps Soviet cinema's most thoughtful exploration of weakness, of its drawbacks and advantages, is to be found in a work by a great *woman* director. In 1977, the Ukrainian film director Larisa Shepitko made her most celebrated film, and the one that would be her last (she died in a car accident shortly thereafter): *The Ascent* (*Voskhozhdenie*), based on the novella *Sotnikov* (1969) by the Belarusian writer Vasil Bykov (published in English as *The Ordeal*). Both these works, which are set during the Second World War, on the face of it would appear to foreground the heroism and sacrifice of Soviet partisans and the brutality of fascism; but they stand apart from most Soviet war dramas in that they *complicate* the weakness/strength binary.

Bykov's eponymous partisan Sotnikov is a bespectacled *intelligent*, with a teacher's diploma. As the plot opens, he has volunteered, despite being ill with the flu, to accompany a fellow partisan, Rybak, on a mission to reconnoiter and get provisions. The novella plays with readerly expectations, albeit not initially: Sotnikov is clearly the weaker of the two. Rybak, a man of peasant background, is burly and agile, physically strong and mentally practical. He has only an elementary level of formal education, but he possesses knowledge far more suited than that of Sotnikov to the situation: he can navigate the forest and, being native to the area, knows it intimately. Coughing, physically weak, and too lightly clad for the brutal winter weather, Sotnikov is a poor match for the mission. He appears to be a liability, a weak link, and indeed his cough and slowness cause the pair to be exposed and captured by the enemy. The reader is naturally inclined to judge Sotnikov harshly for his weakness and inopportune volunteering. But such preconceptions are overturned when it is Sotnikov, and not Rybak, who demonstrates resilience, finds the courage not to give up their partisan group under torture, and meets death with dignity.

In particular, the plot represents an overturning of the maxim, propagandized in Soviet culture as in others, of the "healthy mind in a healthy body." Here the healthy body in no way guarantees a fortitude of spirit—an obvious affront to the Soviet valorization of athleticism. Likewise the relationship between these characters' actions and their class background: readers of socialist-realist novels were trained to expect spinelessness and duplicity from weak *intelligenty*, not from workers or peasants.

But Bykov's exploration of weakness in *Sotnikov* goes beyond this subversion of cultural expectations about class and masculinity. He endeavors, that is, not just to draw a distinction between the two men but to highlight their shared predicament of finding themselves under the condition of total helplessness. Both are in fact victims of circumstance ("such is the power of circumstance," explains Bykov[73]), caught in the whirlwind of the brutal forces of nature and history. Whatever strength, physical or spiritual, either is possessed of—this is no match for the "power of circumstance," the hostile forces that menace them. Both fail to accomplish their mission, and the actions of both lead to the execution of innocent people (who had helped them along the way). Even Sotnikov's refusal to give anything away under torture—a quintessentially heroic act—is ineffective in practical terms: the Nazi captors do not need both men to corroborate their information; it is enough that one of them is ready to talk. Sotnikov and Rybak's situation is thus one of utter failure and disempowerment. Bykov aims to examine what kind of choices remain in the total absence of agency. Both men are doomed, but the one who chooses death over unpalatable collaboration in the end seems the more resilient, less subject to external forces. In a way, this is an experiment: it is their condition of radical weakness that enables the two characters to come face-to-face with who they really are—to understand, viscerally, their relationship to the world.

Explaining her conception of the film's central dilemma, Larisa Shepitko emphasized self-discovery: "The ascent is not to somewhere, but to oneself. Sotnikov ascended [*voznessia*]. Rybak, although he remained alive, destroyed his self in himself [*unichtozhil v sebe sebia*]."[74] Rybak assures himself that his compromise is just strategic; he hopes to escape and rejoin the partisan forces. We could interpret this as a mere rationalization for cowardice, but in a lecture on the novella,[75] Dmitry Bykov (no relation) reads Rybak's choice as problematizing utilitarian thinking: Rybak wants to live so that he can "remain useful" and resume his fight against fascism. But, as we are admonished by Tolstoy with his "nonaction," and by Giorgio Agamben with his "impotentiality," not every situation demands one's action; sometimes abstention has more potential. Tolstoy explains "nonaction" thus: "All the disasters of people, according to the teaching of Laozi, come not so much from what they have not done out of what was needed, as much as what they do out of what they shouldn't."[76] And as Agamben explains his concept, "Impotentiality does not mean . . . only [the] absence of potentiality, not being able to do, but also and above all 'being able to not do,' being able to not exercise one's own potentiality."[77] (Such philosophical and ethical pushback against action and heroism can of course have political and even geopolitical implications; compare, for instance, the connection drawn by John Shelton Lawrence and Robert Jewett between the American preoccupation with superheroes and US military adventurism and folly.[78]) As Dmitry

Bykov notes, Rybak's instrumental reasoning ultimately entraps him in the mere service of brutality. In this view, Sotnikov's resilience comes not despite his status as an *intelligent* but *because* of it—because of his ability to think in complex, even abstract terms, rather than the naked utility of further action.

Critics have noted the Christian overtones of Shepitko's film: its very title, and the marked association of the frequently illuminated Sotnikov with Christ, and of the abject, postbetrayal Rybak with Judas Iscariot. For his part, Dmitry Bykov faults Shepitko's decision to imbue Sotnikov with Christian kenotic and sacrificial connotations. The literary prototype, he argues, is not saintly but ordinary: "[Vasil] Bykov to the contrary tried to highlight the everydayness of his hero, his marked lack of heroism, the idea that anyone could be like him, and moreover that the most pitiable, the most hapless, will in the end turn out to be the most heroic."[79] Why should the most hapless, the one most destined to fail, prove the most heroic? If we follow this reasoning, we might see Bykov's text as proposing a distinction between victory and virtue. As against the mentality of a victor, who *manages*, who *comes out on top*, Sotnikov's acceptance of failure allows him to abstain from ethically perilous compromise. *Managing* at all costs can alienate one from oneself and the world. As Shepitko emphasizes (narratively, but also especially compositionally), Rybak—shunned by the villagers after his self-saving compromise, but hardly fitting in with the fascists either—dooms himself to intolerable loneliness, whereas Sotnikov in his weakness seems to stand, as will be discussed below, for the idea of community.

Dmitry Bykov faults Shepitko's decision to make her Sotnikov extraordinary and saintly, arguing that, in the source novella, the force of this character's depiction lies precisely in his belonging to this world: "Sotnikov is not a martyr, but one of many [*ne muchenik, a odin iz mnogikh*], and the value of this image lies precisely in its mass nature."[80] The religious overtones notwithstanding, however, Shepitko's Sotnikov does not belong to the realm of heroic abstraction. First of all, like his prototype in Bykov's novella, he is not a figure of absolute perfection; he rather appears riddled with guilt and self-doubt, and is hardly at peace with himself. In Shepitko's Sotnikov, integrity and weakness, integrity and self-questioning, not only coexist but appear to buttress each other.[81]

In the novella, what situates Sotnikov's weakness in the post-Thaw USSR of his creation, rather than in some atemporal biblical dimension, is his deliberation, just before being executed, not about the rightfulness of his martyrdom but about the guilt he feels for those he has inadvertently doomed. This preoccupation with one's relationship to the world—the interrogation of one's own behavior vis-à-vis others—links Sotnikov to other weak characters of late Soviet fiction.

Both film and source text clearly represent, aside from a historical fiction about the Soviet-German War, a contemplation of the predicament of the Soviet intelligentsia, or of people generally: Sotnikov and Rybak's situation dramatizes a person's relationship with the various irresistible forces found in life. As Shepitko insisted on several occasions, her film is not just about the war. In one interview, she seems to extrapolate the situation of the artist vis-à-vis power to that of the late Soviet intelligentsia generally:

> Every day, every second prompts us to make a compromise, to maneuver, keep silent sometimes, make a concession in the hope of making up for it later. . . . "I'll say what they want there, I'll try to please them here, and avoid saying it there, here I'll tell only a half-truth, there I'll hush it up altogether. But in my next film, I will make up for it, I'll tell everything I want, in full measure as a creative person should, as an artist, as a citizen. I'll tell it all." It's a lie. It's impossible. It's hopeless to deceive yourself by this illusion. If you stumble once, you'll forget the way there.[82]

Scholars of Soviet subjectivity often see it through the prism of dissimulation, or in Lipovetsky's definition, tricksterism. In this reading, it entails a certain degree of compromise, the practical donning of various masks and discourses appropriate for the given time and place. Shepitko's statement here acknowledges the truth of such assessments but rejects the necessity of this state of affairs. Still more poignantly, she foregrounds the problem of communication, even of *communion*. The dissimulation required by the Soviet system seemed to also require, as a corollary, that everyone find their place in this dissimulation; but through Rybak's predicament, Shepitko demonstrates how compromise atomizes people, leaves them utterly alone. Likewise radically alone is the local collaborator who interrogates Sotnikov; this man, Portnov—himself scorned by the German officers he serves—gives the prisoner a speech about how "everyone breaks in the end," clearly signaling his own desperation for Sotnikov to join him in the category of compromiser, to provide company for his misery.

Looking at this episode through the prism of the Soviet intelligentsia's various compromises, Shepitko emphasizes that constant orientation toward power forecloses communication, makes one incomplete as an artist or a citizen. In the film, contra Dmitry Bykov's objections, communication and community are in fact highlighted. In an atmosphere where verbal communication implicates not just you but also your interlocutor, wordless communication becomes key. Words can betray; under interrogation, the woman in whose house the fascists have found Rybak and Sotnikov almost gives away another woman who has been hiding a Jewish girl, Basya (herself indeed captured), but then finds herself unable to save herself (and her own three children) by naming that harborer. Rybak's pragmatic (and self-serving) words

43

ensure his survival but doom him to radical solitude. In Shepitko's long pans of snow-swept planes and forests that dwarf a human being, in the coldness and desertedness of life depicted, characters communicate wordlessly by huddling together. Earlier, before they are caught, Rybak tells Sotnikov that he is glad to have a companion (even, it is implied, one so unreliable as the coughing Sotnikov), because he would not want to be in the forest alone. At times (again, before their capture), Rybak is forced to carry the ill and wounded Sotnikov on his back, but his doing so can be read as the alleviation of his own potential solitude.[83]

Shepitko's most idiosyncratic technique in this film is her extreme close-ups of her characters' faces. Sometimes, when these faces look straight into the camera, they seem to be attempting to communicate something to the viewer. At other times, when they look past the viewer, it is the viewer's turn to attempt to catch the character's gaze, to make a connection, to try to understand what they are thinking or experiencing. These extreme close-ups put characters and viewer into a situation almost of intimacy, and the characters themselves likewise keep looking at one another intensely, attempting to communicate and relate in silence.

Finally, I would emphasize that Sotnikov's resilience is bound up with the fact that he is specifically *not* alone. He could possibly have saved himself by compromising, but this would disaffiliate him from a world united by its vulnerability. Moreover, to survive would ultimately be unethical. After all,

Fig. 3. The prisoners led to the execution. *The Ascent* (dir. Larisa Shepitko, 1977).

Fig. 4. Sotnikov with the other condemned people. *The Ascent*
(dir. Larisa Shepitko, 1977).

the discovered Jewish girl, Basya, had no opportunity to make such a compromise or negotiate with the enemy. What does victory mean in a world
where some, like Basya, must perish, where the weak are destroyed? In this
predicament, the only ethical solution is to build a coalition of the weak. Sotnikov's weak decision incorporates him, quite physically, into the world; the
mis-en-scène makes the integration palpable (fig. 3). As Rybak, after making
his compromise, collapses and splits from the group, Sotnikov joins an old
man, a woman, and Basya—the captives he is to be executed with—in an embrace. They stand together supportively, keeping one another from falling,
organizing themselves into one human family (fig. 4).

The coalition of the weak might also offer a solution for endurance. As
he stands on the scaffold, about to be hanged, Sotnikov—rather than avert-
ing his eyes toward heaven, as might befit a martyr—gazes at a young boy in
the crowd and steals a quick smile, making a connection. Crucially, Sotnikov
remains, to the very end, a teacher, instructing this boy—not through the
example of self-sacrifice (an act of heroism "proper") but through wordless
communication, through which he might connect with and reassure the boy,
and through him, perhaps, the community of people. What Sotnikov models
for the youngster is an exemplary inseparability, the connectedness of the
vulnerable of this world.

Yuly Kim's *Cinderella in the Concentration Camp*: Performing Kurt Vonnegut's Gender Subversion in the USSR

ON APRIL 3, 1977, the *New York Times* declared, "The most popular American author in the USSR this decade is Kurt Vonnegut." Vonnegut traveled to Russia four times; developed a close friendship with his literary translator, the brilliant Rita Rait-Kovaleva; and was widely published, both in such literary journals as *Novyi mir* (*New World*) and *Literaturnaia gazeta* (*Literary Gazette*) and in stand-alone editions. In 1975, an adaptation of his anti-war novel *Slaughterhouse-Five* was staged, paradoxically enough, at the Theater of the Soviet Army. The production, directed by Mikhail Levitin, was called *The Wanderings of Billy Pilgrim* (*Stranstviia Billi Piligrima*). The script of the play was written by Mark Rozovsky and Yuly Mikhailov (the pseudonym of Yuly Kim). Vladimir Dashkevich, the composer who wrote the play's music, would later recall this production as an ultimately dull affair; but at the time, audiences flocked to it because there was one episode in particular that everyone wanted to see.[1] In his memoir, Levitin identifies the same scene as the very heart of the play.[2] This was a kind of *mise en abyme*: a pantomime of "Cinderella" staged by English POWs in a Nazi camp during the Second World War. I use "pantomime" here in the British sense: a theatrical entertainment based on a well-known fairy tale, and usually staged around Christmas, that involves cross-dressing, music, topical jokes, and slapstick comedy. In the source novel *Slaughterhouse-Five*, the pantomime is described quite briefly; the reader gets only two lines from it. But these lines prove to be crucial to the novel's thematics. This is the moment when the clock strikes midnight, prompting Cinderella to lament, "Goodness me, the clock has struck—Alackday, and fuck my luck," which the novel's protagonist Billy Pilgrim finds so hilarious that, laughing uncontrollably, he ends up being removed from the theater and carried straight to the infirmary.[3] In *The Wanderings of Billy Pilgrim*, these two lines from the novel are expanded into a comic scene by the Russian poet and bard Yuly Kim. The scene resonated with audiences to such a degree that Kim and Dashkevich decided to develop it into a one-act lyric opera called *Cinderella in a Concentration Camp* (*Zolushka v kontslagere*). In his short "Autobiography," Kim mentions it as an unlikely success: "'Cinderella' in a military version hit the spot [*prishelsia po vkusu*] and ran for two seasons at the Theater of the Soviet Army" (figs. 5–6).[4]

This chapter analyzes the significance of Kim's choice to operatically adapt Vonnegut's seemingly throwaway lines about English POWs staging *Cinderella* in a Nazi camp. It is my contention that, recognizing and appreciating the ethics of gender subversion underlying Vonnegut's novel, Kim reaffirms it in his libretto. Both the novel and libretto, I maintain, cast doubt on aesthetically complete, heroic narratives, debunking them as self-aggrandizing and self-rationalizing. Here, gender subversion becomes a method of practicing introspection, entertaining alternate points of view, and, most importantly, interrogating historical forgetfulness. I will first present a brief historical and theoretical background, explaining the fundamental principles of Vonnegut's aesthetics, and why it had such an appeal for late

Figs. 5–6. Cinderella (left) and Fairy (right). Selvinskaia T. I. costume design. For *The Wanderings of Billy Pilgrim*, staged at the Theater of Soviet Army, 1976.
© Bakhrushin Theatre Museum, Moscow.

Soviet readers and theatergoers. I will then discuss the instances of narrative "transvestism" in Vonnegut's novel, explaining their centrality to his poetics and their intimate connection to the issues of literary form and historical memory. Finally, I will demonstrate how Kim picks up this cross-dressing thread and uses it to endorse, from the stage, Vonnegut's resistance to self-righteous forgetting.

VONNEGUT AND THE DISCOURSE OF WEAKNESS

From the standpoint of Soviet propaganda, it was extremely convenient that such an American author as Kurt Vonnegut existed. An "internal dissident" of sorts, an atheist and socialist, he was relentless in his debunking of the conformism, consumerism, and mindless technocracy of capitalist America. His novels explicitly lambasted US imperialism and could be interpreted as a critique of the Vietnam War. These aspects of Vonnegut's writing were emphasized in the introductory articles to the Russian translations of his novels, and in Soviet media discussions of them.[5] However, Vonnegut's works resonated with disaffected Russian intellectuals as much as with the Soviet establishment. Soviet nonconformists' acceptance of Vonnegut's "anti-Americanism" is yet another caution against any binarist thinking that might code this cohort as necessarily pro-Western or procapitalist. In my view, it was Vonnegut's privileging of weakness and irony, in opposition to the prevailing Cold War rhetoric of power and conformity, that resonated with the Soviet (no less than the American) intellectual milieu. Just as neither side in the Cold War had any monopoly on the discourse of power, the counterdiscourse—that of *weakness*—appealed to writers and readers on both sides of the Iron Curtain. The principle of weakness Vonnegut follows in structuring his texts and characters is at once emphatically anti-American *and* anti-Soviet, inimical to the discourse of power central to both national identities. Thus, Vonnegut's writing blurs the boundary between the two inimical camps, contributing to the spirit of détente that, by the mid-1970s, when *The Wanderings of Billy Pilgrim* was staged in Russia, was unfortunately petering out.[6]

Vonnegut himself clearly perceived his literary mission in terms of critiquing dominant discourses. In July 1975, not long after the launch of Apollo-Soyuz, the first joint US-Soviet space mission, *Literaturnaia gazeta* published a conversation between Vonnegut and Chingiz Aitmatov, in which the latter characterized both the shared spaceflight and this dialogue itself as examples of "taking action amid life's contradictions" (*deistviia v usloviiakh zhiznennykh protivorechii*).[7] Here Vonnegut laments the American tendency to "treat life problems as games to be won," but on the other hand remarks on a hopeful change he sees occurring in the American national character, one that might prove beneficial for the cause of international peace and co-operation. This change is the weakening of the ideal man: "Nowadays in our country, the type of the strong, muscular man, who crushes his opponents, is no longer considered attractive. . . . Nowadays there is no need to appear as a threat to those around you. I hope our leaders are taking this change of national character into account."[8] Vonnegut and Aitmatov's dialogue about the need for the two belligerent superpowers to move from competition to cooperation is in line with the theory, then popular among the intelligentsia of both countries, of *convergence*. First conceived in economic terms by the Dutch economist and Nobel Prize laureate Jan Tinbergen (1963), convergence became the central animating concept of the Soviet nuclear physicist and human rights activist Andrei Sakharov, who expanded it to the realm of politics and culture. In his essay "Reflections on Progress, Peaceful Coexistence, and Intellectual Freedom" ("Razmyshleniia o progresse, mirnom so-sushchestvovanii i intellektual'noi svobode," 1968), which was widely circulated in samizdat in Russia and published in the *New York Times*, Sakharov warned that the arms race could lead to global extinction, and proposed that instead the two blocs might peacefully coexist by each adopting the advantages of the other's system: socialist fairness, and capitalist protections of intellectual freedom and civil liberties.[9] The essay made Sakharov an open dissident and the target of attacks by the Soviet political and scientific establishments, and was heatedly debated in various intellectual circles of the time. As Aleksandr Oleinikov highlights in his 2013 poem "To the People of the 1960s" ("Shestidesiatnikam"), many intellectuals at the time pinned great hopes on convergence: "We called for convergence / Cursing the vile party organizer. / We forgive you, intelligentsia, / You eternally lost sheep."[10] The poem, which bemoans the advent of oligarchy in post-Soviet Russia, faults the intelligentsia (hence its need of "forgiveness") for not realizing that *convergence* would mean the victory of global capitalism (without the socialist economic justice envisioned by Sakharov), and the rise of yet another system based on brute force. Leaving aside the retrospective illusoriness of "convergence" as an ideal, it is clear that Kurt Vonnegut shared the belief that international peace could be promoted via the making of concessions, specifically, the reduction of power and the embrace of weakness. As Sakharov showed, there were various preconditions for convergence; for Vonnegut, a key one was the softening of the national character.

In general, in his writing, Vonnegut counters the charisma of power—already well tarnished by the catastrophic events of the twentieth century—with a charisma of weakness. In this, he resonates with the aesthetic and ethical potential of postwar exhaustion, as described by John Barth in "The Literature of Exhaustion": "In an age of ultimacies and final solutions—at

49

least *felt* ultimacies, in everything from weaponry to theology, the celebrated dehumanization of society, and the history of the novel—[novelists'] work in several ways reflects and deals with ultimacy, both technically and thematically."[11] Here, Barth proposes the ethics of embracing one's limits: the exhaustion of certain literary possibilities is an *aesthetic* problem that calls for an *ethical* solution. In *Slaughterhouse-Five*, this aesthetic problem is articulated thus: "[Eliot Rosewater] said that everything there was to know about life was in *The Brothers Karamazov* by Fyodor Dostoevsky. 'But that isn't *enough* any more,' said Rosewater" (101). The first sentence is often quoted without the one that follows it, as if to portray Vonnegut as endorsing Dostoevsky. But the quote's two-sidedness shows that Vonnegut is being polemical; and while it could take another whole chapter to do analytic justice to the disagreement involved, I would just propose here that the quotation articulates an ethical imperative to give up on exhaustive knowledge and embrace, instead, an incomplete, tentative, and self-questioning form of ethical engagement. Dostoevsky's final novel—which, Bakhtin's assertions notwithstanding, constitutes a *theodicy*—creates a picture of moral order that is perhaps too wholesome and exhaustive for Vonnegut, who instead proposes a clear paradox: *the insufficiency of totality or completion.*

BILLY PILGRIM AND THE INSUFFICIENCY OF TOTALITY

Two American models of male subject formation gained currency in the late Soviet cultural imagination: Hemingway's hypermasculinism and Vonnegut's antiheroism. The attraction of Hemingway and his characters for the Russian intelligentsia is clear: the typical Hemingway character is a manly man, complete with a beard, utilitarian turtleneck, and a glass of alcohol. For the Hemingway character, there is no satisfaction in official dogmas or on the field of battle, but he has other routes to self-affirmation, which Petr Vail and Aleksandr Genis, in their analysis of the cultural dominants of the Soviet 1960s, describe as mostly stylistic: "Style demanded aggravated masculinity—readiness for physical pushback, the search for risky situations, and aggressive demonstration of biceps."[12] When the Hemingway character rejects accepted truths and norms, he does so with style. As described by Vail and Genis, the Hemingway character is a "strong, handsome, correct person, who does not know what to do."[13] From this definition, it seems clear that the Hemingway character represents, in the Russian context, a return of the superfluous man, and bears many of the same romantic connotations thereof.

Quite unromantic, by contrast, is the protagonist of Vonnegut's *Slaughterhouse-Five*, Billy Pilgrim. Billy's marked feature is not so much a lack of form, but rather his formal grotesque. His body manages to negotiate opposites: he is extremely tall, but this sheer size does not make him manly. He is lanky and flaccid; one character describes Billy as a "broken kite."[14] He does not drink and is monogamous. At war, he is no hero—he does not even have a gun—and his appearance is so nonmartial and nonthreatening that his enemies think he is mocking them by turning their war into a farce. In peacetime, he is a successful optometrist, leading a perfectly accomplished bourgeois existence. Crucially, Billy is infantile, passive, withdrawn, alienated, friendless, and completely insane. He believes himself capable of traveling through space-time. Progressive time leads to death, so in order to counteract mortality, Billy wishes to arrange all moments synchronically rather than diachronically in his mind. The novel might not present his solution to existential problems as a "recommended" one, but it sympathizes with his efforts.

Having been a POW in the Second World War and having survived the bombing of Dresden, the narrator himself compulsively attempts to rearrange the memories of the events he has witnessed in order to master them. The introduction to the narrative emphasizes this endeavor's impotence rather than importance:

> I think of how useless the Dresden part of my memory has been, and yet how tempting Dresden has been to write about, and I am reminded of the famous limerick:
> There was a young man from Stamboul,
> Who soliloquized thus to his tool:
> You took all my wealth
> And you ruined my health,
> And now you won't pee, you old fool. (2)

Notably, in her translation of this limerick, Rait-Kovaleva transforms the man from Istanbul into a researcher (*dotsent*) with a failed "instrument," thus bringing the problem of impotence even closer to the heart of Russia's "scientific and technical intelligentsia":

> Какой-то ученый доцент
> Сердился на свой инструмент:
> Мне здоровье сорвал,
> Капитал промотал,
> А работать не хочешь, нахал![15]

> A certain learned researcher
> Was angry with his instrument:
> You ruined my health,
> Squandered my wealth,
> And now you don't want to work, you smartass!

From the outset, Vonnegut stresses the intimate connection between the narrative's weak form and Billy's essential frailty; the verbose subtitle—as originally published, much longer than just *The Children's Crusade*—prepares the reader for the novel's "telegraphic-schizophrenic" style. Most eloquently, the character's weakness, his inability to forget the bombing of Dresden, and the nonauthoritative, halting, and stuttering narrative come together in the practice of narrative transvestism, a grotesque clash of opposites that has been overlooked in critical scholarship on the novel. While the term "cross-dressing" may be more neutral or up-to-date, I use the word "transvestism" here advisedly. It has recently fallen into disfavor because originally it was used as a medical "diagnosis" to code this practice as a kind of mental disorder. As such, however, with its connotations of so-called deficiency, the term "transvestism" is a perfect fit for Vonnegut's poetics of weakness.

As employed by Vonnegut, gender subversion is a device to lead characters and readers to humility, which Vonnegut posits as the supreme ethical stance. In an interview with the Russian journalist A. Mirchev, Vonnegut states that humility (rendered in the Russian text as *smirenie*) is entirely absent in today's world, and that all his works try to provoke a sense of it, to imbue and infect his readers with it. He continues: "It would have been incredibly interesting if the pilot who flew to Nagasaki and dropped a bomb there, knowing well what it had done to Hiroshima four days earlier, if this pilot had refused to perform his task."[16] Central to the ethics of narrative transvestism in *Slaughterhouse-Five* is that, when its characters are called upon to retrieve their most crucial memories, and, motivated by them, to perform this kind of *turn-back-from-Nagasaki* ethical abstention, Vonnegut makes them enter archetypal *female* roles.

For example, the narrator, also named Kurt Vonnegut, chooses to identify himself with Lot's wife, who, against the divine prohibition, looks back at her destroyed, unrighteous hometown. This woman's "irrational," compulsive moment of retrospection, it should be emphasized, constitutes an act of *identification* with what she has supposedly been "rescued" from. Her gesture is like that pilot's wished-for refusal—a sort of *abstention from self-righteousness*, which Vonnegut admires, holding it up as the essence of humanness, and then performing it in the process of writing the book. And this is why his book is a "failure":

Lot's wife, of course, was told not to look back where all those people and their homes had been. But she did look back, and I love her for that, because it was so human. She was turned to a pillar of salt. So it goes. People aren't supposed to look back. I'm certainly not going to do it anymore. I've finished my war book now. The next one I write is going to be fun. This one is a failure, and had to be, since it was written by a pillar of salt. (11)

Thus does the book affirm *aesthetic* failure on *ethical* grounds.

This ethical rejection of aesthetic perfection in the face of trauma is marked as a feminine trait in the novel. One of the people to whom the novel is dedicated is Mary O'Hare, who, we learn in the opening chapter, is a friend's wife who was aghast when the narrator mentioned his intention to write a book about the war. Her objection is quoted: "You'll pretend you were men instead of babies, and you'll be played in the movies by Frank Sinatra and John Wayne or some of those other glamorous, war-loving, dirty old men. And war will look just wonderful, so we'll have a lot more of them. And they'll be fought by babies like the babies upstairs" (8). Significantly, the "babies upstairs" referred to here are girls. Mary thus establishes a gender equation in which the masculine element appears aesthetically complete and ethically dubious, while the feminine element is unaesthetic and incomplete (associated as it is with immature "babies"), but ethically eloquent. The author-narrator promised her that, in *his* war story, there would be no part for Frank Sinatra or John Wayne. And he keeps his promise, insofar as the protagonist of his war story, Billy Pilgrim, appears unsightly and ridiculous, particularly when inhabiting the guise of Cinderella.

BILLY-CINDERELLA

Much has been written on Billy Pilgrim as a Christ figure, but nothing on him as a *Cinderella* figure. Billy's transition into Cinderella occurs after the English soldiers stage their drag show. The roles these soldiers enact within the realm of circumscribed play do not in any way compromise their identity as models of virility. It's the end of the war, and the Russian and American soldiers alike are described as starving and "crippled human beings"—that is, in terms that emphasize their deficiencies of *form*—whereas the Englishmen remain "clean and enthusiastic and decent and strong." They are the epitome of masculine perfection: "Their bellies were like washboards; the muscles of their calves and upper arms were like cannonballs" (42). The success of their drag show in fact hinges on the recognition of the contrast between their masculine essence and the feminine role they temporarily play. However, in his madness, Billy cannot differentiate between stage and reality. The world appears both unreal and illegible to Billy, who finds himself performing the role of a soldier, a role for which he is not particularly suited. When he discovers the silver boots that were used as a prop in the panto performance, we are told that "the boots fit perfectly. Billy Pilgrim was Cinderella, and Cinderella was Billy Pilgrim" (65). The English soldiers' perfect masculine form is an aesthetic representation of power as containment. Here, Billy aspires but fails to gain at least some level of containment by fitting perfectly in the English boots.

Crucial here is the difference between the English soldiers, who are capable of entering and exiting drag at will, and Billy Pilgrim, who is not. Vonnegut writes that the English POWs were all masters of various games; the war for them was a game to be mastered like checkers: "They were adored by the Germans" because "they made war look stylish and reasonable, and fun" (42). The Englishmen approach their emasculated experience of imprisonment as a temporary "losing streak" that one need simply bear with a stiff upper lip. Meanwhile, for Billy, the war is an all-encompassing condition of misery and wretchedness, with no redeeming conclusion in sight.

CINDERELLA, OR THE RETRACTION OF GIFTS

When Vonnegut the author returned from war, he enrolled to study anthropology at the University of Chicago. His thesis, which was ultimately rejected by the department, included the argument that "Cinderella" featured an archetypal plot similar to the biblical story of creation, in which God takes back the gifts bestowed on Adam in the book of Genesis.[17] Specifically, Vonnegut was interested in the moment in the Cinderella story where the clock strikes midnight and Cinderella is returned to her rag-clad misery. Vonnegut intended to argue that the end of the story, which provided redemption in the person of the enchanted prince, was akin to the Bible, which promises redemption for Adam's distant progeny.

If redemption is to be calculated in material terms, then Billy is truly a lucky Cinderella, because his is an exemplary rags-to-riches story. Billy miraculously survives the horrific bombing of Dresden physically unscathed and becomes a wealthy optometrist with a "lovely Georgian home" in a small American town. And yet, appropriately enough, this Cinderella seems more at home in the fairy-tale landscape of the Brothers Grimm than in Perrault's iteration or the Disney production that purge this story of its unsettling ambiguities. The Brothers Grimm version is a story of revenge that ends Cinderella's virtuous triumph on a note of unimaginable cruelty. As Cinderella strolls away from the altar with her prince, the stepsisters' eyes are plucked out by the newly minted princess's helpful birds.[18]

As if approaching the "story" of the Second World War from the standpoint that Mary O'Hare had admonished him against—that of a "wonderful" struggle waged by "glamorous" men—Vonnegut stages it as the Brothers Grimm's Cinderella story. Yet, bearing out Mary's concerns, the story of Dresden affords Billy-Cinderella no feeling of victorious or redemptive "closure." By looking back, Billy-Cinderella repeats Lot's wife's ungrateful gesture, in effect demonstrating that good fortune (God-given gifts, gifts received) is insufficient to induce complacent forgetfulness. This Cinderella keeps coming back to the moment where rags and aesthetic formlessness prevailed; this is why the only phrase from the whole pantomime that is retrieved for the reader (and on which the story fixates) is the moment of the clock striking midnight. This Cinderella cannot stop seeing the boiled bodies of young German women in Dresden. And it is here that Cinderella's name, whose etymological origin is literally "incineration residue," must take on its symbolic meaning for Billy. Billy-Cinderella will never be able to clean himself of Dresden's ashes.

Billy strives in vain to construct a symbolic order in which his traumatic compulsion to repeat would at last be mastered, via the eradication of chronological time and the affirmation of a *good* infinity in which "everything is beautiful and nothing hurt"(122). Insofar as riches disappear upon the clock's striking, Billy attempts, unsuccessfully, to create a system of thought in which time is suspended, all moments exist simultaneously, and the clock will never strike. I say "unsuccessfully" because, ultimately, Billy's collage of temporalities can only approach the aesthetically superior image of the final victory, and muddy it with eternally preserved moments of unimaginable loss.

In *The Origin of German Tragic Drama*, Walter Benjamin describes seventeenth-century mourning plays that represented grief allegorically. Benjamin makes a crucial distinction between the symbolic and allegorical representation of history. A symbolic representation attempts to negate the distance between what it is and what it represents, *faking* aesthetic wholeness. By contrast, allegory refuses the consolation of the transfiguration of a horrific reality into art:

> Whereas in the symbol destruction is idealized and the transfigured face of nature is fleetingly revealed in the light of redemption, in the allegory the observer is confronted with the *facies hippocratica* of history as a petrified, primordial landscape. Everything about history that, from the very beginning, has been untimely, sorrowful, unsuccessful, is expressed in a face—or rather in a death's head.[19]

Allegory incorporates the memory of what has passed, what is no longer there—all the lost possibilities—into its very form (hence its fissures and distortions, its uncanny otherness). This refusal to forget the lost, the failed, and the broken constitutes a *backward glance* that harbors, to use a Benjamin phrase from another essay, a "weak messianic power."

In "Theses on the Philosophy of History," Benjamin writes, "The past carried with it a temporal index by which it is referred to redemption. . . . Like every generation on earth, we have been endowed with a *weak messianic power*, a power to which the past has a claim. That claim cannot be settled cheaply."[20] My understanding of this paradoxical combination of power and weakness is this: the promise of redemption endures in and through one's very apprehension of the failure to fulfill it. Benjamin adduces Klee's *Angelus Novus*, the Angel of History, who looks backward:

> His face is turned towards the past. Where we see the appearance of a chain of events, he sees one single catastrophe. . . . He would like to pause for a moment so fair [*verweilen*: a reference to Goethe's *Faust*], to awaken the dead and to piece together what has been smashed. But a storm is blowing from Paradise. . . . [It] drives him irresistibly into the future, to which his back is turned, while the rubble-heap before him grows sky-high. That which we call progress, is this storm.[21]

The same backward glance structures *Slaughterhouse-Five*, written by Lot's wife, the pillar of salt, about a character who is unable to move on, perpetually returning to the moment when time strikes midnight and the bestowed gifts are taken back. Billy might wish to abide in a Cinderella story with an infinite "happily-ever-after," but Vonnegut does not allow him to fully immerse himself in this compelling scenario. Billy's schizophrenia is a marker of his inability to achieve full coincidence with his own self. He finds himself sharing a hospital room with a stereotypical "manly man," Bertram Copeland Rumfoord, who, as they begin to converse, justifies the bombing of Dresden in strategic terms, inscribing, that is, the horror into a perfectly meaningful, aesthetically complete symbolic order. To this, Billy can reiterate a single line: "I just want you to know: I was there" (193). These words, "I was there," underscore the impossibility of escaping temporality, despite Billy's desire to exist in timelessness; and they demonstrate the ethical superiority of memory over forgetting. The subjectivity of a person who witnesses horror particularizes the moment, making it stand out from the perfect whole, rendering it *eventful*. (Hence, by contrast, the objectifyingly *total* aesthetics of totalitarianism.[22]) Suddenly, it is no longer possible to present this catastrophe in an unambiguous, digestible, complete form: "You must have had mixed feelings, there on the ground," Rumfoord eventually concedes (198). In looking back, Billy replays Lot's wife's gesture, which problematizes Rumfoord's would-be righteous view of the mass bombing of Dresden as a necessary evil and encapsulates the novel's ethico-aesthetics.

CINDERELLA IN A CONCENTRATION CAMP REMEMBERS

Kim's *Cinderella in a Concentration Camp* produces the same effect: despite its humor, it provokes moral disquietude. The title of course already suggests the incongruity: no "happily-ever-after" can reduce the horror of a Nazi camp. But the broader implication is that such a setting would, of necessity, militate against the movement of any conventional fairy-tale plot. The librettists clearly saw Vonnegut's critique of forgetfulness and defense of aesthetic formlessness as closely related, as two sides of the same coin; and they understood that the trans-Cinderella plotline would encapsulate this symbiosis of two *disturbances*: one, a disturbance in content (the memory of trauma), and the other, a disturbance in form (collage, polyphony, and disorder).

Before we get to the place and time of the main action, a Nazi POW camp near Dresden in 1945, the opera opens with a preamble that examines the use and abuse of forgetfulness in a series of song-skits. The opera's very first line is, "Why dredge up the past?" (*Zachem byloe voroshit'?*). The question is first posed by a wayward wife whose husband wants to know where she's been, and is then repeated by the chorus, which in unison extrapolates the woman's self-serving thought into the wish for a carefree life, in blissful forgetfulness of past harms. The scene ends with a forecast of the potential result of such forgetfulness: the birth of yet another Genghis Khan:

> Зачем былое ворошить?
> Кому так легче будет жить?
> Новое время по нашим часам!
> Пойдем лучше в гости:
> У наших соседей
> Родился чудный мальчик,
>   Назвали—Чингисхан![23]

> Why dredge up the past?
> Will that make anyone's life easier?
> According to our watches, it's modern times!
> Let's instead go visit friends.
> The neighbors just had a baby, a lovely boy,
>   They named him Genghis Khan.

Kim uses *Cinderella in a Concentration Camp*, then, to denounce the rescinding of the gains of memory achieved during the Thaw—both the government's *re*-whitewashing of history, and the late Soviet intelligentsia's resignation to blasé contentment. This latter stance of "whatever" is prominently featured in Alexei Yurchak's seminal book *Everything Was Forever, Until It Was No More: The Last Soviet Generation*, which describes a form of subjectivity that, somewhat like the "weak subjects" I consider here, straddles the border between full acceptance and complete denial. The average member of the last Soviet generation was not without certain political views; this cohort's primary characteristic, however, was the tepidity with which these views were adhered to, and the meager effort ever made in their defense. In this interpretation, late Soviet identity seemed to base itself on a sense of *measure*.

This late Soviet subjectivity, a *moderate* one, diverges considerably from the weak subjectivity advanced in Vonnegut's novels and adopted in Kim's opera. The former is predicated on the "acceptance of everything," in Yurchak's words,[24] while the latter upholds the principle of ethical questioning. In a variety of texts, Kim—whose father was a Korean communist who immigrated to Russia to join the revolutionary experiment and was subsequently purged—counteracts the prevailing late Soviet mood of easygoing apoliticality with a viewpoint he sums up as *trebovatel'nost' k sebe* ("self-exactingness; the obligation to maintain one's standards").[25] This is, indeed, how Kim portrays dissidence in his later works: not just as critique of the regime but precisely as a form of self-exactingness, self-questioning. Yurchak's picture of late Soviet subjectivity leaves no room for discontent with oneself. Not only political action is discredited as passé and vulgar—the mode of self-questioning is discredited along with it. Both Yurchak and Kim would agree that there was no way to remove oneself completely from the sphere of the political and the performative, so the difference is whether the performance instills you with a sense of moral disquietude, or a sense of just gaming the system. Kim's heretical zeal and critique of dogmatic thinking is considerably more "communist" than any game of "playing by the rules," even if those rules are ostensibly communist ones, established as they were by the Soviet government. To put it another way: there is far more individualist thinking in the blasé cynicism of the late Soviet *intelligent* who finds politics too fanatical, too off-putting, than in Kim's questioning of himself and the society in which he lives.[26]

While Kim recounts in his memoirs the loss of socialist ideals, his commitment to democratic ideals and the concept of liberty in a way instantiates Benjamin's concept of the duty toward what could have been. Benjamin finds allegory politically progressive, precisely because it renounces the idea of a harmonious, aesthetic totality that would transfigure horrific reality and make it seem justified. The essence of dialectical materialism, he asserts, lies precisely in this avowal of past suffering (rather than, say, resignation to the present status quo, or the idealization of historical progress). Benjamin finds this discontent, and the structure of critique it generates, in the epic theater of Brecht. Benjamin connects the revolutionary content of such theater with its revolutionary form, arguing that the montage technique evident in Brecht's theater and Eisenstein's cinema, with its repudiation of illusionism, is the modern iteration of allegory:

> Epic theatre proceeds by fits and starts, in a manner comparable to the images on a film strip. Its basic form is that of the forceful impact on one another of separate, sharply distinct situations in the play. The songs, the captions, the gestural conventions differentiate the scenes. As a result, intervals occur which tend to destroy illusion. These intervals paralyze the audience's readiness for empathy. Their purpose is to enable the spectator to adopt a critical attitude (towards the represented behavior of the play's characters and towards the way in which this behavior is represented).[27]

Benjamin echoes Eisenstein's idea that montage is a dialectical, constructive form because its juxtapositions jolt the viewer out of complacency.

Following Benjamin, Fredric Jameson argues that Brecht's destruction of illusionism, the laying bare of the device as a method, is intimately connected to his understanding of theater as a dialectical combination of contemplation and action; as a means, that is, to reckon with unfulfilled promises and work out alternative possibilities. Defining Brechtian theater as an "experimental space and collective laboratory," Jameson writes, "The spectacle as a whole should try to demonstrate to the audience that we are all actors, and that acting is an inescapable dimension of social and everyday life."[28]

KIM'S BRECHTIAN THEATER AND
THE TRADITION OF BRITISH PANTO

I mention Benjamin's *allegory-based* reading of Brecht here because *The Wanderings of Billy Pilgrim* constitutes just such an allegory, and because Kim's work in theater evinces the influence of Brecht. Around the same time Kim was working on *Cinderella in a Concentration Camp*, he was also writing an adaptation of Brecht's *Threepenny Opera*.[29] *Cinderella in a Concentration Camp* is an exercise in precisely the Brechtian mode of dialectical theater. Levitin, the director of *The Wanderings of Billy Pilgrim*, describes the twenty-minute insert of Kim's *Cinderella* into his play precisely as a device of juxtaposition between existence as it is and as it should be: "All of this went counter to the overall course of the play's action, laying bare its essence [*kontrastno s obshchim khodom deistviia, obnazhaia sut' proiskhodiashchego*]. This is how people live in reality, and here they demonstrate how they would actually prefer to live."[30] Under the guise of British panto, the opera revives the tradition of early Soviet and German-Marxist avant-garde theater. Kim's different historical position—his lived experience under conditions of late Soviet socialism—led to disappointment in Marxism, but his indebtedness to this form of political and dialectical theater helped him find a suitable artistic form with which to probe the contradictions of real socialism.

British panto and the historical avant-garde theater have a common origin in the tradition of harlequinade and commedia dell'arte; the latter, especially, should be seen as a source for such highly stylized mass spectacle as thrives on artifice rather than verisimilitude, and combines raucous entertainment with didacticism. British Victorian panto and symbolist harlequinade theater emerged in reaction against the more grim and dehumanizing elements of the industrial age: regimentation, mechanization, rationalization.[31] However, as theater underwent transformation, becoming less the exclusive bailiwick of elites or the bourgeoisie and acquiring new working-class audiences, both British pantomime and the historical avant-garde theater became more engaged in political critique and topical humor. Furthermore, both thrived on incongruity and buffoonery, physical tricks and stunts. In both, the heightened physicality of the spectacle, bearing out the theories of Bakhtin, was no less subversive of the status quo, and no less of an affront to bourgeois propriety and good taste, than topical political humor.[32]

But for Kim and Dashkevich, there was still another vector by which "Cinderella" in particular would refer viewers to the aesthetics and politics of early avant-garde experimentation. In 1947, just on the eve of the virulent anti-formalist campaign, Lenfilm produced *Cinderella*, written by Evgeny Schwartz and directed by Nadezhda Kosheverova, who had previously been a member of the Factory of the Eccentric Actor (FEKS), and who used the genre of a childlike fairy tale to revive the tradition of Soviet eccentrism.[33] The film's avowed abdication of realism and dedication to the principle of incongruity were especially evident in the king himself, who was played with frenetic, gestural gusto by one of the greatest actors of the Meyerhold theater, Erast Garin. For Kim and Dashkevich, then, to re-create "Cinderella" as a British panto, utilizing its techniques of circus and eccentricity, is also to continue in the iconoclastic tradition of Kosheverova, Schwartz, and FEKS.[34] Levitin alludes to this tradition both in his retelling of Vonnegut's depiction of the war ("Vonnegut described the war as abhorrent, dry to the point of *eccentricity*, laughable to the point of horror, with the *marionette* existence of people who think they make history"), and in his description of the stage design that was supposed to convey this mood: "The whole stage space was 'bandaged' [*perebintovano*]; there were hints of somewhat realistic wounded shapes; the white gauzy space, even the wheelchairs and stretchers, were bandaged, but right in the center there hung a huge box with colorful toys."[35] The use of *toys* on a bare stage must have reminded those in the know of Meyerhold's first staging of *The Magnanimous Cuckold* in 1922, where his actors showcased his theatrical biomechanics wearing Liubov Popova's stark unisex "uniforms for acting," accessorized with children's toys. The absurdity of festive playthings amid the horrors of war in *The Wanderings of Billy Pilgrim* was conditioned, however, by the fact that *Cinderella* was meant to be a British panto.

OPERATIC TRANSVESTISM AND
THE EMBRACE OF THE INCONGRUOUS

In undertaking to expand Vonnegut's brief reference to a staging of "Cinderella" by English POWs, Kim and Dashkevich clearly explored the tradition of British pantomime. Pantos were and still are staged during Yuletide, as ritualistic, communal celebrations of rebirth and transformation. And Kim and Dashkevich's opera, following the rules of British panto, indeed takes place during this season.

This is not, however, a straight-faced holiday celebration; the opera follows the British panto tradition in approaching the holiday via travesty and burlesque. It revolutionizes the Gospel commandments by, first, taking them out of the narrow domain of Christianity and applying them to all humanity, in line with the opera's principle of eschewing factionalism. Levitin explains that the Cinderella episode was meant to be the play's pinnacle, signifying humanity's yearning for accord: "The high point became a play within the play, the performance of *Cinderella* in a camp for American and British POWs at Christmas. . . . From the moment he appears, Pilgrim leads the whole audience and all the characters to *Cinderella* as the most radiant of his memories—about the coming together of people even in inhuman circumstances, about joy."[36] The theme of Cinderella begins with an appeal to all creeds:

О баптисты и католики, лютеране и православные, духоборы и марониты, о мормоны и адвентисты седьмого дня! О сунниты и шииты! О буддисты и агностики, язычники и марксисты! Восславим праздник Рождества . . .—не вопреки каждый своему вероисповеданию, а в строгом соответствии с той заповедью, где сказано:—Ну возлюби же, подлец, ближнего своего хотя бы на час! А это, уверяю вас, сказано везде. (500)

Baptists and Catholics, Lutherans and Orthodox, Dukhobors and Maronites, Mormons and Adventists! Sunnis and Shiites! Buddhists and agnostics, pagans and Marxists! Let's celebrate the Christmas holiday—not each going against our own creed, but rather in strict adherence with the commandment:

"C'mon, love thy neighbor, thou scoundrel, at least for one short hour!" And I assure you, this is said everywhere.

Second, the opera approaches the Christmas miracle via the prism of Brechtian dialecticism—that is, simultaneously advancing an ideal and despairing over the unlikelihood of its fulfillment:

Господа! Нам отпущено ровно шестьдесят минут—на все: на прегрешение и покаяние, на молитву и непристойный фарс, на стриптиз и рождественскую службу. Мы должны успеть, . . . и то и другое, ибо и то и другое в равной степени дорого человеку, да-да, и стыд и бесстыдство—лишь их одновременное наличие придает каждой личности своеобразие, а жизни—смысл. (500)

Gentlemen, we have been allotted exactly sixty minutes for everything: for sin and repentance, for prayer and bawdy farce, for striptease and Christmas services. We must manage to get through both, for both are equally dear to mankind, yes, both shame and shamelessness—for it is only when these exist simultaneously that each personality is unique, that life makes sense.

In professing the embrace of incongruity, Kim's libretto underscores the most subversive element of British panto: cross-dressing. In cross-dressing, the performance of one gender does not eclipse the presence of the other. Both are in plain view simultaneously.[37] In her study *Narrative Transvestism*, Madeleine Kahn observes that "the transvestite is enacting a fiction of gender transformation and directing his audience toward an inherently contradictory interpretation of his gender. Transvestism temporarily suspends the rules of logical consistency. The transvestite is a woman *and* he is a man. . . . The impermanence of the transvestite self is crucial to its meaning and its power."[38] The most unsettling incongruity of the British panto, then, was the one performed by cross-dressed actors, whose complicated gender affiliation pointed to the slippage and inadequacy of all stable categories.

British pantomime foregrounds this collision of opposites, as many jokes nod to the actual gender of the actor, thereby performing his or her symbolic disrobing. Kim replicates this undressing with jokes that underscore the incongruity between the actor and the role:

Зовут меня Фея, за мой талант,
поскольку на войне я военный интендант! (511)

They call me Fairy, for my talent, insofar as,
in war, I am a military quartermaster.

The prince rhapsodizes to his father about Cinderella, who comes with, so to speak, *more* than one could hope for in a bride:

> Ах папочка, ах папочка,
> Какое существо!
> Смотри какая бабочка,
> как много в ней всего! (518)

> Oh, Daddy, oh, Daddy!
> What a creature!
> Look, what a butterfly,
> how much of everything there is in her!

And yet, this formal excess also signifies a *lack.*

Just like the English POWs, the opera's cross-dressed soldiers epitomize masculine hardness. For example, in their self-descriptions, the ugly stepsisters Zhanetta and Zhavotta appear as a collage of military technology: their faces look like "gas-masks," their thighs are made of steel, and their bodies put together make up "a twin-barrel heavy artillery weapon" (518). However, these tokens of masculine strength, which in Vonnegut's novel buttress the English POWs' sense of coherent, unbreakable self, constitute a *liability* in the realm of the opera.

In an opera redolent of war fatigue, power is disavowed; what is pined for instead is *femininity*, which here represents a reprieve from war and metonymizes the realm of love and peaceful coexistence. After all, the prince is markedly uninterested in military conquests, yearning, rather, only to find "a real woman" (512). The stepsisters are equalized with the heroine of the tale, Cinderella, in their shared eagerness for escape from the realm of war. In a conventional panto, only the dame-stepmother and the ugly stepsisters would be played by men, but in the Nazi POW camp, *all* the female roles, including Cinderella herself, are of necessity played by men. The opera, then, playfully hints at the idea of femininity as something rare and precious. Cinderella's frequent assertions of genuineness—"I am little Cinderella, I sing little songs"[39]—suggest the anxiety that she might be only an approximation of that for which the prince yearns. Kim's libretto thus takes Billy Pilgrim's sense of internal incoherence and deficiency and disperses it among all the characters of the panto.

Lest the comic grotesque be misinterpreted as mocking this fraught femininity, Levitin insists that the performance of female roles by male characters was in fact a form of momentary liberation from the hardness and viciousness of war, a fleeting return to the self: "*Cinderella* was obviously acted by men; its text is written in verse, and the method of actors' existence

Fig. 7. Scene from *Cinderella* in *The Wanderings of Billy Pilgrim*, staged at
the Theater of Soviet Army, 1976. Russian State Archive of Literature
and Art, f. 3337, op. 1, d. 44, l. 19.

[*sposob akterskogo sushchestvovaniia*] in this fragment differed radically
from the rest of the play. It was as if throughout the performance, the characters were breaking out toward themselves [*proryvalis' k samim sebe*], and
only here, in *Cinderella*, became truly free" (figs. 7–8).[40]

In "The Play of Eros: The Paradoxes of Gender in English Pantomime," Peter Holland alludes to the rule by which the principal male character is played by a female, and observes that "the heroic male is a heavily
marked gap in panto performance."[41] In this regard, Kim's opera is thus both
truthful to the British panto tradition and to Vonnegut's novel. The discourse
of heroism is gravely undermined. The king and the prince sing a song in
which two models of romantic masculinity (Napoleon and Don Juan) are
compromised:

> Жил на свете Бонапарт,
> Грозный генерал.
> Он когда входил в азарт,
> удержу не знал!
> Бьет бывало
> чем попало
> всех подряд,
> а ему в восторге
> все кричат:
>   Вот это па . . . (502)

> Once there lived a Bonaparte,
> fearsome as hell.
> And when he got into the swing of things,
> No one could him quell.
> He would hit all comers
> with whatever came to hand,
> but everyone would shout at him
> in delight: "What a . . . !"

Here the choir chimes in, at just the right moment, neutralizing a potentially volatile situation. The word abruptly abandoned on its first syllable, after a rather ambivalent assessment of Napoleon, suggests the possibility that instead of praise (*Vot eto paren'!*, "What a guy!"), the singers were actually about to issue a denunciation: *Vot eto padlo!* ("What a creep!"), which would also make a more suitable (albeit still imperfect) rhyme with *chem popalo* ("whatever came to hand"). Kim's opera, then, despite almost entirely

Fig. 8. Scene from *Cinderella* in *The Wanderings of Billy Pilgrim*, staged at the Theater of Soviet Army, 1976. Russian State Archive of Literature and Art, f. 3337, op. 1, d. 44, l. 18.

diverging from Vonnegut's book in terms of actual plot, is faithful to its major themes: its denouncing of machismo and the violent aesthetics thereof, and its debunking of perfection or heroism.

In a study of cross-dressing in ancient Greek drama, Froma Zeitlin argues that emotions are gender identified, and so when a male actor "plays the other," he opens his masculine self to emotions marked as feminine, such as "fear" or "pity." The male performer thus allows himself to experience that which appears to be the other's consciousness.[42] For the purposes of our discussion, it is irrelevant whether these emotions belong "essentially" to the realm of biological womanhood. Rather, these "feminine" emotions are forbidden to men by *culture*, and when performed *by* a man, the female role becomes an exercise in experiencing otherness, while the distance between the actor and the role facilitates critical reflection—a double estrangement. This experience is essential for Vonnegut's novel, which invites the reader to look at *everything* from standpoints alien to cultural norms—a form of total questioning. Kim attempts to reproduce this double estrangement in his own bardic performance of the libretto. He is careful to stay true both to the role assigned and to its actor; his Cinderella, for instance, is sung in a masculine baritone, all the while remaining himself—the bard who sings the song.

This incorporation of discordant elements, which is visibly glaring in the practice of cross-dressing, and *audibly* glaring (pardon the synesthesia) in Kim's polyphony, becomes the crucial organizing principle of the opera's final scene. Right at the moment when a happy future is about to ensue, *Cinderella in a Concentration Camp*, like Benjamin's Angel of History and Vonnegut's Lot's wife, halts the forward movement and *looks back*. When the prince announces that the happy ending will take place in Dresden, the pantomime abruptly ends, literally in midchorus: "I love this city, not a city, but a dream," interrupted by the emcee's untimely announcement that the following day was February 13—the first day of the catastrophic bombardment of the city. The rest of the opera is a fragmentary montage of voices, where exclamations of victory in English, Russian, and French are jumbled with statistics of casualties in Dresden, Hiroshima, and Nagasaki:

Люблю я этот город,

Не город, а мечта . . .

—В январе нас перевели в Дрезден.

—А потом наступило тринадцатое февраля. И четырнадцатое. Оба этих дня мы провели в бомбоубежище. В то время как полторы тысячи самолетов, наших и американских, все сбрасывали и сбрасывали воющую смерть на беззащитный город—всего три тысячи семьсот сорок девять тонн.

—Вместе с нами сидел американский писатель Курт Воннегут.

КУРТ

"Дрезден превратился в огненный ураган. Пламя пожирало все, что
могло гореть. . . . После бомбежки Дрезден стал похож на Луну: одни
минералы."

—Нагасаки—семьдесят пять, Хиросима—сто, Дрезден—сто тридцать
пять тысяч убитых, главным образом, беженцев из других мест Гер-
мании . . .

ХОР

Этот город—там поют и танцуют,

На асфальте—дети солнце рисуют,

И ничем не грозит небосклон . . .

Утешенье, и покой, и отрада,

Если нету—значит, выдумать надо

Этот город, прекрасный, как сон . . .

ПОБЕДА

АМЕРИКАНЦЫ

Вот это парень! Вот это да! Ты наша радость—а ну, давай сюда!

АНГЛИЧАНЕ

Правь, Британия, морями! Правь чем хочешь и владей!

РУССКИЕ

Гремя огнем, сверкая блеском стали, пойдут машины в яростный
поход!

ФРАНЦУЗЫ

Алон занфан де ля Патрие! (522–23)

I love this city,

Not a city, but a dream . . .

—In January we were transferred to Dresden.

—And then came April 13. And 14. We spent both days in a bomb shelter,
while 1,500 airplanes, ours and American, kept dropping howling death
on the helpless city—3,749 tons of it, in all.

—The American writer Kurt Vonnegut was sitting with us.

KURT

"Dresden turned into a hurricane of fire. The flames devoured everything
that could burn. After the bombardment, Dresden looked like the
moon: nothing but minerals."

—Nagasaki—75,000; Hiroshima—100,000; Dresden—135,000 killed,[43]
mainly refugees from other parts of Germany.

CHORUS

People sing and dance in this city,

Children draw the sun on the asphalt,

And the skyline is harmless . . .
Here are solace, peace, and joyousness,
If it doesn't exist, it must be invented,
This city, lovely as a dream!

VICTORY

THE AMERICANS

What a guy! Wow! You are our pride and joy—get over here!

THE ENGLISHMEN

Rule the waves, Britannia! Rule and reign over anything you wish!

THE RUSSIANS

Thundering with fire, and sparkling with steel, the machines shall go on a furious march.

THE FRENCH

Allons enfants de la Patrie!

Kim's opera, that is, emphatically rejects the narrative of the "good war," the facile historical dichotomy of righteous winners and wicked losers. It undertakes, instead, a process of *re-collection* in every sense. Lost amid conflicting memories and historical ruins, all the actors, and the audience, are brought together by the shared predicament of the dream turned nightmare, and by a collective working-out of the tragic complexity of existence. The epilogue foregrounds confusion and ethical questioning, with the emcee and chorus engaging in a debate that echoes the above-cited dialogue between Billy Pilgrim and Rumfoord. The chorus espouses the necessity of compromising one's conscience in the battle for abstract ideals and principles; it declares that the end justifies the means, and that the individual is helpless to resist larger historical forces:

> Идет потоп,
> И он неудержим,
> Он увлекает целые народы,
> То что же может *слабый* человек?
> Идет потоп, исход непредсказуем.
> Что может он, когда безумен век?
> (524; emphasis mine)

> Comes the deluge
> And it is relentless,
> It carries off whole nations,
> So what can a *weak* person do?
> Comes the deluge, the outcome is unpredictable.
> What can he do, in this crazy epoch?

68

Fig. 9. The finale of *Cinderella*: Billy prostrate on the stage as broken toys come crashing down on the stage from the large metallic lantern suspended above it. From *The Wanderings of Billy Pilgrim*, staged at the Theater of Soviet Army, 1976. Russian State Archive of Literature and Art, f.3092, op.1, d.32, l. 22.

Narrated in unrhymed prose, the emcee's rebuttal lacks lyrical pathos, and is admittedly much weaker. He can only repeat that these points are all valid, and that he cannot counter them—"I don't know!" he exclaims—except to note that "conscience is a moral category that allows us to distinguish, unerringly, between good and evil" (524–25). The emcee has no arguments; the chorus's assertions seem to exhaust the knowledge of life; but for the emcee, this exhaustive knowledge appears lacking. The weak emcee has no answers, but his questions provoke the experience of moral disquietude. In this lies their power.

In summary, I have argued here that in Vonnegut's famous novel and Kim's unknown opera, gender subversion acts as a vehicle toward and a symbol of the cultivation of weak subjectivity—a particular form of self, marked by the inability to forget the casualties of one's own good intentions;

the compulsion to recollect elapsed possibilities; the embrace of aesthetic incompleteness; and the voluntary shedding of invulnerability and self-righteousness. This weak self, in turn, appears to be the predicate for building a new solidarity, a new international community.

Russian readers were especially keen on Vonnegut's concept of *karass*, introduced in *Cat's Cradle*. A *karass* is an association of people not based on traditional linkages like family, country, nation, class, or party but formed on the basis of some cosmic, mystical, or philosophical affinity. In the reader responses to Vonnegut published in Soviet newspapers, many Soviet Vonnegut fans expressed the desire to be members of *his karass*. With the help of *karass*, Vonnegut deconstructs the fixed meaning of identitarian categories. What Russian audiences found appealing, then, was precisely his system of secular ethics, which breaches national borders and maps the world's matrix, not with knots of conflict and competition but rather with ties yet to be discovered.

"What a Hero of Weakness!": The Radical Orthodoxy of Evgeny Kharitonov

AT FIRST GLANCE, it might appear that Evgeny Khari-
tonov's persistent celebration of weakness shares the same code with many
other underground Soviet writers of the 1960s and 1970s. In "Tears on Flowers" ("Slezy na tsvetakh"), Kharitonov admits to youthful acquiescence to
normative gender expectations—"Sure, you had to conquer something at
some point, at some age—to get up on the parallel bars and not fear falling
off"—only to disavow it with the subsequent idolization of those who dared
to *not* acquiesce: "But my God, what to do when, later, you find yourself
admiring the people who never conquered anything, never overcame, and
dared to remain nonconquerors [*osmelilsia ostat'sia nepreodolevshim*]! What
a hero of weakness! [*Kakoi on geroi slabosti!*]"[1] Kharitonov's protagonist's
salute to those who "dare to remain nonconquerors" and accomplish nothing
could, indeed, serve as an homage to Erofeev's own eponymous protagonist, Venichka, who (as described in the next chapter) cultivates "chicken-
heartedness" in himself and prescribes it as a panacea for all the world's
ills.[2] Here I will examine Kharitonov's discourse of weakness, and performance thereof, in *Under House Arrest* (*Pod domashnim arestom*), and argue
that, even as he adopts a mode and subject of writing akin to those of his
contemporaries—the weak mode, the weak subject—he uses them, in fact,
for peculiar and paradoxical ends. The previous chapters interpreted weakness in postmodern works as a device for questioning easy certainties, grand
narratives, and false totalities. The indulgence in weakness was read as a
rejection of the very idea of power, and of those who represent it. Notably,
Kharitonov's heroics of weakness complicates the schema proposed by this
book, as it aspires to the very opposite: to buttress and affirm the long-
standing grand narrative of Russian exceptionalism and messianism.

Kharitonov methodically inscribes his precarity and marginality vis-à-
vis Soviet society (both as an experimental writer and as a gay man) into the
Russian literary and cultural tradition, with its emphasis on humility, resig-

nation, and holy foolishness. His is an attempt to make homosexuality this grand narrative's missing link, the most concrete manifestation of Russian specificity and Russian values at a time when these values were threatened not only by mainstream Soviet culture, with its imported Marxism, but also by dissident circles, with their imported cosmopolitanism and liberal democracy. Kharitonov has much at stake, I contend, in marshaling the "big guns" of Russian nationality and the Russian literary and cultural canon. By claiming himself to be a true heir to Russian tradition, he attempts to legitimate his project of life creation, or creation of life as art, which encompasses both his homosexuality and his writing about it.

THE LETTER TO AKSENOV: A SHORT RÉSUMÉ

On June 27, 1981, just prior to his death, Kharitonov managed to send westward a collection of writings he had produced over the course of twenty years, which he gave the title of *Under House Arrest*. The manuscript was sent to the Russian dissident writer Vasily Aksenov, at the time residing in the United States and well connected with the expat literary scene and American presses that published nonconformist Russian writing. In the accompanying letter to Aksenov, amid asking him to attend to the manuscript's publication in the West, Kharitonov nevertheless takes the liberty of articulating the major differences between his own and Aksenov's writing styles, philosophies of dissent, and conceptions of personal identity and communal affiliation.[3] In the letter, that is, what at first appears like an expression of admiration for Aksenov's recent novel *The Island of Crimea* (*Ostrov Krym*) quickly devolves into something more like censure. Kharitonov identifies his position on life, art, and society as resolutely opposed to that of Aksenov, who in that novel cloaks his political dissidence in Hemingway-like machismo. Rejecting Aksenov's aesthetic mode of self-confident righteousness and exaggerated manliness as cosmopolitan and Western, Kharitonov proposes instead his own "weak" dissidence as more innate to Russian culture. Just as Aksenov creates his authorial persona via identification with his protagonist (in his case, a dashing James Bond stand-in), Kharitonov describes his own protagonist and then himself in terms of their shared weak subjectivity, claiming not so much their right to exist—the discourse of *rights* is Western, hence alien to Kharitonov—but the authenticity of their existence as a particularly Russian form of being.[4]

Kharitonov begins his letter by explaining, or justifying, the style of his writing. Its tentative, fragmentary form, which preserves distortions, gaps, and typos and slips of the pen, represents the *process* of writing rather than its end result. In this preference for the means rather than the end, this foregrounding of unfinishedness, Kharitonov appears perfectly in line with the preoccupations of postmodern fiction as an international phenomenon. But then he moves from formal representation of the process of writing to *form as the representation of a particular subjectivity*: "The subject manifests himself in his rhetorical reactions, fatally tied to his own 'karma' and finding artfulness in it, at times with pleasure breaking into 'reactionary conservatism' [*vyryvaiushchiisia v 'reaktsionnost'*]—when touching on an ideological topic."[5] As he is asking Aksenov to publish his work in the West, Kharitonov outlines certain salient characteristics that make him an outsider to the American literary market: "This 'I' is also an inhabitant of a little island of solitude and is not really drawn into social existence, does not feel its swinish pressure [*ne ispytyvaet ee kaban'ego davleniia*], and when he does feel it, he becomes enraged like a schoolboy. . . . This 'I' does not measure out his homosexual descriptions [*ne doziruet gomoseksual'nykh opisanii*]."[6] Aksenov should refrain, Kharitonov warns, from attempting to place his oeuvre within American writing that thematizes gay sexuality: the persona in question "is not Albee, Baldwin, or Tennessee Williams; he is not connected to the laws—even laws making provisions for everything—of the literary market; he does not know how to court the reader."[7] His conception of the outsider, with its aesthetics of resignation and resignation to aesthetics, claims a different genealogy; it alludes to pastness—in particular, to the Russian variety thereof: "He is cloistered, an underground man [*keleinyi, iz podpol'ia*]; and that's his image [*i v etom obraz*]. Nothing is constructed so as to first be conceived by his will, then realized; [rather,] a conscious lack of will, trust in a pattern that will organize everything in the best possible way—that's his genre."[8] Such words as "cloister" and "underground" take us, of course, to Dostoevsky and his appropriation of the Russian tradition of holy foolishness (on which more below).

More importantly, however, these words, in the context of sexual, and specifically homosexual, desire and ardent aestheticism, are anchors to a past in which Kharitonov claims membership: the particular moment, that is, of the fin de siècle, when so many Russian religious philosophers, writers, and poets were keen to reconceptualize sexuality through the prism of Russian Orthodox spirituality and vice versa.[9] In this short résumé, Kharitonov simultaneously makes three contradictory moves: he affirms both his singularity and marginality and, at the same time, his belonging to tradition; upholds a lack of design as design's very feature; and, all at once, both affirms and denies the performative aspect, the mask of constructed subjectivity in his writing, which appears to be autobiographical. That is, by referring to the rules of image construction and genre, he draws a border between author and protagonist, but also blurs it.

This oscillation, however, quickly becomes a structural principle of the whole letter, with Kharitonov jumping willy-nilly in and out of his own weak positionality. Continuing the theme of weakness, he pleads with Aksenov to arrange for the publication of his book, but then abruptly initiates an offensive against Aksenov's own writing. This he does from a position of "power," insofar as he quickly marshals to his cause not only the giants of Russian literature but also the stylistic peculiarities of nineteenth-century polemical writing. In a snide, ironic tone, Kharitonov pits Aksenov against Russian literary greats:

> It seems as though the most esteemed writers of Russia must have been, so to speak, obscurantists [*mrakobesy*], when it comes to their worldviews. But here [in Aksenov's *The Island of Crimea*] is our anti-Solzhenitsyn, anti-Gogol, anti-Dostoevsky. There is no humility, no meekness, no blaspheming with holy foolishness; instead there is humanism, chivalry, cosmopolitanism expressed in everything, in the distribution of power, in symbols, in bons mots, in plot construction, in love of sports and fashion.[10]

Kharitonov thus excludes Aksenov from the canon of Russian literature: everything in Aksenov's novels, from their plot construction to their thematization of humanism, is alien to Russian culture. And so here comes Kharitonov to return to Russian literature its humility, meekness, and holy foolishness:

> Vasily Pavlovich, you can well imagine that, in my poetic sympathies, what is dear to my heart is the world of poor folk, the fear of God in people, the boondocks [*provintsiia*], dreaminess, eternal grief and tears instead of action, and quite Mamleevian and Sologubian heinous nastinesses instead of your free, valiant amorous bouts [*mamleevskie i sologubovskie uzhasnye pakosti vmesto svobodnykh doblestnykh liubovnykh poedinkov*]. Not for me did Hemingway write; as a child I was no reader of *The Three Musketeers*. . . . But yours is a sober point of view—unobscured [*ne pomrachennyi*] by Orthodoxy and politics—on the current distribution of forces, historical and social; the point of view of a humanist and progressive, not a cleric or schismatic. And your novel is an invaluable historical document of this great non-Russian, so to speak [*velikaia nerusskaia, tak skazat'*], position.[11]

Kharitonov's speech here is highly stylized, peppered with Old Church Slavonicisms and grammatical inversions, and modeled on the solemn and mellifluous speech patterns used by Russian monks, church fathers, and religious philosophers; and by nineteenth-century Russian writers in their polemical pieces, written in moments of heightened zeal. Kharitonov does not just claim to be a "cleric or schismatic"; he verbally performs this role. The "heinous nastinesses" he cherishes—*pakost'* is a Church Slavonic word; in the plural and in combination with *uzhasnye*, it sounds comical, borderline illiterate, and somehow antediluvian—are claimed here as part of this role of a deeply Orthodox, truly Russian person, a monk and a holy fool. In the letter to Aksenov, Kharitonov carefully constructs a complex cultural genealogy for himself as a literary phenomenon. And this is not a one-off attempt, but characteristic of all his creative strivings. Elsewhere Kharitonov declares, "A lot had to occur in the world of culture and the world of nature before I could appear. I should be treated with superstitious awe."[12] Kharitonov is deeply invested in positioning himself not as a chance occurrence but as an acme of endemic cultural processes. To accomplish this feat, he has to rely on established, recognizable cultural models. As indicated in the letter to Aksenov, the cultural model he especially identifies with is that of the holy fool—the particular prism through which Kharitonov's heroics of weakness must be understood.

HOLY FOOLISHNESS AND KENOTIC LOVE

Saint Paul was the first, in his epistle to the Corinthians, to establish the virtue of holy foolishness and the paradoxical strength of weakness: "We are fools for Christ's sake, but ye are wise in Christ; we are weak, but ye are strong; ye are honorable, but we are despised." The holy fool spurns societal norms of behavior and embraces marginality as a sign of saintliness. The tradition of holy foolishness is a rich one in Russian culture; it appeared within the church and was a practice of its fringe elements.

Holy foolishness emerged in a monastic setting in both Byzantium and Rus'. It became a fully developed behavioral model in its urban form as practiced in Russian towns and cities beginning in the fifteenth century. The urban fool becomes an apostle of the crucified Christ by living within the city as a vagrant and an outcast. He or she assumes a guise of madness in order to be misunderstood and persecuted.[13]

In the nineteenth century, holy foolishness enjoyed something of a "comeback," as Russian literary and visual culture used it to thematize certain peculiarities of the Russian national character. Westernizers and progressives in this period appreciated holy foolishness as potentially harboring the social protest inherent in Russian common folk, while Slavophiles like Dostoevsky used holy foolishness to connote such non- or anti-Western values as otherworldliness, egolessness, and liberation from instrumental and pragmatic thinking. Scholars have claimed that "the Russian people's collective sense of self has been markedly influenced by this phenomenon."[14]

The symbolics of holy foolishness is paradoxical. Holy fools eschew and scorn social propriety, and behave in blasphemous ways, in order to attain saintliness. Because language is a social phenomenon, and they strive to be antisocial, they use their body as a text (that is, they semiotize their body). Instead of common language, they use muttering, glossolalia, gestures. Holy foolishness, then, would appeal to Kharitonov on multiple levels, not least in its utilization of corporeal signs and gestures. The language of gesture was close to Kharitonov, who developed his own theory of pantomime and defended a dissertation on the subject, and who worked as a pantomime choreographer for the theater of the Moskvorech'e House of Culture. Furthermore, bodily semiotics was also a go-to form of communication in the gay "cruising" culture of Moscow; in his writings, Kharitonov describes a number of chance love encounters that take place in silent anonymity.

Holy-foolish behavior is marked by a recognizable code: holy fools are often naked or bear the stigmata or heavy shackles on their body, thus displaying their imitation of the suffering of Christ on the cross. The *exhibition* of the profane body, by which holy fools show themselves to be the lowest of the low, and invite bullying and beatings, is a paradoxical form of asceticism—a simultaneous rejection of the flesh and a rising *above* one's nature. Hence Kharitonov's utter disinterest in "normalizing" gayness. To present gay love as holy foolishness, Kharitonov must internalize society's prohibition of homosexuality and conceive of it as a form of degradation, the denigration of one's ego. Significantly, his protagonist and lyrical persona invariably portrays his love for men as an impossible love, doomed to remain unconsummated. Throughout the volume, again and again, the protagonist ends in the same predicament for a variety of reasons: Russian cultural taboos that could get one killed; laws, which could get one imprisoned; or the psychological makeup of the protagonist, ever ardently attracted to men who cannot and will not reciprocate his love.

Unrequited, impossible love is Kharitonov's constant motif. Those who knew the writer personally found this perplexing, insofar as, in "real life," Kharitonov was quite charming, and able to find many who were eager to return his love. But for Kharitonov, this doomedness is crucial to constructing the image of the ascetic holy fool: "Everyone has an Isolated Sore Point. It is the focal point of a life, giving it form and keeping it from falling apart; but it also makes a person flip out [*no na nem chelovek i svikhivaetsia*]. That is the point. And the best sore point of all is hopeless, inconsolable love."[15] And, lest the reader not recognize the religious underpinnings of his philosophy of suffering, Kharitonov follows this excursus into the benefits of painful love with an admonition given in the didactic tone of Russian religious writing: "Look after [*beregite*] your unhappiness. [Or 'safeguard,' 'tend to' it.] Do not accidentally swap it for happiness. Never, ever, ever for any money exchange it for happiness, and happiness will be with you forever."[16] The yearning must remain unfulfilled for as long as possible, because the one who yearns is always in the subservient, "weak" position vis-à-vis the one yearned for. The unequal, self-denigrating love is the most effective tool for the cultivation of weakness: "And the most wonderful thing for him, as it is for you, as it is for anyone, is to fall into the arms of someone he can't compare with and open himself up to them and confess that he is nothing compared to them because he too loves loving [*on tozhe liubit liubit'*] because only in love can you be so weak and bow down before someone else."[17]

Painstakingly, Kharitonov builds a theory of love as the practice of humility, self-renunciation, kenosis. The benefit of love for Kharitonov is that it both generates and fortifies the imbalance of forces: love is not just a tool for attaining weakness; it is also an expression of it. Love is a yearning to fill a particular lack, as one of Kharitonov's characters explains in a letter to his paramour in the story "The Viable Infant" ("Zhiznesposobnyi mladenets"):

> There was something lacking in me at the deepest level from the very beginning. You could not fall head over heels in love with me because like you I am weak and you can only fall head over heels in love with a strong, red-blooded young man with rosy cheeks who has in him what you lack and admire and want to possess.[18]

Should, however, the reader assume that Kharitonov thinks of love as a corrective, a mode through which one *gains* what one has lacked, this would be mistaken. Love, as Kharitonov understands it, is not revolutionary; it does not remedy disequilibrium. To the contrary, it exacerbates it. It is an expression and intensification of weakness, not its redress. Kharitonov is clear on this point, for instance in "Alesha Serezha": "People love a person they would like to be and know they never can be."[19]

This unfillable lack has a clear Freudian subtext, as witness its marking as feminine in the poem "Should We Burst into Tears?" ("A ne rasplakat'sia li nam?"):

> Амур лежит спит эта вещь у него через ногу,
> что распаляет Психею, у которой этого нет.[20]

> Eros reclines sleeps this thing across his leg,
> which inflames Psyche who lacks it.

There is precedent for the association of holy foolishness with nonheteronormativity; one of the best-known Russian Orthodox holy fools is Saint Ksenia of Petersburg (d. 1803), who upon the death of her husband gave away all her worldly possessions and dressed in her husband's old clothes, insisted that everyone call her by his name (Andrei), and essentially transformed herself into her husband. In her time, of course, her sanctification was conditioned on the shedding of earthly possessions rather than of gender constraints, but underground poets of the twentieth century, contemporaries of Kharitonov, were inspired by the potential of her gender-bending.[21] With his abundant tears, weak persona, and the construction of love as a hopeless desire to fill lack, Kharitonov consistently adopts a position that in masculinist Russian culture, and for that matter in many such cultures, would be perceived as feminine. However, all these aspects of Kharitonov's love—self-effeminization, self-denial, and submission to the strong ones of this world—are not ends in themselves; as mentioned above, they are ways of raising oneself above one's nature, conquering it. They are a spiritual feat.

THE POWER OF WEAKNESS

Saint Paul's formulation of holy foolishness is quintessentially ironic. His portrayal of himself as weak and his opponents as strong, that is, clearly means the opposite, conditioning as it does his program to conquer the world for a new faith.[22] By the same token, kenoticism is paradoxical: through the emptying and denial of the self, through extreme humility, the holy fool establishes his saintliness and attains significant moral worth. Kharitonov enacts holy foolishness in his manifesto "A Leaflet" ("Listovka"), which begins with an image of frailty and futility—"We are sterile, poisonous blooms"—and ends with the promise of restitution: "And it is also as plain as the light of day that all who are vulnerable, or artful [*lukavoe*], all fallen angels, all who are clothed in spangles or artificial flowers or tears, are closest to God's heart. It is they who will sit at His right hand, they who will receive His kiss."[23]

How does this gay holy foolishness compare with other codings of queer outsiderhood? In *The Queer Art of Failure*, Jack Halberstam argues for the embrace of failure as a critique of "the toxic positivity of contemporary life." In a society devoted to the logic of success, progress, and the accumulation of wealth, *failing*, which the author marks as queer, affords an escape, a way of privileging the alternative, the naive, and the strange: "Being taken seriously means missing out on the chance to be frivolous, promiscuous, and irrelevant."[24] Halberstam alludes to Walter Benjamin and his embrace of unknowing; to celebrate failure, he observes, is to choose to "take a stroll down uncharted streets in the 'wrong' direction."[25] However, Kharitonov's own queer weakness differs radically from Halberstam's conception of queerness as a democratic openness to all such aspects of life as do not fit the master narrative, to potential "roads not taken." Reading Halberstam alongside Kharitonov, and asking ourselves what the aesthetic and political implications of their respective conceptions of queer outsiderhood are, we are struck by how, in the former, the tentative, unfinished nature of existence is the property of a *secular* worldview. By contrast, the religious worldview promises a completion to everything incomplete, redemption to the unredeemed; it transforms foolishness into higher knowledge, and defeat into Paul's all-swallowing *victory* (1 Corinthians 15:55–57). (Incidentally, one famous secular variant of Kharitonov's last-shall-be-first stance comes to mind: Queen's assertion, in what is sometimes interpreted as a "gay anthem," that we who have had "sand kicked in [our] face[s]"—"*we* are the champions.") Kharitonov would not have agreed with Halberstam's version of queer weakness, which embraces defeat without the expectation that this loss will later be recouped. Kharitonov's clairvoyant, apocalyptic vision assigns "higher meaning to the playful and purposeless" (*vysokoe znachenie igrivomu i netselesoobraznomu*).[26] His essay "In the Cold Higher Sense" ("V kholodnom vysshem smysle") refers to the weak as "the chosen people," thus coding weakness not as blunder or transgression but as part of God's design, reflecting the essential Christian conception that the "meek" are "blessed" and "the last shall be first":

> Weakness is a subtle power, inaccessible, invisible to the eyes of imbeciles, and it always wins in the end. Naked power is mindless. That's the power of the idiot red-neck [*eto sila idiota muzhkika*]. Your sort of power, my dears. . . . Only we who don't know how to fight, only we who are cowards, who do not waste our time on futility, we are the chosen people, the defeatists. Not you. Riffraff![27]

This declaration on weakness begins in exaltation and ends in bathos, as the narrator loses control and ends up meting out insults. This register switch from the exalted to the crude is a common element of Kharitonov's poetics. Here, the oral inflection of the last two pithy sentences gives the speech the appearance of incongruent spontaneity. The epithet *bydlo*[28] ("riffraff"; or "cattle," "rabble," or "hoi polloi") sounds out of place—jocular and almost *skaz*-like. This element of travesty suggests the possibility that the whole speech, which at first appears a genuine statement of principles, is in fact an act of performance, a game or role.

If so, however, this role-playing would fit well within the tradition of holy foolishness. In exhibiting his mask, Kharitonov's first-person narrator plays a holy fool. In *Holy Fools in Byzantium and Beyond*, Sergey Ivanov argues that in Eastern Orthodoxy, only those who *feigned* insanity, deliberately *performing* their unruliness, were regarded as *holy* fools.[29] The strange behavior had to appear purposeful in order to be regarded as divine madness. In holy foolishness, performativity and authenticity go hand in hand. Discussing theatricality in *Death in Quotation Marks*, Svetlana Boym describes the use of literary masks not as a subterfuge but as an attempt to tell the very truth about oneself: "The paradox of the mask consists precisely in its ambivalence: in different moments in history and in different theaters, it has been seen as a metaphor for exteriority, as an exterior superficial disguise, and by contrast as a metaphor of a deep, hidden . . . inner self, an image of intersubjectivity."[30] This higher, intersubjective truth is precisely what Kharitonov aspires to in donning the guise of the holy fool. He states that, occasionally, when looking "at my patterns" (*uzory*; apparently a reference to his work, his almost "word-weaving" style of writing), he asks himself: "So, is this all Me, or not Me? . . . It seems to be me. But also seems to be not me. Published in a journal, among other writers—that'd be me; but here on a desert island, with no one else around, that's all me, and for precisely that reason, it's also not me, but rather [everything] in general [*i potomu uzhe i ne ia, a voobshche*]."[31] Holy foolishness justifies withdrawal from societal norms, and in this isolation from mundane superficial relations, more sustaining, more meaningful and enduring bonds are discovered. For Kharitonov, then, the mask, the artifice, is the very truth.

THE PANTOMIME TEACHER

Kharitonov's work as director of a pantomime theater for the deaf, as a choreographer and teacher of pantomime, helps to shed light on his attitude toward performance, the relationship between acting and being. For the deaf, pantomime might indeed present the most organic form of theatrical performance, as it resembles sign language in its utilization of bodily expressivity for communication.

Kharitonov built his literary oeuvre on the foundation of weakness and failure, cultivating, in every line, his status of pervert and outcast, unpublishable writer; but his work in theater was in many ways the opposite of his literary practice. Writing was a form of cultivating seclusion, but speechless pantomime was a form of communication with the public. Kharitonov clearly saw pantomime as a spectacle. This was his opportunity to lead a public life, and he found some success in it. His dissertation, entitled "Pantomime in the Training of a Film Actor" ("Pantomima v obuchenii kinoaktera"), which he defended at the All-Union State Institute of Cinematography (VGIK) in 1972, was received quite favorably, earning the highest praise from all committee members. That same year, Kharitonov's speechless pantomime *Enchanted Island* (*Ocharovannyi ostrov*) debuted at Moscow's Theater of Mimicry and Gesture. A major success among the artistic elite of the city, the play was staged sixty-six times until its closing night on March 31, 1980. In 1977–1978, Kharitonov also worked in the psychology department at Moscow State University to research how the language of gesture and performance might be used to treat stuttering.

Despite the quite public persona donned by Kharitonov in his pantomime as opposed to the outsiderhood of his writing, there are numerous connections between the two activities, especially as seen in an "alternative title" Kharitonov gave his dissertation. On one copy of this work, he wrote a different title for it, by hand. (The phenomenon of handwriting here is crucial, as it constitutes an actual bodily gesture, which a typewritten text does not.) This new title was "A Piece about Life on the Edge and as a Cover-Up [*i dlia otvoda glaz*] in the Genre of Dissertation, with Enlivening Misprints [*s ozhivliaiushchimi opechatkami*], on a Dead, but Enduring Cliché." This new title cannot but put the whole work in a new light, as harboring a secret subtext. The dissertation itself, and the pantomime performance *Enchanted Island* that put its theories into practice, now invariably seem instances of doublespeak. It is as such—as a disruptive, controversial occurrence, in particular, an affront to Soviet *straightness*—that Anastasia Kayiatos interprets *Enchanted Island* in her article "Silent Plasticity: Reenchanting Soviet Stagnation."

Having interviewed the deaf actors involved (despite its many stagings, the play was never recorded), and conveying their reminiscences narrated in bodily language—the most "enchanting" verbal form imaginable—Kayiatos describes *Enchanted Island* as a celebration of "queer-crip" plasticity, and of the stagnation-era plasticity that gave queer-crip expressions an outlet. Kayiatos argues that, given the Soviet state's attempt to enforce vocality, the embrace of *silent* gesture becomes a form of resistance, silencing this compulsory Soviet doxa, and leading the audience to hear, instead, the loaded silence of suggestive gesture, and to discern in it traces of queer presence. Kayiatos sees Kharitonov's play as confirming the theories of Western "queer-crip" scholars: "Pantomime makes room for the body to move through space at an angle and angle toward other bodies in directions not dictated by cultural or political custom. It opens up the plastic 'I' to new sensations that make it affective, per Kharitonov, receptive to its surroundings and other bodies in novel and unnamable ways."[32] In Kayiatos's view, *Enchanted Island* constitutes a stage where the consummate union of actors with audience takes place in the mythic consciousness of nonidentitarian, spiritual communitas. But while this image of a pancosmic embrace is an attractive one, consideration of Kharitonov's writings raises the question: might something have been overlooked in the bodily excess produced by the deaf actors' memories? Could there be some remainder, unintegrated into this picture of the "queer-crip" affirmation of plenitude and discovery thereof in *difference*, in hedonistic experimentation with new ways of life? The language of Kharitonov's descriptions of pantomime suggests a far more ambiguous picture.

81

In Kharitonov's dissertation, the essential traits of pantomime that distinguish it from dance or ballet appear to be drama, conflict, and suffering: "Pantomime is fundamentally unlike a purely choreographic composition, in that its participants are much further separated from one another by their distinguishing plastic traits."[33] Where Kayiatos discerns communality, Kharitonov insists on divisiveness, on conflict. The body in pantomime does not possess the freedom of expression; it realizes its potential in a composition that constrains rather than liberates it. "This is the body under someone's influence."[34] The body copes with its conditionality and contingency as part of the performance; it contends with the rules of the game, the laws of composition.

For Kharitonov, pantomime's state of bodily influence associates it especially with "female roles" and the "passive voice."[35] In Russian, the word "passive" in "the passive voice" is, appropriately enough, *stradatel'nyi* (lit., "pertaining to the sufferer"). The bodily plasticity of pantomime is suffused with suffering; the affective range of pantomime encompasses longing, submission, and resignation. Kayiatos sees *Enchanted Island* as celebrating diversity and mutability through its motif of transubstantiation; and yet, in their attempts to overcome their separation, the featured pair of unfortunate lovers keep turning themselves into various creatures and objects so as to organize themselves yet again into a composition that thrives on the *distance* between them.

The essential compositional element of Kharitonov's pantomime is binary opposition, which creates a dramatic confrontation conducive to the actors' most intense bodily expressivity: a woodcutter and a tree, a hunter and a deer, a hammer and a bell. Clearly, each episode rehearses the structure of dominance and submission, the master-slave configuration. Furthermore, each component of this configuration depends, for its definition, on the composition; each component becomes itself in relation to the other, by acting out the laws of their relationship: "The meaning of a given sign will be its role in a composition; the composition, for its part, is the ability to act out, to express the sensory characteristics of this sign."[36] This means that the actress who plays the tree can only fully develop her treeness in relation to a woodcutter:

> The character reveals herself in action, in relation toward the other. We call these meanings a pair of opposing sides: the one who teaches, and the one who is taught [*obuchaiushchii—obuchaemyi*]; the one who subjects the other to a metamorphosis, and the one who is metamorphized; the one who controls the other's movements, and the one who is controlled; the one who is served and the one who serves; the one who seeks, who chases, and the one who is sought after, who is being chased; the one who is doing something in secret from the other, and the one who hunts the former down [*vyslezhivaiushchii*].[37]

What is striking here is not just that expressive action seems to require disequilibrium but that each pantomime instantiates one and the same predicament—an insoluble repetition of the yearning for and submission to power. Curiously, the list of polarized roles begins with an allusion to a classical structure of gay love, that of teacher and pupil ("the one who teaches and the one who is taught"), and ends with something quite ominous—the hunter-hunted binary, which metaphorically suggests Kharitonov's relationship to the state as an artist and a gay man. There is a clear equivalence between these relationships, the erotic and the political, in terms of power imbalance. Could Kharitonov's pantomime, then, be not so much a site of resistance, as per Kayiatos, but rather a perverse—but cathartic—enactment of the anesthetization, sanctification, and legitimization of one's own abjection?

PRECURSORS I: SAINT JOHN THE EVANGELIST AND OSCAR WILDE

Kharitonov's mask is that of a writer unmade, who pours out his soul along with his tears onto the page. Nevertheless, we can see him as engaged in a quite deliberate project, namely, that of painstakingly resurrecting certain discourses—vessels of intersubjective truth—from the fin de siècle era, refracting them through the prism of late Soviet subjectivity, and organizing them in a radically new thematic knot. Fin de siècle culture—late nineteenth-century religious philosophy, and the writings of decadents and symbolists—provides him with models of subjectivity that combine holy foolishness and aestheticism and that practice self-denial as an expression of individualism, and espouse this individualism as a ticket to spiritual transcendence.

In his essay "In the Cold Higher Sense," just as in his letter to Aksenov, Kharitonov defines his creative genius via comparison with a small number of literary forebears:

> The most unusual, the most poignant [proniknovennyi], the most clear-sighted person on earth has been, undoubtedly, St. John the Evangelist. In second place would be Oscar Wilde. Joyce would give Wilde a run for his money [s nim mog by posporit'], but Joyce was not gay, which, for all his fathomless artistic merits, kept him from being as poignant as Wilde. And in third place—it can't be helped, and I say this without guile—it's me. And glory to those who at times sense this.[38]

The first comparison in Kharitonov's writing of a protagonist with John the Evangelist comes earlier, in an essay titled "Tears for a Person Killed and Strangled" ("Slezy ob ubitom i zadushennom"), which, significantly, also combines the themes of holy foolishness and impossible love. Kharitonov wrote this piece in 1978, soon after being interrogated as a suspect in the murder of his friend Aleksandr Volkov, and it is structured in the form of a mock confession. Kharitonov's protagonist explains how his extraliterary pursuits both impede and simultaneously generate his creative project. His amatory adventures figure as sinful only insofar as they distract him from creative work. And yet they are the source of his creative urgency; it is because of them that his writing must rise to the occasion and fulfill its redemptive potential. They embody the realm of the mundane and private, which writing must transcend, giving it universal significance, incorporating it into the whole:

> The chiefest, most substantial joy is when you stand shedding tears at the abyss. I have composed some words, for instance, and brought them before everybody. Before God? My Redemption is when these words have been heard, but even if they are not heard that is not Sin. . . . My confession is revealing what is personal to myself to make it common property; because my act is in language, and language is the common property of all. It is God's. My longing is to become ultimately a commonplace.[39]

In a way, the transformation of personal experience into writing is a form of self-dissolution (a kenosis befitting a holy fool) and apostolic service to Logos. Kharitonov's forerunner in this respect is John the Evangelist, who was famously explicit on the subject of the sanctity of the word: "According to no less an authority than St. John, in the beginning was the Word, and the Word was God."[40] Like John the Evangelist, who followed Christ and then recorded and spread his word, Kharitonov announces his yearning to be an apostle of truth, transmitting and transcending his personal suffering in service to all.

    In John the Evangelist, an apostle and writer and "the disciple whom Jesus loved,"[41] Kharitonov's protagonist sees the essential elements of his identity: writing, homoeroticism, and the dissemination of truth. There is an inner logic to the jump from writing about the sacred Word to writing a paragraph about fashion: "To restore men to the role of flowers and dazzling jewels we need to bring back the short Greek chlamys, the priestly stole, the old purple mantle, and away with jackets and trousers; no obeisance to the icon of Power (of God or the Tsar), but only to that of the bud-like cherub."[42] Both topics are about transubstantiation: between flesh and word, and between the human being and the sacred flower; both word and flower have a capacity for dispersal and dissemination.

    The turning of a man into a flower conjures Narcissus, who fell in love with his own reflection in water and was subjected to this transformation as punishment. But Kharitonov, while accepting his flowerlike, aesthete's essence, preemptively counters an anticipated accusation of same-sex love as fruitless or narcissistic. Rather, he thinks of his lifework as an apostolic imitation and love of God, a following in his steps and dissemination of his word. The image of the flower allows Kharitonov to conceptualize perpetuation not in the typically procreative sense but as the dispersal of ideas: "all the marigolds and weeds on my balcony completely withered in the sun but I collected seeds from the shriveled flowers re-sowed them and they have come up."[43] The flower's poetics is a catchall, simultaneously covering the protagonist's erotic, mundane, creative, and spiritual preoccupations. Compare the sentiment expressed in the above discussion on gardening with Father Zosima's famous homily in *The Brothers Karamazov*: "God took seeds from other worlds and sowed them on this earth, and raised up his garden; and everything that could sprout sprouted, but it lives and grows only through its sense of being in touch with other mysterious worlds."[44]

The declaration of the primacy of the Word ties John the Evangelist to Oscar Wilde, who held similar beliefs about the primacy of art. The melding of the two projects finds expression in Kharitonov's *chestnolzhivoe slovo*, or "truthful-lying word." This "truth-lying," a neologism of Kharitonov's, may help explain how his sense of mission, of self-sacrificial suffering in the service of all, could coexist with his admiration for Oscar Wilde, known especially for his unapologetic aestheticism.

The connection should be sought within the confines of that infamous Reading Gaol. In "'Next to Christ': Oscar Wilde in Russian Modernism," Evgenii Bershtein argues that Russian modernists, specifically adherents of the Russian symbolist movement, created their own myth of Oscar Wilde as a Nietzschean martyr. Bershtein discusses the strange history of the reception of Oscar Wilde in Russia, noting that "in Russia's Silver Age, Wilde's best-known texts were his prison writings," in which—and this is what especially caught the eye of Russian modernists—Wilde famously admits that in his life before the trials he had been misled by the constant pursuit of pleasure, and that he had not understood the importance of suffering, which he realized only later in prison. "Suffering—curious as it may sound to you," he writes [in a letter to Alfred Douglas]—"is the means by which we become conscious of existing."[45]

This sentiment could be taken straight from Dostoevsky, whose Underground Man (the model for Kharitonov's protagonist) declares, "Suffering—why, this is the sole cause of consciousness. Though I did declare at the beginning that consciousness, in my opinion, is man's greatest misfortune, still I know that man loves it and will not exchange it for any satisfactions."[46] Fin de siècle Russian writers and philosophers, who had recently discovered strong affinities between their own tragic worldviews and those of Dostoevsky and Nietzsche, were disposed to see in Oscar Wilde a kindred spirit, who chose to pursue a doomed aesthetic revolt against morality in full knowledge that it would end in punishment and suffering. Kharitonov is determined to inscribe himself into this tradition of tragic and prophetic aestheticism: "We shall write like Gabriele D'Annunzio, Nietzsche, and St. John (especially in the Revelation)."[47] It is not incidental that this transnational literary canon of decadence should include D'Annunzio, an Italian poet who combined militant aestheticism with militant—and radical—politics, specifically fascism. This inclusion hints at Kharitonov's own consistent blending of aestheticism with devout nationalism.

PRECURSORS II: KUZMIN, ROZANOV, AND THE TRADITION OF PATRIOTIC QUEERNESS

Notably, Russian literary tradition *already had* its "Russian Oscar Wilde"— Mikhail Kuzmin; but even as he seeks his literary forebears in modernism, Kharitonov omits this father of gay Russian literature from his genealogy. Kharitonov does adopt certain aspects of Kuzmin's conceptualization of his sexual identity while rejecting others. Kuzmin had long anticipated Kharitonov in seeking the native roots of his homosexuality in the life and teachings of Russian monks and sectarians. Monks' adherence to the past and ritual, he believed, preserved remnants of Byzantine antiquity, which in turn bore the legacy of ancient Greek society and its sexual mores. Kuzmin moreover looked favorably on monks' eschewing of the mundane life of biological reproduction, and their commitment to a ritualistically organized existence in which art and life were in organic interdependence. This was true also of schismatics (particularly Old Believers), who, furthermore, remained untainted by the alien influences of modern life. Kuzmin's sense of affiliation with such "heretics" allowed him to interpret his sexual identity—likewise marginal, misunderstood, and subject to persecution—as something similarly autochthonous.[48]

And yet, Kuzmin manages to find, in modernistically perceived combinations of the pagan and Christian in early Christianity, remnants of Hellenism, which offered a countermeasure to Christian asceticism. Thus does Kuzmin offer, in his writing in general and especially in his well-known novel *Wings* (*Kryl'ia*, 1906), a vision of same-sex love as blissful and fulfilling, as opposed to impossible and insufferable, as it appears in the works of Kharitonov. Unlike virtually anything by Kharitonov, *Wings* famously features a happy ending.[49] In the novel's finale, the main character Vania chooses to join his soon-to-be lover on a journey, symbolically opening a large window and letting the sunshine in to fill the room. To be sure, Kharitonov follows in Kuzmin's footsteps in attempting to "authenticate" his sexual identity via its inherent connection to the sacred, forgotten mores of Russian antiquity; his above-cited "chlamys," for instance, highlights continuity from Hellenic to Byzantine (hence Russian) civilization. But Kharitonov is unable or unwilling to follow Kuzmin triumphantly out of the closet or underground; his writing, instead, cultivates the pleasure of lying low and suffering deeply.

The different approaches, of course, may have something to do with the respective milieus involved. Kuzmin's emancipatory narrative matched the historical moment in which he wrote, when, even as homosexuality was technically illegal, sodomy statutes were rarely enforced in tsarist Russia;[50] and when—in that first decade of the twentieth century that produced *Wings*—Russian cultural circles were preoccupied with the idea of life creation—of the creation of life as art—and with resistance to the status quo (especially as regarded gender). Any deviation in how one lived one's life thus harbored major aesthetic potential. Sensual apprehension, moreover, was favored over positivism and pragmatics, so any form of heightened sensuality was welcome. By contrast, the Soviet milieu, whether in its mainstream or dissident precincts, was far more prudish and censorious about experimental approaches to identity and the elevation of the sensual above the rational. It made perfect sense, then, for Kharitonov to develop the image of the aesthete-homosexual as an underground man.

In a study of the historical poetics of gay literature in Russia, Bershtein argues that, despite Kuzmin's unprecedented devotion of a whole novel to the theme of gay love, gay Russian literature ultimately took a different, non-Kuzminian path. As Bershtein explains, while Kuzmin's *Wings* fits the tradition of the Western bildungsroman, plotting out the protagonist's fulfillment and emancipation and the normalization of homosexuality, the subsequent gay tradition in Russia has favored a fragmented and contradictory style, with no plot progression or culminative moments to speak of.[51] Such writing dramatizes the theme differently (and, we might add, tracks the dearth of tangible progress in gay rights after Kuzmin's hopeful start): rather than affirming one's identity through the scenario of a taboo lifted or social position improved, it uses brokenness to convey a still-troubled interiority, to communicate one's suffering to the world.

Bershtein traces this fragmentariness, which Russian gay literary culture adopted and which Kharitonov clearly perfected, to another modernist, the Russian religious philosopher Vasily Rozanov. Rozanov is credited with the creation of a new genre, one that combines aphorisms, diaristic records of intimate details, and political opinions, all jumbled in an often-contradictory manner, but held together by the force of the narrator's emotions. Rozanov explicitly identified with Dostoevsky's Underground Man, and like him "blasphemed" against established norms, especially the church's advocacy of asceticism and censure of sexuality. Seeing sexuality as, by contrast, the most concentrated expression of human vitality and individuality, Rozanov sought in his writings to reconcile Christianity with it. His preoccupation with the intimate sides of life—the sheer *physicality* of his prose—became a model for writers who would approach the intimate and the taboo. But Rozanov's significance for gay Russian literature goes further: in his 1911 book *People of the Moonlight: The Metaphysics of Christianity (Liudi lunnogo sveta. Metafizika khristianstva)*, he provided a metaphysical defense of homosexuality, crediting "spiritual sodomites" with an enormous contribution to civilization—nothing less than Christianity itself.

The essence of Rozanov's theory is that gay love is neither a crime (as the government was inclined to treat it) nor a disease (as current medical texts were arguing), but rather a specific constitution of being, characterized by the ability to love deeply and intensely in the absence of sexual desire. Like so many Russian modernists, Rozanov was an admirer of Otto Weininger's *Sex and Character*, published in Russian in 1908, and he subscribed to the idea of universal "bisexuality"—that is, the existence of both masculine and feminine elements in each human being. According to Rozanov, "moon people," or the third sex, already possess the balanced elements of both the masculine and the feminine, and so feel no need or desire to conjoin with the opposite sex. Unlike "sun people," who seek completion in procreative sexuality, moon people feel dread before reproduction, and channel their revulsion into same-sex love and asceticism. Here Rozanov unfolds a complex genealogy that takes us back to ancient Mesopotamia, where Semitic high priests rejected familial life and embraced the life of the spirit; these sacred people reviled sexuality as part of familial, mundane existence. They had numerous techniques of subduing the desires of the flesh, including flagellation and even castration. These high priests also sought to destroy the very idea of sex by cross-dressing and purposefully appearing androgynous. As Rozanov tells it, Judaism first appeared among the Semites specifically as a religion of familial life, of "be fruitful and multiply"; the tradition of the *anti*-procreative high priests was kept alive, meanwhile, by sects of Judaic monks, who dwelled in the wilderness and took vows of celibacy, and whose ranks would eventually include, most famously, Jesus Christ. For Rozanov, Christianity, with its distaste for the body and procreation, and its sanctification of celibacy, is the religion of ascetics.[52] Kharitonov's multiple allusions to a gay subtext in the relationship between John the Evangelist and Christ would seem to derive directly from Rozanov's theory: "I've got to break with homosexuality. It's no good and it leads nowhere. . . . One thing was acceptable, and that was John loving Christ and dedicating his whole life to him. But that was Jesus Christ. Who had a doctrine. Which it was John's job to safeguard and spread."[53] Not only does Kharitonov adopt Rozanov's style of writing, he also instantiates Rozanov's theory in his semi-autobiographical texts that describe the acceptance and cultivation of third-sex identity as a form of asceticism; flowers and tears as stigmata; and the end result: one's role as votary in the service of truth.

Rozanov himself was a heterosexual man and considered the feminine element to be only weakly present in himself. On certain occasions, however, he did perceive in himself a pronounced femininity, and these happened to occur at the height of patriotic zeal. In his 1915 book *The War of 1914 and the Russian Revival* (*Voina 1914 goda i russkoe vozrozhdenie*), Rozanov describes the erotically charged elation he feels at the sight of a squadron of cavalrymen, and concludes that "the essence of the army is that it turns all of us into women—weak, trembling, embracing the air."[54] In response, the philosopher Nikolai Berdiaev wrote a scathing essay titled "On the Eternally Womanish in the Russian Soul" ("O 'vechno bab'em' v russkoi dushe"), in which he scorned Rozanov's easy arousal by power, and readiness to submit to it, as a particular flaw of the Russian national character.

In a sense we have already seen Kharitonov repeat Rozanov's gesture of trembling admiringly before soldiers: the above-cited image of a man as a flower clad in a chlamys—the Greek soldier's cloak later incorporated into Byzantine royal attire (with the also-mentioned *porfira*, the purple mantle). Kharitonov's aesthetics of weakness, rehearsed ironically in that "flower" passage (with appurtenances of war and force cherished right alongside the injunction *not* to pay "obeisance" to "Power" and "Tsar") would seem likewise to harbor a valorization of militancy, of strong rule. As if following Rozanov, Kharitonov's protagonist adopts effeminacy as an intoxicating role, a "feminine" submission of the self to beautiful virile power:

> We are turned on by bow-legged brutal Tatars. A moment of unendurable beauty! . . . I liked waiting sometimes of an evening for a man to arrive and would get myself ready washing dressing in a courtly seductive way applied at great length just a touch of make-up smeared myself and added a hint of shading. . . . This hour of anticipation preparation getting ready for my entrance, then my skilled arousal of the man showing my art clinging invitingly and then, when he had done his bit, I would go off to sleep the rest of my night in my own room and the performance was over, . . . until we meet again, until the next *Führer* [*do svidaniia do novogo* fiurera; emphasis in original].[55]

In *Under House Arrest*, the intoxication of sexual submission goes hand in hand with submissiveness toward the state, toward law and order. For Kharitonov, they are packaged together as constituting his adoption of the "weak" persona of a gay aesthete, his becoming "a hero of weakness." And Kharitonov would perhaps agree with Berdiaev's assessment of the Russian national character, albeit turning a minus into a plus sign, as his works explicitly portray this passive submissiveness as that which distinguishes him as a proud and definitive bearer of the Russian psyche.

Indeed, a constant motif of Kharitonov's is the affirmation of Soviet law and order—a Stockholm-syndrome-like gratitude to his captors, as he explains his rightful categorization among "unprintable authors":

> Let us not feign naivety and ask why our works get banned. They are quite right to ban us. Our life is governed by Law and Order, and there is a Law about what it is proper for people to see in print and what is to be passed over in silence. Law and Order in our Motherland is as it should be. Order is always fatally right for people with an artistic bent. We are tied to it. We need it. Violating it is the whole tenor of our artistic works. Were things to change, our keynote would be taken from us and we should lose the ground we stand on.[56]

Elsewhere in the book, this submissive position is marked as anti-Western: "We have no freedoms and we don't need them. We shall personify an ideal of endurance and of quietly going mad at home."[57] The allusion to "freedoms," a marker of Western democratic discourse, makes it clear that the "we" here who thrive on censorship are not just any writers, but specifically Russian writers. Such statements might appear flippant or ironic; but Kharitonov's all-too-seriousness becomes manifest as he marshals his most effective rhetorical weapon: antisemitism.

THE JEWISH QUESTION

In a two-issue publication dedicated to writings by and about Kharitonov in the journal *Glagol* in 1993, many of the contributors felt compelled to touch on the uncomfortable subject of his frequent pronouncements about Jews, for instance: "How wise of God to endow us with anti-Semitism"[58] (*Ne zria zhe v nas vlozhena Bogom iudofobiia*[59]). Commentators on Kharitonov who acknowledge this phenomenon in his writing typically attempt to excuse or at least explain it. Vasily Aksenov, for instance, reads it as a form of épatage, a rebellious pose by which Kharitonov sought to establish his brave exclusivity. He imagines the author saying, "I make" these statements—what Aksenov calls "strained hints at antisemitism"—"so that people won't think I'm afraid" (*chtoby ne podumali, chto boius'*[60])—(If so, Kharitonov would be engaging in something akin to the modern phenomenon of "ironic" or "hipster racism.")[61] Iaroslav Mogutin explains Kharitonov's "Judeophobia" with reference to a notorious idea of Weininger that Kharitonov may have taken too close to heart. "Weininger advanced the very debatable thesis that for a man of homosexual orientation, Jewishness signifies the feminine, which cannot arouse in him (a homosexual) any positive emotions; this explains a great deal about Kharitonov."[62] Perhaps the quaintest of these attempts is the one made by Evgeny Popov, who seems to imply that Kharitonov simply did not understand what he was saying: when a Kharitonov character uses the word *zhid*, this means that the author himself does not realize that this word "has lost the neutral, nominative connotation" that it had "in the time of Dostoevsky" and "has become a slur."[63] Given that the word *zhid* is indeed used frequently in Kharitonov's writings—including in the context (whether meant "seriously" or otherwise) of "yid-Masonic" machinations to keep Russians low[64]—and given the meticulous scriptedness of his language, and the holistic coherence of his texts, I would propose that we attempt to interpret the "Judeophobia" in question not as an inconvenient character flaw or the result of ineptitude but as a particular discursive practice. Kharitonov's textual antisemitism should not be excused and dismissed, but rather analyzed as a particular device necessary for the completion of his creative project.[65]

Kharitonov revives the discourse of antisemitism, not unfamiliar to a cultured Russian reader, because it is essential for his project of inscribing homosexuality into Russian culture, of authenticating and legitimizing it. If, as I argue, Kharitonov seeks especially to champion gay aestheticism as a form of holy foolishness, hence as the most innate expression of Russianness, then it behooves him to establish a different Other, in contrast to whom his "weak" position would be strengthened. Thus does Kharitonov's manifesto "A Leaflet" allot such prominence to discussion of the similarities and distinctions between gays and Jews. First a parallel is drawn between the outcast nature of the two traditionally reviled groups, Jews and gays: "Our question has points of similarity with the Jewish Question."[66] But then Kharitonov proceeds to establish essential (or essentialized) differences between them. In the process, he constructs a new binary, that of Jew-gay, which effectively replaces the hetero-gay opposition. Since in the Russian cultural tradition the Jew must be the negative element of the equation, gayness is pushed, inevitably, into the positive side of it. Lest this be seen as "unfair" on my part, it should be emphasized that in constructing his Jew-gay opposition, Kharitonov relies on clichés and stereotypes (that is, on essentialization): Jews belong to the sphere of commerce, gays to that of art:

> Just as, for example, in the opinion of most anti-Semites, [Jews'] genius most often flowers in commerce, mimicry, feuilletons, art without pathos, in practical everyday discretion, the art of survival; just as certain spheres of activity may be thought to have been created on purpose by them and for them:
> So too our genius has flourished in, for example, that most ephemeral and flimsy of arts: ballet. Whether it's literally dance, or any pop song, or any other art form based on delectation—it is quite obvious that it is our creation.[67]

At the core of Jewish existence is profit and pragmatism; at the core of gay existence is noninstrumentality, transcendence of the mundane. Both groups represent a "menace," but the Jewish threat is external (they will take over, usher in the apocalypse), while the gay threat is internal: *you* straights are all repressed versions of *us*; but you mustn't all give in to the urge to *become* us, as that too would "hasten the end of the world"—the discontinuance of the human race. (Again, Kharitonov seems to take on the vocation of Rozanov's secret and exclusive "moon people" priests: not *everyone* can follow the directive implied in Matthew 19:12.):

> Just as Jewish people have to be ridiculed in jokes and the image of the crafty yid firmly retained in the mind's eye by all non-Jewish humanity to ensure that anti-Semitism should not perish from the earth, since if it did what would there be to prevent Jews from getting all the jobs in the world? (and there are those who believe that this is precisely how the world will end) . . .
>
> So too our ethereal flower-like sort with its pollen flying who knows whither must be mocked and transformed by the coarse, direct common sense of common people into a term of abuse, so that immature silly boys should not take it into their heads before their masculine drive has finally become established in them to give in to the weakness of falling in love with themselves. Because, of course, and there can be no doubt about this (for us), although the very thought is highly subversive and must not be allowed to circulate freely (in order not to hasten the end of the world from the opposite direction), but for all that it is true: you are all repressed [*zadushennye*; lit. "stifled" or "strangled"] homosexuals.[68]

I quote this section at length because it is key to understanding Kharitonov's competing "poetics" of Jewishness and gayness. While both groups appear marginal to the majority, their relationship to it is, in fact, directly inverse. Jews' genius is in mimicry—that is, in the ability to adapt, to pretend to be like everyone else while being essentially alien; gay genius lies in espousing marginality, while in fact epitomizing the very core of the totality. Jews infiltrate, while gays self-sacrificially stand apart. To choose to be a hero of weakness means to refuse to become a Jew, who attempts to adapt and gain worldly power, and who, in seeking power, moves further away from the apostolic truth, from godliness, from spiritual thoughts.

In "Tears for a Person Killed and Strangled," Kharitonov establishes the core difference between Jews and Russians in much the same terms: one group embodies commerce, fakery, calculation, and adaptation, while the other embodies authenticity and loyalty to higher principle, including to the principle of totality (the whole to which one belongs):

In our culture, where there is a need for diplomacy and palliative care, Jews will get ahead, but a Russian, to avoid being crafty, won't do anything at all, it makes better sense for us and is more godly. . . . Where you are dealing with commodities, even cultural commodities, the Jews are in a class of their own. Wherever there is faking: the cinema; translating literary art from other languages; there the Jews are unbeatable. And in terms of relative valuation, the market agrees that their goods are finer and better made. They have more soul and international humanity in the mix. But when it comes to dogged loyalty to the state and Party, the Jews are hopeless. And where the need is for soul solely, for madness, for unadulterated godliness or monastic seclusion [*gde nuzhna tol'ko dusha, tol'ko bezumie, tol'ko Bog bez podmesi i monasheskoe odinochestvo*], there they can't compete.[69]

In both these works, then, the essence of the Russian national character lies precisely in the same set of principles coded as gay: the rejection of pragmatism and profit in favor of the life of the spirit; the creative urge to transcend the mundane; and monastic seclusion, a self-sacrificial refusal to follow others. Furthermore, while Jews are accused of liberalism and activism (*mezhdunarodnaia chelovechnost'*, or "international humaneness"), Russians are said to be more naturally inclined (so as "to avoid being crafty") to do nothing, which is a variation on the death-orientation that in "A Leaflet" Kharitonov ascribes to gays: "We [gays] are sterile, poisonous blooms"; "you [straights] are all repressed homosexuals," which, if you but knew and embraced it, would "hasten the end of the world." This brings us back to the Kharitonov stance described above of holy foolishness—specifically, to its social conservatism. For indeed, while "gay artist" might theoretically suggest "progressiveness," not necessarily so does "gay artist as *holy fool*." To the extent that holy foolishness harks back to the death-oriented,[70] hence apocalyptic[71] kernel of Christianity itself, it could be seen (at least in Kharitonov's interpretation[72]) to proscribe any sort of social or progressive action. If this life is mere preparation for that imminent end, why bother with sociopolitical tinkering—an activity that, again, "Judeophobia" codes as Jewish?

It is through the abjection of the Jew that Kharitonov can affirm, without a hint of irony or reservation, his cause, which is the validation of the Russian national character, with gayness held up as the apotheosis thereof. But Kharitonov can only integrate his marginal self into a totality by delineating this totality via the exclusion of someone *else*, another Other—which only goes to show the provisional, shaky grounds on which this claim to wholeness rests.

In conclusion, in this chapter I have argued that Kharitonov creatively appropriates a specifically native variant of weakness, holy foolishness.

Constructing his gay weak subjectivity as an instantiation of Orthodox holy foolishness, Kharitonov aims to disassociate his project from Western queer practices of self-determination and, more importantly, to inscribe himself in Russian cultural tradition. What makes Kharitonov's stance particularly (even fascinatingly) radical is that he attempts to claim for himself a rightful place in the Russian literary canon, not despite but precisely because of his gayness. Gay love, which is nonprocreative—"we are sterile . . . blooms" (or "fruitless," *besplodnye*)—and thus technically "impractical," takes its place among the Dostoevskian, especially Dmitry-Karamazovian, impracticalities and nonmaterialisms that make up the vaunted "Russian soul." Kharitonov's performance of weakness and careful construction of his artistic persona should be read, I propose, as a strategic aesthetic project with enormous sociopolitical stakes. In the process, however, Kharitonov recruits weakness in the service of dogma and totality, inviting us to reassess our theoretical understanding of weakness—based on Vattimo's philosophy of weak thought and Halberstam's "queer art of failure"—as a mode of celebrating *difference*. Reading Kharitonov, we are faced with the stark possibility that our supposedly familiar categories ("difference," "queerness," etc.) are hardly as stable as we had thought.[73]

Describing his philosophy of "weak thought," Vattimo posits that at its core lies a desire to avoid partial, exclusionary thinking. It is "an effort to reconstruct a non-partial point of view, one which would thus allow us to grasp totality as such."[74] For Vattimo, ideology masks truth not because it is false but because it is partial; it only pretends to be whole. When one questions one's own ideology, one espouses "weakness" as conceptualized by Vattimo. Weakness is a practice of entertaining the possibility that other points of view exist. Kharitonov's discourse of weakness issues a challenge for a Western academic such as myself to expand her views and question her ideological assumptions—affords her a chance, that is, to practice "weak thought."

"Universal Chicken-Heartedness":
Low Spirits and Immoderate Meditations in
Venedikt Erofeev's *Moskva–Petushki*

INTRODUCTION: EPIC OR TRAGEDY?

Moscow–Petushki (*Moskva–Petushki*; translated into English as *Moscow to the End of the Line*, *Moscow Stations*, or *Moscow Circles*) was written in 1970 but published in Russia only in 1989 in the journal *Trezvost' i kul'tura* (*Sobriety and Culture*). Its first Soviet publishers, that is, saw it, or at least sought to frame it, as an anti-alcoholism pamphlet. But the author must have had a different genre, or, rather, several of them, in mind.[1] The novel's subtitle or genre designation, *Poema* ("An Epic Poem"), announces a certain affinity with an illustrious predecessor—another prose work that refers to itself as a *poema* and features a journey: Gogol's *Dead Souls* (*Mertvye dushi*). In the dedication, moreover, Erofeev calls his poem "tragic."[2] Over time, however, while commentators have recognized the work's epic aspirations, its *tragic* elements—those most glaring to the editors of a *temperance* journal— have gone less noticed.[3] Since the fall of the Soviet Union, *Moscow–Petushki* has attained cult status as the first Russian postmodern novel and provoked a surge of interpretations ranging from political to metaphysical, from religious to existentialist.

Most interpretations engage the myth of the author, which is understandable, insofar as the protagonist (whom I will call as he calls himself, Venichka) shares a name and a great number of autobiographical details with his creator.[4] As myths usually do, the Erofeev legend cloaks the author, and by extension the protagonist of what Eduard Vlasov calls his "immortal *poema*,"[5] in deeply heroic tones: he is a sober drunk and a holy fool, who expresses his resistance to Marxism-Leninism, and to other violent meta-narratives of the twentieth century as well, via his inspired, antisocial drinking, and his postmodern drifting through various quotations, mixing of discourses high and low, and celebration of chance and paradox.[6] More often than not, contradictory elements of Erofeev's narrative are analyzed as befitting a consistently postmodernist worldview. That is, Erofeev is alleged to eschew all certainty, coherence, or order—former virtues long since compromised by twentieth-century experience—in favor of *disorder*, which is less complicit in the evils of modernity.[7] Or, Erofeev's *poema* is said to counter a now negatively coded *energy*, which has fueled wars and revolutions, with the less culpable *entropy*.[8] Drinking, in this latter interpretation, represents a means of slowing down (alcohol being literally a "depressant") and of introspection, of adopting a less brutal and more reflective form of being, of transcending the mundane world and entering a higher plane of existence.

I do not disagree with these influential interpretations, but in what follows I will attempt to propose a less holistic reading, taking as a starting point the consideration that, at some point midnarrative, there occurs in *Moscow–Petushki* a change of perspective. Laura Beraha notes this significant switch in her description of the *poema*'s "inherently paradoxical picaresque dynamic": "It is this relentless, self-annihilating momentum that is invoked to embrace Erofeev's potpourri of genres, and then turned back on itself to expose and exploit the absences latent in the rogue, his world and his entire narrative project."[9] Mark Lipovetsky pinpoints the key shift at the *poema*'s end:

> From this point of view, drinking as a chain of ruptures in consciousness and existence and intoxication as a regular arrhythmic plunging into the dark and chaos together form the poem's narrative and the hero's ragged being as a consistent meaning of approaching God. . . . The paradox of *Moskva–Petushki* consists in the fact that the entire finale—after Venichka has missed his stop at Petushki—reads as an insistent refutation of the apophatic cognizance of God, superimposed on "altered" evangelical scenes and the chain of "renunciation of thyself and all things."[10]

According to this multilayered argument, Venichka the trickster attempts to resist the culture of late Soviet cynicism by recourse to cynicism's counterpoint or further development (borrowed by Lipovetsky from Peter Sloterdijk) of *kynicism*. This ethics demands the hero's perpetual discursive metamorphoses, which allow him to resist conscription into any grand narratives or stable social truths, while at the same time to subscribe to the eternal, inherently valuable "self-generating Logos," what Lipovetsky calls "a shared notion of the sacred."[11] Lipovetsky argues, however, that the sphere of the sacred, the divine Logos, of which Erofeev is a prophet, in the end fails to offer an exit from universal cynicism, cruelty, and violence.

This interpretation is compelling and cogent, but I would nevertheless propose also examining the midnarrative shift toward the tragic from a different angle. In Lipovetsky's reading, the *poema*'s tragedy resides in the "absence of an alternative to cynicism on earth or in heaven, in society and in consciousness: this is the testimony inscribed into the tragic finale of *Moskva–Petushki*."[12] Offering a sophisticated reading of the *poema*'s instantiation of the tragic, this interpretation appears to me wanting in one respect: it transfers the burden of responsibility for the tragic end from the hero to the world around him. In this regard, it is similar to the "classic" *comic* interpretations of the book, wherein Venichka's feats are lionized, his fiascos excused or ignored. If Venichka is portrayed, indeed, as an uncompromising adept of chaos or an obdurate prophet of entropy, his failure to reach Petushki at the end of the *poema* must be explained with reference to the insuperable chaos of the world or at least of Soviet *realiia*, amid which one is better off not "winning," and the human condition appears hopeless. These explanations appear to me perceptive, yet partial. In my view, the narrative's transition to the tragic—the catastrophe of its finale—suggests the possibility that, with *Moscow–Petushki*, Erofeev proposes, but also questions, a particular worldview, one that my study defines as an ethics of weakness.[13] I interpret the *poema* not as an apologia of this worldview but an exploration of its pluses and minuses. In this sense, the *poema* embodies a philosophical tract, testing (and critiquing) Venichka's judgments as to his place in the world.[14]

According to the classical Aristotelian definition of tragedy, events are only tragic if they occur due to a character's error (*hamartia*): "Misfortune is brought about not by vice or depravity, but by some error or frailty."[15] In Aristotelian terms, if a bad turn of events is caused by external forces, then it does not constitute a tragedy, but a mere misadventure. Tragedy requires some fatal gap between a character's intentions and actions. Does not *Moscow–Petushki*, by the same token, address the *internal* as well as external causes of Venichka's fate? Might it be that Venichka's essential weakness is in fact that selfsame Aristotelian "frailty" that leads to tragedy? This chapter will argue that Erofeev uses *Moscow–Petushki* to subject weakness, which he recognizes as symptomatic of his generation and which he himself cultivates, to a fuller consideration, putting its pros and cons to what, as mentioned in the introduction, Erofeev sees as characteristic of contemporary prose: a "piercing questioning."[16] Erofeev's novelistic interrogation of late Soviet weakness, rather than unreserved engagement in it, allows him to simultaneously share in and deviate from the secret code.[17]

TWO DIVERGING JOURNEYS

Erofeev's admiration for the Russian religious philosopher Vasily Rozanov is well known.[18] His notebooks of the 1960s are peppered with Rozanov's proclamations on every facet of life, from literature to Jews to the downfall of European civilization. But one thought that keeps recurring, clothed in various formulas, is a call for solitude. In most cases, Erofeev either shortens or modifies the quotations to befit his own temperament and personal philosophy. For example, Rozanov's "Flee the crowd [*tolpy begai*], or pass it warily by" is truncated by Erofeev into "Pass warily by the crowd."[19] Rozanov's "Solitude is the best guardian of the soul. . . . Out of solitude comes everything— out of solitude comes strength, out of solitude comes purity" is shortened to "Solitude is the best guardian of the soul. Out of solitude comes everything."[20] Importantly, Erofeev here discards "strength," "purity," and the energetic quickness implicit in the act of "fleeing" and retains only solitude.

Likewise, Rozanov's dictum that the people around you "diminish rather than enrich your soul" is both recorded in Erofeev's notebooks[21] and finds its way, in a reworked form, into *Moscow–Petushki*. Venichka, the protagonist of the *poema*, argues with himself: "Do I really need your crowd? Are your people really necessary? Take the Redeemer even, who to his own Mother said, What art thou to me? And, indeed, what do these vain and repellent creatures have to do with me?"[22] This statement is curious: the disavowal of all ties with humanity, and the implication that his journey constitutes a search for something loftier than "mere" connection with people, directly contradict the apparent aim of the trip to Petushki, which is to visit his sweetheart and their son. The central conflict of *Moscow–Petushki*, I believe, exists in the juxtaposition of the two journeys: journey no. 1— the openly apparent journey—is to take the protagonist toward Petushki, where his sweetheart and sickly son reside; journey no. 2, the underlying one, leads toward self-discovery via alcoholic seclusion.[23] Venichka attempts to accomplish the two journeys simultaneously, and in the end fails—but not because of the vicissitudes of Soviet life, nor owing to the postmodern condition in general, nor God's inconstancy, nor the perils of alcoholism. Venichka fails because, at the end of the *poema* and of his life—he dies an untimely death—the philosophical position that salvation can be found in solitude proves unsustainable.

Intoxication in the *poema* is a form of spiritual seclusion, of finding oneself through a process of *vypadaniia*, a "falling-out" of all social systems. It is a form of becoming, based on a radical refusal to fully identify with any one discourse. The travesty-like mingling of all discourses that cancel each other out supports the idea that Venichka does not prescribe any of them. However, his avoidance bespeaks not a postmodern desire to celebrate the death of the author but rather, to the contrary, the urge to establish oneself as a subject. Venichka believes he can, and should, establish his subjecthood by separating himself from others, through seclusion and intemperate individualism. In the end, however, this radical freedom from all affiliations leads to his disorientation. This loss of direction takes him away from the potential salvation that might be located in Petushki or (more generally) reside in other human beings.

Ann Komaromi perceptively pinpoints the lack of interpersonal connection as the *poema*'s central menace: "[Erofeev] went further than Aksenov or Bitov in showing how vulnerable such individual subjectivity remains without the response that would validate it."[24] Detecting Venichka's "need for interpersonal response" and diagnosing his solipsism as an existential threat, she ascribes the breakdown of communication to environmental conditions—that is, the particular underground existence of samizdat writers.

I would emphasize, however, that Venichka does not only desire human communication; he also rejects it. It is not just that late Soviet conditions have hopelessly complicated potential communion with other people; the rejection of others is inscribed in Erofeev and Venichka's shared worldview. My contention, then, is that the *poema* dramatizes Venichka's failed quest to reach salvation via weakness of the will and the solitude that weakness affords. What follows is an attempt to show that the quality Erofeev paradoxically refers to as "firm uncertainty" (*tverdaia neuverennost*[25]) extends to the worthwhileness of Venichka's most cherished state—that is, aloneness.

SOLITUDE AND WEAK THOUGHT

Doubt rather than truth is both the engine and the outcome of Venichka's immoderate meditations. Perhaps the most succinct encapsulation of Venichka's relation to truth is this: "I'm not saying that now the truth is known to me, or that I've approached it close up. Not at all. But I've gotten close enough to it so that it's convenient to look it over."[26] Here Venichka assumes a position conducive to contemplation. This position is marked by its proximity to truth, which however still suggests a certain distance from it. Doubt is, of course, an admission of weakness. It is doubt rather than certitude, and weakness rather than strength, that Venichka cultivates. This self-admittedly partial access to "truth," or at times its complete substitution with the "bitter mishmash" that Venichka carries in himself and conceptualizes his subjectivity around, is a textbook instantiation of Vattimo's "weak thought."[27]

But how can a subjectivity be sustained weakly, with no recourse to power or violence? One way it can be achieved is through negation, the sustained distancing of the self from established systems of thought.[28] Both Erofeev the author and Venichka the protagonist attempt to affirm their authentic selves, via the radical nonaffiliation with any discourse or agenda. Alcohol functions not to enlighten the imbiber but rather to perpetuate his weakened condition, his state of neutrality.

In 1990, Erofeev gave an interview to Leonid Prudovsky for the journal *Kontinent* (*Continent*—an émigré publication that would for a brief time also be published in post-Soviet Russia). Throughout the interview, Prudovsky keeps trying to get Erofeev to express his nonconformism in the form of some sustained political stance, but Erofeev insistently refuses to turn his "weak" persona into that of a fighter or dissident. To the leading question whether in school he was one of the bullies or the bullied, he answers that he was "neutral and assiduously observant."[29] The interviewer then asks to what extent it was possible to sustain such neutrality; Erofeev responds: "It was possible to find such a position, and I managed to find this diminutive and very convenient position of observer. And I took it. Perhaps it was not a very lofty position, but who gives a crap about loftiness?"[30] As the interview moves on to cover the more mature period of Erofeev's biography, the author sticks to his position of nonbelonging, rejecting any association of his life or work with political dissidence. The height of this stance comes as Erofeev makes the shocking assertion that he—who, it should be kept in mind, was expelled from several universities for draft evasion and for keeping a Bible in his drawer, and who long existed as a person "with no fixed abode"—he, this selfsame Erofeev, has a mutually loving relationship with Soviet power:

> Erofeev, what about our dear Soviet power—how great was its sudden love for you when you became world famous?
>
> *It took no notice of me at all. I love my power.* [Here and below, Erofeev's use of "power" is ambiguous, potentially referring to "his" (i.e., allegedly beloved) Soviet power, or to his *own* power.]
>
> What do you love about it?
>
> *Everything.*
>
> Do you love it for letting you be and not throwing you in prison?
>
> *I especially love it for that. I am ready to love my power for everything.*
>
> And what do you love most about it: its lips or its acts, the way it talks or the way it walks?[31]
>
> *I love everything about it. You can discuss my power if you want—be my fucking guest.* [*Eto vam vol'no rassuzhdat' o moei vlasti, ebena mat'.*] *You can fool around if you want. But I don't fool around. I love my power, and no one loves their power as much, not one asshole loves their power as much I love mine.*[32]

Erofeev might seem to be engaging in irony or épatage. But as Mikhail Epstein argues, Erofeev's performance here is complex and multifaceted; it is characterized rather by *anti-irony*, a stance Epstein ascribes to Erofeev's oeuvre generally.[33] In Epstein's definition, anti-irony is a position existing somewhere on the border between irony and earnestness: transforming irony into its opposite, Erofeev arrives at a new level of seriousness. In my view, the difficulty of defining anti-ironic seriousness complicates investigation of a given author's affiliation with it; as Epstein concedes: "[Erofeev's] intonations cannot be engaged with [*ego intonatsii nel'zia angazhirovat'*]."[34]

Calling the interviewer's own ironizing "out of place" (*neumestnym*), Epstein intimates that there might be some moral reasoning, some didactic purpose behind Erofeev's anti-ironic resistance to it. I would suggest a different interpretation: the uniqueness of the vague position Erofeev seeks to occupy—a position that it would be impossible to co-opt—lies precisely in his unwillingness to ascribe some higher purpose to his own negation.[35] Such lofty purpose, service to the demands of virtue, would be, to Erofeev, the kind of license that turns into licentiousness. In this view, any cause becomes a passport to violence, and Erofeev is committed to avoiding violence at all costs. As he writes in one of his notebooks, "The most frequently repeated formulas in Nazi declarations are the love of fatherland, the love of nation, the love of nature, simplicity."[36] Erofeev's cultivation of himself via negation becomes especially pronounced here: what the Nazis did, he would not do. (Indeed, having established that Hitler sincerely loved dogs, Erofeev admonishes himself: "Be sure not to love dogs."[37]) As against the Nazis' extolling of the virtue of simplicity, Erofeev insists on making himself complex. The Nazis were men of action, which Erofeev would have none of.[38] Likewise eschewing such Nazi-valorized concepts as "duty" and "responsibility," he would focus on cultivation of the self.

Erofeev approvingly culls quotations from various religious and philosophical sources on the worthwhileness of renouncing the life of action and duty and concentrating rather on the self. Reading the twelfth-century abbot Saint Bernard of Clairvaux, Erofeev applauds his advice that "your first and last thought should be you, yourself; your only thought should be your salvation,"[39] which he connects with a similar sentiment by the same theologian: "If you take an attentive look at yourself, you will be surprised that you could have thought about anything else."[40] Erofeev reminds himself that the same idea has been expressed by other important Christian thinkers, including Augustine, Luther, and Tolstoy.[41] Later in the same notes, he derives a similar idea from Heidegger and, of course, from Rozanov.

In light of this focus on self-cultivation, we might return to the book's dedication, which, as noted, labels *Moscow–Petushki* "tragic." This dedication is addressed to Erofeev's friend Vadim Tikhonov, whom in his notebook he describes thus: "V. Tikhonov has no heart, no mind, no constancy, no idea; he possesses only individuality."[42] The word "individuality" commonly connotes certain "remarkable" or even "admirable" qualities, but to Erofeev it seems to signal, rather, just distinctness. Tikhonov, that is, was just, irreplaceably, *who he was*, and not, for instance, a person as schematized in the ideological filter of socialist realism. No wonder, then, that the *poema* is dedicated to him: it is devoted, in general, to the exploration of this kind of individuality—the sheer contingency of a particular person.[43] In *Moscow– Petushki*, the hero of this *poema*, Venichka, sums up Erofeev's cultivation of individuality—via, as described above, the avoidance of implication in any cause or affiliation—in the following terms:

> Oh, if only the whole world, if everyone were like I am now, placid and tim-orous and never sure about anything, not sure of himself nor of the serious-ness of his position under the heavens—oh, how good it could be. No enthu-siasts, no feats of valor, nothing obsessive! Just universal chicken-heartedness [*vseobshchee malodushie*]. I'd agree to live on the earth for an eternity if they'd show me first a corner where there's not always room for valor.[44]

This line, of course, can be read as specifically anti-Soviet, directly polemi-cizing as it does with the beloved aphorism of Soviet schoolchildren, "there is always room for valor," borrowed from the story "Old Izergil" ("Starukha Izergil'," 1895) by the father of socialist realism, Maksim Gorky. But despite its demonstrably anti-Soviet tonality,[45] this passage does much more than just poke fun at Soviet values. It succinctly formulates a philosophical position that Erofeev is committed to, and for which his antihero Venichka serves as a mouthpiece. This is the position that serves as a foundation on which the whole *poema* is built and whose viability it explores.

GETTING WASTED, OR
VOLUNTARY DISEMPOWERMENT

Venichka advocates extreme weakness—in his own words, "chicken-heartedness"; in Epstein's diagnosis, entropy—as a precondition for perfec-tion. There exists one main obstacle to this state of sublime timorousness: the natural impetus to activity or action. But notably, just at the moment when Venichka is about to explain how to get around this obstacle, he is interrupted by three persons in white (presumably staff of the Kursk Station restaurant):

> "Universal chicken-heartedness." Indeed, this is a panacea, this is the predi-cate to sublime perfection. And as for nature's activist inclinations . . .
> "Who's getting sherry here?"[46]

The placement of this question about the sherry (whose realistic motivation is that those intending to remove a rowdy patron are identifying him by his latest drink order) appears to give a clue as to Venichka's solution to the problem of "natural activist inclinations": sherry is needed precisely to *suppress* such inclinations, lest one become active, and fail to attain that longed-for state of chicken-heartedness.

Besides being a source of inspiration and reflection,[47] booze is an excellent instrument for the cultivation of weakness. Not only in the *poema*, but in his notebooks as well, Erofeev obsessively enumerates all the physical manifestations of weakness and its accompanying "complex of the lack of initiative" that so appeals to him: "The head is lost, the nerves are shattered, the hands are tied, the heart is broken, the vital signs are low" (*golova poteriana, nervy rasstroeny, ruki opushcheny, serdtse razbito, tonus snizhen*).[48] The perfection of alcohol as an agent of weakness lies precisely in its association with passivity. To drink is not a choice; it is choice's very opposite—weakness of the will. In Russia, it is doubly so, since as Venichka himself concedes, everyone drinks. "This circle, this vicious circle of existence, it has me by the balls. I've only got to read a good book and I can't figure out who drinks for what reasons. The dregs looking up or the bigwigs looking down. Then I can't go on, I drop the book, I drink for a month."[49] If one were keen to stand out or engage in the performance of holy foolishness, then drinking, in Venichka's milieu, would hardly suit such purposes.[50] Rather, drinking is a compulsion, which allows him to assume his characteristic position of negation *passively*. Even his individuality, that is, has to be acquired without his initiative or will.

In his exclusivity and nihilism, Venichka differs crucially from others marked by ostensibly similar traits—Turgenev's Bazarov, for example, or a typical Byronic hero. The nihilism of Bazarov, or the active defiance and arrogance of the Byronic heroes, are counterposed by the passivity of Venichka, who believes that he is greatly misunderstood when his coworkers compare his infrequent visitations of the bathroom facilities to Manfred and Cain's deliberate establishment of their superior exclusivity: "It works out like this, we are nothing but gnats and scoundrels and you are Cain and Manfred."[51] Byron's self-appointed outcasts are strong personalities; in particular, the strength of their defiance of norms (from the heavenly to the social) is measured by their readiness to violate the sixth commandment. Unlike them, or the closer-to-home Raskolnikov, who hoped to prove via murder his status as a Napoleon rather than some kind of a gnat, Venichka does not seek such lethal superiority; it is imposed on him from without. He does not want to prove anything to anyone, least of all any kinship with such homicidal rebels as Cain or Manfred. Repeatedly compared to these Byronic characters by his dormmates, he rejects the association every time, clarifying that "this absence of the deed," as they call it, is not, in his case, an exhibition of extreme willpower, but rather a product of his sense of shame. It's not that he wills himself not to, it's just that he *can't*. This is why he says he is being not simply misunderstood but, rather, understood "antinomially":[52] his shame is being mistaken for pride. And yet, his dormmates are on to *something*: while his delicacy and sensitivity are not intended to elevate him above the rest, they certainly stem from his need for privacy, for separation from others, or as he calls it, for the "infinite extension of the sphere of the intimate."[53]

In this—in Venichka's quest for an exit from mundanity and banality, from the life of politics or commerce, from the life shared with others— alcohol allows him to portray his exclusivity as stemming from weakness rather than strength: "I am sick in my soul. . . . Everything that you speak of, everything that occupies your time, is forever alien to me. While that which occupies me, I'll not say a word about."[54] Venichka's isolation is complete: not only does he refuse to understand anyone else's concerns, but he is unwilling or even unable to communicate his own. (More on Venichka's self-association with muteness below.) Crucially, this absolute freedom from others is achieved weakly, passively, without his initiative. And this weakness of will contains not only an aesthetic potential (as a source of inspiration) but also an ethical one. Like his author, Venichka believes that, whether evinced by the vulgar majority or by willful mavericks, strength leads to violence; Venichka's extreme individuality and drunken nonparticipation represent an attempt to devise an ethics of weakness, encapsulated in the following passage:

> And so I solemnly announce that, till the end of my days, I shall not under-take anything the like of my sad brush with eminence [his position as foreman of a crew of cable fitters, from which he was fired]. I'll remain below and from below I'll spit on their social ladder. . . . To climb up it, you've got to be a hea-thenish, thick-skinned bastard, a pervert, forged out of pure steel from head to foot. Which I am not.[55]

This passage makes clear the dialectic of Venichka's weakness: he does not choose to be weak; he is born that way. Hardly forged from steel (a pos-sible reference to Stalin), he *assents* to his weakness ("I solemnly announce," "I'll remain below"). This double passivity is presented as an ethical choice. Simply to be weak is one thing, but to accept it without a fight is leave-taking.

THE MOTIF OF DYING CHILDREN

And yet, right after Venichka reaches his nadir (or per his code, perhaps his apex) of weakness at Orekhovo-Zuevo station, he has a dream that al-legorizes his voluntary disempowerment and highlights its ethical ambigu-ity. It is at Orekhovo-Zuevo that Venichka is clearly at his ultimate weakest: exceedingly drunk, he comes to the edge of consciousness, which coincides with a quite literal loss of autonomy (as he is borne along with the tide of passengers exiting the train) and loss of direction. (Yuri Levin's explanation seems the most convincing: this must be where Venichka boards the wrong train and begins heading backward to Moscow.[56]) Right after this unfortunate episode, the narrative departs from any parameters of verisimilitude, and Venichka enters a realm of phantasmagoria. The door to this other plane of existence is marked by a revolution, or rather, a dream of it. This dream offers a dramatization of the acquisition and relinquishment of power that had taken place earlier—Venichka's above-mentioned status and dismissal as a crew foreman—and repeats his ascendance and fall. This time, in the dream, Venichka finds himself elected president, declares his power to be absolute;[57] but then, upon the sudden demise of his prime minister (who dies soon after hearing President Venichka's power-grabbing speech, as if killed by its authoritarianism and sacrilege), he immediately steps down from his high position, abandoning the lofty cause of revolution. From this course of events, his resignation might seem to be ethically motivated: in his striving for power, that is, he had supported the revolutionary cause, which demands sacrifices, but the piteous sight of the very first victim shakes him as if from a pernicious spell.

This neat coding of the withdrawal from action as *ethical*, however, is complicated by President Venichka's resignation speech, in which he compares himself to Pontius Pilate—a reference that rather associates retreat from action with *betrayal*:

> Delegates. If I should ever have any children, I'll hang on their wall a portrait of the Procurator of Judea, Pontius Pilate, so that they will grow up neat and clean. Procurator Pontius Pilate standing there washing his hands—that's the right kind of portrait. Such am I also: I stand here and wash my hands. I joined you simply because I was dead drunk. . . . Like Pontius Pilate I'll wash my hands, and before your eyes, drink up all the rest of the Rossiiskaya. Yes. I trample on my authority—I leave you.[58]

Here, Venichka aptly plays with the traditional metaphor of "washing one's hands" to mean evading responsibility, associating his own vaunted delicacy and fastidiousness with an act of betrayal. On the one hand, this dream renunciation of action or authority is presented as an attempt to abstain from bloodshed and avoid the trappings of vanity; on the other, the comparison with the ethically detached "neatness" of Pontius Pilate presents a complication: Venichka's ethical chicken-heartedness now seems somewhat less ethical. What is more, in this dramatic leave-taking (Erofeev's quintessential philosophical position), Venichka forgets that he already *has* a child. Whether born of the urge to use an eloquent trope ("If I should ever have any children"), or just of drunken forgetfulness, Venichka's denial of paternity coincides with Pontius Pilate's act of renunciation. This image of a potential portrait of Pontius Pilate at the ultimate moment of disengagement from ethics, which will hang on a potential wall of Venichka's potential children, serves as an apt metaphor of Venichka's abandonment of his actual son.

From this moment on, Venichka's way to Petushki seems to be forever lost, and the angels who had assisted him on his way prior to the Orekhovo-Zuevo station turn into furies, who mock him and lead him to his ultimate death. The angels' peculiar switch from benevolence to malice should be considered in light of the fact that these angels had been associated early in the narrative with Venichka's loved ones, urging him on his way to his son: "It was the angels who reminded me about the goodies, because I bought them for the ones who are themselves like angels."[59] By the end of the *poema*, these selfsame solicitous angels turn so malignant as to remind Venichka of the cruel children he witnessed laughing at a man cut in half by a train: "Some children ran up to [the accident victim], three or four children, they had picked up a lighted cigarette butt from somewhere and stuck it in the dead man's half-open mouth. . . . And the children ran around roaring with laughter. That's how the heavenly angels laughed at me then."[60]

This grotesque scene with monstrous children is told right before the final scene of Venichka's own execution, and seems to strangely prefigure it: the number of the assassins echoes the number of the cruel children, and the assassins' choice of murder method, an awl stuck into the protagonist's throat, matches the cigarette that the sardonic children stuck into the dead man's mouth.

Once Venichka loses his way and starts moving backward, vengeful spirits haunt him all the way back to Moscow. And along with them, Venichka begins to be haunted by thoughts of guilt. When accosted by the furies, he attempts to appease them by asserting, somewhat without conviction, that "no one is guilty."[61] Then a mysterious woman in black accuses him, in effect, of abandonment: "Right at the door she stopped, turned her husky, cracked, tear-stained face toward me and cried, I hate you, Andrei Mikhailovich!"[62] As Eduard Vlasov explains, Andrei Mikhailovich was the name and patronymic of Kurbsky, at first a friend, then a political opponent of Ivan the Terrible; Kurbsky's wife had reason to hate him, as he went into exile without her.[63] This allusion to a historical episode of abandonment places Venichka in the role of deserter.

The mysterious woman's blaming of Venichka for her misery is strikingly at odds with his own perception of their relationship. This is, in fact, the second of Venichka's uncharacteristically affinitive envisionings of a woman in black. The first such instance comes earlier in the *poema*, when he compares his own sense of grief, which renders everything else in life meaningless, to that depicted in Ivan Kramskoy's painting *Inconsolable Grief* (*Neuteshnoe gore*) (fig. 10). Centering on a woman in an austere black dress who covers her mouth with a handkerchief, the painting places the viewer into a situation in which communion with the bereaved is both called for

Fig. 10. Ivan Kramskoy. *Inconsolable Grief*, 1884. Oil on canvas.
State Tretyakov Gallery, Moscow.

and obviated.[64] The viewer cannot share in the woman's grief. Any attempt at consolation is forestalled, both by the painting's title and by the woman's positioning as she occupies the center of this dark room and looks past the viewer.

When Venichka first mentions the painting, it is with the intention of suggesting that the woman's seclusion (a *falling-out* from the rules of mundane reality in which the rest of humanity resides) is temporary, while his is a permanent state of exception—a kind of *existential* abandonment:

> For instance, do you know Kramskoy's painting, *Inconsolable Grief*? Well, of course, you've seen it. Imagine that some cat or other has just knocked on the floor some kind of, oh, phial of Sevres porcelain belonging to the grief-

stricken princess or young noblewoman, or that it has torn into shreds some priceless peignoir or other. Would she be storming around, or flailing about with her hands? Of course not, because all that would have been nonsense to her, because for a day or three, she is "more elevated" than any kind of peignoir or cat or Sevres porcelain.[65]

Importantly, mourning in this view is marked by Venichka's favored passivity (no "storming" or "flailing about"). Venichka's listeners here are invited to bear witness to the inexpressible without sharing in it, while he himself is in a privileged position: he shares with the woman her inconsolable grief.

Upon the reappearance of a woman in black (who might be the same woman in black, in any case an echo of the first)—the above-mentioned Mrs. Kurbsky—Venichka again attempts to create a sense of identification with her, but she resists this communion. Rather, she identifies him as the cause of her grief, and rejects his desire for connection on the basis of shared experience, exposing him, in the process, as a *doer*—an actor rather than a passive receptacle. Whereas the first woman in black appears as a metaphor, the second seems to have migrated from the world of art to haunt Venichka's drunken dreams. As a product of his delirium, she suggests the possibility of his own doubt, his uneasy conscience. Could he be expressing here the fear that perhaps his passive disengagement, which was supposed to have enabled him to avoid violence, has somehow rather caused suffering, and thereby constituted an act of cruelty, an act of violence—or at least, *some* kind of act?

Kramskoy painted *Inconsolable Grief* soon after the deaths of his two young sons. Relatedly, sick or dying children represent a constant if subtle leitmotif in *Moscow–Petushki*. First appearing in the initial stretch of Venichka's journey, the motif is introduced here somewhat incongruously, via an intertextual analogy. This occurs as Venichka contemplates the specifics and worthwhileness of his latest binge, eventually concluding that such questions are unanswerable, just like a certain unsolved historical mystery: "I just calculated that from Chekhov Street to this hallway I drank up six rubles—but where and what and in what sequence, to good or evil purpose? This nobody knows and, now, nobody will ever know. Just as we don't know to this day whether Tsar Boris killed Tsarevich Dmitri or the other way around."[66] The paradox mentioned seems to be a reference to Mussorgsky's opera *Boris Godunov*, based on Pushkin's eponymous drama. In act one, Godunov is alleged to have ordered the assassination of ten-year-old Tsarevich Dmitry, the son of Ivan the Terrible, in order to seize the throne; in the last act, Boris himself dies, having been tormented by incessant visitations of the dead child's apparition. Early in *Moscow–Petushki*, mention of this historical riddle might appear jocular, especially in the context of Venichka's musing on the unknowability of his own alcohol consumption; but in retrospect, reference to this reciprocal killing is revealed as entirely serious: this was, indeed, a somber reflection on the moral unknowability of one's actions. That is, as the reader reaches the end of the *poema*, and the angels turn into demons, Venichka perceives a reciprocity between his desertion of his loved ones and their own cruel abandonment of *him*. This dynamic suggests that, contrary to Venichka's earlier-expressed belief, one does not gain oneself through separation from others, but rather perishes.

There are multiple allusions to the abandonment and death of children in the text, but perhaps the most extended discussion on the subject appears in Venichka's conversation with the angels about his son. Tellingly, when the angels reproach him for his bingeing, Venichka misinterprets their concern, thinking they merely want him to be happy, even in erotic terms. But the angels correct him, explaining that in watching over him, they are acting on behalf of his little boy:

> *No, we are not silly, we are only afraid that once again you won't get there.*
> "Won't get there? I won't get to Petushki? To her? To my shameless Tsaritsa with eyes like clouds? You're really funny."
> *No, we are not funny, we are afraid you won't get to him and he won't get any nuts.*[67]

Here Venichka's abstention from accountability reaches its peak. He justifies his previous absences with reference to his all-conquering "limpness," then vows to reach the boy, "if only I don't croak, killed by fate."[68] The angels see right through this obvious attempt to "pass the buck" of his own irresponsibility on to the workings of destiny. "'The poor kid,' the angels sighed."[69] Mustering one last attempt to nudge Venichka toward his son as a potential source of contentment, they remind him that he has not smiled the whole day; and he indeed smiles upon remembering his son's smile, this reflection of one smile in the other standing as Venichka's only moment of transcendence of his perpetual narcissism and solipsism, the only moment of the hero's unfreedom from human connection.

Remembering his sickly son, who tends to recuperate when his father visits, Venichka starts praying to God to preserve his son from any calamities or accidents, ending the prayer with "And if he should get sick, let him start getting better the minute he sees me."[70] The murder at the end of the book, we are given to understand, will thus claim one more victim, Venichka's son (since, never again seeing his father, he will be deprived of this remedy).

The last thing Venichka sees before his death is the letter Ю (Iu, or Ju in linguistic transcription), which may signify not just his own demise but also his absence in the life of others, specifically his son. The letter Ю has previously been associated in the *poema* with Venichka's son: specifically, it has been said to be a source of pride to Venichka that a three-year-old knows and can write such a difficult letter. In fact, aside from the boy's sickliness, this early feat of literacy is the only thing we know about him.

THE LETTER *Ю*

The significance of the letter *Ю* in the *poema* has received some critical attention. Vlasov adduces two interpretations, the first of which—advanced separately by Liubov Liubchikova and Igor Avdiev—holds that this letter encodes the name of the woman for whom Erofeev the author felt an unremitting and tormenting love, Iuliia Runova. According to a second contention, *Ю* stands for the Russian verb "to love," insofar as its first-person singular form *люблЮ* features this letter twice.[71] This latter interpretation has been advanced by Svetlana Gaiser-Shnitman, who goes on to suggest that the boy, who "loves his father as himself," embodies the Christian ideal.[72] The first interpretation, referencing Venichka's tormenting love, does not explain the significance of the child's notable ability to recognize and write *Ю*. The second interpretation's association of love with the son seems productive, but the letter's trembling suspension at the moment of Venichka's death calls for further elaboration.

The least satisfying of interpretations of Venichka's final agony, meanwhile, are those that attempt to connect it to his capacity for love. In this religious reading, Venichka's demise becomes a final act of kenosis for the sake of the world, a Christlike self-sacrifice as an expression of enormous love for humanity.[73] But to read Venichka's self-imposed torment so Golgothically would be to ignore his explicit misanthropy, his rejection of valor, his yearning for solitude and freedom from accountability, and his feelings of guilt. This would be to justify our antihero completely.

If, however, for argument's sake we read Venichka as indeed inviting his own death for the sake of humanity, then the behavior of the furies and angry angels can be understood only according to a reading of Christ proposed by Tarkovsky's Andrei Rublev in the eponymous film released in 1966 (i.e., not long before Erofeev's composition of his *poema*). In the section of the film titled "The Passion according to Andrei," the great medieval painter of icons and religious frescoes contradicts his misanthropic teacher Theophanes and argues that empathy for humanity is integral to an artist's vocation. To prove it, he offers, uncharacteristically for a monk, a rendition of Christ's passion from the subjective standpoint of the people who loved him and felt left behind by his after all *voluntary* death:

Jesus comes from God, in other words, he's almighty. So if he died on the cross, it must have been preordained. Both his crucifixion and death were God's doing. And this should have caused people to hate him—not the people who crucified him, but the people who loved him, especially if they were with him at the time. For they loved him as a human being, and he abandoned them of his own free will; it was unfair, even cruel of him.

Scandalized by Rublev's judgment of Christ's behavior as callous, Theophanes responds, "Do you realize what you are saying? For these words, you'll be packed off to the north to touch up icons."

But the camera sides with Rublev. As we hear his "sacrilegious" words, we see Golgotha, transposed to a snowy Russian landscape, a pensive yet determined Russian Christ in peasant garb, and his distraught and uncomprehending followers. The camera chooses to focus on their pain, rather than on Christ's torment, at one point even dipping to the level of a kneeling Mary Magdalene as she tries to cling to the legs of her departing Lord (figs. 11–13). Staying with her, the camera bears witness as Christ's leg briskly shakes off her grasp, as if to demonstrate the cruelty of which Rublev speaks.[74]

It is noteworthy that Venichka, just like Rublev, addresses Christ's separation from people, including, as mentioned above, his rebuke of his own mother Mary; but the inflection is different. Venichka presents this cruelty as worthy of emulation. The angels, however, see it differently. If Erofeev's Venichka is indeed performing an act of martyrdom, then the angels, much like Tarkovsky's Rublev, assume a *human* viewpoint on his actions, siding rather with the loved ones he leaves behind. This martyr, moreover, in his anguished dreams after Orekhovo-Zuevo, appears to have internalized the position of his loved ones, channeling and mirroring their sense of abandonment.[75] When he realizes that he has lost his way, he feels not independent and fulfilled but lonely and incomplete.

In light of these considerations, it would be inconsistent to read the bloody dispersal of the letter Ю in positive terms, as a manifestation of the hero's all-conquering love or a promise of resurrection. Quite the opposite: the quivering of the letter (as if about to dissolve or explode) suggests a certain insolvency, a tragic failure. It might perhaps refer to that one important thought that the protagonist has been chasing, striving to articulate, and that will now remain forever unformed.

If we perform, moreover, a sort of "archaeological dig" in Russian poetry, we discover alternative origins for Venichka's letter Ю, which might clarify its momentous reappearance at the end of the poem. As attested by his notebooks, Erofeev was prodigiously erudite. In the late 1960s, in particular, he was working on compiling an anthology of Russian poetry. The

Figs. 11–13. "The Passion According to Andrei." *Andrei Rublev*
(dir. Andrei Tarkovsky, 1966).

significance of this letter in the Russian poetic canon might thus have been familiar to him.[76]

The lyrical life of *IO*—and in particular, the ascription to it of synesthetic properties—may perhaps begin with Mikhail Lermontov's metapoetic "A Fairy Tale for Children" ("Skazka dlia detei," 1839–41), in which the poet detects a certain moisture in words rhyming with the *-ю* ending:

Я без ума от тройственных созвучий
  И влажных рифм—как например на *ю*.[77]

I am crazy about triple consonances
  And damp rhymes—like for example those for words ending in *ю*.

Ю then reappears, in all its dampness and fluidity, in Konstantin Balmont's *Poetry as Sorcery* (*Poeziia kak volshebstvo*, 1916), where it is described and seemingly etymologized as "climbing like ivy, flowing in a stream":

Ю—вьющееся как плющ, и льющееся в струю.[78] [emphasis mine]

But this letter's greatest attendants were the futurists. In a little book entitled *The Record of Tenderness: The Life of Ilya Zdanevich* (*Rekord nezhnosti: Zhizn' Il'i Zdanevicha*, 1919), which features the letter Ю on its cover, Igor Terentiev continues the association of the letter Ю with softness, tenderness, and fluidity, for his part adding *femininity* to this pantheon (fig. 14). Terentiev first remarks on the pernicious absence of femininity and fluidity in his fellow futurist Zdanevich's poem *Ianko*: "There's not a single woman

Fig. 14. Cover of Igor Terentiev's *The Record of Tenderness: The Life of Ilya Zdanevich* (1919).

there, not a single *ɞ* [a not phonic but almost pictographic approximation of Ю]—not a drop of moisture."[79] He goes on to describe how Zdanevich attempted to compensate for this lack, remedying it with "a compress made out of a woman" in his next work "A Donkey for Hire" ("Asel naprakat"). This "feminine compress" consists of the overabundant use of the letter Ю, with which Zdanevich, in Terentiev's opinion, sets a record of amorousness and tenderness:

> Все неприлично любовные слова в беспричинном восторге юлят, ются, вокают, сяют, преслюняя самого юснаго поэта Велемира Хлебникова: напЯляя клЮсь яслюслЯйка вбильЕ пиизЯти.[80]

> All these unseemly love words play in wanton delight, they whirligig about, they [here follow three transsensical verbs], out-drooling even the most Ю-ish poet Velimir Khlebnikov: *napIAliaia klIUs' iasliuslIAika vbil'E piizIAti* [more transsensical words that cannot be translated, but at least conjure the intimacy of Ю-ness and Я-ness.]

Here, the interaction of the letters Ю and Я are suggestive of the erotic relations between a woman and a man.

Vasily Kamensky's *His-My Biography of a Great Futurist* (*Ego-moia biografiia velikogo futurista*, 1918) devotes a whole section to the letter Ю, building on its associations with femininity and, in his view, "sonority, rosy-morningness [*rozoutrennost'*], suppleness, and arousal."[81] To Kamensky, Ю exemplifies the unity of form and content inherent to all letters: "Every letter is a strictly individual world, whose symbolic concentration gives us an exact definition of its inner and outer essence. For example, Ю."[82]

Kamensky then adduces a poem titled "Ю" from his collection *Barefoot Girls* (*Devushki bosikom*, 1917) to illustrate this acme of individuality, completeness, and unity:

> Ю
> Юночка
> Юная
> юно
> юнится
> юнами юность
> В июне юня.
> Ю—крыловейная лейная
> Ю—розоутрая рая
> Ю—невеста Ста Песен.
>   Ю и Я.[83]

> Ю
> Little Iuna
> The Young
> Youthfully
> Youngifies
> with iunas youth
> While youthening in June.
> Ю is wing-flappingly flowing,
> Ю is rosy-morningly heavenly,
> Ю is the bride of a Hundred Songs.
>   Ю and Я [I].

The poem begins with *Ю*, and ends with *Ю и Я*, or "*Ю* and I." Individuality is thus complemented by unity with and completion via the Other. Since the *Ю* of the poem stands for womanhood, *Я* must represent the poet as an icon of masculinity.

What must have made *Ю* special for the futurists, who were interested both in a letter's sound and in the semantic significance of its form, is that in formal or visual terms, Ю instantiates the harmonious coexistence celebrated in Kamensky's poem. The letter's shape—much like the union of the two sounds it stands for, a consonant (*j*) and a vowel (*u*), categories themselves sometimes coded as "masculine" and "feminine" in culture[84]—epitomizes the connection of opposites: a man (the phallic *I*) and a woman (the labial *O*); a one (1) and a zero (0), which could stand for God and the universe in its potential; and finally, a line and a circle, of which the former, per the theory of Andrei Bely, symbolizes a human life (a string of temporal moments), while the latter symbolizes eternity, existence as a whole.[85] The combination of both in the letter *Ю* is akin to Bely's spiral, that is, the reconciliation of a human life with eternity, of the *I* with Being—a form of transcendence.[86]

With this poetic reconnaissance in view, we could conclude that Venichka's final *Ю* emblematizes neither his erotic nor his kenotic love (although both elements of eros and agape are encapsulated in it), but rather a vision of supreme harmony. And the trembling dispersal of the letter in Venichka's eyes signifies the disintegration of this vision. In this context, the letter's synesthetic color "red," in conjunction with its Russian poetic tradition of being (likewise synesthetically) moist or fluid, unites the blood from Venichka's fatal stab wound with "beer [flowing away] on a table top" after a spill[87]—an image he had conjured earlier to convey, coding as he does all things through his central trope of drinking, a thought he cannot pin down.

But what does all of this have to do with Venichka's son, who has mastered the letter in infancy? To answer this question, we might return to Kamensky's above-cited poem that begins with *Ю* and ends with *Я*.

Kamensky can bring the two letters together so seamlessly because not only is Я the first-person pronoun, it is also the last letter of the alphabet, while Ю is the penultimate letter, the one that precedes Я and stands closest to it. In Kamensky's poem, this closeness to Ю is what leads him to the discovery of his Я, to its manifestation in the end. That is, Kamensky arrives at his Я by writing about Ю. If we read both these works as journeys toward Я—Я being the journey's "last stop," its destination—then Kamensky does indeed reach it via Ю, but Erofeev's *poema* never quite gets there.

The *poema*'s premature ending on the imperfect vision of the quivering, blood-soaked penultimate Ю rather than a final Я brings to mind one more futurist work, the ego-futurist Vasilisk Gnedov's *Death to Art* (*Smert' iskusstvu*, 1913). Constructed of fifteen *poemas*, Gnedov's masterpiece is generically similar to *Moscow–Petushki*. The fourteenth, penultimate *poema* famously consists of just one letter—Ю, while the fifteenth, last one, entitled "A Poem of the End" ("Poema kontsa"), contains no words at all, thereby signaling the end of language, speech, and art. Just like Venichka, ego-futurists were seekers after self-definition, the realization of their ego, their Я. In Gnedov's case, where Я should have been, there is emptiness and silence, which relates it to the end of Erofeev's *poema*.[88] Perhaps muteness is the point. Perhaps silence is the very realization of Gnedov's ego, the separation of the self from the rest of humanity being the precondition of individual existence. Venichka might have wanted to believe this, to espouse his final association with muteness—his killers' stabbing of him through or near his voice box—as the ultimate declaration of independence and individuality.

But the very tragedy of Venichka's journey may lie precisely in the unsustainability of this freedom. The very centrality of the letter Ю, as the emblem of Venichka's connection with his son,[89] as the emblem of wholeness and harmony, suggests that in this potential debate between the cubo-futurist Kamensky and the ego-futurist Gnedov on the relationship between the ego and its Others, Erofeev might have sided with Kamensky. To judge from the counterexample or "cautionary tale" of Venichka, that is, one's self-realization is predicated on the intrinsic union with you/Ю. Despite his protagonist's self-associations with muteness (at the outset and the very end of the journey), Erofeev's text, unlike Gnedov's, contains a whole host of words, perhaps exposing yet another of Venichka's weaknesses: the compulsion to speak, as well as the impossibility of the existence of *I* in a state of complete isolation.

Enjoy Your Symptom!: Sasha Sokolov's *A School for Fools* as an Artist's Guide to Psychosis

IN A NOTEBOOK he kept between 1967 and 1978, the Soviet writer Sergei Dovlatov recorded the following series of quarrels that supposedly took place between several well-known figures of the late Soviet literary underground:

> Once Naiman and Gubin got in an argument. They argued over which of them was lonelier. Konetsky and Gorbunov almost got into a scuffle. They argued over which of them was more dangerously ill. Shigashov and Gorbovsky stopped saying hello to each other entirely. They argued over which of them was less normal. "How normal you have recently become!" Shigashov reproached his friend. "I am the one here who is abnormal," Gorbovsky defended himself. "Absolutely abnormal. I even have a document from the psych ward to prove it. And what about you? I don't know . . . I don't know about you."[1]

The escalation of these arguments suggests that the most valuable trait for a Russian underground writer or poet in the late Soviet period was insanity, with certification from the psychiatric ward being a veritable badge of honor.

While the list appears to be tongue in cheek, it does reproduce the state of affairs quite faithfully: many writers did in fact respond to the Brezhnev-era practice of treating dissidents with punitive psychiatry by turning a minus into a plus. In *State of Madness: Psychiatry, Literature, and Dissent after Stalin* (2018), Rebecca Reich provides a meticulous and fascinating account of the struggle waged between state psychiatrists and artists in their respective definitions of insanity and its relationship to art. To be sure, the association of creativity with madness existed long before the advent of Soviet psychiatry; it is found in Plato, and it veritably courses through European Romantic poetry.

Soviet psychiatry co-opted this association for its own purposes when it began to diagnose nonconformists with psychiatric disorders and compulsorily hospitalize them. This practice had a famous historical precedent in the case of Petr Chaadaev, who was declared insane and placed under house arrest by the tsarist authorities for attempting to explain, in his *Lettres philosophiques* (*Philosophical Letters*, 1827–31), Russia's backwardness in comparison to western Europe. Chaadaev was eventually forced to produce an "Apologie d'un fou" ("Apology of a Madman," 1837), in which he put a more hopeful, patriotic spin on his theory. Chaadaev's letters precipitated what would be the most enduring debate of Russia's intellectual history—the Westernizer versus Slavophile dispute on the country's place in the world—but his case may also have contributed to the emergence, in the Russian literary tradition, of a strong association between intellectual, creative, or sociopolitical dissidence and madness.[2] Beginning with Pushkin's "Bronze Horseman" ("Mednyi vsadnik," 1833) and Gogol's "Notes of a Madman" ("Zapiski sumasshedshego," 1834), Russian characters' rejection of extant power structures and yearnings for freedom manifested in unusual behaviors coded as "mad." Equally robust is the literary exploration of characters diagnosed with psychiatric disorders and institutionalized for questioning accepted societal beliefs, including the cases of Ivan Gromov in Anton Chekhov's "Ward n. 6" ("Palata n. 6," 1892) and Ivan Bezdomny in Mikhail Bulgakov's *The Master and Margarita* (finished in 1940, first published in 1967). Both cases introduce an essential epistemological ambiguity; heightened clarity of vision is a rare phenomenon, and as such often presents as madness.

Building on this long-standing history, Soviet psychiatrists expanded the medical definition of mental pathology to include such characteristics as "heightened conflictedness; yearning for self-assertion; rejection of traditions, conventional opinions, and norms of behavior; a tendency toward philosophizing; and the use of metaphorical language."[3] Predictably, many artists exhibited these traits, and by the late 1960s, the psychiatric hospitalization of underground writers was a common phenomenon. In this chapter, I will analyze Sasha Sokolov's novel *A School for Fools* (1973) in the context of what we might call the Soviet "dissident schizophrenia craze." What interests me specifically is how Sokolov's novel reappropriates both political and medical discourses, identifying with the symptomatology of the disease and transforming it into a precondition for the creation of art.

Sokolov's novel, written at a time when writers were being diagnosed with schizophrenia and institutionalized, is narrated by a sufferer of dissociative identity disorder, a condition that was included in the loose operational definition of schizophrenia used in Soviet psychiatry.[4] The afflicted protagonist is, furthermore, unable to perceive linear or chronological time, a classical symptom of schizophrenia.[5] The novel offers no discernible plot, blurring the lines between past, present, and future, and between fantasy and reality. Readers learn to disregard these narrative deficiencies and acclimate themselves to what *is* there: a keenness of observation; a depth of perception, feeling, and sensual apprehension; insight into how the self is constructed vis-à-vis the surrounding world. The reader cannot but recognize in the mentally disabled student So-and-So (this is his "name" in the novel: *Uchenik takoi-to*) an artist's sensibility, imagination, and ability to conjure impressions and metamorphose them into fanciful and poignant patterns.

Interestingly, when the novel was first published in the United States, it was interpreted as an apolitical text, dedicated solely to questions of metaphysics and aesthetics. But in broaching the very politicized subject of schizophrenia, the novel is of necessity political. Discovering an artist in a mentally ill protagonist and elevating his ramblings to the sphere of art, the novel performs an operation directly counter to the basic mechanism of Soviet punitive psychiatry, which diagnosed artists as mentally ill and deprecated their works as tantamount to disease.

SOVIET PUNITIVE PSYCHIATRY AND DISSIDENTS

At the 20th Congress of the Communist Party in 1956, first secretary Nikita Khrushchev delivered his famous "secret speech" denouncing the "personality cult" of his predecessor Joseph Stalin, who had died in 1953. The speech ushered in the policy of de-Stalinization, significantly loosening the repression regime. The "thawing" of mass terror, however, made the use of punitive psychiatry more rather than less common.[6] As explained by the brothers Zhores and Roy Medvedev in *Who Is the Madman?* (*Kto sumasshedshii?*, 1971),[7] after the 20th Congress, it was no longer possible to incarcerate a political dissident for a minor infraction. Many dissenters' "misdeeds" were not grave enough to warrant the accusation of "anti-Soviet" or "slanderous" activity (per articles 70 and 190-1 of the Criminal Code of the RSFSR), but their removal from the public sphere was nevertheless desired. (It was precisely the relative mildness of their offenses that rendered them "dangerous.") Psychiatric hospitalization now presented a convenient solution to this problem. Dissidence became an asymptomatic psychiatric disease. The absence of obvious manifestations (for instance, hallucinations) was in a way essential to the diagnosis; the line between mental health and pathology having been blurred or effaced, anyone could be diagnosed as insane and institutionalized. Dissidents typically received two diagnoses: one (paranoia) that already existed in the sphere of international psychiatry, the other devised by Soviet psychiatrists specifically to cover asymptomatic cases. This latter was the so-called *vialotekushchaia shizofreniia*, "torpid" or "sluggishly progressing" schizophrenia (a diagnosis formulated by Prof. Andrei Snezhnevsky in 1969).

In a country where human rights were already severely curtailed, a person diagnosed with a however "sluggishly progressing" schizophrenia could be institutionalized, without any due process, for extended periods of time. The epidemic proportions of this "torpid" schizophrenia among nonconformists, and the great difficulty of foreseeing all the possible traps of this murky diagnosis, prompted some dissidents to conceptualize strategies for surviving it.

Samizdat articles offered specific advice for those under threat of this diagnosis; two texts in particular gained some currency. The first, titled "Juridical Instructions for Those Facing Interrogations" ("Iuridicheskaia pamiatka dlia tekh, komu predstoiat doprosy"), by the biologist, poet, and activist Aleksandr Vol'pin, began circulating in 1968. The second, "A Manual on Psychiatry for Nonconformists" ("Posobie po psikhiatrii dlia inakomysliashchikh"), was coauthored by two political prisoners eminently well positioned to give such advice: Vladimir Bukovsky, a former victim of punitive psychiatry, and Dr. Semyon Gluzman, a dissident psychiatrist, with the two working in tandem from their respective labor camps in 1975.[8] These two texts modeled two possible strategies. Vol'pin's "Instructions" recommend that persons undergoing interrogation should familiarize themselves with psychiatric discourse so as to be able to counterpose it to the law. Specifically, Vol'pin proposes that one use legalistic precision to question the authority of one's psychiatrist questioners—to emphasize how rife their discourse is with ambiguity.[9] The second strategy, proposed by the "Manual on Psychiatry for Nonconformists," is less confrontational; here one is to learn the ins and outs of psychiatric discourse in order to maneuver around it, to play along with interrogators while avoiding saying anything that could be construed as insane. For example, the authors advise against using metaphorical or figurative language, citing the famous case of the general turned dissident Petro Grigorenko, who, when asked about the motives for his "antisocial" activities, answered that "he could not breathe."[10] Such fanciful use of language could lead, as in Grigorenko's case, to a conclusion of paranoia.

Thus, while the first text advocates the use of logic to break a code, the second's solution is to accept the code as it is, acclimating to it in order to avoid being ensnared by it. For nonconformist artists, these two routes offered a difficult choice: either they could accept impossibly "legalistic" conceptions of what is "normal" in art, or they could repossess and repurpose madness as a code word for nonconformism and the creative impulse, while temporarily disavowing that same nonconformism. In what follows, I will read Sokolov's *A School for Fools* against these two manuals, as still another "instruction booklet." Specifically, and perhaps counterintuitively, Sokolov teaches how to get out of the diagnosis of "sluggishly progressing schizophrenia" by presenting symptoms of a more precipitous course of this disease. In categorizing this work among such manuals, I do not mean to suggest that it shares with them the intended end result—avoidance of institutionalization. On the contrary, the character named the Author actually admits that the greatest risk he runs in writing his book is that it might land him in the psychiatric ward: "And I am afraid that after [this] there will be great unpleasantness for me, up to and including the most unpleasant, I'm afraid they'll immediately ship me off *there*, to Doctor Zauze."[11] Rather, reading this work as an instruction for use, a manual for developing a schizophrenic sensibility, I propose that the novel actively engages with the official discourse on the dissident "disease," attempting to conceptualize an active attitude toward it—a complex subject position that would neither reject nor negate the diagnosis, but rather own up to it, and in doing so, paradoxically affirm one's limited, liminal, and fragile autonomy. I will use Lacan's concept of the *sinthome* to offer a new approach to psychosis and schizophrenia within the context of the Soviet punitive-psychiatry apparatus. Sokolov's novel demonstrates how the subject's perpetual dislocation, his incessant attempts to find his bearings, result in a text that maps out this very self with all its pitfalls, detours, and dead ends. The self finds itself in the schizoid split; and the record of the disease, embedded as it is in the collective structures of meaning, embodies the self as the story of its dislocation. Finally, in claiming that the title signals an instruction for use, I mean that the novel proposes a certain mode of communication with the reader, a form of "schooling," in which readers learn not only to appreciate the creative potential of "schizophrenic" discourse but in fact are induced to adopt it as a heuristic tool, becoming "schizophrenic" themselves.

THE TITLE

The title of Sokolov's lyrical novel about a perpetually adolescent, lovable individual with split-personality disorder and schizophrenic experience of time has been interpreted both metonymically and metaphorically. The former interpretation would see the title as referring to a particular special-education school, which the protagonist attended, attends, will attend (time being a supremely fluid concept in the novel) and which is the locus of all his sorrows and desires. In the metaphorical reading, the title would refer to a state of being in the Soviet Union, or just *being* in general, the human condition. But the title has not been interpreted as a manual for *training* fools, which is how I propose the book be read. After all, this is the interpretation prompted by the narrator himself: "Dear author, I would call your book *A School for Fools*; you know, there is a School for Piano Playing, a School for Playing the Barracuda [*na barrakude*; the narrator's confused-associative term for the Barcarolle accordion he plays], so let yours be a school for fools, especially since the book is not just about me or about him, the other one, but about all of us together, students and teachers, isn't it?"¹²

In contrast to the Romantics or decadents, who put their faith in the idea of divine madness, of the spiritual transcendence effected by the poet-prophet, artists of the 1960s and 1970s embraced madness as metaphor. The old organic link between madness and creativity was replaced by the use of madness as a code word for nonconformist artistic practices (with a wink). In their "Manual," Bukovsky and Gluzman recommend using this equation of nonconformism with mental illness as a tactic, a means to avoid saying anything poetically or politically suspect, which avoidance would project sanity as understood by the authorities. Many artists, however, used the code defiantly, to project freedom and noncompliance—hence the title of the first samizdat collection of Leningrad underground poetry: *An Anthology of Soviet Pathology* (*Antologiia sovetskoi patologii*).¹³ In his memoir—that is, outside the context of advising how to pass a psychiatric evaluation, and describing rather the stance of the dissident artist—Bukovsky himself sounds a similar note of defiance: "We weren't at all afraid to be called psychos—on the contrary, we were glad of it: let these fools consider us psychos, or rather the other way around, let these psychos consider us fools."¹⁴ In such instances, pathology loses its direct meaning entirely. In *A School for Fools*, however, Sokolov is doing something completely different. As a proper postmodernist, he holds—as is evident from his texts—that both normalcy and madness are verbal constructs. But he uses madness as more than just a code; he seeks to turn it into a precondition of artistic existence. The question Sokolov's novel poses is not epistemological, not how to know what is normal and what is not. Nor do I think it offers, as Cynthia Simmons proposes, an aesthetic solution to a political problem: how to covertly, safely espouse nonconformist ideas.¹⁵ It might be too reductive to read the novel (as does Alexandra Karriker¹⁶) as essentially a political argument against the practice of ostracizing and punishing introspective individuals and eccentrics for their unpopular hypotheses or allegedly antisocial behavior. The central aim of the novel is not to trace how deviance, abnormality, and madness are constructed by society, à la Foucault; nor is it to propose psychosis as the only freedom, the sole escape from a society gone mad, a return to the rhizomatic structures of desire, a substitution of one schizophrenia with another, à la Deleuze and Guattari. Rather, the question is: What individual action is possible under the conditions in which madness, albeit constructed, appears unavoidable? The novel conceives of madness as neither merely a signifier nor merely a signified; neither just a code for different-mindedness, nor a creative tapping into the primordial roots of existence. Rather, madness here functions as something in between. *A School for Fools* teaches its readers to use the very discourse of illness to supplement and reconfigure it; acknowledging the constructedness of the disease, readers will nevertheless find its creative potential contagious.

LEARNING THE LANGUAGE

When Sokolov was young, he "feigned mental illness" and admitted himself into a psychiatric ward in an attempt to evade military service. In fact, he used metaphorical language to get himself committed, saying that he sometimes felt that his chest was a "taut drumhead, with an internal Aeolian harp whose strings awaited plucking," while other times he felt like "an unexploded bomb."[17] Even as he presented these feelings as delusions, they sound suspiciously like metaphors for an artist in the making.

This encounter with the mental health apparatus informed the writing of his first novel. During his time in the ward (as he would later mention in an interview), he keenly observed the speech patterns of patients around him being treated for schizophrenia. These same patterns constitute the linguistic peculiarity of his narrator's mode of expression. The narrator's speech contains all the markers of schizophrenic speech, as outlined by both Lacanian psychoanalysis and current neuroscientific research.

A central characteristic of psychotic speech is prolific and extravagant metaphorization.[18] According to Jakobson, linguistic, metonymic relations are logical, causal, syntagmatic, and diachronic; metaphorical relations create shifts in meaning and produce discontinuity.[19] As already noted, the narrator has an undifferentiated conception of time, and his thought process is associative; the structure of the novel as a whole is paradigmatic.

Furthermore, the narrator's approach to metaphorization would be defined as schizophrenic, even by nonpunitive psychiatrists today. First, he gravitates toward concretism, interpreting the figurative language of others literally. For example, he uses concretism to dumbfound his own father, a prosecutor, turning the latter's bilious complaint about all the "scoundrels" in the world into an act of political dissent:

You know our father, he does not believe anyone, and when I said something about that to him once he replied that the whole world is made up of scoundrels and nothing but scoundrels, and if he were to believe what people said, he'd never have become the town's chief prosecutor, and at best he'd be working as a building superintendent like Sorokin, or a dacha glazier. And then I asked father about the newspapers. What about the newspapers?—he responded. And I said: you're always reading newspapers. Yes, I do, he replied, I read newspapers, and so what. Isn't it true that there is nothing written there?—I asked him. Why do you say that, said father, everything is written there, whatever is needed—is written. And if, I asked, something is written there, then why read it: it's scoundrels that write it. And then father said: what scoundrels? And I replied: those who write. Father said: write what? And I replied: the newspapers. Father was silent and looked at me, and I looked at him, and I felt a little sorry for him, because I saw how disconcerted he was. (64)

All media in the Soviet Union was state owned. Drawing a logical inference from his father's hyperbolic outburst about the unreliability of human nature (that this would vitiate, along with everything else, the newspapers everyone reads), the student So-and-So in effect accuses him of political incorrectness. Furthermore, So-and-So demonstrates that, since to utterly avoid nonconstative speech acts is impossible, the father, just like his son, is constantly at risk of being deemed politically suspect and therefore mentally unstable.

Second, the protagonist also has a predilection for autonyms, referring to himself for example as Nymphaea Alba (the white water lily), and for autonomic neologisms such as *skirly* (a self-referential word for an unnameable reality—*skirly* is a terrifying word that refers to the sound of sex). Finally, most of the narrator's associations are made on the level of the signifier. For instance, he dubs one of his teachers "Vodokachka" (Russian for a "water-pump station") not because of the way she looks or sounds, but because her initials are VDK; a railway branch becomes a branch of acacia becomes the narrator's beloved teacher Veta Akatova on the basis of sound similarities (Veta Akatova—*vetka akatsii—zhelezno-dorozhnaia vetka*). Ultimately, the protagonist's thought process is homonymic. Inasmuch as the unconscious does not differentiate between various meanings (does not filter out those not befitting the context, but allows them to coexist with those that do), the principal multiplicity and coexistence inherent to the protagonist's language is structured like the unconscious.

THE PRINCIPLE OF SUPPLETION

And yet, the narrator's lyrical and excessive metaphorization and homony-mization do not allow the metaphoric chaos to completely overtake the mimetic order. The metaphoric and homonymic operations that the protagonist's mind performs introduce just enough equivocation (ambiguity, indirectness) to ever so slightly twist the discourse that defines and imprisons him. In the novel, the narrator's poetic musings are meant to coexist with commonsense, normative language; the two modes are related by suppletion (the supplying of a necessary exception to a rule, which presupposes irregularity). It is not for nothing that one of the epigraphs to the novel lists irregular Russian verbs as if they constituted some rhythmic verse: *gnat', derzhat', bezhat', obidet', slyshat', videt', i vertet', i dyshat', i nenavidet', i za- viset', i terpet'* ("to chase, to hold, and to rotate, to hear, to see, and to offend, to run, to breathe, likewise to hate, and to endure, and to depend"). This was a typical mnemonic device to help Russian schoolchildren learn these verbs. Given how common are the actions they express, it is easy to see how ubiqui-tous these exceptions are, how essential they are to Russian speech, and thus how important it is for schoolchildren to learn them. Like the exception to any rule, the narrator's poetic language is both contingent on and excessive to the patterns of normative speech.

To illustrate the suppletion principle in the text, we might consider the episode with the slippers. The repressive headmaster at the protagonist's special-education school orders the students to bring slippers. We know that the protagonist's beloved teacher Norvegov, who is now dead and thus epito-mizes (as will be discussed further below) pure freedom, would always walk barefoot. His prosecutor-father, epitomizing the law, is always shod in boots. Slippers are of course somewhere in between bare feet and official boots. Slippers are meant to suppress noise, to so to speak domesticate the un-ruly pupils of the special school; in an interview, Sokolov said that when he was in the psychiatric ward, a secret police infiltrator sought to buy his trust with the offer of nice new slippers.[20] In the novel, via the slippers, the state's school defines these students, placing them in the category of "patient," in need of domestication by the system. And to make this function of the slip-pers as clear as possible, the headmaster orders the students to carry the slippers in a special pouch that identifies their owner and his belonging to the "Special School." Hearing this dictate, the narrator raises his hand to ask whether it would be all right for his mother to make just one pouch for his *two pairs* of slippers. That is, he believes there are two of him, which would require two pairs of slippers, but he is willing and able to compromise on the number of pouches. He thus simultaneously concedes that he is what society deems him to be—that is, mentally ill, since he requires two sets of slippers—and controverts his diagnosis by insisting on one pouch for both pairs, thereby respecting the rules of common sense and expediency. The headmaster, however, refuses to indulge in such doublethink. He insists that if the student So-and-So believes himself to be two people, he must carry two pouches. The protagonist's madness operates on the principle of supple-tion; it does not eradicate the rule but builds on and amends it. As if meeting the law halfway, it asks the lawmaker-headmaster to grant just a partial ex-ception. But the repressive state apparatus will not countenance *any* excep-tions to its laws; it demands unity.

Suppletion is at the core of the artistic bifurcation ("split personality")

125

experienced by the protagonist. The working principle behind becoming a "fool" is hinted at in the book's dedication, which reads: "To the feeble-minded boy Vitia Pliaskin, my friend and neighbor, from the Author." It is hinted that Vitia Pliaskin is indeed the schizophrenic protagonist of the novel (student So-and-So), as he sometimes speaks directly to another character called the Author. *Pliaska* in Russian means dance; Vitia Pliaskin thus encodes "St. Vitus's dance," the traditional term for the symptoms (rapid, uncoordinated movements) of the childhood ailment of chorea. Saint Vitus was the patron saint of persons affected by rabies, epilepsy, and nervous disorders, but a curious occurrence significantly expanded his area of patronage. Chorea sufferers and their parents would gather around a statue of Saint Vitus and offer a prayer, which due to their jerky movements often resembled a dance. Thus did Saint Vitus, originally a patron of nervous disorders, eventually become also a patron of dancers and artists. In the process, form gave birth to content; an accidental formal similarity cemented the connection between the dance and the disease. The symptom was imitated in the cure and led to a celebration via art, a self-sufficient form of being. Crucially, this is a matter of supplementation: mimicking jerky movements, dance supplements disease, becoming more than just it. The lack of control inherent in the disease is rounded out by the controlled movements of the dance. Sokolov likewise adopts the symptom of madness and attempts to treat it via mimicry, in the process propelling it into the sphere of art.

CREATIVE IMPATIENCE: THE RIVER LETHE

In his essay "A Mark of Illumination" ("Znak ozaren'ia"), Sokolov pinpoints what in my view may be the central problem of *A School for Fools*—the phenomenon of artistic mastery, or rather, the impossibility of its attainment. He defines "the lofty madness of art" as "the lifelong attempt of the master to convince himself that life exists; a futile but beautiful attempt."[21] This quote suggests that Sokolov sees artistic mastery as a validation and substantiation of existence; a prospective breakthrough, transcending ideologies, politics, and social constructs and norms; and an impatient search for an authentic expression or mode of being. Sokolov concedes that the futility of such attempts to escape social coercion can lead to apathy. Therefore, he exudes impatience; art is an attempt to overcome the apathy prompted by the thought of futility, to impart life with substance. Sokolov conceives of art as an act, or an action:

> Ask any pharmacist for the pills against apathy [*vialost'*, which could also be rendered as "sluggishness"]. And meanwhile the internist from the verses

of your teacher about the unhappy love [apparently a reference to a poem by Rilke]—which is a sort of apathy—recommends showers and exercises. One can also try to get better through starvation and deprivation. Or through death. Clinical or ordinary. It's miraculous, sir, a veritable resurrection. But that—later, in spare time. And now—now it's better not to ruminate but to create, to act. You were impatient.[22]

In the same essay, Sokolov repeats the line about impatience several times, owning up to this marker of the diagnosis of psychiatric abnormality. What he does not own up to, however—and hardly would—is sluggishness. Dissident "schizophrenia" should be anything but sluggish; on the contrary, apathy and sluggishness are conditions of conformist social existence. Elsewhere discussing his *School for Fools*, he counterposes the speed and energy of art to the sluggishness and apathy of the Soviet regime: "And while there in times of economic problems the word replaces currency, in years of sluggishly progressing repressions it replaces lead bullets."[23] The most "sluggish" character in the novel is the train conductor, an embodiment of authority who likewise incarnates apathy—the description of his checking of tickets and interaction with passengers includes three instances of the word "sluggishly" (*vialo*)[24]—even as the protagonist and his mother are on their way to energetic enterprises: he to his music lesson, she to an illicit affair with the music teacher.

Thus it would hardly suffice, for the creative work of lunacy that this novel is, to just mimic the mild symptoms of "sluggishly progressive schizophrenia" (especially since there is little difference between the behavior of the sufferer of this "disease" and that of a regular Soviet citizen). To act, to create an artistic act, Sokolov needs to ramp up the course of the disease. The excessiveness of the symptoms displayed takes the disease out of the sphere of mere code (i.e., madness = covert dissidence) and turns it into something more: the artistry of life. This is why the river at the center of the novel's cosmology is ever surging, on the brink of overflow.

As many of the novel's commentators have observed, the river is a key symbolic landmark on the map of the world inhabited by the schizoid narrator. Just as in Dante's *Purgatorio*, the river bounds a paradise—in this case, the dacha town that for the narrator represents a kind of Eden. The dacha home of his father, the Soviet prosecutor, with all the connotations that this position implies, is located on one bank of the river; and the opposite bank is the dwelling place of the narrator's beloved geography teacher Norvegov, an iconoclast and a madman, who also happens to be dead. At times in the text referred to as Lethe, this river signifies forgetfulness; other times it has no name.

The narrator identifies himself metaphorically with *Nymphaea alba*, a species of water lily that flows in the river. The river enables the narrator's

partial disappearance into Nymphaea Alba. This river of forgetfulness reminds us that the narrator possesses only a selective memory, a trait that
serves as an impetus for imagination. As Sokolov scholars have noted, *Nymphaea alba* has traditionally been associated with such phenomena as purity,
androgyny, and fecundity;[25] but for the purposes of this discussion, the most
important association is that of the Egyptian sun god Ra, himself an avatar of
resurrection and reincarnation. *Nymphaea alba* has two particular abilities
that prompt this association: it can resurface after being submerged deep in
the water, and it can regenerate after having wilted. The liminal position of
the water lily, its combination of fragility and endurance, characterizes the
positioning of the narrator, who manages to generate as much movement as
possible without giving in to complete chaos. The novel is likewise preoccupied with the quest to generate energy—in particular, of a subversive variety,
and yet, an energy that would be subject, like the flowering of the water lily,
to aesthetic form.

From the very beginning, the narrator is drawn to the river, while all
other inhabitants of the dacha avoid it, fearing its "whirlpools and strong currents, wind and waves, bottomless pits and grasses at the bottom" (8). The
same vortex that terrifies others appeals to our narrator because it enables
the river to unnaturally flow simultaneously in two opposite directions. The
balancing act that the narrator pursues is to float in this perpetually moving
river, amid its whirlpools and currents, without eddying out on either bank.

The two banks of the river both connote oblivion. The prosecutor-
father signifies the symbolic order; elsewhere Sokolov refers to Soviet Russia
as a Lethe-like oblivion, in which law-abiding citizens placidly spent their
lives. The bank where the narrator's father resides represents this state of
stagnant order. His teacher Pavel Norvegov, meanwhile, dwells on the other
bank. In psychoanalytic terms, the prosecutor-father is a neurotic (his vision
of reality fully coincides with the social order and societal dictates), whereas
the teacher Norvegov is a psychotic (his vision of reality fully corresponds
to his own desires and dreams, with the symbolic order fully foreclosed).
Norvegov is ultimately free, and this freedom is death. The narrator is split
in a schizoid balance between the two. While the narrator greatly admires
his teacher's energetic rebellion, a part of him desperately wishes to avoid
ending up in the same proverbial "there," which could refer both to a psychiatric ward or to death, the ultimate oblivion. (The school that the student hopes never to leave is located, just like the river Lethe, precisely on
the border between two realms: the collective normative existence of Soviet
reality and a complete exit out of it.) Norvegov, moreover, is a namesake
of Saint Paul; the narrator tells us that *this* Paul's other name, too, is Saul
(*Savl*), which conjures the religious fanaticism and extremism of the famed
apostle. So-and-So is torn between the two urges pulling him to either bank

of this river. His therapist, Dr. Zauze, probably modeled on Freud, advises him to attempt to merge the two sides in one common act. But the *two* So-and-Sos are unable to achieve such a union, and the novel is a record of this failure. Success, however, would have resulted in the complete negation of So-and-So as a person: his full incorporation into either the Soviet family or into psychotic oblivion. The measure of his therapeutic failure is, paradoxically, the measure of his success.

According to Jean-Luc Nancy, Hegel's definition of subjectivity involves irreconcilable contradiction, the subject being that "which is capable of maintaining within itself its own contradiction."[26] By this, Nancy means that consciousness relies on that which is exterior to it—that is, existence—to define itself, just as, in the realm of grammar, to fulfill its position in a sentence, a subject requires a predicate. In *Tarrying with the Negative: Kant, Hegel, and the Critique of Ideology* (1993), Slavoj Žižek, discussing Hegel's conception of an act as stemming from his conception of subjectivity, writes that the risk involved is not the act's ultimate failure but rather its success: *"a wholly successful act (an act 'corresponding to its notion') would bring about catastrophe*, i.e., either a suicide (the accomplished self-objectification, the transformation of the subject into a thing) or a lapse into madness (the 'short-circuit,' the immediate sign of equality, between Inside and Outside, i.e., the (mis)perception of the Law of my Heart as the Law of the World)."[27] For their endurance, subjects must experience a degree of failure. In his book *Parallax View* (2006), Žižek continues to search for a dynamic version of truth and proposes that it can only exist in the form of two sides that can never be bridged, enacting the "insurmountable parallax gap" as the displacement of an object seen from two points of view.[28] I am reminded of this parallax view by Sasha Sokolov's narrator, who is bifurcated, and whose bifurcation conditions a perpetual shifting between two closely linked but different perspectives—the only movement, according to Žižek, that does not lead to catastrophe.

As mentioned above, the narrator lovingly calls his literature teacher Vodokachka ("water-pump station"); the waters of writing, like those of the novel's river Lethe, must move energetically (rather than sluggishly), and in both directions, so as to ensure rather than alleviate the perpetual split: "From this time forth I belong to the dacha river Lethe, which streams against its own current at its own desire [*protiv sobstvennogo techeniia po sobstvennomu zhelaniiu*[29]]" (192). The narrator is torn between his two personas—the engineer and the pupil simultaneously—the one more censorious, the other more creative and nonconformist:

Dear mama, I don't know if one can be an engineer and a schoolboy together, perhaps some people can't, some are unable, some haven't been given the gift, but I, having chosen freedom, one of its forms, I am free to act as I wish and to be whoever I want either simultaneously or separately, can it be you don't understand this? (107)

His split personality is the only condition for the possibility of art (that which allows one to move simultaneously in two opposite directions). In two of the novel's episodes, the principle of the synchronous coexistence of two contradictory points of view becomes most vivid. These instances resemble Escher's self-referential lithograph of two hands drawing one another. One is when Nymphaea turns into the water lily that he has plucked, thereby getting plucked by a boy. The other is the parable of a carpenter who crucified himself on the cross of his own creation.

In "A Mark of Illumination," the author outlines his solution to the anxiety of influence—the desire to become the one you emulate while remaining yourself: "And if the question is put point-blank: to be the same as the lyricist or not to be—the answer will sound ingenious in its unprecedented simplicity: to be and not to be. Simultaneously."[30] This answer could also be expanded to form a general rule for the creation of art or life.

THE *SINTHOME*

This paradoxical reliance of selfhood on that which is external to it is present in the Lacanian concept of *sinthome*, which I believe is useful for understanding the mechanism behind Sokolov's complex identification with schizophrenia. In his later work, Lacan amends his concept of *symptom* and arrives at this new idea of the *sinthome*. In the period when Lacan believed that the unconscious was structured like language, he put the symptom in the category of the symbolic; it was a coded message received from the Other and decipherable by the analyst. The *sinthome*, however, retains its undecipherability. It is not just the coded message, but also a glitch within the code, an error that cannot be analyzed, narrated, or solved. This symptom has no resolution, because in resisting the symptom, the subject experiences pure enjoyment. The new theory explains why the symptom, even after its decipherment, does not disappear: the subject is too invested in it; the symptom is the wound around which the subject constitutes him- or herself. The subject arises through the process of trying to work out this symptom, and in the process, their whole being depends fully on its presence. In *A School for Fools*, student So-and-So, also known as Nymphaea Alba, explains it thus:

And if someone were to propose to us that we transfer to . . . an ordinary school for normal people, and inform us that we had gotten better and become normal—no, no, we don't want to, don't force us out!—we would weep, and wipe away the tears with our cursed slipper sacks. Yes, we love it, because we are used to it, and if we ever, after spending several so-called years in each class, if we ever graduate from it with its graffiti-covered black and brown desks, we will be terribly dismayed. For in leaving it, we would lose everything—everything that we had. (179)

Compare this to Žižek's discussion of Amfortas's wound as a *sinthome* in Wagner's *Parsifal*: "All his being is in this wound; if we annihilate it, he himself will lose his positive ontological consistency and cease to exist."[31] It is precisely where the symptom is at its most unresolvable that So-and-So can avoid being fully symbolically constituted. Or, to put it another way: the school, state, or societal symbolic structure determines the position of student So-and-So in society, diagnoses him, and attempts to school him out of his condition; but in doing so, it schools him *in* it. He acquires a taste for it; he discovers and enjoys himself in the school's and his own failure to doctor him out of his deficiency.

Žižek describes the *sinthome* as a double deception, likening it to an episode from the Marx Brothers' *Duck Soup* in which "Groucho defends his client before the court of law with the following argument in favor of insanity: 'This man looks like an idiot and acts like an idiot—but this should in no way deceive you: he *is* an idiot!'"[32] Žižek elucidates: "The final deception is that social appearance is deceitful, for in the social-symbolic reality things ultimately are precisely what they pretend to be."[33] The mechanism of this double deception is operative in the episode in which So-and-So tells one of his teachers that he has not done his homework because he was busy collecting "winter butterflies." The teacher is annoyed at this: "Since it's winter what kind of butterflies can you be speaking of . . . are you crazy?" The student replies "with unshaken dignity": "In the winter one can speak only of winter lepidoptera, those which are called snow butterflies. . . . [To] the second of the questions you posed my reply is this: the fact of my insanity is of no surprise to anyone, otherwise they would not keep me in this damned school along with others who are fools" (108–9). The student thus attempts to get out of the punishment for not doing his homework by seemingly going along with society's definition of him as insane; what complicates the issue, however, is that he does not just *seem* to believe in winter butterflies but actually does believe in them. We are dealing, then, with a double deception: his professed love of winter butterflies is predicated on his environment, the "school for fools," as well as on the broader schoolchild scenario in which missing homework has to be (however fictitiously) justified. But the explanation devised in this case is not fully a lie, a verbal construct (like "the dog ate my homework"). It is not fully coterminous with the appropriate social scenarios, nor fully outside of them. It is both socially constructed and the pupil's very own.

MONSTROUS SURPLUS: THE SCREAM

In psychoanalytic theory, this moment of autonomy that cannot be co-opted within the symbolic order is both a void and an excess: a void in the symbolic structure and "an anamorphic surplus."[34] How can the novel demonstrate this unrepresentable surplus? In her book *The Prose of Sasha Sokolov: Reflections on/of the Real*, Elena Kravchenko argues that the novel constitutes "a quest for a 'former self,'" and that via linguistic metaphorizing and metamorphosing, via playing with the material qualities of language, and the creative re-collection of the self, So-and-So manages to acquire critical distance from "things that are normally taken for granted" and to construct and complete himself.[35] Kravchenko's reading of the novel is illuminating and compelling, but I cannot agree with her assessment, based on Bakhtin's theory of authorship, that So-and-So finds his autonomy via the unification and re-collection of his self. His autonomous self is located, I would emphasize, in the places where language fails, in the gaps of communication, in the perpetual oscillation, the noncorrespondence, noncoincidence of his two selves, student So-and-So and *Nymphaea alba*, the engineer and the child, the subject and the object. Language in the novel does not serve as a narrative prosthesis that might compensate for the deficiencies of the self and the surrounding world by filling the void. On the contrary, Sokolov's text operates by inscribing the gaps in which the subject exists into its language, such that this language bears the traces of the protagonist's deficiency. The most obvious moments of the return of the repressed, the reader's encounter with the real, come with So-and-So's extraordinary bellowing screams, screams "of a new type," "fierce and spellbinding" (136, 138). These screams are properly proleptic in that they are able to exit linear time and move simultaneously like the river Lethe forward and backward:

> I wanted [my father] to hear and understand what the cry of his son meant: aaaaa! Wolves on the walls even worse on the walls there are people, people's faces, they are the hospital walls that when you are dying quietly and terribly aaaaa huddled up in the fetal position faces which you have never seen but which you will see years later these are the preludes to death and life for it has been promised to you that you will live in order to be able to sense the reverse movement of time. (121)

On the one hand, the screams signify a rupture in language. Existing outside language or in its margins, they often constitute pure sound; yet student So-

and-So perceives them to be the acme of his creative expression, his most successful attempts at communicating his anguish and his impotence, all that encapsulates his innermost self. While So-and-So delights in the beauty of his scream and its almost literal voluminousness (there is an episode when he screams into an empty barrel, trying to fill it with his scream), it is ultimately unsettling and monstrous. It unnerves the teachers and parents, and agitates the other "fools."

The rest of the novel, however, seems to echo these screams, replicating and redoubling the protagonist's deficiency, his existence in the split between his two personas—between the school and the dacha, between engineering and botany—resisting their resolution and finding the self in the permanent oscillation between the two irreconcilable sides of his being. The form of the novel itself, its constant metaphoric mutation and distortion, its inability to sustain a coherent point of view, is grotesque in its replication of the narrator's monstrosity. Kravchenko persuasively argues that the conceit behind the novel is the story of Narcissus from Ovid's *Metamorphoses*.[36] The classical Narcissus is a beautiful boy who falls in love with his own reflection in a pond and is transformed into a flower. Kravchenko reads our protagonist as such a Narcissus, whose self-reflexive musings and solipsistic encounter with himself transform him into an object of his own reflection. But this would seem to call for an important qualification: Sokolov's plot represents a distorted version of the common tale. Our Narcissus is markedly not a beautiful boy, and when he sees his own reflection, he is not drawn to it, but recoils, experiencing not love, but an excruciating pain:

> I am howling sir howling for I have been betrayed I Nymphea 'tis I bald [*az esm' lysaia*[37]] weak flatfooted with a high forehead like on a real cretin and a face old from doubts look I am absolutely awful my nose is all covered with disgusting blackheads and my lips puffed forward and flattened as if I were born of a duck and it makes no difference that once upon a time in the flower of my crucial age I learned to play on a mother-of-pearl three quarters Barcarolle that didn't help me nevertheless it is excruciatingly painful. (142)[38]

Just like the howl itself, the image is grotesque. The protagonist's transformation into a flower, *Nymphaea*, is not de facto a complete metamorphosis, but only a partial one. Nymphaea is simultaneously a female flower, a flatfooted teenager with blackheads, and a cretinous old man. Furthermore, the photograph in which So-and-So finds his likeness was taken when he was a pupil of the school, making his baldness doubly or triply incongruous. (That is, he is too young to be bald; and his baldness grammatically feminizes him: *az esm' lysaia*—"I am bald," even as this condition is not typically associated with women; and baldness is likewise not usually a topic befitting description via Biblicisms or Old Church Slavonicisms like *az esm'*).

To read this grotesque mixture of forms as the Bakhtinian coherence of the world in the process of becoming (Kravchenko's interpretation[39]) would miss the mark. In Sokolov's fondness for everything that is deficient, monstrous, and grotesque, his texts pursue transcendence of the mundane not through the discovery of coherence but, paradoxically, through the failure to find it. Sokolov's predisposition toward deficient characters has been acknowledged by many scholars, and often interpreted as a thematizing of holy foolishness and its attendant removal of the self from the world.[40] I would propose a different reading: that of grotesquerie as a driving mechanism of Sokolov's art.

THE GROTESQUE

The grotesque texture of Sokolov's writings attests to the presence of the sublime in their manifest inability to grasp it. Having come to serve as a catchall term for the bizarre, the grotesque is in fact a specific form of aesthetic expression, characterized by the mixture of incongruous natural forms. Etymologically, "grotesque" comes from the Italian *grottesco* ("of or pertaining to a cave"), and originally signified the ancient Roman decorative art found on the walls of basements of Roman ruins in the late fifteenth century. This featured extravagant configurations of tiny fantastic hybridic creatures intertwined with one another via spiraling vines and garlands (arabesques).[41] A *School for Fools* is structured around all three of the main tropes that Remi Astruc identifies as essential for the grotesque: doubleness, hybridity, and metamorphosis.[42] Lipovetsky calls Sokolov's branch of postmodernism neo-baroque, insofar as it revitalizes the baroque relationship with spectacle and its emphasis on "the unfinished and unfinishable process of creation itself."[43] In that respect, grotesque incongruity is very much a part of the Sokolovian baroque, as it contributes to the rough, incomplete surface of the whole and exhibits the seams of its imperfect assemblage. According to John Ruskin, it is precisely the grotesque's imperfection that renders its effect on the spectator similar to the perception of the sublime. In this view, the noble or symbolic grotesque reveals the presence of a truth exceeding the human capacity for understanding; it arises "from the confusion of the imagination by the presence of truths which it cannot wholly grasp."[44] It makes perfect sense to Ruskin, then, that the grotesque nature of human comprehension in the face of inexpressible truths should best be represented by distortion:

> The fallen human soul, at its best, must be as a diminishing glass, and that a broken one, to the mighty truths of the universe round it; and the wider the scope of its glance, and the vaster the truths into which it obtains an insight,

the more fantastic their distortion is likely to be, as the winds and vapors trouble the field of the telescope most when it reaches farthest.[45]

According to Ruskin, the distortion exhibits an awareness of truths beyond human ken, thereby pointing to them. This distortion exists, however, not as a promise of prospective enlightenment; in the grotesque, it always appears retroactively, as a failure to grasp the truth, and proleptically, as an anticipation that truth will remain ungraspable in the future as well. Justin D. Edwards and Rune Graulund observe that "for Ruskin, the grotesque is distortion, delineating the gap between imagined possibility and reality."[46] The mind delights, however, in the sublimity of being able to imagine the existence of something it cannot properly imagine (in the sense of comprehend). One derives a particular enjoyment from one's failure, since the apprehension of this failure is the closest one can get (short of literal death) to a ticket out of the mundane. This is how the grotesque operates in Sokolov's texts.

Indeed, all Sokolov's texts feature characters who are patently weak in one way or another. All of them attempt to find a way to live with their weakness, to locate themselves in time and space and find themselves via writing, which records their attempts and situates them within their deficiency (rather than allowing them to transcend or exit it). Their lack brings them both terror and delight. Being in this gap is what makes them *them*. All Sokolov's texts, even those not told from the point of view of a schizophrenic narrator, feature unstable narrative perspectives—for example, *Palisandriia*, the fictional life-writing of one Palisandr Dalberg, is written at times in the first, at times in the third person—and they resist chronology. The time warp in which the past, present, and future coexist renders the gap between imagined possibility and reality, placed in close temporal proximity, that much more poignant.

The grotesque might offer a more fitting framework for Sokolovian characterization than holy foolishness. Holy fools are sanctified; they exhibit their belonging to another, more sacred, more transcendent existence by their demonstrable inability to belong to this one, to fit in or thrive in it. Sokolov's characters are not holy fools in that respect; they suffer from a double weakness: they are poorly adjusted to the environment, but their belonging to any other reality is equally tenuous. Their grotesqueness does not guarantee admission to some higher reality. They present the reader not with sacred alterity but with its demonstrable absence. The mode by which the grotesque operates is similar to the uncanny: you feel both recognition and recoil; you recognize the familiar in the strange. Encountering a holy fool, you recognize the transcendent in the deficient human form; encountering the grotesque characters of Sokolov, you recognize yourself and your own existential struggles in the deficient human form. Holy foolishness creates distance from the perceiver; the uncanny grotesque reduces it. Significantly, So-and-So is able to transform into or reflect whomever he is looking at or talking to: he becomes old when speaking with Academician Akatov; he takes on the form of his teacher Norvegov when looking at him, or his ghost. Holy fools resist intimacy with onlookers and affirm their difference and alterity, whereas Sokolov's grotesque monsters create a space of intimacy with the reader.

BLINDNESS

Sokolov's early, pre–*School for Fools* writings include two stories that feature blind protagonists. He published both in *Zhizn' slepykh* (*Life of the Blind*; subsequently *Nasha zhizn'* [*Our Life*]), the Soviet national magazine for the blind. While Sokolov's "The Old Helmsman" ("Staryi shturman," 1971) received the magazine's prize for best story about the blind, I would like to focus here on the other piece, "All the Colors of the Rainbow" ("Vse tsveta radugi," 1968). This story-essay[47] features a complicated narrative structure, in which the narrator recounts the protagonist's own story to him: the protagonist, that is, does not yet know his own story, because it still has not transpired; like all-seeing Tiresias, the narrator foretells this future fate. The conversation takes place the day before the outbreak of the Soviet-German War, during which the protagonist will lose his sight from a blast injury. Prior to the injury, the protagonist had played the accordion, and the narrator tells him that music is a key to his selfhood. The story that follows can be interpreted as one of salvation via either music or blindness: either his music will help him get through his blindness, or his blindness will prompt him to develop his musicianship. However we choose to read it, the protagonist is to end up an accomplished musician—composing, learning to play numerous other instruments, and teaching children. In this future, the blind protagonist is told, he will play the piano, and thereby the narrator will synesthetically learn to hear the hitherto unnoticed colors of reality: "I enter the twilight of his room, where stands a black, graceful instrument and where all the colors of rainbow and dawn reveal themselves to the composer."[48] So not only will music infuse the blackness in which the protagonist dwells with color, it will color the narrator's world as well.

But the story does not end here. The blind protagonist's music will trigger the narrator's recollection of his own childhood. The narrator tells us that as a child, he was unaware of, or de facto blind to, the repercussions of the war. In particular, he had eagerly awaited one particular neighbor's return from the front. Prior to the war, this neighbor had been a pianist. In his anticipation, the narrator-as-child glamorized this combination of war hero and musician, and nurtured an especial love of war songs. But the pianist returned home without a left arm, which made it impossible for him to continue playing.[49] The narrator tells us that the disabled musician put his piano out on the street, hoping someone else, at least, might find use for and take it. But it just stood there untouched, its tragic story having made it somehow unapproachable. "All the Colors of the Rainbow" would seem to contrast one story of triumph over disability with another story of failure. It might be read affirmatively as enabling the narrator to deal with a childhood disappointment by at last discovering someone able to play him the war songs he so longed to hear from his neighbor. I choose to read it as the inscription of a persistent trauma into a story of triumph. The stories of the two musicians are not different, but similar, and only by remembering that at the heart of the blind musician's amazing triumph is the incurable loss of his vision can one approximate an understanding. The reader is left primarily with the impression not of all the colors of the rainbow, but of the blackness of the discarded piano that everyone feared to touch. In this journal for the blind, the story-essay was accompanied by a picture of the blind musician; seeing it in black and white rather than the colors of the rainbow on which the title insists, the seeing reader could share the experience of being unable to see with the journal's blind audience (fig. 15).

Fig. 15. Photo accompanying Sasha Sokolov's "All the Colors of the Rainbow" in the journal for the blind, *Life of the Blind*, 1968. Caption: Mari Composer M. S. Stepanov.

Sokolov's *A School for Fools* has been compared to Nabokov's works, although Sokolov insisted that he had not read Nabokov prior to writing his first novel. Even so, his story-essay of the two disabled musicians makes me think of Nabokov's "A Guide to Berlin" ("Putevoditel' po Berlinu," 1925), in which a Russian émigré inscribes himself into the alien city by exchanging glances with a boy in a window across the street from a pub he often patronizes. The émigré hopes that he will persist in the boy's memory as part of the landscape of his childhood. Nabokov must have felt that the story was missing something, that it needed something that might ensure the boy's memory on which the future fate of the émigré rests, because when translating the story into English, he added to it the element of a missing limb. It is in the proleptic rendition of the boy's memory that the reader learns that the émigré is missing an arm.[50] His memorable disfigurement will thereby make him an indelible part of mutilated post–First World War Berlin. This strange moment of intimacy on the basis of shared disfigurement strikes me as operative in Sokolov's story of the blind musician.

SOKOLOV'S TERATOLOGY

Sokolov's second novel, *Between Dog and Wolf* (*Mezhdu sobakoi i volkom*, 1980), diffuses thematic blindness from a property of one character to that of the whole work. Blindness powers the plot. Sure enough, one of the secondary characters, Nikolai Ugodnik(ov), is a lame, deaf-mute, and blind hunchback. This extravagant combination makes him unwelcome in hospices and shelters, which limit their beneficence to particular categories of disability. A vagrant ragpicker, he shares his name with Saint Nicholas the Miracle Worker (*Nikolai ugodnik*), the patron saint of vagrants and travelers. And he is indeed characterized by miraculous movement: in life, he is an avid skater on the invalid-house skating rink, and in death (from alcohol overdose) he is transformed into a soaring eagle. But being "the cripple of all cripples" (*kaleka sred' kalek*[51]), he emblematizes the existential condition of all the "crippled" and homeless characters in the novel, the persistence of life in the perpetual dusk referred to in the title—a Latin-derived Russian expression (appearing, for instance, in Pushkin's *Eugene Onegin* [*Evgenii Onegin*]) for twilight—that is, when a shepherd cannot distinguish between the dog that guards his flock and a wolf that threatens it.

It is this ostensibly temporary blindness that generates the plot of the novel, which Kravchenko calls essentially "a crime story."[52] The reader, in the role of detective, attempts to discern what took place in the story, whose narrative texture is akin to twilight itself, simultaneously concealing and revealing the key to the puzzle. The reader thus takes part, along with the characters, in existence "between dog and wolf." Sokolov wrote the novel while serving as a gamekeeper on a hunting preserve, and the story revolves around an essential misrecognition. A knife grinder kills a gamekeeper's dog, mistaking it for a wolf. The gamekeeper responds by stealing the knife grinder's crutches, which restricts the latter's movement, insofar as he has only one leg. After a series of escalating clashes, the knife grinder is drowned. In a twist, it then appears that the knife grinder and gamekeeper were father and son. This complicated familial relationship suggests yet another reading for the title: the ambiguity as to whether your kin is a protective dog or a menacing wolf.[53] The title suggests that the ontological position of the other vis-à-vis oneself lies somewhere in between: the other is simultaneously a dog and a wolf. The novel oscillates between the perspectives of the alleged father and son, making it that much harder to discern the essential mystery. The densely allusive, disjointed, and arcane language adds a layer of incomprehensibility. The reader is made to feel both horror at the brutality of the characters' lives and pity for their suffering; this is once again the performance of existence between dog and wolf, which the gamekeeper describes in a poem as the encounter between *laska* ("care," "affection") and *toska* ("melancholy," "despair"): "I love the hour between wolf and dog, as if care were mixed with despair [*slovno laska peremeshana s toskoi*]."[54]

PALISANDR DALBERG AS NYMPHAEA'S DOUBLE

In *A School for Fools*, the protagonist, despite his obvious deficiencies, nevertheless possesses many endearing traits: his tender, unrequited love for his botany teacher Veta Akatova; his devotion to his deceased geography teacher Pavel/Savl Norvegov; and his ability, akin to that of a natural scientist, to observe and experiment—in particular, to grow and generate metaphors, transforming language into a live thing. Due to all these characteristics, the protagonist's resistance to deadening reality and his search for the self have invariably been read as successful and transcendent. Beginning with Nabokov, who declared the book "charming . . . and most touching," commentators (e.g., Kravchenko and Lipovetsky) have typically seen the book as affirming the protagonist's aesthetic sensibility and creative ability to rise above his dismal environment. But Sokolov's other two novels received a very different assessment. While *Between Dog and Wolf* is often considered too abstruse to afford any "message" to speak of, *Palisandriia* (1985; translated into English as *Astrophobia*) is read as a complete negation of the possibility of a message, of any insight or revelation—a pure historical farce. The authors of *A History of Russian Literature* remark that, with the latter work, Sokolov "moves from the tragic to the parodic, from metamorphoses to pastiche and grotesque."⁵⁵ In this view, while *A School for Fools* demonstrates the postmodern ability to creatively transcend the narratives that make and maim us, *Palisandriia* is about the "postmodern defeat of the creative imagination."⁵⁶ But while *Palisandriia* is indeed a much less "charming" book, I would argue that its eponymous monster Palisandr Dalberg is not so different from the student So-and-So.⁵⁷ They share not only some of their most defining characteristics but also their most crucial failures, and they author their own selves via these failures. Despite his radical nonconformism, So-and-So is an offspring of his prosecutor-father, and as such, of the Soviet system. Like So-and-So, Palisandr is intimately related to a henchman of the repressive state apparatus, in this case one of the most notorious: he is a nephew, that is, of Lavrentii Beria, the chief of the secret police and first deputy chair of the Council of Ministers under Stalin. Palisandr also happens to be a grandson of Grigorii Rasputin, the "mad monk" adviser to the tsar's family at the Russian Empire's collapse. In fact, he is closely linked to any number of major historical figures. Both So-and-So and Palisandr exist in a state of timelessness, the latter due to his Uncle Lavrentii's suicide on one of the Kremlin's clocks, which stops time.

Both are engaged in the process of autobiographical recollection and composition of the self. Both have an affinity for older women: taking So-and-So's schoolboy crush on his teacher several levels beyond, to the point of sexual deviance, *Palisandriia* relates its main character's Casanova-like conquests of quite elderly women. Palisandr's gerontophilia is not just a clever parodic inversion of Humbert Humbert's pedophilia, but represents a particularly Sokolovian treatment of time. Nabokov's Humbert wishes to aesthetically freeze time, erasing the distinction between immortal art and mutable reality. He would preserve reality from change by freezing it in art, and in the process he destroys a thirteen-year-old girl. Existing in immutable reality, Palisandr wishes to make time move backward and forward simultaneously, like the river in *A School for Fools*. In his love of older women, he aspires to return to a mother's womb. He thus yearns to enact both progression and *re*gression, just as the embryonic state signifies at once life's development and preformation. Like student So-and-So, Palisandr appears, in his own narrative, at times heroic and potent, irresistible to his conquests; and at times he appears pitiful and vulnerable, suffering from extra digits, cross-eyedness, and alopecia. And last but not least, Palisandr's hermaphroditism is yet another element that closely links him to So-and-So, who is both a male human and a female flower/*Nymphaea*. Once Palisandr's greatest secret, his androgyny, is revealed, he begins speaking of himself using the neuter ending *o*, which now appears at the end of *its* name and of the past-tense verbs describing *its* actions. Kravchenko traces the grapheme *o* in the novel, arguing that it haunts the text much prior to its first appearance at the

end of Palisandr's name.[58] She sees it in this context as an oval-shaped menace, topologically representing the abyss of time and space into which everything must descend; it is the shape of the beckoning womb, the vortex of
time, and the Kremlin stairwell. The grotesque union of opposites, marked
graphically by the attachment of the fraught *o* to Palisandr, may thus be read
as the erasure of all differences and the neutralization of all discourses into
meaningless nothingness. Boris Groys, for example, argues that the world
Sokolov constructs in his novel is far from pluralistic, as in it all discourses
and ideologies ultimately converge into one pattern:

> Like many other contemporary Russian writers, Sokolov shows that the ideo-
> logical pluralism of our time is in itself an illusion, an ideological construct.
> Contemporary "theories" may contradict each other or even be incommen-
> surate, but their narratives are all the more similar for it. One and the same
> plot can tell about the artist who discovers the feminine side of his soul, the
> wage laborer's alienation, the KGB agent in a hostile environment, the dis-
> sident searching for the truth outside the Soviet world, and so on. They all
> perform the same ritual of individuation by proceeding beyond what "exists,"
> is usual, traditional, and given, and by crossing this boundary they discover a
> new truth, which they proclaim to humankind. To be aware of this ritual is to
> realize the inevitability of history and historical narrative, which can be over-
> come neither by a single and final flight from history into the space of extra-
> historical truth, nor by the timelessness of pluralism.[59]

It is this reading that the authors of *A History of Russian Literature* build on
to suggest that, "personified by Palisandr Dal'berg, postmodernism becomes
a post-historical monster that sucks the life and energy from diverse cultural
discourses."[60] Groys and these authors alike thus read Palisandr's monstrosity as an ultimate negation. In his monstrous mimicry, in the failure of his
attempts at originality, they see a condemnation of any pretense of saying
something new, individual, one's own.

To this I would counter that Palisandr's self materializes precisely in
and through this failure. His self is located in this very *o*, which acts as a
Lacanian *sinthome*. Attached to his very name, the *o* is not just a void; it is
also a surplus (being, quite literally, a suffix). It graphically echoes student
So-and-So's scream "Nymphaea!" into the abyss of the empty barrel. This
scream is both an act of rebellion and an admission of impotence. This story
is radically different from the story of Narcissus, who looks at his reflection,
becomes one with it, and takes on the form of a flower. Student So-and-So
is condemned to only partial transformation. His scream, identifying him
with the flower, is not a substitution but an appendix—an excessive appendix to his usual form. Just as in the case of student So-and-So/*Nymphaea*,

Palisandr's hermaphroditism is not a reduction of all differences to naught or devaluation of all matter to nothing. Though he makes a rhetorical move to embrace his own inner contradictions, his distortion of the rules of grammar appears to us as a monstrous suppletion akin to student So-and-So's unsettling use of the feminine gender when speaking of his own baldness. Confusing his allegiances and accumulating kinships, Palisandr's narrative appears schizoid (in the sense of "split between antagonistic or contrasting states") and schizophrenic.[61]

Thus I cannot agree that Palisandr's autobiography reduces all different ideologies and points of view to one narrative, simply replicating the same narrative over and over again. If, as Groys says, all narratives are narratives of discovering individuation, of finding one's own unusual truth, then Palisandr's narrative differs from all other narratives precisely because it is about his failure to find his truth, or rather, about his discovery of his truth via the negation of its possibility (a radically different position from the one common narrative). Symbolically, this is represented in the novel's final act, in which Palisandr forces himself to vomit. This purging of the self is a remainder in which the self resides, as we get the hint that the autobiographical account we have just finished reading is the very vomit emitted by our monster. The mechanism of simultaneous expulsion and appropriation of regurgitated matter from the depth of his being returns us to Sokolov's espousal of the schizoid form of being.

SCHIZOID EXISTENCE

The dissident scholar Yury Glazov argued that a normal citizen of the Soviet Union was "a kind of a schizoid":

> A man who manipulates his behavior between what is officially allowed and what he personally and in a close circle reveals as his beliefs is in Soviet society considered a sane man, though actually he is a kind of schizoid. If any person is unable to behave himself on these two watertight levels of official and non-official thinking, speaking and behavior, and proclaims his real thoughts in an unofficial way, he is considered by the officials to be an abnormal man and suffers from one of several possible forms of persecution, including confinement to a mental hospital.[62]

Glazov argues that the state promoted behavioral bilingualism among its citizens, and that what set dissidents apart was their determination to be "monolingual in a society which allows only a schizophrenic existence."[63] In her above-mentioned study *State of Madness*, Reich complicates this opposition, suggesting that dissidents "inhabited the overlap of insanity and *inakomyslie* in what might also be described, to develop Glazov's terminology, as distinctly 'bilingual' ways."[64] Theirs, Reich argues, was a position on the ambivalent border between the two conceptualizations of their behavior.

Although Reich does not discuss Sokolov's writing in her book, his tactic would certainly match her assessment of dissident activity. In his works, official and unofficial thinking, speaking, and behavior are connected in more ways than just via contrast. Rather, they feed off one another; to eliminate bifurcation would be both impossible and undesirable. Sokolov's recipe is to embrace this rupture, cultivate it to the point of excess, and transform schizoid existence into an art form, thereby affirming its viability, even necessity—as monolingualism would connote the death of the subject.

The Weakling, the Genius, the Bomb, and the Globe: Writing as Weakness in Andrei Bitov

I F   O N E   had to pick the quintessential herald of weakness in late Soviet culture, this honor would go, without question, to Andrei Bitov. Numerous scholarly articles and critical responses have sought to pinpoint the exact nature of Bitov's weak hero, a creature both familiar and yet new to Russian literature. If, in our previous case studies, weakness always had a specific cause and manifestation—PTSD and gender subversion in Vonnegut and Kim, alcoholism in Erofeev, mental illness in Sokolov, marginality associated with sexual orientation in Kharitonov—the weakness of Bitov's heroes is a thing in itself, a state of being. This weakness disorients Bitov's reader, as his *text* (as Marina von Hirsch terms the composite of all his works[1]) complicates any attempt to assign fault for it. Who is to blame—the character himself, the family, the Soviet state, the postmodern condition, or the human condition in general? Further complicating this task is the weakness of the text itself, its lack of resolution, its exposure of its creator's misgivings and perpetual teetering on the brink of dissolution.

Time and again, Bitov constructs his narratives around characters who appear perpetually uncertain, unable, unoccupied, and uncomfortable: "I'm ashamed and depressed that I am not like everyone else, that I am so weak and have no will power, and that I so much want but cannot force myself to be good, to be like everyone, so that I could be calm and righteous," as the eponymous protagonist of "The Idler" ("Bezdel'nik," 1968) describes himself.[2] The protagonist of "The Bus" ("Avtobus"; written in the 1960s, first published in 1988) suffers from the same inability to synchronize his life with others: "Sometimes I cannot get in the right phase. Periodically. Rather often. Not in the right phase means that nothing I do turns out right, all of it is vile, everything slips through my hands, I must do one thing, but I want to do another."[3] In this reminiscence with Dostoevsky's Underground Man, the inability to bring to conclusion one's ideas, plans, and dreams is connected with the failure to write a book this aspiring writer would have liked to write:

"I've been thinking for a month already, if I could only write such a book."[4] Many of Bitov's works feature complaints regarding the exhaustingness and fruitlessness of the creative process: "Some months ago I suddenly wanted to write a poem and, of course, did not risk it. Then yesterday it came back to me. There weren't enough words and I did not and will not write it, but something like a prose translation remains."[5]

Most telling, then, of Bitov's particular quality of weakness are those characters and narrators who languish as dissatisfied writers, marked, first and foremost, by their perpetually blocked desire to formalize and finalize their thoughts on paper. Paradoxically, however, these writerly difficulties, of which Bitov's characters and narrators eternally complain, appear to instantiate both the failure *and the accomplishment* of their creative practice. For example, the book envisioned by the aspiring writer in "The Bus" represents a lifelong project: "It would be nice to begin the sort of book that you'd have to write your whole life. . . . That is, not that you'd have to, but could write your whole life. You just write it and write it. And when you end, the book ends."[6] This passage, with which the story begins, demonstrates precisely how one might go about accomplishing the task of writing something continuously (or at least of extending it): by always failing to express oneself fully, making mistakes, self-correcting ("that is, not that you'd have to, but could") and then failing again. If the aspiration is indeed to write a book that never ends, then these accumulated failures paradoxically represent the fulfillment of the ultimate design.[7]

For Bitov, writing is not just a tool by which one describes or registers weakness; writing itself becomes a weakness—that is, a compulsion one would be advised to give up but cannot. In "Notes from the Corner" ("Zapiski iz-za ugla," 1963; first published in English, in 1986), the writer confesses, "Inevitably I will now write about exactly this and only about this. About futility. I write this useless and harmful opus."[8] With these sentences, Bitov begins a circuitous, almost impossible-to-follow passage, one that again demonstrates how this compulsion toward fruitless writing is both bemoaned and endorsed, since it provides that continuity aspired to earlier by the writer from "The Bus":

> I'm secretly hoping . . . I'd get all tangled up in the lines, having tied them all together, and, already despairing, confusing their order and interrelationship, pull on the first one that comes to hand. Then somehow suddenly by a miracle I'd wind up with the right line, the one with the right fish, and everything will come together and take form so that in the end I'll come to a real affirmation which will fill me with a belief in the necessity of continuing my efforts, I'll swim across, fly over, land, and come out on the other shore in complete certainty that this is not that old one, but a wholly different land I've been

heading towards, where at last I'll go forward, and all this only because the shore is the opposite one, and at first, it won't hit me that there is no qualitative difference in their opposition.[9]

This writer begins the passage with the metaphor of an elusive fish he hopes to land, but then, midsentence (a very *long* sentence), he forgets the fish and his aim to catch it, and instead plunges into the water himself. Somehow, by way of water, we have switched metaphors. The need to catch something is abandoned in favor of swimming, ostensibly to reach the other shore. But there's a catch (pun intended): the writer seems to know a priori and even desire—"I'm secretly hoping" must apply to everything in the sequence of this long sentence—that the other shore will be no different from his shore of origin. Therefore, we are to understand that it is neither the fish nor the shore (neither the result nor the destination), but the fishing and swimming itself, the very process of moving toward something perpetually out of reach, that is the secret authorial aim. The fruitlessness, the very lack of success of which Bitov's characters ever complain—is not a deterrent, but quite the opposite, a driving impulse: "It's the same with a writer—even when it's unendurable for him, he is ready to do anything just to keep from being deprived of this very unendurability."[10]

This unbearable condition, a quixotic cross between graphomania and writer's block,[11] is precipitated by a low-grade *horror vacui*—the constant apprehension of the void and the end that, as this chapter will describe, is the invariable background for Bitov's characters' aspirations and desires, as the condition of their unceasing striving; what they unceasingly strive to do, that is, is avert, or at least postpone, this end. It is through the prism of this fear of the ultimate end, made particularly palpable in the atomic age by the possibility of total annihilation at any moment, that the writerly difficulties of Bitov's paradigmatic hero—a weakling who can scarcely start or finish a piece of writing—should be examined and ultimately justified.

Fixation on *the end* undermines human agency, casting doubt, in particular, on the worthwhileness of any creative act. The thoughts of futility that plague Bitov's characters and weaken them are not unreasonable. Furthermore, the apprehension of the ultimate end of thought, of the human race, of the earth, of the sun—the perception of the ultimate fragility of everything, which permeates Bitov's writing—raises his characters' marked weakness to a prophetic manifestation. The impotence of a Bitovian writer-character, that is, gives him insight into the essential condition of being: helplessness in the face of death. Weakness is a state of recognition of one's finitude, and that of all life and the world. Bitov is often described as a Christian thinker, yet his awareness of the end and, along with it, the difficulty this awareness presents for a creative person, is burdened by the secularism of his catastrophic imagination, in which the end is final and unrecoverable—there is no immortality for humanity or human thought, no everlasting Kingdom of God.

And yet, while featuring the foibles and adventures of weaklings, who seem unable to accomplish much of anything, many of Bitov's works center on the concept of a demiurgic genius, who just might succeed in becoming both immanent and transcendent, overcoming the limitations of ordinary human life, and enduring beyond the end. The genius is always an aspirational figure for Bitov's weakling; the genius is a model and promise of continuity and endurance in a world otherwise bereft of it. While the weakling, mired in idleness, would seem to be the polar opposite of the potent genius, this chapter makes the case that Bitov's weakling-writer, who is aware of and tries to avert or rather defer catastrophe, stands far closer to *genius* than any normatively abled or "well adjusted" character. It is precisely the protagonists' weakness that brings them closer to their ideal of genius, and that just might offer its own, perhaps even preferable, solution to the problem of the end.

DISPERSAL AND CONTINUITY,
PERMANENCE AND METAMORPHOSIS

From its earliest beginnings, Bitov's prose had unstable boundaries. There was something indefinite about its generic parameters; it gravitated toward the uncertain genre of the long short story (in Russian, *povest'*). It did not help that the author kept tinkering with and rewriting elements of his stories, renaming characters, transforming settings. He was fond, moreover, of mixing and matching stories, recombining them into different collections, or forming them into longer pieces; for instance, all the chapters of his 1990 *The Flying Away Monakhov* (*Uletaiushchii Monakhov*), which Bitov gave the genre designation *roman-punktir* (i.e., a "novel-dotted line on a map"), were first published as discrete stories beginning in the 1960s, when they were written, and over the years. Or sometimes, on the contrary, he would take a chunk from a longer text and publish it as a separate piece on its own; *Pushkin House* (*Pushkinskii dom*), for example, was originally written as a novel but first published in seemingly disjointed pieces. This genre play yet again underscores the doomedness of writing as a finalizable project with discrete boundaries. Which is fittingly Bitovian; as Wai Chee Dimock persuasively argues, no literary category is less conclusive than genre, or so emblematic of *weakness*:

> Far from being a done deal, a complete catalog of what exists and what is to come, genre is a mixed attempt at cataloging, doomed to come up short

because there will always be more specimens coming its way, inconvenient specimens, unforeseen and unrecognizable on its terms. Genre cannot ban such evidence or deny its empirical force. It's a taxonomy that never quite taxonomizes. . . . Ontologized out of habit but in practice without an ontology, it's "weak" in the sense Gianni Vattimo would use the term.[12]

Bitov's protean text seems ever on the brink of falling apart into smaller elements or reorganizing itself into different compounds, but we sense its various segments coalescing around a single nucleus: Bitov's character. Whether named Monakhov, Infantiev, or Odoevtsev, or unnamed altogether, the character possesses certain qualities that make him particularly Bitovian. And yet, this ur-character, too, while retaining most salient characteristics and concerns, does not stand still but keeps metamorphosing, taking on different incarnations.[13]

In the early stories, this composite character is a young man who often feels like life is passing him by. The usual image associated with this man is a public bus, which he rides endlessly and aimlessly, always in limbo between an origin and a destination, both thriving in and suffering from the transience of this in-transit stage. Surrounded by strangers, the man on the bus acutely feels his alienation from them. Their bustling about and eagerness to reach their destinations is juxtaposed with his dreamy sense of aimless languishing. The limbo in movement, the state of transient inactivity, is a perpetual motif in Bitov's characters' lives, who often suffer from but also savor the experience of being taken somewhere and, more importantly, *from* somewhere, in buses, planes, trains, and the back or passenger seats of cars. Being transported nourishes both their inactivity and passivity, while at the same time makes them more attuned to the condition of living on this earth, which is, after all, in perpetual movement to nowhere.

The main character of Bitov's early stories is an idler, as the above-mentioned story's title so aptly designates him. Like the protagonist in Dostoevsky's "White Nights" ("Belye nochi"), the idler drifts through life filled with aimless dreams and impressions, deriving from them both pleasure and pain. And, like Dostoevsky's dreamer, the idler generates many ideas that he is then unable to realize. The state of perpetual idling, anticipation, and postponement in the early stories gives way to a slightly different form of failure in such works as *The Flying Away Monakhov* and *Pushkin House*. By now the protagonists have somewhat changed. As the writer himself ages, so do his characters, who have turned from good-for-nothings to restrained go-getters, their modest successes—reached without much initiative on their part—endowing them with a sense not so much of accomplishment as of emptiness and their own phantomlike existence. Both Monakhov and Odoevtsev are faced with the sense of "having been," dissatisfaction with lost time, lost moments, lost self. If the previous iteration of the character felt as if life were passing him by, the new version is plagued by the sense that this has already occurred. As Monakhov muses about himself, "People, thoughts, feelings, and now this place—all of it had already been. Is it possible that I too have already been? That was the question Monakhov had not wanted to allow into his consciousness."[14] This realization of life as not a continuity but rather a series of irreversible stages leading to the irrevocable end is deeply felt by *Pushkin House*'s Lev Odoevtsev, who sees the age of twenty-seven as a border dividing a human life between the inhabitance of the present-continuous and present-perfect tenses. The perception of time's implacable flow, of separation from one's youth, which suddenly constitutes an irretrievable past, is so palpable for Leva that he dedicates to this problem of being in time his infamous article "Three Prophets," of which much more will be said later in this chapter.

Suffice it to say here that Odoevtsev, a literary scholar, raises discontinuity from the level of one's personal life to the problem of culture: the question for Leva, a scion of an illustrious family of renowned literary scholars, is not just how to compensate for the sense of one's lost life, how to endure despite and beyond the end, but also, and more importantly, how to preserve and revitalize culture, to ensure its endurance despite the historical cataclysms assailing it. In "The Birds, or, The Catechizing of Man" ("Ptitsy, ili Oglashenie cheloveka"; written in the early 1970s, but then included by Bitov in his novel *The Catechized* [*Oglashennye*, translated into English as *The Monkey Link: The Pilgrimage Novel*] in the 1990s), the scale of fragility and finitude expands to encompass the whole organic world, whose continuity is under threat due to both human and suprahuman causes. One might think that the Bitovian character's anxieties have bled into the environment around him, or conversely, that despite his weakness and self-absorption, his concerns have now risen to the occasion of the all-threatening ecological crisis. It is, therefore, a natural progression of Bitov's preoccupation with weakness that, from worries about his character's flaws and failures, it grows into ethical questioning and larger environmental concerns about everything around us that cries out for preservation.

FISSION AND FRAGMENTATION

When Bitov's stories first appeared, critics immediately recognized the protagonists' divergence from the socialist-realist ideal of the positive hero but were unsure whether these anemic characters should be read as a purposeful challenge to the literary status quo, or just an accidental failure to reach it. Bitov kept the 1961 *Smena* review of his story "The Sun" ("Solntse") and included it in the commentary section of one of his collections. In harshly critiquing the story, the reviewer ascribes the main character's weakness to Bitov's weakness as a writer: "Again we sense some deficiency, something not just unsaid, but not thought out, not understood by the writer himself."[15] Another writer might have taken it as a great demerit to be found lacking in understanding; but in Bitov's worldview, recognition of one's incomplete understanding is in fact a much-valued quality of thought. Bitov's wise characters, from Odoevtsev's genius grandfather to the sage painter in "Man in a Landscape" ("Chelovek v peizazhe"), are vociferous advocates of the idea that human thought is insufficient to comprehend the totality of existence, and that *recognizing* its own insufficiency is thought's redeeming quality (more on this below).

And yet, both Russian and Western commentators cannot but disparage Bitov's incompleteness-sensing characters. Soviet critics tended to fault not only Bitov's flawed characters—"the main character of his works is 'a bad son, husband, father. As well as, probably, an unreliable comrade and a lousy friend'"[16]—but their author himself, who, they believed, must have condoned and identified with this insupportable behavior. In particular, Soviet critics saw Bitov as employing literature to self-analyze his own deficiencies.[17]

Not so with Western and post-Soviet Russian scholars, many of whom read Bitov's text as socially critical but nevertheless lament the lack of agency and integrity that distinguishes his characters from the positive hero of Soviet literature. Such interpretation strikes me as logically inconsistent: if self-assurance, ambition, and the focus on action at the expense of introspection are characteristic of the Soviet positive hero—whom Bitov finds an overall sham—then why should commentators bemoan Bitov's characters' failure to live up to this phony ideal? That is, critics seem inclined both to denounce the Soviet cult of heroism and action and also to diagnose Bitovian weakness as a symptom of societal malaise—"he is 'hollow'"—a nonhero of not-his non-heroic no-time ('standstill,' 'stagnation' [*'bezvremen'e,' 'zastoi'*])"[18]—hence a phenomenon to be overcome rather than cultivated. For example, Ann Komaromi interprets Leva Odoevtsev's deficiency as reflecting the Soviet failure to "eliminate the contradictions that had produced . . . superfluous men."[19] As Komaromi puts it, Leva "proves in most cases to be intellectually and morally weak."[20] Hers is unquestionably a negative assessment; indeed, it seems more censorious and harsher than Bitov's own. Komaromi finds Leva suffering by turns from "comfortable conformity" and "smugness," then from shame, "the sense of himself not coinciding with his ideals."[21] In this interpretation, Leva's failure appears to lie in his being both like and unlike everyone else.

Commentators' inclination to see weakness in a solely negative light reflects our general (albeit often unconscious) subscription to the charisma of power. For example, when whoever is speaking in the appendix of *Pushkin House* tells us that "I am guilty of this 'allusion,' as it is stylishly called now, and helpless against it,"[22] Pekka Pesonen interprets this literally: "In Bitov's world, there reigns a wild and free carnival, but the constant uncertainty and ambivalence generated by this carnival are oppressive."[23] Others, too, would prefer to see Bitov extricate himself from this injurious uncertainty. In their approach to a Bitovian character's lack, they tend to view the progression of the text as *filling* it, at least temporarily. For example, I. Rodnianskaya reads the arc of Bitov's text as a progression from fragmented existence to spiritual wholeness or composure (*dukhovnaia sobrannost'*).[24] Ellen Chances discerns a similar advance in "The Gamble" ("Azart"): "The movement away from a human being's self-destructive behavior toward a self-affirming approach to life."[25] Komaromi would likewise see Leva save himself, find "that creative and ethical potential [he] possesses and which might be realized in life," and ingeniously arrives at the principle of cubist discontinuity. This principle allows Komaromi, on the one hand, to see Leva's managing to finish an article as an admirable accomplishment, but on the other, to appreciate the wisdom of Leva's recognition of "the inability ever to realize oneself fully in a finished form."[26] This latter point, on the unrealizability of one's potential, is well put and incontrovertible, and Komaromi's idea of cubist discontinuity strikes me as eye-opening; but I tend to doubt we should see Leva's ability to complete an article as necessarily praiseworthy. Despite the many discontinuities in the narrative, the text remains consistent on one point: the ethics of incompletion.

The widespread desire to see Bitovian works and characters overcome rather than abide in their weakness leads many to read the apex of Leva Odoevtsev's life in *Pushkin House*—his "duel" with his archnemesis Mitishatiev and the collateral destruction of the museum that he is supposed to guard—as the result of his sudden capacity to overcome, for a brief moment in time, his constitutive weakness, to rise above it. Andrianova speaks of Leva's transformation at the moment when he leaps to the defense of his idol Pushkin's honor by dueling with the offender: "Leva's moral instability, spinelessness, and inability to resist the manipulations of others suddenly turn into the complete opposite; this is no longer a pitiful modern Eugene trying to ride a lion, but a real horseman, a knight of honor, whose speech now features uncharacteristic turns of phrase and harsh intonations."[27]

The scholar admires Leva's plucky challenge to Mitishatiev, but it seems notable that it is only in response to Mitishatiev's provocation that Leva summons this courage. That is, he is once again unable to resist Mitishatiev's manipulations. Nor does his act show any deliberateness or strength of will; in fact, Leva is described as *bezumen* ("out of his mind"), and thus still has much in common with Pushkin's hapless Eugene, whose infamous mounting of the lion statue, as Andrianova reminds us, he copycats earlier. Nor is his duel particularly original, but rather precisely an act of hackneyed repetition. The duel was practically an institution, almost compulsory for all nineteenth-century gentlemen, whenever occasion demanded.[28]

It has been noted by many (and with reason) that in his mad lunge to fight Mitishatiev, Leva's physical appearance miraculously and recognizably assumes traits of Pushkin. It is almost as if Leva becomes possessed by Pushkin. This acquisition of Pushkinian features is presented in a nonlinear, collage-like manner, so that the reader is forced to attempt to reconstitute the fragments into a coherent image, as when looking at a cubist portrait: "His eyes had moved wide apart, they swam on the sides of his face like two cold fish. Stubble had sprouted on his death mask. He suddenly had a lot of hair—tangled curls. His neck had grown thin, and it stuck up loosely from his collar."[29] From these textual fragments, we could say that the subsequent burst of energy resulting in the museum's destruction stems from two simultaneous nuclear reactions: fusion with another nucleus, that of Pushkin, and fission—that is, Leva's dissolution of the boundaries of the self, a kind of falling apart. Leva's merging with or transformation into his idol Pushkin is an exultant loss of self (rather than a moment of self-discovery).

Notably, the portrait concludes with a trait that in fact reminds us of Leva's spinelessness and impotence: "His hands just dangled, unnecessary [*ni k chemu*]."[30] This burst of energy, accompanied by a loss of self, lacks a conclusive end that would give meaning to everything that precipitated it: after all, in the end, no one dies in this "duel," not even Leva. Indeed, if read as a reenactment of Pushkin's own duel, which was lugubrious and so supremely meaningful as to be almost Golgothic in Russian culture, then it would be hard not to see this repetition as an embrace of failure.

Despite, then, the positioning of this duel and museum destruction as the book's most momentous action, its climax, it nevertheless shares with all other aspects of Leva's life the same transience and inconclusiveness. Haven't we been prepared throughout the novel precisely for this? Cannot we read this incident as the latest, most glaring manifestation of Leva's weakness, rather than as its overcoming? And Leva's integration and identification with Pushkin, his loss of himself in the latter—isn't this, rather than some apotheosis in the grand tradition of literature (i.e., some communion with genius), rather just a function of his profession, that of literary scholar (rather than writer), someone who lives by literature, but is not a writer? ("But what a profession I've picked for him!" says Bitov in an appendix. "Don't be a writer, but write anyway. Live by literature, on literature, with literature, but not in it."[31]) And doesn't this moment of the historic explosion of Leva, his rupture from the boundaries of the self and violation of the museum's wholeness and order, epitomize all the crumblings that Leva has so far undergone due to his constitutive weakness?

In fact, the very influence of others on Leva (which Andrianova adduces to describe his spinelessness) is described in the text as fission, decomposition:

Our Faina and Mitishatyev are also that same Lyova: either they compose Lyova's soul, or his soul splits into two parts, three parts, [splinters on] them [*razdvaivaetsia, rastraivaetsia, rasshchepliaetsia na nikh*]. Using the rules of the parallelogram of forces, we have substituted from the numerous forces affecting Lyova two or three equivalent vector arrows, thick and bold, which lie across Lyova Odoevtsev's amorphous soul and crystallize it under pressure.[32]

Curiously, this very crumbling that Leva constantly exhibits stems from his sense of shame, as for example, in this episode where Leva crumbles when his two "friends," the antisemitic, vulgar Mitishatiev and the Semitic, genteel Blank, finally and fatally intersect: "And while old Blank, on the other end, was crumbling in compliments [the literal meaning of *rassypalsia v komplimentakh*, "showering *X* with compliments" or "complimenting profusely"], Leva, on this end, was crumbling, but crumbling literally [*rassypalsia, no rassypalsia bukval'no*], as Mitishatiev could see."[33] And, finally, crumbling is associated with love. In the novel, the topic of love as a weakness and the lover as a weakling is brought up in a conversation between Leva and his beloved tormentress Faina. But the sensation of crumbling from love is experienced by Leva in his last encounter with the unloved Albina, for whom Leva suddenly and belatedly feels a futile depth of feeling, *after* she has finally disentangled herself from him. This sudden burst of feeling is described as crumbling to bits: "But had he suddenly disintegrated, crumbled, cracked [*raspalsia, rassypalsia, raskololsia*], and turned to her at last with feeling—it would already have been too late. The irreversibility staggered Lyova."[34] The novel would thus seem to make a direct connection between Leva's propensity for fission and a particular relationship with another, a kind of openness to becoming pervaded or invaded by the other, which is what occurs when Leva "duels" on behalf of Pushkin, in effect becoming him.

Could we then perhaps read the climactic episode of Leva's uprising as an instance of living up to the potential of his weakness? After all, early on the novel prepares us for the explosion at the end by telling us of Leva's inner tension, stemming from his aristocratic marginality, his secret nonbelonging, which from a different perspective appears as chosenness (both weakness and strength): "Lyova, then, would be hauled to the surface and blown to bits [*razorvat'sia na kusochki*] by the intolerability of his own internal pressure!"[35]

Curiously, Leva's very potential for fission and explosion metaphorically associates him with genius, which in several of Bitov's works is defined precisely by this ability for radical dispersal. In *Pushkin House*, for example, Leva's distinctive contribution to literary scholarship is his paper "Three Prophets," in which he compares three approaches to the poet's craft—Pushkin's suprapersonal consciousness, his godlike immanence in all; Lermontov's individualism, his precious attachment to his discrete *I*; and Tiutchev's envious yearning but inability to be like Pushkin. Pushkin's capacity to exit the parameters of his discrete *I*, to exist in everything, is a quality he shares with the figure of a genius as described by a loquacious painter in "Man in a Landscape," who adduces dispersal, in a far more pessimistic vein, as a genius's distinct fate:

> The genius's fate is a cosmic catastrophe, but not in the sense that we pity him on the same scale, or that it has a cosmic bearing on us; nor in the sense that he would've given us much more if he hadn't burned in the denser atmospheres; but in the sense that [geniuses] share a cosmic nature. They have all exploded and dissipated into dust, much like our little globe is going to burst any minute. Humanity is nearing a catastrophe of the same scale that every genius has lived through.[36]

Here the ultimate destiny of both genius and the world is radical dispersal. What makes the fate of a weakling like Leva akin to that of a genius and the universe itself, then, is their tenacity and continuance under the threat of dispersal.

THE BOMB AND "THE IDLER"

In his Nobel Prize acceptance speech in 1950, William Faulkner explained the problem of literature in the atomic age: "Our tragedy today is a general and universal physical fear so long sustained by now that we can even bear it. There are no longer problems of the spirit. There is only the question: When will I be blown up?" Faulkner continues that a human being cannot be in conflict with himself when he is preoccupied with the thought of impending death.[37] In order to accomplish anything, one must forget about death; but this is impossible when the prospect of imminent annihilation becomes a condition of everyday life. This sense of living at the end of time would go on to permeate postmodernist writing, resulting in a symptomatically vexed relationship to futurity.

In his famous attack on postmodernism in *Postmodernism, or the Cultural Logic of Late Capitalism*, Fredric Jameson charges postmodernism with "a new depthlessness, which finds its prolongation both in contemporary 'theory' and in a whole new culture of the image or the simulacrum" and "a consequent weakening of historicity."[38] In this view, the postmodernist artist or writer is capable only of reproducing their own (postmodern) condition. Echoing Jameson's argument, Dale Peck decries Rick Moody's *The Black Veil* as part of "a tradition that has systematically divested itself of any ability to comment on anything other than its own inability to comment on anything."[39] And yet, while such a description might also seem perfectly applicable to Bitov's writings, with their consistent reprise of writerly failure, Ellen Chances argues, convincingly in my view, that Bitov hardly embraces postmodern depthlessness, and indeed would rather counter it.

In her book *Andrei Bitov: The Ecology of Inspiration*, Chances explains how Bitov's background in geology influences his writing: in his works, he invariably imagines the present world as an accumulated history of layers of past experience. According to Chances, Bitov insists on the need to preserve cultural continuity.[40] How does one write, then, when this continuity is threatened, when one exists without the prospect of futurity? How to continue in the absence of continuation?

Most scholars pinpoint the great rupture in continuity that Bitov grapples with as the October Revolution, which made a fundamental break in Russian history—the forcible abandonment of the previous culture, and the creation of a new one as if from scratch. The Stalinist purges showed the catastrophic proportions of the disruption, and the vicissitudes of life in post-Stalinist Russia indeed supplied Bitov's characters with the traumatic baggage they struggle to bear in *Pushkin House* and the author's other works.[41] However, perhaps due to Bitov's geological training, his writings exhibit symptoms of preoccupation with other kinds of ultimacies and finitudes as well.

In particular, the dread of nuclear war is manifest in Bitov's works in the form of metaphors of explosion, allusions to bombs, and recurrent discussions of the prospect of nuclear winter. In fact, global nuclear war on the one hand, and the Soviet project on the other—as the purported triumph of human reason and final end of the progressive movement of history—are often presented by Bitov as stages of the same historical process, in which the latter, geographically limited end, offers a preview of postapocalyptic things to come once nuclear winter arrives. For example, before undertaking to describe a perfectly ordinary Soviet suburban locale in "Man in a Landscape" that is so ordinary as to not even warrant a name—"I won't name it. Its anonymity will be my excuse"—the narrator prefaces with the comment: "No, this isn't a description after an atomic attack."[42] Tracing allusions to nuclear destruction in Bitov's works will allow us to understand how the author conceives of the problem of culture, its succession and endurance, in conjunction with the problem of life as an ecological network of ties between humans and their environment, in general.

Among Bitov's early stories, there are several instances of the topic of nuclear catastrophe broached in conversation between protagonists and their fathers; the former typically recall these exchanges amid ruminations on the purpose of writing and the possibility and necessity of communication.[43] In "The Idler," the morbidly indolent protagonist, suffering from his unmanly lack of action, is juxtaposed to his father and the latter's circle of friends, who demonstrate their masculine activeness by admiringly discussing scientific "progress," especially the nuclear bomb. This father, like the fathers of other of Bitov's protagonists, enjoys reading popular science magazines and discussing remarkable tidbits found in them. The idler's father expresses awe over the recently discovered chemical element that would allow a bomb the size of a walnut to devastate a continent. The father delves deeper into antimatter-related musings about the possibility of devising a still more impressive miniaturization: a bomb the size of, say, a pinhead destroying the whole planet:

> "And that's not all," says father, "furthermore," he says, "but this is secret," father says, "other elements have been found beyond the hundredth . . . !" So they, these elements, according to what father says, have exhibited such amazing explosive capacity that take a bomb the size of a walnut—and a continent's gone. Suppose some journalist brings it in in his pocket, drops it somewhere—and that's it. And rockets aren't necessary . . . "Aren't necessary?" I say. "Aren't necessary," father says. "But in general—are they necessary?" I say. "You puppy [or "punk," *shchenok*]," father says, "I've been through the whole war." "So that's why you don't understand," I say. "[Punk]!" father says. "And that's not all," says the old man. "If there were some antimatter from the anti-world—then one pin head would suffice for the whole planet."[44]

Just as in other stories, these discussions inevitably cause intergenerational discord, as the son fails to find such a feat of absolute creativity, which leads to absolute destruction, in any way appealing. In response to the father's narrative of total annihilation, the son tells his own story that only appears to come out of nowhere:

> "And I was told," I say, "of course this was in America . . . in one of the secret places there were five submarines, side by side. And on one of them a sailor was sent above to shovel the snow. But he refused categorically. Then they sent another one. It's his—the other's—brother, who was telling me. So he shovels, and under him, on the boat, a fire had started and just couldn't be stopped. And the commander isn't there—he's on shore. And the fellow upstairs still does not know anything (he is shoveling snow), but he just feels: there is something heating up under his feet—but he pays no attention to it. And suddenly, there's this ga-asp! The boat blew up. And everybody else with it, and the fellow who was shoveling was thrown up in the air and flew off a

few kilometers—and straight into a pile of snow. And the captain was walking along the shore at this time and was just then passing a street light. His forehead bumped into the pole—and he fell dead on the spot. And there were no survivors. Only the one in the snow pile—he alone remained."[45]

Bewildered by this narrative, the father asks the son its relevance to the conversation. When the son cannot find an answer, the father predictably attributes the son's seemingly non sequitur story to his characteristic fragility: "You don't know how to drink."[46]

And yet, despite the slapsticky detail of the commander's forehead-on-lamppost demise, the story aptly responds to the father's awesome tale of all-destroying power. The son parries the father's annihilation narrative, that is, with one of his own, but told not from the sublime, suprahuman perspective of planetary conflagration but from the standpoint of a hapless human being, a sole survivor. It sounds like an anecdote: the most unfortunate and lowliest sailor, who could not even dodge the universally despised task of shoveling snow, ends up being the only one to survive the explosion. And yet, the emphasis on being left alone, via the repetition of "there were no survivors" and "he alone remained," suggests a terrifying sense of abandonment. We are to understand that from this perspective of an ordinary human being, sole survival would be a horrific rather than desirable outcome. Bitov here seems to be exploring the implications of the neutron bomb that so amazes the father—its "selling point" is that it destroys all local life but leaves property intact, to be theoretically used by subsequent invaders—and showing its "practicality" to be, in fact, the height of absurdity: "It suddenly seems to me that this terror of [father's] is feigned and that, actually, he even admires it. That a bomb like that will fall—and all that's alive will perish, but that even the windowpanes in houses will remain intact. And no contagion—come in, help yourself."[47]

The son's story obliquely expresses his dissatisfaction with his father's seeming acceptance, even appreciation, of the idea of going on with one's life after such destruction of human (or even all organic) life ("come in, help yourself"). Along similar lines, one of the very first ecocritical texts, Joseph Meeker's *The Comedy of Survival* (1974), makes an interesting observation on the detrimental effect of tragedy as a genre on human self-conception vis-à-vis the world. According to Meeker, tragedy raised the moral concerns of its hero over the biological imperative of survival:

As Aristotle puts it, comedy imitates the actions of men who are subnormal or inferior to the social norm and tragedy imitates the actions of superior men. . . . Tragedy shows man's potential strength and greatness. This is true only if it is assumed that the metaphysical morality that encourages man to rise above his natural environment and his animal origins is mankind's best hope for the future.[48]

In this interpretation, tragedy contributed to pernicious Western anthropocentrism, since the tragic hero's story is that of a valiant attempt to rise above one's environment, disregarding human life—in fact, all life—in the process. Meeker, a biologist turned literary critic, maintains that tragedy valorizes the human mastery of nature, of the environment, and is thus implicated in the ecological crisis we find ourselves in: "The tragic view of man, for all its flattering optimism, has led to cultural and biological disasters, and it is time to look for alternatives which might encourage better the survival of our own and other species." Meeker believes that comedy represents such an alternative: "Comedy demonstrates that man is durable even though he may be weak, stupid, and undignified. . . . Comedy is concerned with muddling through, not with progress or perfection. . . . In the world as revealed by comedy, the important thing is to live and to encourage life even though it is probably meaningless to do so."[49] In prioritizing its hero's adventures in muddling through life, claims Meeker, comedy ascribes great value to life, both human and nonhuman, and as such it integrates humans into their environment, rather than distancing humans from it.

The truth of Meeker's distinction may be seen in the juxtaposition of Bitov's weak son's comedic story and his dignified father's tragic imagination. Epitomized in the tale of the latter is the awesome and grotesque tragedy of human hubris, of the aspiration to master nature leading to its annihilation; all life is devalued for the sake of some metaphysical victory. As a rebuttal, the son offers his story of the most undignified, most comedic hero, who in the proper Aristotelian fashion is unworthy of his lucky fate and unable to appreciate it. It is completely in line with Meeker's argument that in the son's comedic tale of survival, it is precisely the life of all that becomes the key value, the most important aim.

THE BOMB AND WRITER'S BLOCK IN "LIFE IN WINDY WEATHER"

A similar interaction between a father and son takes place in "Life in Windy Weather" ("Zhizn' v vetrennuiu pogodu," 1967). Here again, the son, Sergei, is an ineffectual writer, suffering from writer's block, and the father is an aficionado of popular science and nuclear power who enjoys regaling his son with stories of awesome discoveries and technological advances. In one of the most memorable moments of the story, the writer and his father have yet another Bitovian conversation on nuclear war. The father remarks that in such a conflict, the most important day is the second one, because the remaining humanity will be so dispersed that the technology of communication would be key. Symptomatically, the writer-son objects: "Why . . . would you need these communications on the second day when on the first no one would be left alive anyway?"[50] The writer's thinking is conditioned by this radical finitude that makes everything superfluous; this thinking also marks a key ideological difference of his generation from that of his father, the "manly men" inclined to "win" a nuclear conflict, to attempt the reconciliation of human ends with the end of (most) humans. The conversation abruptly ends, as the father feels insulted and embarrassed by the force of his son's logic, and the son feels superior to yet alienated from the person he loves.

Importantly, the son's triumph is not experienced as such, but rather as a failure; after all, it leads to blockage of the conversation and a weakening of connection: "They drove for a while in silence. His father tried to think of a new topic, and not finding one, took up his most pointed and cunning subject: his son's work and affairs. [Sergei[51]] continued to think about his father with the same sadness and tenderness and was not at all irritated (and this was a complete exception to the rule) when his father stepped into his field and began to make up some absurd, hostile thing."[52] Here, the theme of disconnectedness and loneliness intersects with the son's difficulties with writing, which the father surely brings up to regain the upper hand.

The father's search for a new theme, in a story dedicated to the writer's own difficulty in finding a theme to write about, demonstrates why one would want to write in the first place—namely, to establish connection and continuity. (Fittingly, Bitov's characters are often in possession of fathers, grandfathers, and sons with whom they are perpetually trying to arrive at an understanding; the emphasis on familial ties makes it clear that Bitov thinks of connectivity both synchronically, as the togetherness of the living, and diachronically, as a succession.) There must be, we gather, a connection between the son's writer's block and his desire to establish contact and connection, to overcome loneliness. After all, right after the sad conversation with the father, Sergei is visited by a nightmarish vision that not only repeats the sailor's predicament discussed above, but is also apparently the most persistent, recurrent terror to plague Sergei's own life. Just as often occurs with him, that is, he now once again imagines an atomic mushroom cloud rising in the distance in front of the family car, signaling the demise of everything except for one sole, wretched survivor—himself: "the destruction of everything dear to him . . . and his own empty, useless preservation."[53]

Being with others, then, is an essential precondition of living for Bitov. In his chapter on Bitov's graphomania, Richard Borden sees this author's oeuvre as exemplifying extreme solipsism. There is, to be sure, some justice in Borden's assertion that Bitov's circular writing—that is, his writing about what it means to write—is introverted by definition. But it seems that in "Life in Windy Weather," Bitov rather establishes the interdependency of writing and *living*, and living for Bitov means being with others. In Bitov's universe, one cannot live disconnectedly (this is what Chances calls Bitov's ecological thinking—the interdependence of everyone and everything within the universe[54]). Furthermore, in this particular text, Bitov's writer attempts to arrive at the kind of writing that, instead of precluding life (i.e., connectedness), facilitates it, establishes connections.

"Life in Windy Weather" represents the fictional diary of a young writer who moves with his wife and infant son to a summerhouse. This move is supposed to take the writer out of his usual surroundings, so that in solitude, in communion with nature, far from the deadening hum of city life, he can rekindle his ability to write. The summerhouse was to bring him in contact with life itself, with authentic existence in a Tolstoyan vein. But in particular, the process of simplification, of reducing the elements of life to their bare essentials, necessitates understanding what those essentials really are. For example, the protagonist realizes that the first precondition of creating is simply to be alive: "Consciously, he had already understood for a long time . . . that the main thing is simply *to live*, to be alive, and therefore no matter what your condition is—fruitful or unfruitful—as long as you are alive, not benumbed."[55]

Like other of Bitov's characters of this period (e.g., Monakhov and Odoevtsev), Sergei senses his own maturation as a kind of atrophy, a deadening. He has already reached the age of twenty-seven, and so "has already been." The sense of being truly alive emanates from the writer's tiny son, who is continuously reaching out to the world and is deeply invested in everything that takes place around him. The writer cannot but be stirred by his son's artless, spontaneous joy at the sight of him, by the child's "outstretched hand and [by how] his face lit up with joy at the mere fact that they saw and recognized one another."[56] The same indiscriminate joy and urge for contact overtake the son at the sight of everything around him: "He stretched his hand out to what he saw before him and said all the words he knew: 'Mama, papa, wawa, goo, all.' 'All, all, all!,' he said joyfully, pointing to what he saw."[57] The infant son's impulsive attempt to reach everything, through touching and naming it, is described as both boundless altruism ("He was truly grateful to his son for so generously sharing his life with him") and utter dependency ("the exactions of weakness struck Sergei").[58]

Experiencing this flood of sensations and feelings, the son is somehow able, without any special effort, to be fully present in himself, yet fully oriented toward others, evincing the complete symmetry between inner being and outward orientation for which not just Sergei but many of Bitov's characters yearn.[59] Sergei finds that the son helps him to overcome his own

160

finitude, not in the conventional sense of procreation as self-replication but in the intensity of feeling toward everything that the son awakens in him: he begins "to feel a tenderness for everything . . . [begins] to live."[60] These feelings of tenderness toward his son, and toward the world that brings the child so much joy, make him perceive his own life as not yet over, as if he has endured beyond, or at least postponed, his own end: "He . . . thought with surprise and ecstasy that it hadn't broken off, hadn't stopped, that it could still happen to him."[61]

GENIUS, RISK-TAKING, FUTURITY

The predicament of the genius described earlier in this chapter is a fraught one. We are given to understand that the genius's thought and creativity is expansive and explosive: expansion beyond the boundaries of the self ensures its endurance, but also threatens the self with fragmentation, dissipation. In "Life in Windy Weather," creativity, especially when still extant *in potentia*, at the moment of its conception, is described as this kind of expansion, as a kind of brimming with ideas. This may be precisely why Sergei is unable to register them on paper, as it would require the abandonment of this state of fullness, the artificial limitation of this plenitude. Thinking of creative avenues available to him, the author describes himself as bursting with directions he can potentially take: "The variety of projects he thought of tormented him and he just couldn't decide which to take up first. And if he forced himself by great effort to settle on just one thing chosen at random, he still didn't know where to begin; too many things rose up before him, too many things filled his head to the bursting point."[62] The question becomes how to keep this balance—how to continue expanding without exploding.

At one particularly poignant moment, Sergei imagines a scenario opposite to the usual one in which he is the sole survivor while the world around him explodes. In this new, reverse vision, everyone survives except him. He has taken in so much of the surrounding world and expands to such a degree as to explode, infusing everything with himself. This contemplation of expansion beyond the boundaries of the self, both catastrophic and salvific, suffuses the protagonist with fulfillment rather than dread. In an otherwise rather temperate narrative, this exhilarating, explosive moment occurs when Sergei is surveying the countryside with his son, Adamically naming things:

And all of this as if lying on one axis which coincided with his gaze and the wind, united by the cupola of the sky, as by a legato, and brought to a completion within him, Sergei—all of this and the seemingly endless continuation of the axis beyond visible bounds—the feeling of the symmetry was the happiest of all feelings. It was a pinnacle, a summit, an explosion, and in the next moment, whether the train left or the boy moved from his place or the cow . . . the axis fell apart, and [Sergei] felt a blissful emptiness: he existed now in the greenery of the meadow, in the boy in the meadow, in the train moving away, in the sky, in his son, in each and every thing. His life exploded, sprayed out, and seemed to flow away and fill everything with meaning and life. He felt like a god, nowhere and in everything, embracing and permeating the world.[63]

Sergei feels godlike in this selfless existence in everything, and we are reminded of the fate of the godlike genius, who is doomed to likewise expand, explode, and find continuity or endure in the world he left behind.[64] It is not surprising, then, that preceding this sublime moment, as Sergei talks to his son, pointing out phenomena in the world and naming them, he perceives in this use of language "a kind of genius."[65] Specifically, what makes this act of naming seem like a work of genius to him is its sense of beginning; naming means calling into existence that which is yet to come: "He felt as if he were on some higher threshold beyond which everything truly begins."[66]

In Western philosophy, the understanding of genius, especially its exceptionality, stems from the idea of genius's prematurity, an ability to see something yet to come. According to Kant, genius "is a talent for producing that for which no definite rule can be given, and not an aptitude in the way of cleverness for what can be learned according to some rule."[67] Vis-à-vis rules, genius is of necessity exceptional. On the other hand, according to Kant, only that which complies with certain rules of artistry can be called art, and so a genius must then be a creator, a model of a future rule. Art, moreover, harbors the possibility of, and an openness to, this coming of genius, this rupture in its system of rules—otherwise no invention would be possible. In his article "Genius Is What Happens: Derrida and Kant on Genius, Rule-Following and the Event," Michael Haworth draws a lineage from this train of thought to Derrida's paradoxical assertion that "the only possible invention would be the invention of the impossible."[68] It is the purview of genius to make possible that which does not exist—that is, the impossible. Similarly, Arthur Schopenhauer associates genius with futurity, with an ability to see into the future, which is precisely what separates it from talent: "Mere men of talent always come at the right time . . . . The genius, on the other hand, lights on his age like a comet into the paths of the planets, to whose wholly regulated and comprehensible arrangement its wholly eccentric course is foreign. . . . Talent is like the marksman who hits a target which others cannot reach; genius is like the marksman who hits a target . . . which others cannot even see."[69]

It is this unique power of foresight that Pushkin senses in himself and articulates in his poem "The Prophet" ("Prorok"), hence the title of the poem. And according to Lev Odoevtsev's interpretation in his article "Three Prophets," it is this very poetic gift that Tiutchev envies and casts doubt on in his poem "Madness" ("Bezumie"). And Leva's point is well-taken,[70] since Tiutchev's poem does in fact contain an almost direct echo of Pushkin's, especially at the very end, where it exposes prophetic gift as a delusion: "It thinks it hears the roiling streams / In subterranean light / The cradled murmur of their dreams / Their strident surge to light!"[71] And yet, Leva's article informs us that despite calling this prophetic ability into question, deep down Tiutchev recognizes its presence in others and its unbearable absence in himself. To corroborate this point, Leva cites another poem by Tiutchev: "Others are given by Nature / An instinct prophetic and blind, / They can feel, they can hear the waters / Even in earth's dark depths."[72]

Furthermore, the loquacious painter in "Man in a Landscape," in his impromptu lecture on the essence of genius, makes a pronouncement that might suggest that, for Bitov, the presumption of this gift, even if erroneous and possibly delusional, is already a sign *of* genius. Discussing Bitov's beloved topic of genius, the painter remarks that this label applies to a person who *mnogo dopustil*. This wording has been translated as "made large assumptions," but importantly, the Russian *dopustit'* has a broad range of meanings, from "to presume" or "assume" (in the sense of imagining a possibility) to, when used with *oshibka*, "make a mistake." The painter explains: "The greatness of the design is the greatness of its primordial error. The artist's design always conceals in its foundation an *assumption*, something that cannot be. . . . The genius's sufferings in this struggle with his primordial assumption are immeasurable, but a genius is a man who has made large assumptions. Without the design's original falsehood, there would be nothing, only lifeless matter is exact."[73] Similarly, in Leva's article, Pushkin's genius is in this risk-taking, this daring—the ability to rise above the quotidian and petty worries about the opinion of others, or even personal safety.

Let us compare this genius to our Sergei in "Life in Windy Weather," who, brimming with possibilities, is mortally afraid of making a mistake or wrong choice. This is not a fear that stops the genius. According to the philosophizing painter, the genius is always overproductive, precisely because he allows himself this risk; he is not deterred by the fear of being wrong: "From the underlying incorrect assumption, endlessly rectified inaccuracies are diffused over the whole creation as the design is executed. This labor of correction and sharper definition is what creates a work of art."[74]

But there exists a still greater risk: when Sergei settles on one choice out of the multitude of possibilities, does he not, of necessity, limit himself, his limitless imagination? As already discussed, Bitov's writer-characters are constantly oscillating between the urge to complete something and the urge to keep going—to postpone completion by all means. Stopping too soon would mean denying oneself further self-realization, the further burgeoning of life. Yet, according to the painter in "Man in a Landscape," every genius, despite enormous overproductivity, stands as the "incarnation" of "ultimate failure."[75] We can interpret this unexpected assertion of genius as maximally unrealized potential through Derrida's above-mentioned paradox. If, indeed, a genius makes the impossible possible—and the impossible should be a far larger category than the possible—then the genius's sphere of action must be truly inexhaustible, and his potential, therefore, maximally unrealized. In his writerly failure to live up to his potential, to produce, the weakling then approximates the genius, even if his degree of failure is much less catastrophic—because he has much less, that is, to lose. Most importantly: in the radical unrealizability of their potential, the weakling and the genius are kin.

With the one difference that the genius is not hampered by the worry of a premature, personal end. This imaginative leap, which according to Schopenhauer allows the genius to see what others cannot, stems from, in the philosopher's opinion, the power of genius's thought to resist the personal, subjective, and isolating will to live, and to assume the suprapersonal view that transcends limited self-interest:

> Now, as this demands a complete forgetting of our own person and of its relations and connexions, *the gift of genius* is nothing but the most complete *objectivity*, i.e., the objective tendency of the mind, as opposed to the subjective directed to one's own person, i.e., to the will. Accordingly, genius is the capacity to remain in a state of pure perception, to lose oneself in perception, to remove from the service of the will the knowledge which originally existed only for this service. In other words, genius is the ability to leave entirely out of sight our own interest, our willing, and our aims, and consequently to discard entirely our own personality for a time, in order to remain *pure knowing subject*, the clear eye of the world; and this not merely for moments, but with the necessary continuity and conscious thought to enable us to repeat by deliberate art what has been apprehended.[76]

According to Schopenhauer, this incredible ability to overcome one's personal interests, including the egotistical will to live, is something that a genius can experience "not merely at moments, but for a sufficient length of time." By contrast, in the case of our weakling, such breakthrough moments as the one that occurs with Sergei, when he somehow manages to apprehend life in its entirely and without himself in it, is a temporary affair. It is to be expected that this moment of exalted expansion does not last. And, indeed, in a brief second, Sergei's imagination, via some kind of defense mechanism, puts the whole scene in reverse, and he manages to regain the individual borders that make him a definitive, limited, and ordinary human being: "Then as if by the reversal of a strip of film in which they play back an explosion, where all the fragments fly back and the smoke and flame flow back, thicker, and disappear like a genie into a bottle and only a smooth space remains as if nothing had exploded, Sergei separated himself off into a tiny point in space and felt as if he were drunk."[77] The impossible task of a creator is how to enjoy both the state of explosive, godlike being in everything and the stable fixity of being human.[78]

THE EFFORTS OF THE WEAKLING IN "NOTES FROM THE CORNER"

Lacking the awesome strength and intrepidity of the genius, what, then, can a weakling do to avert catastrophe, to, if not generate then at least record, preserve, and prolong life both in himself and for others? This is the question Bitov explores in the companion piece to "Life in Windy Weather," "Notes from the Corner," arriving here at the realization that the weakling-writer might just be able to persevere not through strength (*sila*) but through something approximating it: *usilie* ("effort"). Luckily, effortful creation is precisely the weakling-writer's forte.

"Life in Windy Weather" ends in peaceful contentment. But it is a semifictional piece, and Bitov published it in conjunction with journal entries that narrate the same events—the seclusion in the summerhouse and attempts at writing—from a slightly different perspective. As a counterpart to the Tolstoyan "Life in Windy Weather" (which oscillates between apathy and contentment, between dissolution and reassemblage of the self in others), the actual diary, which bears the Dostoevskian title "Notes from the Corner," is markedly more pessimistic. The epigraph to the story is taken from Bitov's "The Bus," discussed earlier in this chapter, and prepares the reader for what is to come: "What should I write about? About this? Or that? Or about that? But, there's no point [*Ni k chemu*]"[79]—which yet again initiates the theme of the futility of writing, or for that matter doing anything, in the face of the imminent end.

If the main sentiment of the fictional narrative is discontented apathy, the prevailing affect of the diary is terror—provoked once more by the prospect of annihilation and the impossibility of preserving life via the force of writing. At one point, the writer ponders how to respond to disaster:

If millions of whatever it is, be it Jews or artists or simply live people, were to be collected and led off somewhere under convoy to a cliff to be shot, to be destroyed, and one of them (it's not hard to make a mistake on such a large scale!) suddenly turns out not to be a Jew but an Urdmurt, not to be an artist but a plumber, not to be alive but a corpse, then he would yell, "What an injustice!" I'm not speaking on his behalf.[80]

The analogy points to the fear that under the condition of the common predicament of all (annihilation), to write about anything else—that is, to imagine that discontinuity does not concern you—would mean failing to speak on behalf of humanity, excluding oneself from this predicament, being already a corpse rather than a living being. The nightmarish terror, worse than the terror of annihilation itself, is to be irrelevant, in the meaning of "unrelated," "standing apart,"[81] although it seems impossible to be relevant during a catastrophe, and for that matter attempting to exclude oneself from it seems delusive. Everyone will eventually end in the ditch.

The historical cataclysmic event becomes a sign of existential condition. From the standpoint of doomed humanity, or, even more so, doomed organic life (the collective we), the writer ruminates:

> We must, or maybe we had better never, understand that our perfectly natural internal resistance to and indignation with the implacability of nature cannot be taken as a proof of the existence of a goal, of meaning, or of progress. Our scrambling [*karabkanie*], overshadowed by the lies of the goal, is essential for the life of consciousness in nature but shouldn't be taken as a confirmation of our ideas, because the ideas gave rise to the scrambling, not nature. Winter naturally ends the year. Death naturally ends life. Humanity will naturally come to its end. As will the solar system.[82]

The writer finds himself in a peculiar position where he both affirms as true, and denies as harmful, the realization that a creative personality cannot do anything ("We must, or maybe we had better never") to prevent the inexorable course of humanity into the ditch. "We must understand"—because it would be delusional to fancy oneself as possessed of agency. "We had better never understand"—because apprehension of the futility of everything would plunge one into a state of despair and stupor: "Such a desert and death arose that only weakness was left, weakness that made social life into bookkeeping, love into lust, friendship into the desire for self-confirmation, and creativity into vanities. I couldn't even shoot myself except with my finger-gun."[83] Bitov's writer is torn between two opposing dicta: one that calls for delusional agency, the other calling for a knowing weakness (*knowing* in the sense that it discerns, behind all lofty words and ideas, only void—the kind of despondent wisdom that Bitov would clearly very much like to counter).

166

Finding himself in this dead end, Bitov arrives at the idea of God, which sounds here like a kind of conceptual loophole, a call to some entity extant beyond himself that would allow him to keep going, would validate the "scrambling" that is life and help him contribute to the scrambling of all: "And the feeling was such that if death did pass, it would pass not in the way a disease passes and not in the way that feelings are forgotten, but only by a miracle, only if that of which I had not even an inkling were to help me. And I said, Help me, God!"[84] Curiously, it appears here as if the weakling-writer suddenly acquires a genius-like ability to invent that which does not exist ("that of which I had not even an inkling"), to invent God. The idea of God gives permission to turn writing into an activity that one can do in spite of its apparent futility, validating the writer's persistent efforts as worthwhile. Importantly, the newfound idea of God does not eradicate the previous nihilism. There is still no teleological aim posited. Writing in no way contributes to any kind of progressive movement forward, any kind of conception of becoming. On the contrary, the idea of becoming is suspicious in Bitov, especially since, if any progression can be discerned in his writings, it is always the movement away from childhood, from the time when one is most alive, and toward always unwelcome death. Writing represents an attempt to "scramble" in the face of this process, to stay as much alive as possible and as long as possible, and God here is that authority that validates these efforts at scrambling. (Which not incidentally recalls the above-mentioned metaphor of the fishing turned floundering in the same text.)

The author who, from the very beginning of his writing career, continuously ponders his own and others' weaknesses, and questions the very idea of strength, thus arrives at a concept that exists somewhere in between weakness and strength—namely, *usilie*. In English, the word would be translated as "effort" or "exertion," but the root of the Russian word establishes a connection between *sila* ("strength" or "force"), the provenance of the strong, and *usilie*, the provenance of the weak.

The cornered writer's very strength lies precisely in his capacity to go on with his fruitless efforts, increasing and prolonging them, and by these means offering resistance to death, understood here both as the ultimate cessation of life and the intermittent despair that might lead to the deadening of feeling ("the crisis and death of consciousness"[85]). The writer comes to realize that by writing about one's weakness, one does not decrease, but in fact increases this sense of despair. But any sense or sensation connotes life. One awakens oneself by making oneself *feel*, by increasing one's feelings, even if the feelings awoken are of one's own weakness and failure. For example, the writer explains the effect of having written about some extremely shameful event that occurred in his past and the accompanying sense of social demise:

I . . . created the image not only of a powerful storyteller, but also of a man capable of being so shaken and stunned that he can't get over his pain, as though the recollection of my "murder" tormented me and wouldn't leave me. . . . I was completely sincere in my game and believed in it, and after all it wasn't only a game, there was also what had really happened that I was telling everyone about at the time, only it was weak, just a bit weak, and I dramatized it in my exposition and repetition. We intensify our feelings by expressing them, after all. . . . Perhaps this is what creativity is.[86]

For the diary writer, then, writing is not just some compulsion, as it might seem from this interminable dilation on one's difficulties with writing, but a continuous effort, a search for strength: "Here I find the strength to write this emptiness" (*vot nakhozhu ia sily pisat' etu pustotu*[87]); "I'd like to say something about [this]—something more detailed and particular—below, if only we can make it to this 'below.'"[88] This search for strength is a priori doomed to failure; human beings are by definition weak, and no effort on their part can prevent their eventual end. But instead the writer will attain a sort of "second prize," will strengthen his weakness, and in doing so will postpone "deadening," to acquire what Bitov calls *protiazhennost'* ("long-drawn-out-ness"[89]). Consider this passage: "I am all the more often unable to take up the pen because all the shapes converging around its tip make me feel ashamed . . . even this word 'pen' I've just written—it's been a year and a half since I began writing directly at the typewriter and haven't been using a pen."[90] Here, writing about one's inability to write does not decrease this inability or mitigate its effect on the writer; on the contrary, it increases the very shame his own writing produces in him, as he makes a botched word choice, in this case "pen" (*pero*), which makes him cringe and evinces the very difficulties he is experiencing with writing just as he is writing about them. Yet, this mode of looking over one's writing, retracing, retracting and correcting what you just said, creates that desired *protiazhennost'* that the writer believes provides life with some kind of meaning.

Earlier in the work, the writer discusses the difference between a sudden death—from a bullet, a holocaust, or an atom bomb—and the lawful, ordinary death from "natural causes" that awaits anyone. The distinction that makes the former seem random, "unreasonable," "absurd," even "criminal," and the latter, a matter of course for all humanity, a norm, lies in this concept of *protiazhennost'*, a *process*, of which the "natural causes" death is a "natural" completion. The latter death, that is, despite its cruel implacability, appears as the culmination of some kind of "meaningful" process, of which the former seems like a violation: "Everything changes its color if you imagine the terrifying outcome occurring suddenly and immediately, crushing you in such a fragment of a second that you don't have time to feel anything, you're deprived of your previous afflictions, of the false logic which you can't even begin to imagine, of the surrounding society, of the vicious bits of paper [*svirepye bumazhki*] with signatures, and the long-drawn-out-ness [*pro-tia-zhen-no-sti*]."[91] In this quote, the writer breaks down his concept syllable by syllable—*pro-tia-zhen-no-sti*—hyphenating and fragmenting this final word so as to extend it, to make *extension* itself lengthier.

LENGTHENING, LONG-DRAWN-OUT-NESS, AND OVERDETERMINATION IN *PUSHKIN HOUSE*

Fragmentation, along with periphrasis, retelling, mumbling, self-correction, and revision are central to the narrative structure of Bitov's crowning achievement, *Pushkin House*. According to an authorial admission, the original plan was to focus on the climactic destruction of the museum, which was discussed earlier in this chapter, but the novel takes a quite circuitous route to this event, with numerous detours and dead ends on the way. The novel begins in the aftermath of the event, describing Leva Odoevtsev's demise—or at least, this is the impression his supine, motionless body makes on the reader—and, after a concise description of the postapocalyptic setting, proceeds to move back in time, to the very beginnings of Leva's life, reassembling it after the fact, in effect reanimating this seemingly lifeless body. In a way, we can read the whole novel as analogous to the moment of hitting the mental rewind button in "Life in Windy Weather," when the writer recollects himself from dispersed nonbeing into a singular being.[92] Ranging as far as possible from the climactic moment, the narrative gives a thorough account of the protagonist's familial background and relationships, devoting considerable space to Leva's parents and to two grandparental figures, the aristocratic and punctilious Uncle Dickens and the eminent but psychologically broken philologist Grandfather Odoevtsev. The latter are both victims of Stalinist repressions, returnees from the Gulag who, as Mark Lipovetsky argues, personify the ideal of individual and modernist freedom, which is deeply alien to Leva's post-Stalinist generation, raised on the ideal of conformity in an atmosphere of ever-abiding fear.[93] It is Leva's admiration for and kinship with these two figures that prepares us for his defining feat, in which, in the name of Pushkin and his honor, he destroys the Pushkin House. To understand Leva's act, it's enough to think of Grandfather Odoevtsev's theory that the Soviets "preserved" prerevolutionary culture by shutting it safely away in a museum—that is, in the past, well-packaged, explained, and frozen in time, preempting any possibility for its continuous, organic development: "Now you think that '17 destroyed, devastated our previous culture. But it didn't; it canned and preserved it. What matters is the break, not the destruction. The authorities froze there untoppled, unmoving: they're all in their places, from Derzhavin to Blok—the sequel [*prodolzhenie*] won't shake their order, because there won't be a sequel [*prodolzheniia ne budet*]."[94] Leva has clearly inherited Grandfather Odoevtsev's preoccupation with continuity and his understanding of the distinction between a fundamental break (a sudden end) and, on the other hand, destruction (a process that allows for come-backs, linkages, and liminal survival techniques), as Leva's article on "Three Prophets" attempts to theorize the possibility of discontinuous continuity, as discussed above. Leva's destruction of the museum represents an effort to demummify the culture that has been entombed there, in accordance with Grandfather Odoevtsev's theory.

The narrative accomplishes a similar feat: it attempts to open up the museum and extricate Leva himself from it. The author does so by keeping the edifice of *Pushkin House* (the novel) in a state of perpetual renovation, continuously oscillating between the erecting, demolition, and reconstruction of the narrative structure with ever-proliferating variants. Just when the narrative of Leva's life is supposed to progress to its fatal end—to culminate, that is, in the body in the museum—the author opts to retell his biography from another angle: that of his love life. Finally, when this part of the novel arrives, inevitably, at the day of Leva's untimely death in the museum, the novel retraces its steps yet again to tell us, this time, about Leva's career, his academic interests, and his competition with his archnemesis Mitishatiev. Moreover, each part, upon ending, offers a variation, an alternative to the given narrative of Leva's family life, love life, and professional life. These variants are pithier, and while they differ in many substantive ways from the ur-variants, they nevertheless end in the same way, leading us to the scene at the museum. Finally, the author can no longer stave off that fateful night. We then go through the events that lead to Leva's duel with Mitishatiev (discussed earlier in this chapter), and just when the reader thinks that there can be no further continuity, that the character has finally and irrevocably died, the author predictably supplies another variant—one that leaves Leva alive and well and walking away.

Not only does Leva survive, but before his escape he manages to re-compose both himself and the museum, almost completely erasing the signs of damage. This *near* complete erasure is significant, as Leva himself is still able to see the cracks and patch-ups (even if they are not visible to anyone else). These cracks remind him that, although the effects of destruction were reversed, it did leave traces; it did make a difference. Critics often characterize Leva's return to conventional, dutiful, tame existence as a mechanized kind of life—in effect, just another form of death. But the patched-up walls of the museum attest to his rebellion, and they are visible to him. They thus create a possibility of balance, a form of incompletion—or more specifically, of a completion that was not perfectly executed, such that Leva's life is now opened up to continuation. Moreover, these walls enable other narratives; after all, someone might just notice a patch or crack in the otherwise perfect facade of the museum and wonder what caused it.

Discussing the structure of Bitov's "versions and variants," Maria Savel'eva argues against buying into the illusion of choice they might suggest. In her view, Leva's life inevitably leads him to the same end:

> In the novel *Pushkin House*, the "versions and variants" never lead to a change in the idea of the work; the main thing is that, at any turn of the plot, the same thing remains—the amorphous character of the protagonist and the limitedness of his choice in any field: both in personal and social life. . . . The novelty of Bitov's technique is that he shows, through formal variability, the absence of variability in content. Bitov does not want to change his hero, who is highly constrained by his family, country, and upbringing; rather, at any turn of the plot, he faces only a dead end, and the whole point of the pseudovariance of the plot is to show the absence of variants.[95]

Savel'eva argues, then, that the novel's open-endedness, seemingly espousing the existence of choice, is only seeming; according to her, since none of the variants change the end result, and the hero remains himself, practically unchanged, the novel thus posits itself, and the life it mirrors, as closed systems. For my part, I discern different implications in this structural peculiarity.[96]

In my view, this seriality, stemming from the author's persistent and perpetually unsatisfactory attempts to fix something in a narrative, *does* in fact introduce variability into an otherwise invariant structure, opening it up. The fact that these variants lead to the same result shows not that the structure is fixed and finite, as one might suppose, but that it is, to borrow a term from genetics and systems theory, "equifinal." The founder of systems theory, Ludwig von Bertalanffy, adopts this embryological term to explain the difference between closed and open systems: "In any closed system, . . . if either the initial conditions or the process is altered, the final state will also be changed. This is not so with open systems. Here, the same final state may be reached from different initial conditions and in different ways."[97] An open system, then, is flexible enough and resilient enough not to collapse from alterations in pathways to the end result, while no such detours are possible within a closed system. Anthony Wilden refers to this redundancy, this multiplicity of pathways that an open system has at its disposal to reach the same result, as overdetermination. Wilden adopts this concept from Freud's theory of dreams and applies it to language in general, explaining that the most open system of all, according to this principle of overdetermination, is the linguistic one:

> Overdetermination may be read to mean "determined" in some classically causal fashion, but in fact the notion is quite different from causal explanation. All it says it that, because of the semiotic freedom of the system of communication in which the symptom occurs, "there is more than one way of getting there." In other words, although the system is indeed determined in some sense by the repertoire or the code from which the possible elements of the message are drawn, and by the syntactic laws of combination in the message itself, this determination is similar to that of language itself. In language, there is a very large number of ways of saying the same thing, and an infinite number of possible messages. Determined as it is by its code and by its syntax, language is perhaps the most semiotically free of all representational and communicational systems—and is not ruled by causality, but by possibility, constraints, and by its pragmatic-semiotic function, that of the transmission and reproduction of variety in the system.[98]

It is, then, precisely this principle of redundancy, its incorporation of elements that are considered superfluous, that ensures the system's longevity, its long-term reproducibility (continuation in the sense of teleonomy, not teleology). In his study of the relationship between play and evolution in the philosophy of Derrida, Christopher Johnson explains this mechanism thus:

> If systems theory, like all modern science, rejects traditional teleological explanation (the system does not know where it is going), the open system does have a "direction": it is goal-seeking (or teleonomic) in that it seeks primarily to persevere, to reproduce itself, that is, to perpetuate and reproduce an invariant structure (the code or programme). The code is, in a very special sense, the memory of the system, and its function is essentially a conservative one: to transmit an invariant structure. But what the code promises is always liable to interference or, to use the terminology of information theory, *noise*. There is no such thing as a channel of information devoid of noise, a pure message. In fact, pure message is unthinkable, and the very condition of possibility of (new) information is noise. The process of morphogenesis, the production of new forms or structures, is dependent upon noise, both internal and environmental, which via natural selection is integrated into the code as new information. This integration of noise is possible precisely because of the "looseness" of connections in the system, the property of equifinality or redundancy defined above.[99]

I take this lengthy excursion into systems theory in order to explain how Bitov's variants and variations—this structure of graphomaniacal excesses and redundancies that appear effortful and weak, and seem to lead nowhere, ever failing to avert the end—in fact accomplish the impossible; namely, they produce a book (not just *Pushkin House*, but the amalgamation of all his works) as open as the most open systems: human language and human life.[100] And as in all open systems, what matters here is not the beginning or the end but the process itself, what lies in the middle, and how much it can be stuffed with noise, debris, and interferences.

The same defense that the "author" of *Pushkin House* offers for Leva's eccentric article "Three Prophets" could be applied to Bitov's novel itself: "There is so much brashness and bluster in it." This "bluster" (in the original Russian, *shum*, "noise")—the interference of Leva's personal concerns and worries—might seem, in a scholarly work, like a defect; but the author begs to differ: "It has one indisputable advantage. It will never be legitimized."[101] We are to understand that the article will never become an "official," lawfully accepted version of literary history, precisely because there is so much personal interference in it. Herein lies the difference between Leva's article and official Soviet cultural history, which Leva's grandfather sees as having completely mummified prerevolutionary culture, providing a single authorized reading of the past, and sealing it off from the present in a closed, dead system. The author voices his opposition to such a system thus: "We have assimilated the fact that the greatest evil, for us personally, is to live in a ready-made, explained world."[102] By contrast, Leva's version of this culture is vital precisely because it is so openly specious, because so much of what is still unknown shines through its lacunae.

Like the grandfather's theorizing, the article itself, then, can be interpreted as both a lament and defense of the constitutive gaps in life and one's knowledge of it. Leva's article offers an interpretation of the intertextual relationship between Pushkin's "The Prophet," Lermontov's "The Prophet," and Tiutchev's "Madness" through the prism of his own relationships with the people around him and the sense of his own inadequacy that they provoke in him. In Leva's version, Tiutchev's "Madness" represents a barb against Pushkin's conception of his own poetic gift in "The Prophet"; instead of the fullness of meaning envisioned by Pushkin, Tiutchev finds emptiness, a lack of vision, even delusion.

This lunge at Pushkin's presumption of his own immortality, which in Leva's interpretation in fact reflects back on Tiutchev's own lack, is something that Leva abhors precisely because he recognizes his own insufficiency and self-doubt in Tiutchev's. We gather, however, that, unlike Lermontov— who issues a complaint in his "Prophet," whimpers about the limitations of his mortal self, and dies—Tiutchev is of interest to Leva specifically as the epitome of a peculiar resilience: "Pushkin chose God (or he had the genius to live uninterruptedly until the age of thirty-seven, which amounts to the same thing). Lermontov preferred death to interruptedness, repetition, spiritual death; Tyutchev went on living *interruptedly*."[103] Tiutchev realizes his lack vis-à-vis Pushkin's suprapersonal, godlike being, but learns to live with it, in fragmented temporality. Resentful and envious, he realizes that he does not "have that which Pushkin has": "They were of the same class, but Pushkin was more the aristocrat, he *had* it [u nego *bylo*], without pondering where it came from; Tyutchev was more the upstart intellectual, he *wanted* to have it but did not."[104]

But, crucially, even as he does not "have it," Tiutchev still keeps plugging away. Despite the fact that Leva possesses his own sense of aristocratic exclusivity, his feelings of inadequacy vis-à-vis his truly aristocratic and exceptional grandfather, Uncle Dickens, and Pushkin himself are fairly accurately represented in this summary of Tiutchev's predicament. And yet, the author defends Leva's version, saying that it is infinitely preferable to a scholarly or "scientific" (Bitov's quotation marks) work that supposedly has no factual mistakes and that therefore "legitimizes and subsequently prescribes for everyone its own skimpiness and poverty of understanding."[105] The difference, then, is not that one is complete and the other is not. Both are incomplete, yet the official version makes a parlous pretense of completion, while Leva's exhibits its own shortcomings, wherein lies its peculiar strength, its advantage. Characteristically, the novel ends with a fragment from Leva's grandfather's article "The Sphinx," which serendipitously issues a defense of life's evasive holeness, argues for the advantageousness of our patchy knowledge of it. Like Leva's article, the genius grandfather's piece represents yet another instance of a fragment that asserts and defends its own fragmentariness. Both authoritative and incomplete, the grandfather's statement asserts that life exists only in its ability to escape our grasp, and calls on us, failing to grasp it, to let it be: "To be misunderstood [or "not understood," *neponiatoi*] is the sole condition for the existence of culture. . . . To exist on the honesty of authentic reasons is beyond a man's strength now. It voids his life, since his life exists only through error. Level judges level. Men ponder God, Pushkinologists Pushkin. Popular experts in nothing *understand* life. . . . What a mess! What luck, that it's all so far off the mark [*chto vse eto mimo*]!"[106]

This is a very interesting moment, insofar as Bitov frequently uses this word *mimo* (going "past," "missing," being "off target)" to describe the sense of deficiency his protagonists feel as they invariably miss their goals, let some vital landmark or destination pass them by—as they feel *life* passing them by, or having already passed them by.[107] For example, this out-of-placeness connects Leva to Tiutchev (in Leva's conception of him): they have both arrived too late and have no future; both see themselves as misfits, and experience both awe and envy toward those whom they perceive as belonging to their time and to eternity. But by the very end of *Pushkin House*, on the authority of the sage grandfather, their failure to establish themselves fully—this gap between intention and result—is validated on two counts.

First, this failure is, in fact, a kind of success: it ensures the preservation of life, since the full knowledge of life would prove fatal. What the grandfather calls "the great cunning of the alive"[108] (*velikaia khitrost' zhivogo*) is what we earlier described as overdetermination. The structure of versions and variants, the fragmented, repetitious, overdetermined reproduction, on the one hand conveys the sensation of what, in *The Flying Away Monakhov*, the narrator terms the "multiplicity" or "divisibility" of being (*kratnost' bytiia*[109]): "We wander in time present, where each next step is the disappearance of the preceding one, where each, in this sense, is the finale of the whole journey. Therefore, the present of the novel is the chain of finales, the line along which the past rips away from the nonexistent future, tracing out the discontinuity of reality which has riddled us with holes."[110] This mental operation, by which the narrator divides time into a series of discrete moments that are separate entities in and of themselves, gives meaning to every lived moment, however fleeting and seemingly insignificant; and yet again, this understanding of time can be seen as a resistance against any teleological, progressive conception of life—an affirmation of its value, despite its futility and aimlessness.[111]

On the other hand, the failure in question allows life to escape fixity, and conveys its potentiality by omission. Leva's life escapes totalization precisely because of the author's numerous unsuccessful and unfinalizable attempts to grasp it, to pin his character down. Like a remainder, Leva exists somewhere *in between* all these versions of his life. And since we will never know which version of Leva is the definitive one, he will forever abide, expanding and contracting, in this zone of discontinuity and indeterminacy. What allows Leva to be, then, is precisely the series of unsuccessful attempts on the author's part to give a full picture of him—in other words, to finish him off. This is, moreover, just like Tiutchev's version of success: to live fragmentarily and discontinuously means to keep on going, to keep "scrambling" (as the narrator of "Notes from the Corner" calls it) in full knowledge that life is aimless and doomed.[112]

Second, the novel validates this scrambling, not only because it is paradoxically successful (at failing to grasp life, thereby preserving it) but also because this effortful existence demonstrates deep ecological affinity with the human condition in general, which makes it an ethical position. Neither Pushkin in his transcendence and immortality (belonging to all), nor Lermontov in his pitiful surrender to mortality, the demise of his discrete *I* (belonging to none, or belonging only to self), get as close to the core of the human condition as do Tiutchev and Leva in their endurance of discontinuity and their effortful scrambling to overcome its effects (most notably, the effect of not belonging).

In one of his numerous asides, the author of *Pushkin House*, A.B., defines human life as basically a series of lost opportunities, a perpetual outsidedness vis-à-vis time:

> What can you do if life and time have hopelessly different velocities: either you break free of time or you lag behind your own life. By the end of the second month, the fetus is sick of waiting to be born, and if it should appear by the end of the ninth, it will do so out of a hopeless indifference to the question of existence and nonexistence. It has failed to become a fish at the right time, a bird a little later, all opportunities have been let slip. A human being is born [*vse propushcheno—chelovek rodilsia*].[113]

In this radically nonanthropocentric description, human life is not the apogee of creation but a belated arrival. It is thus not just Leva and Tiutchev who came too late, but all people, who as a species are defined precisely by their poor relationship to time, perpetually late vis-à-vis the past and early vis-à-vis the future. It is this sense of heart-wrenching discontinuity, this scrambling to find one's place, that brings one into a relationship with everyone and everything alive—that is the basis of connectedness.

Justifying his seemingly compulsive series of postponements of Leva's end, his inability to once and for all finish Leva off, the author adduces life, in which "any point in the present is the end of the past, but also the end of the present, because there is no possibility of living on, and yet we live [*zhit' dal'she net nikakoi vozmozhnnosti, a my zhivem*]."[114] Here, moving from the third person to the first, the author compares the discontinuous existence he has fashioned for Leva to "our" common predicament. And several pages later, the author repeats the same sentiment, this time mobilizing the second-person pronoun: "That's just the point, that if we tell the story of any life with a degree of truthfulness, from an outside viewpoint and at least partially from within, then the picture will be such that the man hasn't the slightest chance of living on. A sequel [or "continuation," *prodolzhenie*]? Inconceivable. But you live [*a ty zhivesh'*]." The author concedes that whereas life resists finality, literature has form (is formed), and therefore naturally resists life's amorphousness: "Only in literature will it really happen: an ending that's the end. By its decency, literature compensates for life's shoddiness and lack of principle."[115] But then the author proceeds, in an unprincipled yet ethical move, to gift his Leva with the same endurance that one could expect from a living being (rather than a character in a novel).

The expression of wonderment at the miracle of a person's persistence in the face of the existential dilemma they find themselves in—an expression that becomes almost an adage in the novel—takes us back to one of Bitov's earliest pieces, in which this idea becomes the starting point from which he revises conventional notions of heroism and the Soviet "positive" character. This story, called "A Journey to a Childhood Friend (Our Biography)" ("Puteshestvie k drugu detstva (Nasha biografiia)," 1963–64), begins with Bitov's narrator, a writer, being encouraged by the editor of a literary magazine to submit, for a change, an article about a positive Soviet hero of his choosing. To such an assignment, the writer responds, in his characteristically timid yet noncompliant fashion, that not only are all his characters already positive ("I don't have the strength for negative ones") but that all people, in his view, are heroic: "They live, and that's their heroism."[116] This story has received considerable scholarly attention, because in it Bitov's anti–socialist-realist stance appears most pronounced. Written early, the story reads almost like a manifesto, offering a critique of the cult of the positive hero. Agreeing, in the end, to write about someone he knows who fits the bill, Bitov uses the occasion to deconstruct this idealized image, to show the dodgy underside lurking beneath the perfect facade. Scholars highlight, for example, the inclusion of a memory in which the positive hero in question, the intrepid volcanologist and eponymous childhood friend Genrikh, asked the narrator to help him cheat on an exam by taking it in his place. This memory appears to discredit the hero. But I believe the intention behind it is exactly the opposite: to save poor Genrikh from his monumental image, making him more rather than less heroic, in line with Bitov's own alternative interpretation of what constitutes heroism, outlined above: one's effortful "scrambling" at life, at enduring it. The story is, after all, called "A Journey to a Childhood Friend," and there is no reason to read this title ironically. Standing the notions of heroism, strength, and weakness on their head, Bitov attempts to breach the distance between them, to reach his friend in more senses than one.

On his way to visit Genrikh, the narrator gives us, through his recollections, an overview of his erstwhile friend's heroic past and present, at the same time attempting to pinpoint something that might connect the two men. He thinks of the resentment he has always harbored for this hero, how much he has always envied Genrikh's exemplary life. In some ways, the writer's attitude toward his friend presages Tiutchev's toward Pushkin in Leva Odoevtsev's interpretation. In pondering his old acquaintance, the narrator begins to deconstruct the perfect picture of him conveyed by newspaper chronicles of his amazing feats. Yet, paradoxically, Genrikh, with all his epic proportions and prodigious abilities, appears distant and bland, like a statue frozen in time. In attempting to bridge the distance between them, to bring back his old friend, the narrator revives Genrikh from his monumentality by infusing him with insufficient, gap-filled human life.

For example, the narrator recalls an occasion when he caught a glimpse of Genrikh's face when no one else was looking at him. At that moment, Genrikh's face held the expression of disorientation and slackness we would associate with Bitov's typical *loser* characters. To the narrator, Genrikh's face seemed "scattered" (*rassypannoe*). But such formlessness does not go to discredit Genrikh, or make us feel that he is hiding something; to the contrary, it seems to save him, transforming him from a hackneyed, one-dimensional socialist-realist image into one of Bitov's compelling weaklings. This awkward glimpse *includes* Genrikh, creating a point of contact.

It is likewise for this purpose that the writer-narrator reverses the conventional understanding of the concepts of strength and weakness, disturbing the boundary between them:

> External, sculptural courage [*skul'pturnoe muzhestvo*] puts me on edge. Actions that take on a textbook heroic form do not inspire confidence in me. Like tempered steel, they are too hard and brittle upon impact. It's the good swimmers who most often drown. Athletic people may be physically quite strong, but [they] cannot withstand hunger. And I find it easier to believe in the courage of physically weak and sick people, in their resilience: it is forced on them, it is justified.[117]

Espousing the frailty of strength and the resilience of weakness, this passage makes clear that when the narrator retrieves moments of Genrikh's weakness from his memory, he does so not to "unmask" the man as, contra his reputation, deficient, but rather to grant him a better chance for viability. In singing the praises of weakness, the narrator wishes to forestall any impression that he might be attempting to shift the balance in his own favor, to elevate himself to some higher plane, in his weakness, than his legendary mountain-scaling friend, with his prodigious strength. Making a gesture of reconciliation and generosity, the protagonist concedes that his own mask of weakness is as tenuous as his hero's facade of strength: "We manage, several times in our lives, to get tired of ourselves, at least in our givenness, we turn into our opposite. And the strong are suddenly human and weak. And the weak are hard-hearted and strong."[118] This is not, on the writer's part, some attempt to snatch a victory from his ever-victorious friend, but rather an attempt to eschew the victor-loser dialectic entirely, because victory would be yet another form of failure:

> What if I, a person who has suffered defeat since childhood, got tired of it, took a pause, and suddenly felt victory in all of this, and turned into a win-

ner, setting specific, brief, insular little goals for myself? And only then understood how empty and lonely and bitter it is to win, if the goal disappears along with the win? And what if you, who have been a winner all your life, always coming in first, suddenly felt the tiredness and bitterness of defeat in all your victories?[119]

The writer, an eternal loser, manages to put himself in Genrikh's place, to feel the insufficiency of victory, and this leap of imagination allows him to establish connection with his friend, to break down the distance between them. Significantly, the story ends at the moment when, having retrieved his recollections and revived his friend from heroic statuary, the narrator finally "arrives." In this space of memory, they are not estranged and afar, but together: "Hello, my friend! It is at home that we are opposites. But here, we have everything in common: the roof here and the house there, in memories. . . . In coming to see you, I didn't just take a plane flight; it is as if I also returned. You ensure my return [*ty—zalog moego vozvrashcheniia*]."[120] In this movement back in time—a retrieval of such memories as would allow for identification and bonding on the basis of mutual weakness—the author recovers not only his friend but also their friendship, and thus his own childhood, his own past self.

STALLING AND RESTRAINT IN "THE BIRDS"

In perhaps his most ecocritical work, "The Birds, or, The Catechizing of Man" (1971–75),[121] Bitov expands this attempt at building a limited understanding with the Other; now it is about establishing connections, not just with other people but with the surrounding world, other species, God. In some ways, making connections here means also forging continuity, but an expanded version thereof that would encompass not just diachronic but also synchronic relationships. And this process, like any attempt at overcoming the discontinuities of life, demands immense effort. Ostensibly, the novella is about the narrator's trip to the biostation at the Curonian Spit reserve and his attempts to build a rapport with the ethologist Doctor D. and with a crow named Clara.[122] As Bitov observes, birds are a constant but barely noticed presence in our lives: "I will venture to assert that we have less contact (in the physical sense) with birds than with any other living creatures. It's hard to imagine that you have touched and caressed one, or that one has pecked you. They just fly around."[123] Both Doctor D., as a no-nonsense, just-the-facts scientist, and the crow Clara are rather standoffish and deeply alien to the protagonist, and yet he treats them with the utmost sensitivity, trying to understand their unique points of view.

By virtue of their difference, the Other is radically apart from and unknowable to us, making understanding practically impossible; but this should not imply the unworthiness of that aim. On the contrary, according to Bitov, attempting such a connection is the most ethical and noble of all efforts: "Man's capacity to know another nature strikes me as catastrophically small, yet there is nothing nobler, or more necessary for human consciousness, than to spin our wheels in this effort [*buksuiushchee usilie*]."[124] What makes this effort ethical is precisely its tentative, *buksuiushchee* nature: it involves skidding and stalling, and is inevitably inadequate.

The narrator attempts to arrive at a nonanthropocentric way of thinking in which the conventional urge to *master* nature gives way to a recognition of *affinity* with it. An approach to establish closeness with the Other should consciously preclude the possibility of making the Other too familiar and thereby subsuming it. One needs to approach understanding without arriving at full knowledge, without merging with the Other completely.[125] Bitov thus again describes the ethics of realizing one's limitations: "This science has . . . an unavoidable ethical aspect. Its limitation is an ethical limitation. Not everything is permitted. Not everything is worth thinking, not everything is worth understanding. . . . The spiritual meaning of a scientific discovery lies not in broadening our sphere of knowledge but in overcoming its narrowness."[126] This last distinction might seem slight, but for Bitov it is essential. The understanding that we invariably operate from a position of weakness rather than of strength is an ethical understanding. It is hubristic pride in the human mind and in the advancements of human knowledge that leads to catastrophes. Approaching human knowledge as imperfect and plagued by shortcomings, being mindful of one's limitations, encourages ethical doubt and imposes restraints on one's otherwise overentitled range of action.

This ethical consciousness of one's perpetual inadequacy must orient persons in their relationship with the Other, and with the world; this becomes especially critical in the face of potential all-annihilating catastrophe, of which Bitov in his writings is ever aware. To give an example of such cognizance of one's merely approximate understanding of the Other's predicament, I will here briefly discuss an earlier text.

Keenly aware of his Circassian ancestry, Bitov was particularly pulled toward the Caucasus and wrote three remarkable travelogues about his journeys there. In one of these travelogues, *Lessons of Armenia: A Journey out of Russia* (*Uroki Armenii: Puteshestvie iz Rossii*, 1969), there is a curious place where Bitov yet again touches on the topic of mass annihilation—in this case, the Armenian genocide. Bitov describes reading a book about the genocide, opening it to different places at random; wherever his gaze would fall, there would be a graphic description of some horrific atrocity. To drive home his point, he quotes liberally from certain harrowing passages from the book.

But then, suddenly, right after one such citation, Bitov offers a metanarrative self-commentary, informing the reader that the ordering of events in the travelogue camouflages a temporal gap. He explains, in particular, that his reading of this book about the Armenian genocide and his writing about it did not temporally coincide; when writing about it, he did not have the book in his possession, and was thus unable to adduce sufficient supporting evidence. His solution was to leave empty pages in his narrative and then return to them later. Borden reads this authorial aside as an example of poor taste:

> Ideally, perhaps, the reader is induced to feel he is actually participating here in the creative act. But, then, let us recall the context: the Armenian holocaust. Can pursuit of any metaliterary goal, to say nothing of the mere need to scratch a self-conscious itch, justify switching off horrifying accounts of genocide as if this were just another topic, rather than the most traumatic event in the modern Armenian consciousness?[127]

In Borden's view, this episode exemplifies Bitov's ultimate drawback: his solipsistic preoccupation with the writerly act at the expense of everything else. I would like to attempt to defend Bitov from this accusation. His inopportune detour strikes me as not at all callous and self-indulgent but the opposite, an instance of the postmodern "den[ying] itself the solace of good forms" (Lyotard[128]), forgoing the temptation to camouflage a rupture of catastrophic proportions with a coherent, well-constructed narrative. This would be in keeping with Adorno's dictum that "there can be no poetry after Auschwitz."

Let us retrace our steps. Bitov's controversial authorial aside follows a quote from the book in question, one that cites a 1917 document issued by censorship authorities of the nascent Soviet state advising the avoidance of any discussion of the Armenian genocide so as not to compromise the fledgling country's friendly relations with Turkey. Silence, therefore, is compromised; while it might be politically expedient to avoid talking about the holocaust, ethics demands the very opposite. But how does one write about a holocaust?

A coherent narrative that clothes horror of such proportion in harmonious form represents yet another misguided tactic. Bitov mocks the aesthetic considerations that went into the creation of the book's table of contents, with its gapless ordering: "1. The Massacre of the Armenians under Sultan Abdul Gamid (1876–1908) 2. The Mass Slaughter of the Armenians by the Young Turks (1909–1918). That is the entire table of contents. How neatly 1908 fits next to 1909! As the last page of the first volume fits alongside the first page of the second."[129] There is something impervious to pain and suffering in this pithy table of contents and its attempt to establish continuity between events that should have none of that quality. Instead of this progressive, chronologically ordered time that propels Armenians to extermination, Bitov scrambles and segments time. He refuses to be silent, but also refuses to be exhaustive or fluent in his description of the genocide. After all, all he can talk about is his limited knowledge, his narrow encounter with it. He registers trauma by compulsively returning again and again to this painful book. This authorial aside, then, bespeaks not self-indulgence but precisely the opposite: the honest admission that there are things the author simply lacks the authority to give a full picture of. His access to, his experience or knowledge of this event, however haunting, can never be represented as complete or authoritative.

In "The Birds," this self-restraint becomes the centerpiece in the narrator's quest for proper balance in his relationship with the surrounding environment. The main topic of the narrator's dialogue with the scientist is the consequences of humanity's insatiable desire for knowledge and whether it can or should be restrained. The topic of nuclear disaster is, predictably, broached, and, also predictably, the narrator offers an anti-humanist opinion on the matter. For him, the nuclear bomb is the logical end of the hubris of human thought, which imposes itself on the world, destroying it in the process. The writer asks the scientist, "Can you really believe that man is capable of stopping? . . . he is no longer nature, but her doom."[130] The writer, a proponent of the ethics of self-restraint and incompletion, questions the scientific zeal to forge ahead, to explore at all costs, and doubts whether humanity can find a way to restrain itself before it's too late. The scientist's response, however, raises a logical inconsistency in the narrator's anti-humanist thinking, which, in highlighting the "dark side" of reason's mastery, at the same time seems to grant this mastery's all-encompassing reach. The scientist offers an optimistic alternative, which might in fact happen to align with this text's overall espousal of an alternative to anthropocentrism. He reminds the narrator that in his apocalyptic imaginings, he has discounted the auspicious (salutary?) inadequacy of human thought: "Don't be too quick to drop the bomb you have in your heart. We don't know everything."[131]

The critique of reason as hubristic and mechanistic was a central theme of nineteenth-century Russian literature, and Bitov is an inheritor of this tradition. We have already discussed the variations on this theme in Bitov's earlier works. Curiously, here, in "The Birds," it is the scientist who reiterates the philologist Grandfather Odoevtsev's insight in the finale of *Pushkin House* that, thankfully, life exceeds thought. Preoccupied with the question of ecological catastrophe, Bitov again returns to the idea of reason's inadequacy, but its implications here are both far more concrete than in *Pushkin House* (since it deals with the question of *physical* survival) and far more general (since its aim is to save everything, the whole universe).

Moreover, in light of this focus on the universe as one organism, and on the individual as a cell thereof, Bitov reorients his thinking about the genius and the weakling in favor of the latter.

The conversation about weapons of mass destruction occurs after one of those nightmares of nuclear holocaust that frequently befall Bitov's characters. In the context of this particular work, dedicated to humankind's fraught relationship to the natural environment, the narrator's visceral experience of extinction is described as a sensation of reduced distance between him as a human being and the rest of the organic world. Human consciousness and reason are subtracted, and only survival instinct remains: "In the pitch dark, it was so sudden that I didn't realize or remember where I was, what was happening to me—or even who I was. A living thing, capable of feeling fear and not wishing to die, had awakened in terror: it didn't know that it was I."[132] In this dream, the narrator loses the distinct borders of the human "I," becoming "a living thing," or "something alive" (*nechto zhivoe*), a part of everything alive and threatened. Although the narrator does not share his dream with Doctor D., in their conversation the following morning, the latter seems to respond to it when he suddenly reinitiates their earlier talk about nuclear conflagration, and in particular disparages the "rich imagination" that can lead one to a hopeless pessimism: "The thought occurred to me that there is nothing poorer than a rich imagination. It hypnotizes its possessor with the brilliance of its very first picture—the most banal and primitive, as a rule. In the same way, the pessimistic eye naturally sees a more convincing view."[133]

This statement seems calculated to counter the narrator's seductive move to reduce, in his imaginings, the distance between himself and the natural world. This is a consistent viewpoint to which Doctor D. is committed. For example, while the narrator carefully considers the various ways in which people anthropomorphize birds in fables, fairy tales, and film, the scientist warns about the pitfalls of the opposite mental operation: *biomorphism*, in which humans make analogical conclusions about their own nature by observing animals and plants. The implication is that in attempting to escape the former, the narrator risks slipping into the latter. Here, too, Doctor D. finds the narrator possessed of *too much* imagination. Meanwhile, whether made from a position of strength (anthropomorphism) or of weakness (biomorphism), the attempt to effect some merger between the human and the natural world is misguided, according to the scientist: "Such is man's time span—unequal to either history or life."[134] In this discontinuous existence, this radical human outsidedness, Doctor D. paradoxically finds cause for optimism.

In his view, it is precisely the lack of continuity, the eternal gap between human thought and life, that is the predicate of universal salvation:

"Since our earth is still large and sufficient for life, isn't our consciousness that she's catastrophically diminished (by instant communications, information technology, and so forth), and likewise our consciousness that she's appallingly denuded and ravaged, merely a form of defense for her? A warning sign, a signal, switched on far ahead of irreversible danger, so that we'll have time to take heed."[135]

The gap between intention and execution, which has previously been conceived by Bitov as the characteristic quality of a weakling, is here transferred not just to the whole of humanity but to the very quality of reason (the proud possession of Enlightenment man), and is deemed fortuitous. The scientist comforts the writer, who feels doomed by the lethality of human thought, with the idea that thought is unable to grasp the totality of reality, and that his own totalizing imaginings must of necessity be fallacious and premature. This assertion in no way represents a renunciation of human responsibility or a call for quietism; rather, it calls for thought to exercise humility in relation to its own domain. The apprehension of the gap between forward-leaping thought and the realization of its designs offers time to question, to stall, to find an escape. As the scientist puts it, "We always have a gambit in reserve"—a notion the writer at first rejects indignantly, but upon further considering its implications, seems to warm to: "The idea that our conceptualization of reality might prove swifter than reality, and that this was our guarantee."[136]

And well might, at first, the narrator feel indignant: Doctor D. has indeed called out his prophetic dream as hogwash, just as Tiutchev had cast aspersions on Pushkin's ostensibly awesome gift of prophecy in *Pushkin House*. This work thus has something new to say about Bitov's beloved concept of genius. Doctor D.'s assessment of human thought as limited—a viewpoint perhaps paradoxical in a scientist, but perhaps not—leads him not only to declare an embargo on prophesying but also to disagree with the narrator's assessment of Pushkin as an infallible genius. Instead of the awesome workings of genius, Doctor D. sees in Pushkin's poetry merely the evidence of precision. The point seems to be that while clarity is something definitely to be strived for, it does not constitute evidence for the totalizing potency of vision inherent in the idea of genius. Indeed, the idea of all-encompassing knowledge and mastery of the world should be abandoned in favor of a clarity of (localized) focus. For Doctor D., failing to strive for precision is akin to a "sin," the abnegation of responsibility. It is this clarity of focus, this self-restrained (rather than boundless) agency, that the narrator must agree with as, using this as a new characteristic of genius, he arrives at a different model: "The only absolute genius was a monk who sowed two beds of peas . . . the amateur gardener Mendel."[137]

In this interpretation, the absolute genius does not elevate himself above reality, does not imagine he could fully cognize it, but, quite the opposite, works from the position of absence, an astute apprehension of his limitations. To Bitov, Mendel is a dilettante, an amateur, who by definition cannot approach his interest authoritatively, from the position of authority; he can only cultivate it as a labor of love. And it is this dilettantism of Mendel that is the precondition of his ingenious discovery, because professionalism, which implies the assurance of absolute knowledge and authority, is a dead end.

> The zeal and splendor of an upstart thought, as it strives in isolation to rise above the surface of reality, are evidence, first and foremost, of how rarely a thought enters its triumphant possessor's mind (where every notion has necessarily been immobilized and named). Paradoxicality, slowness, and sophistication begin to emerge as all but independent features—the thought's desire to be recognized and accepted supplants its function, the brilliance of its secondary characteristics dazzles its meaning. . . . In sum, only if we begin from the beginning, over and over again, can we say something new. It cannot be learned, it has to be *unlearned*. . . . The amateur waves the white flag of ignorance at us: Come here, here I am! On the flag, a haphazard rag knotted to a branch, is the inscription *I love the alive*. In our world so ceaselessly in motion, spinning its wheels in its constant development—*progressing*—if there is anything with the power to regain its own meaning, which has been complicated to the point of loss, it is amateurism.[138]

Here, the genius's vision is not boundless and transcendent; rather, the genius relates to his object of inquiry personally, as a lover (*liubitel'*, "amateur"; "I love the alive")—loving here not in the sense of erotic possession but rather of tenderness and care. It is significant that love in this story is not reciprocal: the crow Clara remains mostly aloof to the narrator's attention, but this kind of well-disposed and tentatively responsive relationship, in the end, satisfies them both.

It is not coincidental that Mendel's love of tinkering, his amateurish tending, portrayed by the image of him planting patches of peapods (only two patches, to boot), ultimately results in the discovery of *discontinuous* genetic variation. Mendel's ingenious discovery is completely in line with Bitov's theory of discontinuous continuity, of which Tiutchev and Leva Odoevtsev, and for that matter all weaklings, are adepts. Thereby, Bitov affirms discontinuous continuity—be it in the form of a halting writing, of partial understanding, cautious making, or provisional (tentative) living—as both the only feasible and the only ethical mode of being in the world.

185

A Manifesto

AFTER THE ousting of Nikita Khrushchev, the new Brezhnev leadership proclaimed the arrival of "mature" or "developed" socialism (*razvitoi sotsializm*). The adoption of this term signaled a shift in ideological self-positioning: whereas the Soviet Union and other countries of the socialist bloc were clearly still a long way off from communism, they nevertheless could be considered to have, in some sense, already arrived. A significant benchmark had been achieved; the project of building socialism was accomplished. Soviet citizens, it was now understood, could stop bracing themselves for impact from the whirlwind of Khrushchev's extravagant aspirations. Khrushchev had been keen on underscoring the persistent distance between Soviet realities and ideals. His preoccupation with accelerating economic growth might have meant that, had he managed to stay in power longer, Soviet citizens would have to sacrifice their present for his visions of the future communist abundance—its arrival by the 1980s, the proverbial "catching up to and overtaking" of the capitalist West. Brezhnev interpreted the current state of affairs to the contrary: as a point of arrival rather than departure. This meant that, while the ideal of communism was still theoretically "out there," somewhere beyond the horizon, in point of fact there was no need for the Soviet Union to rush getting there at breakneck speed. Its citizenry could stop feeling unsettled, as if they were the subjects of some ceaseless economic experiment, and begin rather to enjoy the fruits of living in a country of *developed* socialism.

On one hand, this ideology of arrival put the Soviet artist in an unenviable position: that of *belatedness* vis-à-vis the Soviet state. Unlike early avant-garde artists—self-assured demiurges, bursting with creative power and resolve to transform the world, whose errors had to do with risk-taking and prematurity, and whose failures were always ahead of them—late Soviet artists arrived at the scene when everything had already been said and done, and were thus reduced to the position of epigones and copyists, entrusted with the duty of reiterating established truths, which made them, a priori, a failure. On the other hand, the country's condition of maturity—with its decrease of tempos of development, its acquiescence to stasis, and content-ment with a life short of perfection—seemed to signal some larger, cultural processes of decline, or *stagnation*. What looked like provisional completion and permanency to some, to others appeared rife with shortages, scarcities, and deficiencies.

And it is this general exhaustion of possibilities, this overwhelming sense of insufficiency and failure, both of one's own and of the country at large, that late Soviet writers found to be a fruitful topic of exploration. Strength and completeness were fraught with a sense of violence, of impos-ing one's will on the world—fraught, in particular, with the recent totalitarian systems of oppression that artists were disinclined to be conscripted into. And yet, as this book has attempted to show, accepting one's weak position in the world was in no way tantamount to resignation. It rather signaled resil-ience, an attempt to build ties to the world weakly, through shared aesthetics, shared vulnerability, and shared *scrambling*, rather than pressure and force. It also represented an attempt to find modes of expression better suited to the time of mature socialism than socialist realism, which had demanded idealized positive heroes and teleological grand narratives, and whose vigor had been belied by historical reality. Late Soviet weakness, both of texts and of characters, stands as fertile ground for scholarly query, because it dena-tured established models of writing and identity formation—by weakening them. As explored in this book, weakness was radically experimental.

In the foreword to *The Material Culture of Failure: When Things Do Wrong*, Dimitris Dalakoglou discusses the state of political and ecological decrepitude we are experiencing at this particular historical moment and compares it to the twilight years of the Soviet system:

> Matter on earth (and off world, too) fails due to friction and atmospheric conditions: stuff falls apart, but this statement never held as much truth as it holds today at the present stage of the crisis of late capitalism. It is of course a matter of speed and temporalities, namely, things fail much faster than ever before within the Western World. This fragility implies a more general situa-tion; it signifies the end of the entire political and economic system, as we knew it for so many decades. We live in a condition similar to the one that people experienced when socialism was collapsing; it is just that there is no enthusiasm, expectation and optimism of the sort that happened at the end of socialism.[1]

This outlook may seem dire, but it cannot but hit a chord. We find ourselves in the midst of persistent ecological cataclysms, of a volatility wrought by the climate change of our own doing. At the same time, the crisis of democratic systems, the rise of authoritarian regimes, ever-increasing mass migration and uprootedness due to ever-increasing scarcity and unequal resource distribution mean that, on top of ecological collapse, we can "look forward" also to economic and political breakdowns. And yet, even as we continuously witness the world around us not so much ending as falling apart, it seems to me that we often, and perhaps now more than ever—at least in the United States, the country where I live—prefer to silence frailty or flaws as a topic. Amid all these maladies, we often choose to disavow, at least rhetorically, any sign of weakness, opting instead to posture as ever more "normal," "healthy," and "whole." I understand the political and sometimes emancipatory potential of the rhetoric of wholeness, health, and strength, but this persistent disowning of our weaknesses both physical and psychological strikes me as living falsely. It is inconsistent with all observable (and crumbling) reality to conceive of ourselves as complete and independent rather than partial and contingent. And while social constructivists are right to say that language often serves to isolate and oppress us, and while it is understandable that some disability activists are motivated to combat ableism and inequity by attempting to purge categories that cast whole groups of people as being "the ones with the problem," I also find wisdom in philosopher Giorgio Agamben's warning that our estrangement (characteristic of mature capitalism) from our own impotentiality, this faith in our ability to do everything, ultimately serves to discourage consideration of meaningful action:

> Separated from his impotentiality, deprived of the experience of what he can not do, today's man believes himself capable of everything, and so he repeats his jovial "no problem," and his irresponsible "I can do it," precisely when he should instead realize that he has been consigned in unheard of measure to forces and processes over which he has lost all control. He has become blind not to his capacities but to his incapacities, not to what he can do but to what he cannot, or can not, do.[2]

As I was writing about the various weaknesses of the characters and texts covered in this book, it increasingly struck me that many of the forms of physical and mental disjuncture that postwar writers found productive— precisely because these forms resisted harmful Nazi and Stalinist prescriptions of neoclassical harmony and completion—have since been culturally reconceptualized into an alternative vision of wholeness.

I encountered a particular difficulty in writing my chapter on Vonnegut's *Slaughterhouse-Five* and Kim's *Cinderella in a Concentration Camp*, in which I argued that the ethical potential of the gender subversion therein lies precisely in its formal disjuncture and incompleteness, which befit the trauma laid bare after the cataclysms of the twentieth century. In modern terms, the thorniness arises in treating gender subversion as a disjuncture at all. I was advised against using the word "transvestism" because of its offensive clinical history. However, I reasoned, these texts' choice of adopting femininity was made due to trauma, and "transvestite" has a close etymological connection to "travesty," with its transgressive absurdizing of accepted norms.[3] I did not want to use the term "cross-dressing," which would reduce the practice of assuming another gender (inwardly becoming someone else) to the level of appearance. For the purposes of describing the rejection of masculinity as implicated in violence, "cross-dressing" seemed too defanged an option. The idea was not just to change appearance but rather to adopt precisely that aspect of the world that was considered lesser—the feminine—and to reclaim its aesthetic, ethical, and ontological potential. Eliminating the link between gender subversion and travesty means likewise eliminating the correlation between cross-dressing and the act of queering—that is, purposefully and transgressively adopting strange and unusual behavior.

Presenting my findings at the conference "Divergent Masculinities" in Berlin in the summer of 2022, I was asked why I chose to discuss the hybridity of the masculine and feminine in terms of internal disjuncture and incongruity, rather than of Platonic complementarity, in which the masculine and feminine complete rather than clash with one another. This is certainly a fair question, but the laudable motivation behind it—to affirm nonbinarism—would also impose contemporary patterns of thought and would elide the different kind of affirmation operant in the practices I discuss. Reading late Soviet works through the prism of our current thinking would keep us from seeing how the incorporating of nonnormative behaviors ("deviancies") was understood when these writers made the choice to do so; it would only obscure the aesthetic and ethical motivations for this choice—the premium that was placed on incompleteness and weakness, which I try to rehabilitate.

In discussing Sasha Sokolov's artistic investment in various forms of mental and physical disability, I encountered another potential minefield. Most of Sokolov's most poignant characters are mentally and physically impaired, and in no way does he present them in terms of "differing ability"[4] or "normality." Blindness, a loss of limbs, or, most memorably, a mental disorder in the case of the remarkable student So-and-So, also known as *Nymphaea alba*, are portrayed as a lack or wound, a painful insufficiency—and yet it is precisely this insufficiency that is precious and generative to them; as the very core of their being, they form and author their own selves around it. It is from this standpoint that these characters most keenly reflect on the human condition in general, as the human subject (as psychoanalysts teach us) is defined by *lack*, the human psyche being a mechanism of generating unsatisfiable desires and of working out mechanisms—perpetually inadequate ones—of compensation for the sense of loss.

It is my understanding that within the field of disability studies there is much debate over how to approach disability. While the medical model of disability had treated disability as a physical property, a problem a person must deal with or try to fix, the social model of disability was advanced in which disability became the product of a social system that privileges or excludes the needs of some groups of people over others. While this model has been tremendously politically effective in removing material and social barriers for people with physical and mental impairments, some recent critiques of this model have brought up its insufficiency. Specifically, these criticisms advance the idea that what the social model fails to consider is the diversity of embodied experiences, which could be debilitating but could also be rewarding and even fulfilling, and the identity and agency with which one's experience of one's body is invested.

In his book *Enforcing Normalcy: Disability, Deafness, and the Body*, Lennard Davis, with an empathy befitting his status as a CODA (a child of deaf parents), discusses the trend by which deafness is increasingly not categorized as a disability. He begins his analysis thus: "Some may argue, and indeed many in the Deaf community will argue, that deafness is not a disability. It has become increasingly common for deaf people to deny the term 'disabled' and to disassociate themselves from other people with disabilities."[5] Davis explains this cohort's departure from definitions imposed on them from outside, definitions by which others have characterized them as *lacking*. Some among the Deaf choose to discount the unpossessed sense of hearing as something irrelevant to their situation, and instead define themselves as a community with its own traditions and language, like a particular ethnic group, for example. And yet, having proposed to examine all the social constructs that oppress and disable, rather than unite and empower, Davis nevertheless believes that the concept of disability, while certainly fraught, should not yet be dismissed as obsolete.

Emphasizing that disability is an unstable and fluid category, Davis argues that this instability may yet constitute its advantage:

> The category "disability" begins to break down when one scrutinizes who make up the disabled. The obvious cases are seen by most observers as disabled: the blind, the Deaf, people using wheelchairs, prostheses, and so on. But when we include learning impairments, dyslexia, obesity, and then compound these categories with disease-generated disabilities—AIDS, tuberculosis, multiple sclerosis, arthritis, chronic illnesses—the instability of the category "disabled" begins to appear. The fact is that most citizens will have some form of impairment, some degree of physical difference from others.[6]

Even if we were to successfully expunge concepts of disability, illness, or weakness from our vocabulary, it seems to me that ableism and disableism would hardly disappear; most likely, we would rather, in bad faith, compete with one another for the right to define "health" or "the norm." Susan Wendell describes ableism as "a structure for people who have no weakness,"[7] but there are no such people. Living means coming to terms with one's differing abilities and continuously acquired weaknesses. Those fortunate enough to live to old age will confront some form of acquired disability one way or another. I wholeheartedly subscribe to the importance of examining the social construction of disability, and of combating its stigmatization and oppression, which is so often wrought through language; but I do not think we can do so by, in effect, rehabilitating the concept of *normalcy*, so fruitfully deconstructed by Foucault more than half a century ago. It seems to me the most effective premise for equity and social justice in this regard is not that everyone is "healthy" and "normal" (which simply elides reality), but that we are all in one way or another unhealthy and disabled. The emphasis on affirming everyone's wholeness is unrealistic and would seem to militate against our banding together on a basis that *is* realistic: to address our weaknesses rather than strengths. (The foregrounding of *strength*, indeed, harbors antisocial potential. For example, as part of a culture-wide addressing of the problem of low self-esteem among young women, at some point in the early 1990s it became common for the producers of popular culture— whether in good faith, co-optatively, or some combination of the two—to promote the concept of female *strength* and *confidence*, but often to do so via exemplars—superheroines, "girlbosses," smug butt kickers, etc.—whose qualities are hardly relevant to sociopolitical reality, and simply replicate problematic masculinities.) Insofar as the human condition is one of ontological finitude and gradually acquired decrepitude, our weakness is indeed the only condition we all share, and the only one from which we can begin to develop both radical empathy and political action. As Davis argues, "To develop a working politics, one has to accept that the subject position one occupies is to some extent capable of being shared by others in parallel circumstances."[8] My point here is not to relativize or diminish the experiences of people with disabilities but rather, on the contrary, to understand that we are all implicated and therefore should all work on fostering networks of care and responsiveness.

Twenty years ago, when I was still rather young and carefree, I suddenly and unexpectedly became seriously ill. I was told it was a chronic progressive disease with a poor prognosis. A year prior to the crisis, I had married the man I loved, was working on my PhD at one of the most prestigious universities in the world, and till that moment had never given a thought to the possibility that something catastrophic could happen to me. I thought of myself, I guess, as fully complete, de facto immortal. Like Tolstoy's Ivan Ilyich, I understood the validity of the proposition "To be human is to be mortal" when applied to other people, but not to me. Now suddenly I crossed the boundary to join those less fortunate others to whom this proposition applied; my enchanted life seemed to be slipping away in front of my eyes, and I could not recognize myself. The doctors ended up being wrong; my body unexpectedly and controversially decided to self-correct against all forecasts, and even though I will be monitored by medical professionals for the duration, I am now placated by the thought that this "duration" will be ended by something other than this condition.

Until now, I have rarely told anyone about this vulnerability of mine. But I have learned to appreciate it. That encounter with my own radical weakness transformed how I relate to people and what I value in life. I'd like to think it made me kinder and more attuned to the vicissitudes of the human condition in general. This is why I find it unfortunate that there exists a disavowal of vulnerability and fragility—not just among those who delusionally imagine themselves strongmen and strongwomen, the kings and queens of this world, and among those who would follow them—but also among those who hardly support that sort of politics. I regret that, in the name of human plurality, the latter somehow oftentimes also try to expunge weakness. As a respite from the widespread and relentless focus on strength, I offer my book about the benefits (and to be sure, vagaries) of weakness.

Notes

INTRODUCTION

1. According to the film's credits, all the verses cited in it are by Fedor Tiutchev or Arsenii Tarkovsky (the director's father).

2. *Stalker* uses the nineteenth-century Russian translation of this passage that first appeared as an epigraph to Nikolai Leskov's "The Buffoon Pamphalon" ("Skomorokh Pamfalon," 1887). The English translation here is cited from *Lady Macbeth of Mtsensk and Other Stories*, trans. David McDuff (London: Penguin, 2015), 255. I would like to thank Alec Brookes and Jinyi Chu who, on separate occasions, drew my attention to this moment in the film.

3. Geoff Dyer, *Zona: A Book about a Film about a Journey to a Room* (New York: Pantheon Books, 2012), 107.

4. Lao Tzu, *The Sayings of Lao Tzu*, trans. Lionel Giles (London: John Murray, 1905), 46.

5. The turn toward Eastern religious and philosophical thought was a marked feature of the late Soviet countercultures. In *Flowers through Concrete: Explorations in Soviet Hippieland*, Juliane Fürst describes how "hippies copied and studied books on Buddhism, Shamanism, Orthodoxy, and even the Kabbalah" ([Oxford: Oxford University Press, 2021], 147). Soviet hippies' search for spirituality led them to explore various Eastern systems of thought, although Fürst concedes that ultimately they tended to favor Orthodox Christianity. The Soviet religious renaissance likewise affected underground literary circles, which incorporated Eastern religious philosophies into their sphere of exploration. Viktor Krivulin describes the syncretism—the "active inclusion of motifs of sectarian and religious-cosmic ideologies, and elements of Buddhism"—of the theological studies of underground Leningraders (cited from V. E. Dolinin, B. I. Ivanov, et al., eds., *Samizdat Leningrada, 1950e–1980e* [Moscow: Novoe literaturnoe obozrenie, 2003], 35). In particular on Taoism in Soviet underground poetry, see Boris Kolymagin, "Kitaiskie motivy v poezii andergraunda," *Novoe literaturnoe obozrenie* 135, no. 5 (2015), https://www.nlobooks.ru/magazines/novoe _literaturnoe_obozrenie/135_nlo_5_2015/article/11629/.

6. Like Leskov, Lev Tolstoy became quite taken with this passage, and even produced his own Russian translation of the French translation of it; see Jinyi Chu, "The Aphoristic Way: Lev Tolstoy's Translations of the *Dao de Jing*," *Comparative Literature Studies* 51, no. 1 (2021): 146–75. Leskov's and Tolstoy's praise of weakness will be discussed in chapter 1.

7. On Leskov's sources, polemics, and subversions of hagiographic topoi in the story, see Inna Mineeva, "Neizvestnye fakty iz istorii sozdaniia povesti I. S. Leskova 'Skomorokh Pamfalon (Starinnoe skazanie),'" *Uchennye zapiski petrozavodskogo gosudarstvennogo universiteta*, no. 7 (2015): 74–80.

8. Venedikt Erofeev, *Moscow to the End of the Line*, trans. H. William Tjalsma (Evanston, IL: Northwestern University Press, 1994), 21.

9.. Cited from Stanislav Savitskii, *Andergraund: Istoriia i mify leningradskoi neofitsial'noi literatury* (Moscow: Novoe literaturnoe obozrenie, 2002), 315.

10. Venedikt Erofeev, *Zapisnye knizhki* (Moscow: Zakharov, 2005), 1:519.

11. Rejecting the Soviet model of masculinity as unduly derived from ideology, Aksenov experimented with constructing a new model of masculinity (one clearly influenced by Hemingway's characters) that did not eschew masculine strength, just divorced it from socialist-realist precepts. Hemingway and Aksenov will be discussed further in this introduction, and in chapter 2.

12. Ivan Astakhov, "Ne po-gor'kovski," *Literatura i zhizn'*, August 25, 1961.

13. According to sociologist Daria Franklin's fascinating data sourced from six leading Soviet journals (*Novyi Mir, Iunost', Zvezda, Znamya, Nash Sovremennik, and Oktiabr'*), female-authored fiction texts constituted between 9% and 18% of the journal's output in the Thaw years and between 3% and 15% in the years of stagnation. Franklin's data shows that, remarkably, the era of *perestroika* and *glasnost'* witnessed the decrease of the female representation in these journals. Daria Franklin, "Soviet Journals Content and Authors, 1956-1990," https://github.com/dariafrank/Soviet-journals, data released May 7, 2024. Rather, in the late 80s-early 90s women writers found other ways to make themselves heard. For example, in the early 1990s the newly created group "New Amazons" published two anthologies of new women's prose: *Ne pomniashchaia zla* (The one who remembers no evil, 1990) and *Novye Amazonki* (New Amazons, 1991). But to say that the uncensored culture of the late Soviet period completely lacked women authors would be unjust. Samizdat circulated poetry of Anna Akhmatova and Marina Tsvetaeva, as well as by newcomers like Natalia Gorbanevskaya, Olga Sedakova, and Elena Shvarts. Some of the most important memoirs of the period were penned by women (Evgenia Ginzburg, Nadezhda Mandelstam, and Lydia Chukovskaya). It might be worthwhile to examine the ways in which these women writers participated in—embraced or rejected—the discourse of weakness. But insofar as weakness is stereotypically associated with the feminine gender (or "weaker sex"), in this book I have opted to attend in particular to a phenomenon that is, perhaps, less intuitive or expected, hence less easily acknowledged: instances of weakening in texts written by men.

14. Elena Zdravomyslova and Anna Temkina, "Krizis maskulinnosti v pozdnesovetskom diskurse," in *O Muzhe(N)stvennosti*, ed. Sergei Ushakin (Moscow: Novoe literaturnoe obozrenie, 2002), 432–51. Zdravomyslova and Temkina argue that this discourse eventually resulted in a resurgence of hegemonic (and toxic) masculinity.

15. See, for example, George Fredrickson, *The Inner Civil War: Northern Intellectuals and the Crisis of the Union* (Urbana: University of Illinois Press, 1993); or John Higham, "The Reorientation of American Culture in the 1890s," in *Writing American History: Essays on Modern Scholarship*, ed. John Higham (Bloomington: Indiana University Press, 1970), 73–98.

16. Sergei Ushakin, "'Chelovek roda on': Znaki otsutstviia," in *O Muzhe-(N)stvennosti*, ed. Sergei Ushakin (Moscow: Novoe literaturnoe obozrenie, 2002), 7–40.

17. Ushakin, "'Chelovek roda on': Znaki otsutstviia," 26.

18. John Barth, *The Friday Book: Essays and Other Nonfiction* (New York: Putnam, 1984), 67.

19. See Gianni Vattimo, "Dialectics, Difference, Weak Thought," in *Weak Thought*, ed. Gianni Vattimo and Pier Aldo Rovatti (Albany: SUNY Press, 2012), 39–52.

20. Lyotard famously defined postmodernism as "incredulity toward metanarratives." Jean-François Lyotard, *The Postmodern Condition: A Report on Knowledge*, trans. Brian Massumi and Geoffrey Bennington (Minneapolis: University of Minnesota Press, 1984), xxiv.

21. Gianni Vattimo, "Conclusion: Metaphysics and Violence." In *Weakening Philosophy: Essays in Honor of Gianni Vattimo*, ed. Santiago Zabala (Montreal: McGill-Queen's University Press, 2007), 402.

22. Vattimo, "Conclusion: Metaphysics and Violence," 403.

23. "Weak thought" was formulated in the eponymous collection of articles edited by Vattimo and Pier Aldo Rovatti in 1983.

24. Gianni Vattimo, *Nihilism and Emancipation: Ethics, Politics, and Law*, trans. William McCuaig (New York: Columbia University Press, 2004), 91, 55.

25. Richard Rorty, foreword to Vattimo, *Nihilism and Emancipation*, xix.

26. Mark Lipovetsky, *Russian Postmodernist Fiction: Dialogue with Chaos* (London: Routledge, 1999) and *Charms of the Cynical Reason: The Trickster's Transformations in Soviet and Post-Soviet Culture* (Boston: Academic Studies Press, 2010). Mikhail Epstein, *Postmodern v Rossii: Literatura i teoriia* (Moscow: Izdaniie R. Elinina, 2000).

27. In her textbook on Russian postmodernism, Irina Skoropanova notes in late Soviet culture a definite, albeit "haphazard and very incomplete," awareness of postmodernist practices on the other side of the Iron Curtain; writers and artists, she argues, assuredly sought as much information as possible about artistic developments abroad, and found themselves sharing aesthetic predilections with their Western creative counterparts. On the other hand, Skoropanova

emphasizes that the Soviet version of postmodernism had its specific features: "Given shared aesthetics and even, to a significant degree, poetics, the Eastern variant of postmodernism is more politicized, and includes the language of socialist realism/pseudo-*sotsrealizm* as one of the languages of popular art, and as among the targets to be deconstructed" (*Russkaia postmodernistskaia literatura* [Moscow: Flinta, 1999], 71). While I attempt to contextualize late Soviet writing historically and culturally, and account for the particularities of Russian postmodernism, I am interested primarily in how writers sought to use art for the purpose of proposing new principles of relating to one another and the world at large.

28. See Ann Komaromi, *Uncensored: Samizdat Novels and the Quest for Autonomy in Soviet Dissidence* (Evanston, IL: Northwestern University Press, 2015).

29. Komaromi's groundbreaking research marked the first in a series of recent reexaminations of late Soviet culture. Amid a resurgence of interest in "real socialism" in the USSR, recent studies have examined in depth the diverse ways in which community and communal behavior were conceptualized in the late Soviet period, among them: Polly Jones, *Revolution Rekindled: The Writers and Readers of Late Soviet Biography* (Oxford: Oxford University Press, 2019); Mark Lipovetsky, Maria Engstrom, et al., eds., *The Oxford Handbook of Soviet Underground Culture* (Oxford: Oxford University Press, 2021); Klavdia Smola, "Community as Device: Metonymic Art of the Late Soviet Underground," *Russian Literature* 96–98 (2018): 13–50; Juliane Fürst and Josie McLellan, eds., *Dropping out of Socialism: The Creation of Alterative Spheres in the Soviet Bloc* (Lanham, MD: Lexington Books, 2017); and Alexey Golubev, *The Things of Life: Materiality in Late Soviet Russia* (Ithaca, NY: Cornell University Press, 2020). Disclosing the multiplicity of late Soviet cultural expressions, subcultures, lifeworlds, and communities of belonging, this trend in scholarship has complicated previously established binaries like "Western global modernity versus Soviet socialism" or "official communitarianism versus dissident individualism." My own work attempts to build on this momentum and contribute to these powerful reframings of late Soviet life and art.

30. Brian Naylor, "Read Trump's Jan. 6 Speech, a Key Part of Impeachment Trial," *NPR*, February 10, 2021. https://www.npr.org/2021/02/10/966396848/read-trumps-jan-6-speech-a-key-part-of-impeachment-trial.

31. Sheera Frenkel and Alan Feuer, "A Total Failure: The Proud Boys Now Mock Trump," *New York Times*, January 20, 2021.

32. On the rhetoric of avenging perceived insults and defending one's honor, see Riccardo Nicolosi, "Paranoia, Resentment, and Reenactment: The Russian Political Discourse on the War in Ukraine," *Ab Imperio*, no. 3 (2022): 247–61.

33. In this arrangement, my goal was to present various methods of cultivating weakness in late Soviet prose rather than to provide an exhaustive record of

all the authors practicing the poetics of weakness at the time. Among the works meriting consideration through the prism of weakness but excluded due to considerations of time and word count are Yuri Trifonov's *The House on the Embankment* (*Dom na naberezhnoi*, 1976) and Aleksandr Vampilov's *Duck Hunting* (*Utinaia okhota*, 1970).

34. "Introduction: The Era of Soft Matter," *Tackling Global Issues: Soft Matter, Material of the Future* (Hokkaido Global Campus Initiative Report), vol. 1 (2018): 5.

CHAPTER ONE

1. Kevin M. F. Platt, *Terror and Greatness: Ivan and Peter as Russian Myths* (Ithaca, NY: Cornell University Press, 2011), 84.

2. Marko Dumančić, *Men out of Focus: The Soviet Masculinity Crisis in the Long Sixties* (Toronto: University of Toronto Press, 2021), 19.

3. Andrew Kahn et al., *A History of Russian Literature* (Oxford: Oxford University Press, 2018), 461–62.

4. Lydia Ginzburg, *On Psychological Prose*, ed. and trans. Judson Rosengrant (Princeton, NJ: Princeton University Press, 1991), 241.

5. Ginzburg, *On Psychological Prose*, 247.

6. Dumančić, *Men out of Focus*, 19.

7. Jesse V. Clardy and Betty S. Clardy, *The Superfluous Man in Russian Letters* (Washington, DC: University Press of America, 1980), v.

8. Clardy and Clardy, *Superfluous Man*, v.

9. Clardy and Clardy, *Superfluous Man*, 13.

10. Nikolai Dobrolyubov, "What Is Oblomovism?," in *Readings in Russian Civilization*, ed. Thomas Riha (Chicago: University of Chicago Press, 2009), 2:336; trans. adjusted slightly by me.

11. Dobrolyubov, "What Is Oblomovism?," 336.

12. Dobrolyubov, "What Is Oblomovism?," 339.

13. Clardy and Clardy, *Superfluous Man*, 95.

14. Alexander Herzen, *My Past and Thoughts: The Memoirs of Alexander Herzen*, trans. Constance Garnett and Humphrey Higgins, ed. Dwight Macdonald (Berkeley: University of California Press, 1982), 620.

15. Herzen, *My Past and Thoughts*, 621; trans. adjusted slightly by me.

16. Ellen B. Chances, *Conformity's Children: An Approach to the Superfluous Man in Russian Literature* (Columbus, OH: Slavica, 1978), 23.

17. Chances, *Conformity's Children*, 20, 80.

18. Mikhail Epstein, "Malen'kii chelovek v futliare: Sindrom Bashmachkina-Belikova," *Voprosy literatury*, no. 6 (2005): 193–203.

19. A. A. Faustov and S. V. Savinkov, *Universal'nye kharaktery russkoi literatury* (Voronezh, Russia: Izdatel'skii dom VGU, 2015), 272–73.

20. Fyodor Dostoevsky, *Poor People*, trans. Hugh Aplin (London: Hesperus Press, 2002), 70.

21. Mikhail Epstein, "Malen'kii chelovek v futliare," 194.

22. On the little man's orientation toward the other, see Faustov and Savinkov, *Universal'nye kharaktery*, 245–48. Notably, little men find a different incarnation in the Czech literary canon. Like their Russian counterparts, they are marked by a modest station in life, unprepossessing qualities, and meager ambitions. But Jaroslav Hašek's famously imbecilic good soldier Švejk, or Bohumil Hrabal's persevering and loquacious Dite, appear to submit to power and follow its orders; yet somehow, through the principle of overdetermination, in the process of being zealously fulfilled, these orders get travestied and sabotaged, and power relations are subverted. Unlike the Russian little men, who are victimized and all-suffering, these Czech characters evince a certain exuberance of smallness and the potential advantages thereof. (One might hypothesize that these scrappy little men are metonymic of the small country itself; their resilience is symbolic of its resilience; perhaps because geographic smallness could not have been a preoccupation of the Russian Empire, its literary canon was less invested in disclosing the hidden powers of little men.) Quite adaptable to inhospitable circumstances, they manage to navigate coercive institutions without being beaten by them. They could be considered in the light of Mark Lipovetsky's concept of *tricksterism*, in which a trickster is a liminal, ambivalent figure, existing on the border of the accepted and unacceptable, and possessed of a transgressive vitality. The trickster relies on the "artistic hyperidentification with, and a grotesque parody of, a social role, a set of values, or a discourse" (Lipovetsky, *Charms of the Cynical Reason*, 28). It is also possible, however, to imagine these characters not as some masters of double identity but rather as innocents who nevertheless unwittingly exceed the social roles assigned to them, thereby demonstrating that, however "little" a person might be, they will still exceed the other's perception of them. As Karel Kosik puts it, "Hašek . . . shows that man, even in a reified form, is still a man, and that man is both the object and producer of reification. He is above his own reification. Man cannot be reduced to an object, he is more than a system." Cited from Peter Steiner, "Tropos Kynikos: Jaroslav Hašek's *The Good Soldier Švejk*," *Poetics Today* 19, no. 4 (1998): 470.

23. Harriet Murav, *Holy Foolishness: Dostoevsky's Novels and the Poetics of Cultural Critique* (Stanford, CA: Stanford University Press, 1993), 25, 28.

24. A. M. Panchenko, "Laughter as Spectacle," trans. P. Hunt, S. Kobets, and B. Braley, in *Holy Foolishness in Russia: New Perspectives*, ed. Priscilla Hunt and Svitlana Kobets (Bloomington, IN: Slavica, 2011), 41–147.

25. Murav, *Holy Foolishness*, 26.

26. Murav, *Holy Foolishness*, 14.

27. Cited from Dina Fainberg and Artemy M. Kalinovsky, "Stagnation and Its Discontents: The Creation of a Political and Historical Paradigm," in *Re-*

considering Stagnation in the Brezhnev Era, ed. Dina Fainberg and Artemy M. Kalinovsky (London: Lexington Books, 2016), vii.

28. See the above-cited collection edited by Fainberg and Kalinovsky.

29. With regard to the latter, Western part of the equation, see, for example, David Simmons, *The Anti-Hero in the American Novel: From Joseph Heller to Kurt Vonnegut* (New York: Palgrave Macmillan, 2008). Among reasons for the wave of antiheroic characters in American literature of the 1960s, Simmons adduces a revolt against Second World War–era hero worship (11), and against such homogenizing tendencies of postwar US society as the rise of suburbia and consumer culture (14–15). In *Rebels: Youth and the Cold War Origins of Identity* (Durham, NC: Duke University Press, 2005), Leerom Medovoi traces the reaction against the culture of conformity to the 1950s. The postwar suburb was "a primary Cold War ideological apparatus" (19), meant to stand for American freedom and national abundance in contrast to the bleakness of the socialist bloc; but it also came with deep anxieties about a lack of agency, and helped to feed a widespread culture of youth rebellion, evident in such phenomena as the Beat movement; films like *Rebel without a Cause*, starring James Dean (1955), and *King Creole*, starring Elvis Presley (1958); and books like Ralph Ellison's *Invisible Man* (1952) and J. D. Salinger's *The Catcher in the Rye* (1951). The latter's protagonist, Holden Caulfield, is a quintessential midcentury "weak" American hero, who flaunts his weakness and despises Hollywood movies for their polishing of reality and promotion of idealized hegemonic masculinity: "I just don't see what's so marvelous about Sir Laurence Olivier, that's all. He has a terrific voice, and he's a helluva handsome guy, and he's very nice to watch when he's walking or dueling or something, but he wasn't at all the way D. B. said Hamlet was. He was too much like a goddam general, instead of a sad, screwed-up type guy" ([New York: Bantam Books, 1964], 117).

30. Faustov and Savinkov, *Universal'nye kharaktery russkoi literatury*, 53–55. As will be discussed in chapter 6, later this very propensity to *crumble* becomes the constituent quality of Bitov's characters.

31. Ivan Turgenev, "Hamlet and Don Quixote," trans. Elizabeth Cheresh Allen, in *The Essential Turgenev*, ed. Elizabeth Cheresh Allen (Evanston, IL: Northwestern University Press, 1995), 550.

32. Pavel Annenkov, "The Literary Type of the Weak Man (Apropos of Turgenev's Story 'Asya')," trans. Tatiana Goerner, *Ulbandus Review* 1, no. 2 (1978): 80.

33. Annenkov, "The Literary Type of the Weak Man," 84–85.

34. Leo Tolstoy, *War and Peace*, trans. Louise and Aylmer Maude (New York, NY: Collector's Library, 2004), 1:54.

35. Tolstoy, *War and Peace*, 1:425–26. It is telling that at the moment when Pierre begins to soberly evaluate his own actions, the weak character stipulated by the narrator before has now been reduced to the "appearance" of it.

36. Boris Eikhenbaum, *Molodoi Tolstoi* (Petrograd: Izd. Z. I. Grezhbina,

1922), 20–21. In my view, this Tolstoyan/Bezukhovian self-inventorying is the same thing as Foucault's concept of the "care of the self"—"those intentional and voluntary actions by which men not only set themselves rules of conduct, but also seek to transform themselves, to change themselves in their singular being, and to make their life into an oeuvre" (Michel Foucault, *The History of Sexuality*, vol. 3, *The Care of the Self* [New York: Pantheon Books, 1986], 10). According to Mark Olssen, Foucault's ethics, so far from amounting to the mere moral relativism seen by detractors, wisely takes into consideration life's contingency, its tendency to "constantly escape or exceed the techniques that govern and administer it" (*Constructing Foucault's Ethics* [Manchester, UK: Manchester University Press, 2021], 74). Despite Foucault's insistence on the formulation of one's ethical responses outside any normative system of morality, Olssen contends—examining Foucault's indebtedness to Georges Canguilhem—that the principle of life in the latter's thought grounds Foucault's ethics and differentiates it from total subjectivity. According to Canguilhem, there exists, above all norms, "one norm of norms": life, and the right to it, and the condition that this right must be shared by all. Citing Canguilhem, Olssen explains, "A common basis in life constitutes a ground for dialogue over a world with finite resources that must be shared in common. . . . While there is thus a relativity of norms to social structures, 'the norm of norms remains convergence'" (*Constructing Foucault's Ethics*, 80). As I see it, this necessity to work out one's personal ethical relationship to life through trial and error, while adhering to one essential principle—that of convergence, the unity of all with all—is Tolstoyan in its essence. That Tolstoy calls this principle "God," while in Canguilhem and Foucault it is the "fundamental norm," does not seem so substantive a difference.

37. Ginzburg, *On Psychological Prose*, 253.

38. Lina Steiner, *For Humanity's Sake: The Bildungsroman in Russian Culture* (Toronto: University of Toronto Press, 2011), 110.

39. Ginzburg, *On Psychological Prose*, 39. In particular, Ginzburg describes how this reorientation under the influence of Masonry affected Stankevich and his circle. Following the example of Benjamin Franklin, one of the most well-known American Free Masons, Tolstoy himself kept a meticulous diary, scrupulously recording all his weaknesses: "I am unattractive, clumsy, and unrefined. I am irritable, dull around others, immodest, intolerant, and bashful, like a child. I am practically an ignoramus. What I know, I have learned on my own, in fits and starts, unsystematically, uselessly, and meagerly. I am intemperate, indecisive, fickle, stupidly vain and hotheaded, like all spineless people. I am not brave." Lev Tolstoy, diary entry of July 7, 1854. Lev Tolstoi, *Polnoe sobranie sochinenii* (Moscow: Khudozhestvennaia literatura, 1937), 47:8.

40. Citing passages from letters in which Stankevich, like, later, Tolstoy and his character Pierre, subjects himself to intense self-analysis and enumerates his own weaknesses (e.g., the "tormenting thoughts" that "I am still unable to free

myself of," cited in *On Psychological Prose*, 56), Ginzburg sees Stankevich as re-
fusing to assume an idealized self-image—how we would *prefer* to be seen by
others—but rather registering, in writing, all internal (and inevitable) doubts:
"Stankevich knew that a person passes through a great number of impulses, desires, and momentary reactions before he reaches the point of action or of behavior that is apparent to those around him. If he is someone of an analytical
bent, he judges, condemns, or justifies those impulses, but by no means does he
ever discount them as irrelevant to any ideal definition of himself. A person cannot regard himself from within as a crystalline, pure, and ideally harmonious personality, and not merely from modesty or an aversion to the crudeness of such
self-admiration. He cannot see himself as such because saintliness, purity, and
harmony are not psychological definitions at all, but completely judgmental for-
mulations of a behavior that has been generalized and abstracted from the empirical complexity of inner life" (*On Psychological Prose*, 51).

41. Tolstoi, *Polnoe sobranie sochinenii*, 49:62.

42. In "Thoughts of Wise People for Every Day" ("Mysli mudrykh ludei na
kazhdyi den'," 1903), it appears in this form:

"Слабейшее в мире побеждает сильнейшее, поэтому велико преимуще-
ство смирения и выгода молчания. Только немногие в мире могут быть
смиренны. Человек, когда живет, нежен и гибок. Когда он умирает, он де-
лается жестким и сухим. Все вещи, трава, так же как и деревья, нежны и
гибки, пока они живут. Когда они умирают, они делаются черствы и сухи.
Поэтому жесткое и крепкое—это спутники смерти. Мягкое и нежное—
спутники жизни. Поэтому тот, кто силен руками, не победит. Когда дерево стало крепко, оно обречено на смерть. Сильные и большие *находятся
внизу, нежные и мягкие наверху их*." Tolstoi, *Polnoe sobranie sochinenii*,
40:168.

The weakest in the world defeats the strongest, therefore great are the advantage of humility and the benefit of silence. Only a few in the world can be
humble. A person, when he lives, is gentle and flexible. When he dies, he becomes hard and dry. All things, grass as well as trees, are tender and flexible
while they live. When they die, they become callous and dry. Therefore, the
hard and strong are companions of death. The soft and tender are companions
of life. Therefore, the one who is strong with his hands will not win. When a
tree becomes hard, it is doomed to die. The strong and big are at the bottom,
the gentle and soft are at the top.

In Tolstoy and Popov's translation published in 1910, the passage appears thus:

Человек входит в жизнь мягким и слабым. Он умирает жестким и креп-
ким. Все существа, растения и деревья входят в жизнь мягкими и нежными
и умирают засохшими и жесткими. Жесткость и сила—спутники смерти.

Нет ничего в мире мягче и слабее воды, и нет ничего, что бы превосходило воду в ее разрушительном действии на жесткое и крепкое. Слабое побеждает крепкое, мягкое побеждает жесткое." Tolstoi, *Polnoe sobranie sochinenii*, 40:350.

A person enters life soft and weak. He dies hard and strong. All creatures, plants and trees come into life soft and tender and die withered and hard. Rigidity and strength are companions of death. There is nothing in the world softer and weaker than water, and there is nothing that is superior to water in its destructive effect on that which is hard and strong. The weak defeats the strong, the soft defeats the hard.

43. Described by Tolstoy in an 1893 article of this name; see Leo Tolstoy, "Non-Activity" (1893), https://www.marxists.org/archive/tolstoy/1893/non-activity .html. On this influence, see Michael Denner, "Tolstoyan Nonaction: The Advantage of Doing Nothing," *Tolstoy Studies Journal* 13 (2001): 8–22.

44. Tolstoi, *Polnoe sobranie sochinenii*, 40:350.

45. Tolstoi, *Polnoe sobranie sochinenii*, 64:114.

46. The first published translation of Lao Tzu into Russian, performed by Daniil Konissi, appeared in 1894. It is thus possible (though I cannot say for sure) that, in order to include this passage as an epigraph, Leskov had to attempt his own Russian rendering of it, perhaps using an English translation. (It is unlikely that at this point he had access to Tolstoy's rendering, which so far seems to have existed only in the latter's diary.)

47. Cited from Mineeva, "Neizvestnye fakty," 79.

48. Mineeva, "Neizvestnye fakty," 77.

49. Catriona Kelly has examined the Soviet acculturative practices of eradicating thoughtfulness and inculcating steeliness or toughness (*zakal*). She highlights the popularity of the Russian translation of Jules Payot's *L'éducation de la volonte*, with its valorization of willpower, as in this passage she cites: "Our passiveness, thoughtfulness and dissipation of energy are only so many names to designate the depths of universal laziness, which is to human nature as gravity is to matter" ("The Education of the Will: Advice Literature, *Zakal*, and Manliness in Early Twentieth-Century Russia," in *Russian Masculinities in History and Culture*, ed. Barbara Evans Clements, Rebecca Friedman, and Dan Healey [New York: Palgrave Macmillan, 2002], 135). Numerous initiatives, including Gastev's Central Institute of Labor and Kerzhentsev's League of Time, were organized to cultivate physical and mental strength and expunge weakness. But despite these efforts, Platonov's characters evince precisely this latter characteristically modern drawback.

50. Eliot Borenstein, *Men without Women: Masculinity and Revolution in Russian Fiction, 1917–1929* (Durham, NC: Duke University Press, 2000), 237.

51. Borenstein, *Men without Women*, 236.

52. Borenstein, *Men without Women*, 207.

53. Andrey Platonov, "On the First Socialist Tragedy," in *Happy Moscow*, trans. Robert and Elizabeth Chandler (New York: NYRB, 2012), 154.

54. Andrei Platonov, *Chevengur* (Moscow: Vysshaia shkola, 1991), 246, 164, 55.

55. Jonathan Brooks Platt, "Postsocialist Platonov: The Question of Humanism and the New Russian Left," in *The Human Reimagined: Posthumanism in Russia*, ed. Colleen McQuillen and Julia Vaingurt (Boston: Academic Studies Press, 2018), 218–43.

56. Pavel Khazanov, "Honest Jacobins: High Stalinism and the Socialist Subjectivity of Mikhail Lifshitz and Andrei Platonov," *Russian Review* 77, no. 4 (2018): 576–601.

57. Khazanov, "Honest Jacobins," 600.

58. Khazanov, "Honest Jacobins," 595.

59. Igor' Gulin, "Korit—znachit liubit," *Kommersant*, March 6, 2020, https://www.kommersant.ru/doc/4268824.

60. Gulin, "Korit—znachit liubit."

61. Cf. Kaganovsky's reading of the appearance of women's cinema during the Thaw, as a different, gendered form of seeing. If for Gulin, men are diminished, Kaganovsky finds them entirely absent: "Soviet films from the sixties . . . imagine masculinity as a dream. What is missing from films of the 1960s are the men, which is not to say that sixties cinema focuses exclusively on women—though it does so to a larger extent than either the cinema of the Soviet avantgarde or of Stalinism—but that over and over again narratives are centered around missing or absent men: fathers, husbands, lovers." Lilya Kaganovsky, "Ways of Seeing: On Kira Muratova's *Brief Encounters* and Larisa Shepit'ko's *Wings*," *Russian Review* 71, no. 3 (2012): 497.

62. Sianne Ngai, *Ugly Feelings* (Cambridge, MA: Harvard University Press, 2005), 26–27.

63. See above, note 61.

64. Natal'ia Lesskis, "Fil'm *Ironiia sud'by* . . . : Ot ritualov solidarnosti k poetike izmenennogo soznaniia," *Novoe literaturnoe obozrenie* 76, no. 6 (2005): 314–27, https://magazines.gorky.media/nlo/2005/6/film-ironiya-sudby-ot-ritualov-solidarnosti-k-poetike-izmenennogo-soznaniya.html.

65. Cited from Lesskis, "Fil'm *Ironiia sud'by*."

66. Jack Halberstam, *The Queer Art of Failure* (Durham, NC: Duke University Press, 2011).

67. Lesskis, "Fil'm *Ironiia sud'by*."

68. Lipovetsky, *Charms of the Cynical Reason*, 205.

69. Michel Foucault, *The Essential Works of Foucault*, ed. Paul Rabinow, trans. Robert Hurley et al., vol. 1, *Ethics. Subjectivity and Truth* (New York: New Press, 1994), 131.

70. Lipovetsky, *Charms of the Cynical Reason*, 205.

71. Lipovetsky, *Charms of the Cynical Reason*, 204–5.

72. Adam Phillips and Barbara Taylor, *On Kindness* (New York: Farrar, Straus and Giroux, 2010), 4.

73. Ales' Adamovich and Vasil' Bykov, "Dialog v pis'makh," *Sibirskie ogni*, no. 11 (2013). https://www.sibogni.ru/content/dialog-v-pismah.

74. Larisa Shepit'ko, "Voskhozhdenie k pravde," *Sovetskii ekran*, no. 1 (1978), https://chapaev.media/articles/8936.

75. Dmitrii Bykov, *Vremia izoliatsii: 1951–2000 g: Sto lektsii o russkoi literature XX veka* (Moscow: Eksmo, 2018), 204–11, https://ru-bykov.livejournal.com /2865531.html.

76. Tolstoy, "Non-Activity."

77. Giorgio Agamben, "What We Can Not Do," in *Nudities*, trans. David Kishik and Stefan Pedatella (Stanford, CA: Stanford University Press, 2011), 43. For a discussion of how "impotentiality" relates to Agamben's view of weak messianic power according to St. Paul, see Michael O'Sullivan, *Weakness: A Literary and Philosophical History* (London: Continuum, 2012), 90–91.

78. John Shelton Lawrence and Robert Jewett, *The Myth of the American Superhero* (Grand Rapids, MI: Wm. B. Eerdmans, 2002).

79. Bykov, *Vremia izoliatsii*.

80. Bykov, *Vremia izoliatsii*.

81. As Russell Scott Valentino observes, the translation of the concept of "virtue" into Russian is often gendered: a man's virtue is often rendered as *sila* ("strength," "force"), while a woman's virtue is often rendered as *vernost'* ("faithfulness"): "The virtue of the Greek or Roman soldier is more likely translated as 'force' or 'power'—as in the word *sila*, whose direct connection to virtue is evident in the translation of the English phrase "by/in virtue of' as *v silu* (literally 'in the force/power [of]'). . . . A woman's virtue, in the sense of sexual constancy, is named by a different word, *vernost'*, or perhaps *tselomudrie* (chastity, as applied to women or men), but not *dobrodetel'*, which tends to designate good action in general" (*The Woman in the Window: Commerce, Consensual Fantasy, and the Quest for Masculine Virtue in the Russian Novel* [Columbus: The Ohio State University Press, 2014], 17). Both Bykov's book and Shepitko's film, then, skew away from the traditionally masculine understanding of virtue as *power* toward the more traditionally feminine understanding of it as *constancy* and *integrity*, and imbue Sotnikov with the latter.

82. Cited from Shari Kizirian, "*The Ascent* (1977): Larisa Shepitko's Final Word," *Senses of Cinema*, no. 90 (2019), https://www.sensesofcinema.com/2019/ cteq/the-ascent-1977-larisa-shepitkos-final-word/.

83. The repeated instances of these two men's physical entanglement in the snowy wilderness are reminiscent of the pivotal scene in Tolstoy's "Master and Man" (*Khoziain i rabotnik*, 1895) with all the import of the mutual interdepen-

dence and inseparability at the heart of it. I am grateful to Yuri Leving for alerting me to this possible allusion.

CHAPTER TWO

1. See Dashkevich's reminiscence in Ian Smirnitskii, "Fotosimfoniia odnoi zhizni: 75 let kompozitoru Vladimiru Dashkevichu," *Moskovskii komsomolets RU*, January 19, 2009, https://www.mk.ru/culture/cinema/article/2009/01/19/3928-fotosimfoniya-odnoy-zhizni.html.

2. Mikhail Levitin, *Menia ne bylo* (Moscow: Izdanie teatra "Ermitazh," 2005), 180.

3. Kurt Vonnegut, *Slaughterhouse-Five* (New York: Random House, 1991), 98; further citations in the text are to this edition.

4. Iulii Kim, *Antologiia satiry i iumora Rossii XX veka* (Moscow: Eksmo, 2005), 38:15–16.

5. *Novyi mir* ran Rait-Kovaleva's translation of *Slaughterhouse-Five* in 1970 (a mere year after its first publication in the United States), emphasizing, in an introduction to the text, the novel's "sharply drawn anti-war orientation and truthful reflection of American reality, with its atmosphere of cruelty and indifference to human suffering" (*Novyi mir*, no. 3 [March 1970]: 79). Vonnegut would be typically portrayed in Russian media as an author who spoke truth to power, and who was thus silenced and censored at home. For instance, in 1979, the *Literaturnaia gazeta* correspondent Iona Andronov cited an instance in which Vonnegut's masterpiece had been removed from libraries in the New York State on the grounds that it "besmirched America" ("Shedevry absurda i neugodnye muzy," *Literaturnaia gazeta*, no. 4 [January 24, 1979]: 15).

Vonnegut's undoubted forthrightness in his critiques of the culture and politics of the United States did not translate to some unequivocally positive view of its Cold War rival. In his letters, Vonnegut states that he always remained "polite" when in Russia, so as not to cause problems for his translator Rait-Kovaleva. But back in the United States, he was outspoken in public interviews regarding the dictatorial aspects of the Soviet Union and the poor treatment of its writers and dissidents; see Kurt Vonnegut, *Letters*, ed. Dan Wakefield (New York: Delacorte, 2012).

6. In his introductory article to a 1978 edition of *Slaughterhouse-Five* and other works, A. Zverev characterizes Vonnegut as, in effect, the détente author par excellence: "The very lofty thought that humanity will be able to withstand contemporaneity's powerful tendencies of self-destruction, only as one family (and not as a crowd of lonely people), belongs to the art of true humanism." "Signal predosterezheniia," in Kurt Vonnegut, *Boinia nomer piat', ili krestovyi pokhod detei*, trans. Rita Rait-Kovaleva (Moscow: Khudozhestvennaia literatura, 1978), 19.

7. Chingiz Aitmatov and Kurt Vonnegut, "Vstrecha nad planetoi Zemlia: Dialog sovetskogo i amerikanskogo pisatelei," *Literaturnaia gazeta*, no. 30 (July 23, 1975): 2.

8. Aitmatov and Vonnegut, "Vstrecha nad planetoi Zemlia," 2. On behalf of all Soviet people, Aitmatov here reciprocates by expressing his belief that this joint space venture will set a great precedent for the overcoming of Cold War disagreements: "We will remember this historical moment as a burst of illumination, when the mighty forces of the human spirit met one another halfway, not for destruction, but for unity" (Aitmatov and Vonnegut, "Vstrecha nad planetoi Zemlia," 2).

9. Andrei Sakharov, *Progress, Coexistence, and Intellectual Freedom* (New York: W. W. Norton, 1970).

10. Aleksandr Oleinikov, "Shestidesiatnikam," *Literaturnye izvestiia* 96, no. 4 (2013): 10.

11. Barth, *Friday Book*, 67.

12. Petr Vail' and Aleksandr Genis, *Shestidesiatye: Mir sovetskogo cheloveka* (Ekaterinburg, Russia: U-Faktoriia, 2004), 586.

13. Vail' and Genis, *Shestidesiatye*, 587.

14. The Russian actor playing Billy, Andrei Maiorov, tried to express all these elements of Billy's character through his performance. In the review of the play that appeared in *Komsomol'skaia Pravda*, V. Turovsky writes, "Andrei Maiorov (this is his first serious theater role) plays Billy somehow very timidly and touchingly; his Billy is broken and childishly awkward (*kak-to ochen' robko i trogatel'no, izlomanno i po detski uglovato*)." "Liudi i teni" ("People and Shadows"), *Komsomol'skaia Pravda*, no. 30 (June 2, 1976): 2.

15. Vonnegut, *Boinia nomer piat'*, 2.

16. A. Mirchev, "Interv'iu s Kurtom Vonnegutom," *Kontinent*, no. 51 (1987): 440–41. In "Bartleby, or the Formula," Gilles Deleuze discusses the revolutionary power of Bartleby's formula of refusal, "I would prefer not to." According to Deleuze, "This formula is devastating because it eliminates the preferable just as mercilessly as any nonpreferred." In Deleuze's radical reading, Bartleby's refusal does not just "break the pact with the Father" (the superego, power), but also, in ruling out entirely any sort of unequal binarism or hierarchy, affirms "universal fraternity" (*Essays Critical and Clinical* [New York: Verso, 1998], 71, 78). For Deleuze, Bartleby is a paragon of revolutionary formlessness.

17. Marc Leeds, *The Vonnegut Encyclopedia* (New York: Delacorte, 2016), 142.

18. Wilhelm Grimm and Jacob Grimm, *The Complete Grimm's Fairy Tales* (New York: Random House, 1972), 128.

19. Walter Benjamin, *The Origin of German Tragic Drama*, trans. John Osborne (London: Verso, 1998), 166.

20. Walter Benjamin, "Theses on the Philosophy of History," in *Illumina-*

tions: Essays and Reflections by Walter Benjamin, trans. Harry Zohn (New York: Schocken Books, 1968), 254.

21. "Theses on the Philosophy of History," 257–58.

22. Cf. Katerina Clark's observation on Stalinist aesthetics: "[The] privileging of the general over the particular or contingent, of a character or a person's role over historical detail or individual psychology, was . . . defining for Stalinist culture" (*Moscow, The Fourth Rome: Stalinism, Cosmopolitanism, and the Evolution of Soviet Culture, 1931–1941* [Cambridge, MA: Harvard University Press, 2011], 72).

23. Iulii Kim, "Zolushka v kontslagere," in *Stikhi i pesni* (Moscow: Vremia, 2007), 494–95; further citations in the text are to this edition.

24. Alexei Yurchak, *Everything Was Forever, Until It Was No More: The Last Soviet Generation* (Princeton, NJ: Princeton University Press, 2006), 239.

25. Iulii Kim, *Odnazhdy Mikhailov* (Moscow: Vremia, 2004).

26. Kim himself situates late Soviet dissidence within the Russian tradition of revolutionary progressivism and emancipation movements: dissidents "could not put up with the monstrous system and its dictates. In Russia it's an old tradition. Rebellion against the enormous state apparatus gave birth to the People's Will, and the Decembrists" (cited from Aleksandr Arkhangel'skii, ed., *Svobodnye liudi: Dissidentskoe dvizhenie v rasskazakh uchastnikov* [Moscow: Vremia, 2018], 115). Discussing his wife Irina Iakir's work for the "Chronicle of Current Events" ("Khronika tekushchikh sobytii"), the first bulletin of samizdat, devoted to recording human rights violations, Kim compares it to Herzen's *Kolokol* (*The Bell*) and *Poliarnaia zvezda* (*The Polar Star*)—"just like them, uncensored and doggedly documenting the crimes of the regime" (Arkhangel'skii, *Svobodnye liudi*, 114).

27. Walter Benjamin, *Understanding Brecht*, trans. Anna Bostock (London: Verso, 1998), 21.

28. Fredric Jameson, *Brecht and Method* (London: Verso, 2011), 32.

29. As recently as 2019, Kim again returned to Brecht, with a new variation on that well-known play, titled *The Beggars' Opera* (*Opera nishchikh*).

30. Levitin, *Menia ne bylo*, 152.

31. See Jeffrey Richards, "E. L. Blanchard and 'The Golden Age of Pantomime,'" in *Victorian Pantomime: A Collection of Critical Essays*, ed. Jim Davis (London: Palgrave Macmillan, 2010), 21–41; and the introduction to Michael Green's *Russian Symbolist Theater: An Anthology of Plays and Critical Texts* (New York: Abrams, 2013), 9–21.

32. For more on the politics of British panto, see Jill A. Sullivan, *The Politics of the Pantomime: Regional Identity in the Theatre, 1860–1900* (Hatfield, UK: University of Hertfordshire Press, 2011) and Millie Taylor, *British Pantomime Performance* (Bristol, UK: Intellect Books, 2007). On the politics of buffoonery in Russian avant-garde theater, see Robert Leah, *Russian Futurist*

Theatre: Theory and Practice (Edinburgh, UK: Edinburgh University Press, 2018) and (particularly with regard to Meyerhold) Julia Vaingurt, *Wonderlands of the Avant-Garde: Technology and the Arts in Russia of the 1920s* (Evanston, IL: Northwestern University Press, 2013), 54–83.

33. Larissa Rudova argues that in its formal deviations from the trappings of socialist realism (its great difference from "the numerous shock worker/collective-farmer 'cinderellas' of the Stalinist musical comedies of the 1930s"), Kosheverova and Schwartz's film revived the avant-garde theatrical tradition and instantiated the art of freedom and dissent. Larissa Rudova, "Embracing Eccentricity: Zolushka and the Avant-Garde Imagination," in *A Companion to Soviet Children's Literature and Film*, ed. Olga Voronina (Leiden, Netherlands: Brill, 2019), 417–30.

34. Moreover, Kosheverova, Schwartz, and others may have been aware of the tradition of the British panto and its foregrounding of Cinderella in its productions. While it would not have been possible to openly experiment with cross-dressing in a 1947 Soviet film, there are homages, perhaps unintended, to the British tradition. The enormous Faina Ranevskaya, playing the wicked stepmother, looks very much like a man in drag, complying with the requirements for the dame of British panto tradition, while the prince, who in the British panto would have been played by a young woman, is slender, ethereal, and as dainty as Cinderella herself.

35. Levitin, *Menia ne bylo*, 180.

36. Levitin, *Menia ne bylo*, 180.

37. See the chapter titled "Is She or Isn't He? Gender and Identity" in Taylor, *British Pantomime Performance*, 105–22.

38. Madeleine Kahn, *Narrative Transvestism: Rhetoric and Gender in the Eighteenth-Century English Novel* (Ithaca, NY: Cornell University Press, 1991), 14.

39. An allusion to a well-known song of the 1940s: "I'm a little girl, / I sing songs, / I've never seen Stalin, / But I love him."

40. Levitin, *Menia ne bylo*, 180.

41. Peter Holland, "The Play of Eros: The Paradoxes of Gender in English Pantomime," *New Theatre Quarterly* 13, no. 51 (1997): 198.

42. Froma I. Zeitlin, "Playing the Other: Theater, Theatricality, and the Feminine in Greek Drama," *Representations*, no. 11 (1985): 80.

43. Incidentally, while it hardly detracts from the moral force of Vonnegut's novel, this number (popularized to generations of readers of *Slaughterhouse-Five* as almost an "official" Dresden death toll), turns out to have been based on an overestimate; see Wikipedia. 2024. "Bombing of Dresden." Last Accessed June 26, 2024. https://en.wikipedia.org/wiki/Bombing_of_Dresden_in_World _War_II#In_art_and_popular_culture.

CHAPTER THREE

1. Evgenii Kharitonov, *Pod domashnim arestom* (Moscow: Glagol, 2005), 305; this and further citations from this edition are in my translation.

2. Venedikt Erofeev, *Moskva–Petushki* (Paris: YMCA Press, 1981), 15.

3. It's reasonable to imagine that Kharitonov pursued programmatic rather than strategic purposes in writing this letter all along.

4. This move of validating one's alternative existence on the basis of its *traditionalism* was likewise made by writers of the 1960s "village prose." Vasily Shukshin's characters are typically weak figures who retreat to rural areas to avoid participation in the bustle of modern life. The combination of weakness with moral superiority firmly places these characters within the holy foolishness category (see chapter 1).

5. Kharitonov, *Pod domashnim arestom*, 498.

6. Kharitonov, *Pod domashnim arestom*, 498.

7. Kharitonov, *Pod domashnim arestom*, 498.

8. Kharitonov, *Pod domashnim arestom*, 498.

9. On the merging of the mystical and the erotic in Russian modernism and the role of same-sex love in these endeavors, see Olga Matich, *Erotic Utopia: The Decadent Imagination in Russia's Fin de Siècle* (Madison: University of Wisconsin Press), 2005.

10. Kharitonov, *Pod domashnim arestom*, 499. Of particular note here is Kharitonov's use of *mrakobesy*. In his *History of Words* (*Istoriia slov*), Viktor Vinogradov discusses the use of this word in nineteenth-century Russian progressive writing. In his famous letter to Gogol, Belinsky pairs *mrakobesie* with its more international synonym "obscurantism": "What are you doing, you preacher of the knout, apostle of ignorance, champion of obscurantism and *mrakobesie* [*pobornik obskurantizma i mrakobesiia*]?" Kharitonov's preference for *mrakobes* over *obskurantist* or *reaktsioner* takes strategic advantage of the former word's particularly archaic sound. As Vinogradov observes, although *mrakobes* was a neologism of the nineteenth century, it was coined on the same OCS compound-structure pattern that bequeathed the Russian language such archaisms as *idolobesie, chrevobesie*, and *gortanobesie*. V. Vinogradov. "Mrakobesiie, mrakobes." In *Istoriia slov*. Moscow: RAN, 1999. http://wordhist.narod.ru/mrakobesie_mrakobes.html.

11. Kharitonov, *Pod domashnim arestom*, 499.

12. Yevgeny Kharitonov, *Under House Arrest*, trans. A. L. Tait (London: Serpent's Tail, 1998), 197.

13. Pricilla Hunt, "Holy Foolishness as a Key to Russian Culture," in Hunt and Kobets, *Holy Foolishness in Russia*, 5.

14. Hunt, "Holy Foolishness as a Key to Russian Culture," 16.

15. Kharitonov, *Under House Arrest*, 147–48; trans. adjusted slightly by me.

16. Kharitonov, *Under House Arrest*, 148. The formula "Safeguard your unhappiness" has religious overtones—see, from a homily of Father Zosima (Zakhariia Vasilievch Verkhovsky, 1768–1833): "Safeguard the pearl of faith [*beregite zhemchuzhinu very*], which is the way to our eternal bliss" (cited from I. A. Popov, *Pravoslavie sviatykh i inkvizitorov* [Moscow: Obshchina Pravo-slavnoi Tserkvi Bozhiei Materi Derzhavnaia, 2003], 148)—but also ingeniously remixes two admonitions from Dostoevsky: "Safeguard your soul [*beregi dushu*], believe in the truth" (*Pis'ma* [Moscow: DirectMedia, 2015], 1:393) and, as Father Zosima preaches to Alesha in *The Brothers Karamazov*, "Here is a com-mandment for you: seek happiness in sorrow" (trans. Richard Pevear and Larissa Volokhonsky [New York: Farrar, Straus and Giroux, 1992], 77).

17. Kharitonov, *Under House Arrest*, 3.

18. Kharitonov, *Under House Arrest*, 23.

19. Kharitonov, *Under House Arrest*, 2.

20. Kharitonov, *Pod domashnim arestom*, 64.

21 On how the reception of Saint Ksenia's hagiography shifted over time, see Sergei Shtyrkov, "The Unmerry Widow: The Blessed Kseniia of Petersburg in Hagiography and Hymnography," in Hunt and Kobets, *Holy Foolishness in Russia*, 281–304.

22. Here we could recall Nietzsche's fulminations in *The Antichrist* against Paul's recoding of weakness as virtue—the great "sneaky" "seduction," in Nietzsche's view, that felled proud Rome (trans. H. L. Mencken [New York: Al-fred A. Knopf, 1931], 126, 127).

23. Kharitonov, *Under House Arrest*, 186.

24. Halberstam, *Queer Art of Failure*, 6.

25. Kharitonov, *Under House Arrest*, 186.

26. Kharitonov, *Pod domashnim arestom*, 313.

27. Kharitonov, *Under House Arrest*, 197–98.

28. Kharitonov, *Pod domashnim arestom*, 328.

29. Sergey A. Ivanov, *Holy Fools in Byzantium and Beyond*, trans. Simon Franklin (Oxford: Oxford University Press, 2006), 1.

30. Svetlana Boym, *Death in Quotation Marks: Cultural Myths of the Modern Poet* (Cambridge, MA: Harvard University Press, 1991), 31.

31. Kharitonov, *Pod domashnim arestom*, 311.

32. Anastasia Kayiatos, "Silent Plasticity: Reenchanting Soviet Stagnation," *WSQ: Women's Studies Quarterly* 40, nos. 3–4 (2012): 117.

33. Kharitonov, *Pod domashnim arestom*, 467.

34. Kharitonov, *Pod domashnim arestom*, 455.

35. Kharitonov, *Pod domashnim arestom*, 455.

36. Kharitonov, *Pod domashnim arestom*, 468.

37. Kharitonov, *Pod domashnim arestom*, 470.

38. Kharitonov, *Pod domashnim arestom*, 327. Unlike in the letter to Ak-

senov, where the precursors are all markedly Russian, this genealogy claims belonging to world culture. However, as will be discussed below, the otherwise unusual pairing of John the Evangelist with Oscar Wilde in one cultural paradigm may be seen as a particularly Russian (specifically, Russian modernist) practice. The ironic self-positionality of oneself as a genius recalls a similar declaration by the conceptualist poet Dmitry Prigov in *Alphabet 1*: "Pushkin—pure genius, Prigov—also genius." Lipovetsky and Kukulin read such moments as Prigov's engagement in hypersacralization. The parodic hyperbole deconstructs both official sacral regimes and the author's own claims, but it also enacts his authorial agency, his freedom to undertake such discursive operations. It thus both limits and defines his subjectivity as an author. ("'The Art of Penultimate Truth': Dmitrii Prigov's Aesthetic Principles," *Russian Review* 75, no. 2 [April 2016]: 186–208.) In general, the preoccupation with the figure of a genius became an important cultural marker of the postmodern period, since official Soviet culture on the one hand cultivated the mythologies of certain individual geniuses while simultaneously denying the category of individual exclusivity. Andrei Bitov was obsessed with the conceptualization of "genius," arriving at several different definitions of it throughout his career, as will be discussed in chapter 6.

39. Kharitonov, *Under House Arrest*, 58.

40. Kharitonov, *Under House Arrest*, 57.

41. The phrase "the disciple whom Jesus loved" is repeated in the Gospel of John six times: John 13:23–25; 19:26–27; 20:1–10; 21:1–25; 21:20–23; and 21:24. Kharitonov must have found this insistence significant enough to add John the Evangelist to his triad of "most poignant" gay writers. On the homoerotic subtext of the phrase "the disciple whom Jesus loved," see Martti Nissinen, *Homoeroticism in the Biblical World: A Historical Perspective* (Minneapolis: Augsburg Fortress Press, 1998), 121–22.

42. Kharitonov, *Under House Arrest*, 59.

43. Kharitonov, *Under House Arrest*, 74.

44. Dostoevsky, *Brothers Karamazov*, 320.

45. Evgenii Bershtein, "'Next to Christ': Oscar Wilde in Russian Modernism," in *The Reception of Oscar Wilde in Europe*, ed. Stefano Evangelista (London: Continuum, 2010), 293.

46. Fyodor Dostoevsky, *Notes from Underground*, trans. Richard Pevear and Larissa Volokhonsky (New York: Vintage Books, 1994), 35.

47. Kharitonov, *Under House Arrest*, 192.

48. In their biography of Kuzmin, John Malmstad and Nikolai Bogomolov observe, "The 'marginal,' 'outsider' status of the Old Believers, hounded by the authorities and in some cases driven totally underground (in this resembling the early Church), may also have offered a deep psychological attraction for him. His letters to Chicherin, though chary of details about his actual activities, illuminate yet another dimension of his decision to turn to the Old Believers: his conception

of contemporary Russian culture and his place in it" (*Mikhail Kuzmin: A Life in Art* [Cambridge, MA: Harvard University Press, 1999], 51).

49. In one passage, young Vania Smurov, visiting an older man he is drawn to, encounters a gay gathering and hears the following ecstatic speech: "People go about like the blind, like the dead, when they might create for themselves a life burning with intensity in every moment, a life in which pleasure would be as poignant as if you have just come into this world and might die before the day is done. . . . We are Hellenes, lovers of the beautiful, the bacchants of the coming day. Like Tannhauser's visions in the grotto of Venus, like the clairvoyance of Klinger and Thoma, there is the land of our forefathers, flooded in sunlight and freedom with beautiful, bold people, and across the seas, through mist and murk, we are going there, Argonauts!" Mikhail Kuzmin, *Wings*, trans. Hugh Aplin (London: Hesperus, 2007), 29–30.

50. As Dan Healey explains, "Despite the enactment of legislation designed to impose a conservative European moral norm, the law enjoyed little force. Enforcement was naturally difficult to implement without adopting the policing methods (entrapment, routine surveillance) favored by the authorities in Berlin and Paris. Russia's police, while duly concerned with maintaining order and public decency, lacked the resources to devote to the active detection of sodomy" (*Homosexual Desire in Revolutionary Russia: The Regulation of Sexual and Gender Dissent* [Chicago: University of Chicago Press, 2001], 98).

51. Evgenii Bershtein, "Anglichanin v russkoi bane: K postroeniiu istoricheskoi poetiki russkoi gei-literatury," *Novoe literaturnoe obozrenie*, no. 111 (2011): 158, 160–61.

52. Furthermore, while Rozanov himself was a great promoter of sexual revolution and fruitfulness, other important Russian religious philosophers of the time sought virtue in the sublimation of erotic desire into creativity and spirituality. For example, the embrace of asceticism by Rozanov's "moon people" matches the prescriptions given in *The Meaning of Love* (*Smysl liubvi*) by another highly influential Russian religious philosopher, Vladimir Soloviev; one is advised in this tract to inflame one's erotic desire as much as possible, but then avoid consummation, so as to pour this pent-up erotic energy into art. The period of Russian high modernism saw no few inclined to follow such precepts, observing abstinence in their erotic relationships so as (hopefully) to transform the carnal into the spiritual.

53. Kharitonov, *Under House Arrest*, 87–88; trans. adjusted slightly by me.

54. Cited from Bershtein, "Anglichanin v russkoi bane," 156–57, which is the source of my knowledge of this particular interaction between Rozanov and Berdiaev.

55. Kharitonov, *Under House Arrest*, 85–86; final words of this trans. adjusted by me.

56. Kharitonov, *Under House Arrest*, 206–7; trans. adjusted slightly by me.

57. Kharitonov, *Under House Arrest*, 130.

58. Kharitonov, *Under House Arrest*, 168.

59. Kharitonov, *Pod domashnim arestom*, 301.

60. Vasilii Aksenov, "E. Kharitonov—podpol'nyi zhitel' Moskvy," *Glagol* 10, no. 2 (1993): 95.

61. On "hipster racism," see Steven Threadgold, *Youth, Class, and Everyday Struggles* (London: Routledge, 2018), 109–10.

62. Iaroslav Mogutin, "Katorzhnik na nive bukvy," *Glagol* 10, no. 1 (1993): 8.

63. Evgenii Popov, "Kus ne po zubam: Rassuzhdeniia o knige Evg. Kharitonova *Pod domashnim arestom*," *Glagol* 10, no. 2 (1993): 105.

64. For instance: "The Russian nature without a monastery in its soul [*russkaia priroda bez monastyria v dushe*, i.e., Russia under communist atheism—JV] is a yid institution. Secretly established by the overall yid-Masonic secret mind, so as to officially present Russians in the beggarly churlishness [*tainstvenno uchrezhdena obshchim zhidomasonskim tainym umom, chtoby russkikh ofitsial'no predstavit' v poskonnom polozhenii*]. Which is a devilish rigging by the yids [*Kotoroe est' d'iavol'skaia podtasovka zhidov*]." Kharitonov, *Pod domashnim arestom*, 262.

65. In discussing antisemitism as an aspect of Kharitonov's aesthetic agenda, I do not mean to suggest that he has invented the practice by which antisemitism is used to define what is authentically Russian. That discourse certainly existed prior to Kharitonov, for instance in the writings of Rozanov. Kharitonov's pitting of gays against Jews, however, strikes me as an innovation.

66. Kharitonov, *Under House Arrest*, 184.

67. Kharitonov, *Under House Arrest*, 184–85; trans. adjusted slightly by me.

68. Kharitonov, *Under House Arrest*, 184–85; trans. adjusted slightly by me.

69. Kharitonov, *Under House Arrest*, 109; trans. adjusted slightly by me.

70. "Because the notion of holy foolishness derives from Saint Paul (who also establishes condemnation to death as a metaphor for human mortality in general), the holy fool is associated with death." Liza Knapp, *Dostoevsky's* The Idiot: *A Critical Companion* (Evanston, IL: Northwestern University Press, 1998), 14.

71. As foregrounded for instance in Albert Schweitzer's *The Quest of the Historical Jesus* (1906).

72. Kharitonov's particular stance, indeed, may be seen in the context of the "queer apocalypses" discussed by Lorenzo Bernini (*Queer Apocalypses: Elements of Antisocial Theory* [London: Palgrave Macmillan, 2017]); cf. also the writings of Leo Bersani and Lee Edelman.

73. In *Queer in Russia: A Story of Sex, Self, and the Other* (Durham, NC: Duke University Press, 1999), Laurie Essing narrates a similar moment of estrangement—her encounter with the improbable yet unmistakable merger of queer sexuality and nationalism in post-Soviet Russia: "The intersection of

nationalism and queer sexuality disturbs our sense of the world. For queers to be nationalists and nationalists to be queers, history must have fallen through the looking glass. We know the history in the United States—queers are marginalized and therefore ally with other marginalized groups. Women, queers, persons of color go together like love and marriage. Nationalistic/fascistic politicians cannot be queer, since they seek to eliminate all otherness, including sexual otherness. Yet, once on the other side of the looking glass, we realize there are other histories circulating" (153).

74. Vattimo, "Dialectics, Difference, Weak Thought," 40.

CHAPTER FOUR

1. For an in-depth analysis of the generic multiplicity and intermixing in *Moscow–Petushki*, see O. V. Bogdanova, *"Moskva–Petushki" Venedikta Erofeeva kak pratekst russkogo postmodernizma* (St. Petersburg: Filologicheskii fakul'tet Sankt-Peterburgskogo gosudarstvennogo universiteta, 2002), 5–19; and A. N. Bezrukov, *Retseptsiia khudozhestvennogo teksta: Funktsional'nyi podkhod* (St. Petersburg: Giperion, 2015), 210–20.

2. "To Vadim Tikhonov, my beloved firstborn, I dedicate these *tragic* pages" (emphasis mine). Erofeev, *Moscow to the End of the Line*, 7.

3. Recently, two significant attempts have been made to exit the celebratory mode and account for the *poema's* tragic aspects: Ann Komaromi, "On the Knife's Edge: Venichka's Performance in *Moscow Stations*," in her *Uncensored: Samizdat Novels and the Quest for Autonomy in Soviet Dissidence* (Evanston, IL: Northwestern University Press, 2015), 102–28; and Mark Lipovetsky, "Venichka: A Tragic Trickster," in his *Charms of the Cynical Reason*, 153–92. I will return to the arguments of both scholars later in the text.

4. Yuri Levin, the author of one of the two commentaries to *Moscow–Petushki*, warns against the "common mistake" of conflating the author with the character bearing his name (Iurii Levin, *Kommentarii k poeme "Moskva–Petushki" Venedikta Erofeeva* [Graz, Austria: Grazer Gesellschaft zur Förderung Slawischer Kulturstudien, 1996], 23). The distinction between author and protagonist is central to my argument; the incommensurability between Erofeev and Venichka enables the former to use the latter to interrogate his own most cherished views.

5. Eduard Vlasov, "Bessmertnaia poema Venedikta Erofeeva *Moskva–Petushki*. Sputnik pisatelia," in V. Erofeev, *Moskva–Petushki* (Moscow: Vagrius, 2001), 121–574.

6. On Erofeev's holy foolishness, see Svetlana Gaiser-Shnitman, *Venedikt Erofeev: "Moskva–Petushki" ili "The Rest is Silence"* (Bern, Switzerland: Peter Lang, 1989), 116–20; Lipovetsky, *Russian Postmodernist Fiction*, 66–82; Irina Paperno and Boris Gasparov, "Vstan' i idi," *Slavica Hierosolymitana*, no. 5–6 (1981): 389–400.

7. See Lipovetsky, *Russian Postmodernist Fiction*, 66–82. Lipovetsky's revision of this argument in "Venichka: A Tragic Trickster" is motivated by recognition that the *poema's* tragic end conflicts with the interpretation of Erofeev as unreservedly espousing apophatic negation (whether of the postmodern or holy-foolish variety): "The poem's tragic finale . . . is itself at odds with the now classical interpretation of *Moskva–Petushki* as an apophatic (holy-fool-like) affirmation of the Christian 'transcendental signified' in the midst of drunken hell and universal chaos" (180).

8. Mikhail Epstein, "Posle karnavala, ili vechnyi Venichka," in *Ostav'te moiu dushu v pokoe: Pochti vse*, by V. Erofeev (Moscow: Kh. G. S., 1995), 3–30.

9. Laura Beraha, "Out of and into the Void: Picaresque Absence and Annihilation," in *Venedikt Erofeev's "Moscow–Petushki": Critical Perspectives*, ed. Karen L. Ryan-Hayes (Bern, Switzerland: Peter Lang, 1997), 20.

10. Lipovetsky, *Charms of the Cynical Reason*, 173.

11. Lipovetsky, *Charms of the Cynical Reason*, 167. At one point in the narrative, Venichka defines himself as "a phenomenon" in possession of "self-generating Logos" (*samovozrastaiushchii logos*). Erofeev, *Moskva–Petushki*, 100.

12. Lipovetsky, *Charms of the Cynical Reason*, 191.

13. I have no intention, of course, of moralizing on Venichka's (and by extension, Erofeev's) alcoholism. My point of departure, rather, is the consideration of alcoholism in the novel as an expression of a particular worldview—not an individual worldview, but one representative of the intelligentsia of Erofeev's generation.

14. Some argue that the novel's end is not tragic at all—that with it, rather, the Christlike Venichka kenotically sacrifices himself for the sake of humanity. I will discuss this interpretation later in the text.

15. Aristotle, *The Poetics of Aristotle*, trans. S. H. Butcher (New York: Cosimo Classics, 2008), 19.

16. The generational aspect is touched on in the study of O. V. Bogdanova. Remarking on the crisis of the positive hero in the late 1960s and early 1970s, she differentiates among several categories of "nonheroes" (*ne-geroi*) that sprouted in Russian prose at the time, dubbing Eroveev's Venichka the first postmodern example of this figure: "Almost simultaneously with the nonheroes of the Village Prose ('passive' nonheroes), nonheroes of urban prose ('conformists'), and nonheroes of the prose of 'the forty-year-olds' ('marginals,' 'ambivalent' heroes), Venichka was the first literary representative of the nonhero to belong to the generation of watchmen and janitors, stokers and plumbers, the future postmodernist writers, who followed the writers of the early twentieth century in discovering that 'in vino veritas'" (*"Moskva–Petushki" Venedikta Erofeeva kak pratekst russkogo postmodernizma*, 21). While Bogdanova does not state it explicitly, her list of manual-labor jobs, undesirable for members of the intelligentsia, is meant to demonstrate that these characters establish their nonheroism by avoiding markers of social success, by being "losers" in careerist terms.

17. This is not to suggest that other late Soviet writers who employed the code of weakness embraced its ethics wholeheartedly, nor that they invested it with the same significance as Erofeev. Among the authors mentioned so far, Aksenov ultimately rejects this code, while Bitov, as will be discussed in chapter 6, continues to experiment with "weak" aesthetics throughout his writing, weeding out its questionable aspects and cultivating its strengths.

18. Savitsky notes the return, in the Soviet literary underground of the 1970s, of the genre of diary, with its allowance for fragmented, meandering form and the expression of private emotions and impressions, and he remarks that Vasily Rozanov's prose was seen as a modernist prototype for this genre (*Andergraund*, 64–65). It is thus hardly surprising that, for two of this book's case studies, Erofeev and Kharitonov, Rozanov became a particularly important predecessor and interlocutor.

19. Vasilii Rozanov, *Opavshie list'ia* (Moscow: Iurait, 2018), 8; Erofeev, *Zapisnye knizhki*, 1:629.

20. Rozanov, *Opavshie list'ia*, 81; Erofeev, *Zapisnye knizhki*, 1:624.

21. Rozanov, *Opavshie list'ia*, 8; Erofeev, *Zapisnye knizhki*, 1:629.

22. Erofeev, *Moscow to the End of the Line*, 16.

23. The authors of *Venedikt Erofeev: Postoronnii* likewise highlight this central conflict within *Moscow–Petushki*, calling it "a dialectic contradiction between the theme of seclusion and the theme of meeting." In their interpretation, during the drunken feast on the train, the book takes on the shape of the Platonic symposium, dialogic in form and relational in content (with the subject being love). According to the scholars, this symposium, the acme of Venichka's encounter with the world, quickly devolves back into the Munchausen-like travelogue: "At this peak of accord, the hero cannot help himself and slides back into estrangement" (Oleg Lekmanov, Mikhail Sverdlov, and Il'ia Simanovskskii, *Venedikt Erofeev: Postoronnii* [Moscow: AST, 2019], 251).

24. Komaromi, *Uncensored*, 116–17.

25. Erofeev, *Zapisnye knizhki*, 1:513.

26. Erofeev, *Moscow to the End of the Line*, 46.

27. Erofeev, *Moscow to the End of the Line*; Vattimo, "Dialectics, Difference, Weak Thought," 39–52.

28. This principle of negation, or what Lipovetsky calls the "categorical anti-imperative," (*Charms of the Cynical Reason*, 164), is what leads so many commentators to see in Venichka a postmodern iteration of apophatic holy foolishness.

29. Venedikt Erofeev, *Zapiski psikhopata* (Moscow: Vagrius, 2000), 427.

30. Erofeev, *Zapiski psikhopata*, 427.

31. Prudovsky sounds a rhyming, poetic note here: *ee slova, ee usta, ee postup' i postupki*. Notably, Soviet power, *sovetskaia vlast'*, is grammatically feminine.

32. Erofeev, *Zapiski psikhopata*, 441.

33. Epstein, "Posle karnavala," 16.

34. Epstein, "Posle karnavala."16.

35. In the notebooks, Erofeev records Rozanov's attitude toward loftiness: "Everything lofty [*velichestvennoe*] was permanently alien to me. I did not love and did not respect it" (*Zapisnye knizhki*, 2:70).

36. Erofeev, *Zapisnye knizhki*, 1:540.

37. Erofeev, *Zapisnye knizhki*, 1:476.

38. This stance is echoed in the 2000 film *The Tao of Steve* (dir. Jenniphr Goodman), whose protagonist formulates his "slacker" worldview thus: "Doing stuff is overrated. Hitler, he did a lot. But don't we all wish he would've just stayed home and gotten stoned?"

39. Cited in Erofeev, *Zapisnye knizhki*, 1:45.

40. Erofeev, *Zapisnye knizhki*, 1:45.

41. Erofeev, *Zapisnye knizhki*, 1:45.

42. Erofeev, *Zapisnye knizhki*, 1:471.

43. In his notebook, Erofeev remarks (*Zapisnye knizhki*, 1:562) that "All the Riveras, Mussolinis, Francos, Goebbelses, and Zhdanovs do not favor 'art for a select few.'" In contrast to these authoritarians (and Diego Rivera, who apparently made this list because of his political commitments *to* authoritarian communism), Erofeev resolves to create precisely this kind of art, embracing and cultivating artistic individuality.

44. Erofeev, *Moscow to the End of the Line*, 20.

45. In one of his notebook entries, Erofeev codes weakness in ideological terms as a form of anti-Leninism, alluding, that is, to "Lenin's hated word 'spinelessness' [*beskhrebetnost'*], 'spineless scum'" (*Zapisnye knizhki*, 2:170). Curiously, Erofeev here transfers Lenin's sentiment from the quality the word describes to the word itself, despite the clear implication that Lenin was, to the contrary, fond of using this word. Registering the affective charge with which Lenin imbued it, Erofeev demonstrates that he himself does not find *beskhrebetnost'* particularly objectionable—neither the word, nor especially what it signifies.

46. Erofeev, *Moscow to the End of the Line*, 20.

47. On alcohol as the source of inspiration in *Moscow–Petushki*, see Vlasov, "Bessmertnaia poema," 350.

48. Erofeev, *Zapisnye knizhki*, 1:513, 399.

49. Erofeev, *Moscow to the End of the Line*, 20. In his perceptive article "In Praise of Booze: *Moskva–Petushki* and Erasmian Irony" (*Slavonic and East European Review* 88, no. 3 [2010]: 437–67), Oliver Ready argues that drinking in the *poema* functions much like folly in Erasmus's "In Praise of Folly": Erofeev presents a "lengthy demonstration—as erudite and silly as Stultitia's argument that all people are fools—that all men . . . are drunkards" (459–60). In Ready's view, these respective assertions of universal folly and drunkenness speak to the human condition generally: the fact that truth remains elusive or inaccessible to

people, who would be wise to abstain (so to speak) from believing in their own wisdom and infallibility.

50. Lipovetsky writes that "getting wasted" allows Venichka to "accomplish ritualistic expenditure" and thereby gain symbolic power (*Charms of the Cynical Reason*, 169–70).

51. Erofeev, *Moscow to the End of the Line*, 31; trans. revised slightly by me.

52. "Antinomially" (*antinomichno*) is the word used in the original. "All my life this nightmare has haunted me, this nightmare of being misunderstood not just wrongly, but in exactly the opposite way to what I intend" (Erofeev, *Moscow to the End of the Line*, 34).

53. Erofeev, *Moscow to the End of the Line*, 30. Venichka's sense of shame is perceptively explained by Komaromi, who categorizes it with that of the protagonists of Aksenov and Bitov: "In all these novels, the feeling of shame signals a broken social connection. We can relate this to the dissident decision to refuse the general illusion and take up a stand apart, making oneself an object of ostracism, misunderstanding, censure, and ridicule" (*Uncensored*, 120). Komaromi does not elaborate on this point, but it seems to approach my own view of the text's betrayal of a sense of dissatisfaction, or at least incomplete satisfaction, with its own proposed "solutions."

54. Erofeev, *Moscow to the End of the Line*, 46.

55. Venedikt Erofeev, *Moscow Stations*, trans. Stephen Mulrine (London: Gardners Books, 1998), 25.

56. Levin, *Kommentarii*, 75.

57. Venichka's mock election as president might recall another pseudocampaign in Soviet literature: Ivan Babichev's "conspiracy of feelings" (in particular, of outdated, non-Soviet sentiments), preached in drunken speeches in Moscow bars in Olesha's *Envy* (*Zavist'*, 1927). Ivan Babichev and Nikolai Kavalerov, the novella's main protagonist and bearer of the eponymous feeling, derive their subjectivity from adherence to the perceived values of yesteryear, and from their concomitant rebellion against the moral and aesthetic *completeness* of the new Soviet world, which they are determined to unmask as, despite its loud claims, still incapable of doing away with all vulnerabilities and "weak spots." But aside from the similarity of drunken musings, Kavalerov is a radically different character from Venichka. The former, like Dostoevsky's Underground Man from whom he descends, harbors quite romantic hopes about himself; he and Ivan alike envision their lives via the prism of a romantic plot. (For a discussion of this, see Vaingurt, *Wonderlands of the Avant-Garde*, chapter 5.) For his part, Venichka stands resolutely apart from such romanticism.

58. Erofeev, *Moscow to the End of the Line*, 126–27.

59. Erofeev, *Moscow to the End of the Line*, 17. This has been noted by Valentina Baslyk: "Throughout Venichka's journey [angels] have been associated with his beloved, but sickly three-year-old." "Venichka's Divided Self:

The Sacred and the Monstrous," in Ryan-Hayes, *Venedikt Erofeev's "Moscow–Petushki": Critical Perspectives*, 74.

60. Erofeev, *Moscow to the End of the Line*, 163.

61. Erofeev, *Moscow to the End of the Line*, 149.

62. Erofeev, *Moscow to the End of the Line*, 145.

63. Vlasov, "Bessmertnaia poema," 521.

64. Discussing the significance of Kramskoy's painting in the *poema*, Karen Ryan-Hayes associates it with "a recurrent theme of *Moscow–Petushki*": "the impossibility of emotional and spiritual bonding," in particular, the "profound privacy of the experience of grief" ("Erofeev's Grief: Inconsolable and Otherwise," in Ryan-Hayes, *Venedikt Erofeev's "Moscow–Petushki": Critical Perspectives*, 104–5). Konstantin Kustanovich continues this train of thought in his contribution to the same volume ("Venichka Erofeev's Grief and Solitude: Existentialist Motifs in the Poema," in Ryan-Hayes, *Venedikt Erofeev's "Moscow–Petushki": Critical Perspectives*, 123–51). Kustanovich categorizes the possible causes of Venichka's grief: psychological—depression over his alcoholic intemperance; ideological—disconsolateness over his complex relationship with the Soviet system; philosophical—sorrow over the human condition, its transcendental homelessness, and existential abandonment. Both critics oscillate between locating Venichka's grief within or externally to him, although Ryan-Hayes leans more toward the latter explanation, reading him as evincing "the widespread ennui of the zastoi period" ("Erofeev's Grief," 118), while Kustanovich leans toward the former, the idea that grieving, solitary Venichka stands for the existentialist worldview and the agonizing search for authentic and unherdlike being.

65. Erofeev, *Moscow to the End of the Line*, 47.

66. Erofeev, *Moscow to the End of the Line*, 14.

67. Erofeev, *Moscow to the End of the Line*, 48.

68. Erofeev, *Moscow to the End of the Line*, 48.

69. Erofeev, *Moscow to the End of the Line*, 48.

70. Erofeev, *Moscow to the End of the Line*, 49.

71. Vlasov, "Bessmertnaia poema," 242.

72. Gaiser-Shnitman, *Venedikt Erofeev*, 121.

73. See, for example, E. A. Kozitskaia, "Put' k smerti i ee smysl v poeme Ven. Erofeeva 'Moskva–Petushki,'" in *Analiz odnogo proizvedeniia: Moskva–Petushki Venedikta Erofeeva: Sbornik nauchnykh trudov*, ed. I. V. Fomenko (Tver, Russia: Tverskoi gosudarstvennyi universitet, 2001), 17–22.

74. On the cruelty of the divine in the *poema*, see the brilliant discussion in Lipovetsky, *Charms of the Cynical Reason*, 187–91. Lipovetsky reads Venichka's demise as the killing of "the individual voice, in accordance with the logic of power," thus as evincing the cruelty of the divine Logos (187). I would emphasize rather the cruelty associated in the book with the self's devaluation of others, of human attachments.

75. Venichka's internalization of the sense of abandonment his sweet-heart and child must have felt is conveyed, among other ways, by certain of his drunken metamorphoses; that is, in his delirium, he experiences his own trans-formation into (or very like) those he has abandoned, with one passenger ad-dressing him as if he were a little boy ("You'd better stay home and do tomor-row's lessons. Probably you haven't done tomorrow's stuff yet; your mama'll get mad"), and another calling him "my wandering lovely" (or "lovely wanderess [*milaia strannitsa*]) (*Moscow to the End of the Line*, 129). On Venichka's an-drogyny as an attack on stable gender identity, see Beraha, "Out of and into the Void," 40.

76. I cannot prove Erofeev's knowledge of the poetic history of *IO*, but his *poema* is of course densely intertextual.

77. Mikhail Lermontov, *Poemy* (St. Petersburg: Azbuka-klassika, 2008), 313.

78. Konstantin Bal'mont, *Poeziia kak volshebstvo* (Moscow: Skorpion, 1915), 64.

79. Igor' Terent'ev, *Rekord nezhnosti: Zhizn' Il'i Zdanevicha* (Tiflis, Georgia: Izdatel'stvo 41, 1919), 10.

80. Terent'ev, *Rekord nezhnosti*, 12.

81. Vasilii Kamenskii, *Ego-moia biografiia velikogo futurista* (Moscow: Kitovras, 1918), https://ruslit.traumlibrary.net/page/kamenskiy-biografia.html.

82. Kamenskii, *Ego-moia biografiia velikogo futurista*.

83. Kamenskii, *Ego-moia biografiia velikogo futurista*.

84. "Vowels are women," declares Balmont (*Poeziia kak volshebstvo*, 57–58), "consonants are men. Vowels are our very voice, the mothers who bore us, the sisters who kissed us, the original source from which, like drops and burst-ing current, we flowed out in our verbal countenance." There is also attested a trend in American primary education by which children first learning the alpha-bet were taught to conceive of consonants as "boys" and vowels as "girls"; see for instance Ann E. Kammer, Cherlyn S. Granrose, and Jan B. Sloan, *Science, Sex, and Society* (Women's Educational Equity Act Program, US Department of Health, Education, and Welfare, 1979).

85. Andrei Belyi, "Liniia, krug, spiral'—simvolizma," *Trudy i dni*, no. 4–5 (1912): 13–14.

86. On Bely's spiral, see "Liniia, krug, spiral'—simvolizma," 17.

87. Erofeev, *Moscow to the End of the Line*, 131.

88. On the motif of silence and muteness in the whole *poema*, and especially in the finale, see Lipovetsky, *Charms of the Cynical Reason*, 185–86.

89. As Komaromi perceptively observes (*Uncensored*, 119), the son not only represents a singularly important human relationship in Venichka's life but also models the connection between author and reader: "The little boy represents a more serious hope for the real human results of the connection made at the site of the text, fruit of the union of author and reader that must, like the boy, grow into maturity and independence."

CHAPTER FIVE

1. Sergei Dovlatov, *Sobranie prozy v trekh tomakh* (St. Petersburg: Litmus Press, 1995), 2:37.

2. This may also be considered a remarkable case of life imitating art, as by this time, Aleksandr Griboedov had already published his famous play *Woe from Wit* (*Gore ot uma*, 1825), in which the romantic figure Chatsky, having returned from abroad, eloquently decries the customary behaviors of Russian high society that he has come to find odious, and is declared "mad" by that society.

3. This quote from Prof. N. N. Timofeev's "The Deontological Aspect of Identifying Schizophrenia" ("Deontologicheskii aspekt raspoznavaniia bol'nykh shizofreniei") is cited in V. Bukovskii and S. Gluzman, "Posobie po psikhiatrii dlia inakomysliashchikh," in *Antologiia samizdata. Nepodtsenzurnaia literatura v SSSR (1950-e–1980-e)*, vol 3, *Posle 1973*, ed. V. V. Igrunov (Moscow: Mezhdunarodnyi institut gumanitarno-politicheskikh issledovanii, 2005), 149, 147–59. Significantly for the trajectory of Putinist Russia, a long-available version of this samizdat anthology has recently been removed from the .ru domain.

4. Theresa C. Smith and Thomas Oleszczuk report that "the Soviet operational definition of schizophrenia has been so diffuse as to include conditions which would either be diagnosed as other mental disorders elsewhere, or would not be diagnosed as pathological at all." Theresa C. Smith and Thomas Oleszczuk, *No Asylum: State Psychiatric Repression in the Former USSR* (New York: New York University Press, 1996), 7. Zhores Medvedev was, reportedly, diagnosed with schizophrenia for "what physicians described as his 'poor adaptation to his social environment' and the 'split personality' evident in his wide range of interests." Rebecca Reich, *State of Madness: Psychiatry, Literature, and Dissent after Stalin* (DeKalb: Northern Illinois University Press, 2018), 96.

5. Valentina Ciullo, Gianfranco Spalletta, Carlo Caltagirone, Ricardo E. Jorge, Federica Piras. "Explicit Time Deficit in Schizophrenia: Systematic Review and Meta-Analysis Indicate It Is Primary and Not Domain Specific." In *Schizophrenia Bulletin* 42, no. 2 (2016): 505–18.

6. However, institutionalization as a milder alternative to "corrective labor" or execution was already explored in Ilya Ilf and Evgeny Petrov's *The Little Golden Calf* (*Zolotoi telenok*, 1931), where various characters try to sit out purges by checking themselves into a psychiatric hospital.

7. *Who Is the Madman?* is a memoir of the ordeal of Zhores Medvedev, a prominent geneticist and essayist who in 1970 was forcibly hospitalized in effect for embodying this duality (scientist-humanist): the diagnosis was schizophrenia with symptoms of "split-personality disorder." His twin brother Roy Medvedev was a dissident historian of Stalinism. Zhores Medvedev and Roy Medvedev, *Kto sumasshedshii?* (London: Macmillan, 1971), 35, 133.

8. For an account of how the two managed this remarkable feat, see Re-

becca Reich, *State of Madness: Psychiatry, Literature, and Dissent after Stalin* (DeKalb: Northern Illinois University Press, 2018), 88.

9. A. S. Esenin-Vol'pin, "Iuridicheskaia pamiatka dlia tekh, komu predstoiat doprosy," in *Filosofia. Logika, Poeziia. Zashchita prav cheloveka: Izbrannoe* (Moscow: Rossiiskii gosudarstvennyi gumanitarnyi universitet, 1999), 356–72.

10. Vladimir Bukovskii and Semen Gluzman. "Posobie po psikhiatrii dlia inakomysliashchikh," in *Antologiia samizdata. Nepodtsenzurnaia literatura v SSSR (1950-e–1980-e)*, vol. 3, *Posle 1973*, edited by V. V. Igrunov. (Moscow: Mezhdunarodnyi institut gumanitarno-politicheskikh issledovanii, 2005), 157.

11. Sasha Sokolov, *A School for Fools*, trans. Carl R. Proffer (New York: Four Walls Eight Windows, 1988), 219; further citations in the text are to this edition.

12. Sasha Sokolov, *Shkola dlia durakov* (Ann Arbor, MI: Ardis, 1983), 163.

13. Compiled by K. Kuzminsky, Gr. Kovalev, and B. Taigin in 1962.

14. Cited from Reich, *State of Madness*, 63. This reciprocal diagnosis of Soviet apparatchiks and the whole regime as psychotic recalls an episode in *The Little Golden Calf*, when one of the characters, Kai Iulii Starokhamskii, commits himself to a psychiatric ward "for ideological reasons," arguing that "in Soviet Russia . . . the insane asylum is the only place a normal person can live. Everywhere else is worse than bedlam." Ilya Ilf and Evgeny Petrov, *The Little Golden Calf*, trans. Anne O. Fisher (Montpelier, VT: Russian Life Books, 2009), 218.

15. See Cynthia Simmons, *Their Father's Voice: Vasily Aksyonov, Venedikt Erofeev, Eduard Limonov, and Sasha Sokolov* (New York: Peter Lang, 1993).

16. Alexandra Heidi Karriker, "Double Vision: Sasha Sokolov's *School for Fools*," *World Literature Today* 53, no. 4 (1979): 610–14.

17. D. Barton Johnson, "Sasha Sokolov: A Literary Biography," *Canadian-American Slavic Studies* 21, nos. 3–4 (1987): 206.

18. See Gregory Bateson, "Minimal Requirements for a Theory of Schizophrenia," *AMA Archives of General Psychiatry* 2, no. 5 (1960): 477–91; Jacques Lacan, "On a Question Prior to Any Possible Treatment of Psychosis," in *Écrits*, ed J. Lacan and J. A. Miller, trans. Bruce Fink (New York: W. W. Norton, 2004), 445–88; Michele Ribolsi, Jasper Feyaerts, and Stijn Vanheule, "Metaphor in Psychosis: On the Possible Convergence of Lacanian Theory and Neuro-Scientific Research," *Frontiers in Psychology* 6, article 664 (2015): 1–12.

19. See Roman Jakobson, "Two Types of Language and Two Types of Aphasic Disturbances," in *Language in Literature* (Cambridge, MA: Harvard University Press, 1987), 109–11. On excessive metaphorization and other linguistic traits of aberrant discourse, as well as their relation to Jakobson's theory of language poles, see Simmons, *Their Father's Voice*, 136–39.

20. Natal'ia Kochetkova, "'Ia vsegda znal, chto uedu iz Sovetskogo Soiuza': Sasha Sokolov o roditeliakh-razvedchikakh, psikhbol'nitsakh i Kanade," *Lenta. ru*, February 11, 2017, https://lenta.ru/articles/2017/02/11/sokolovfilm/.

21. Sasha Sokolov, *In the House of the Hanged: Essays and Vers Libres*, trans. Alexander Boguslawski (Toronto: University of Toronto Press, 2012), 62.

22. Sokolov, *In the House of the Hanged*, 62.

23. Sokolov, *In the House of the Hanged*, 14.

24. Sokolov, *Shkola dlia durakov*, 144.

25. See, for example, Simmons, *Their Father's Voice*, 136.

26. Jean-Luc Nancy, introduction to *Who Comes after the Subject?*, ed. Eduardo Cadava, Peter Connor, and Jean-Luc Nancy (New York: Routledge, 1991), 6.

27. Slavoj Žižek, *Tarrying with the Negative: Kant, Hegel, and the Critique of Ideology* (Durham, NC: Duke University Press, 1993), 32; emphasis in original.

28. Slavoj Žižek, *The Parallax View* (Cambridge, MA: MIT Press, 2016), 4.

29. Sokolov, *Shkola dlia durakov*, 142.

30. Sokolov, *In the House of the Hanged*, 63.

31. Slavoj Žižek, *The Sublime Object of Ideology* (London: Verso, 1989), 84.

32. Slavoj Žižek, *Looking Awry: An Introduction to Lacan through Popular Culture* (Cambridge, MA: MIT Press, 1991), 73.

33. Žižek, *Looking Awry*, 74.

34. Žižek, *Sublime Object of Ideology*, 86.

35. Elena Kravchenko, *The Prose of Sasha Sokolov: Reflections on/of the Real*. MHRA Texts and Dissertations, vol. 86 (London: Modern Humanities Research Association, 2013), 19–43.

36. Kravchenko, *Prose of Sasha Sokolov*, 19–21.

37. Sokolov, *Shkola dlia durakov*, 104.

38. The pain of seeing the self is so excruciating that it exceeds language, as emphasized by Sokolov's halting reference here to wording from one of the pillars of the socialist-realist canon, Nikolai Ostrovsky's *How the Steel Was Tempered* (*Kak zakalialas' stal'*). The phrase in question, *muchitel'no bol'no*, figures in the protagonist Pavel Korchagin's injunction—famous to all of us former Soviet schoolkids—about the well-lived life: "[Life] is given but once, and one must live it such that it will not be excruciatingly painful to look back on one's misspent years . . . such that, dying, one might say: 'All my life, all my strength, has been given over to the most wonderful thing in the world: the struggle for the liberation of humanity'" ([Moscow: Detskaia literatura, 1979], 448). Living for the future, such that future you will not be ashamed, is all well and good; but Sokolov's protagonist, for whom past and future exist simultaneously, is denied this opportunity.

39. See Mikhail Bakhtin, *Rabelais and His World*, trans. Hélène Iswolsky (Bloomington: Indiana University Press, 1984), and Kravchenko, "Metaphor of Origin: Narcissism as a Constructive Principle in *School for Fools*," in *The Prose of Sasha Sokolov*, 19–44.

40. See for instance Lipovetsky, *Russian Postmodernist Fiction*, 83.

41. Fittingly, the cover of Sokolov's latest collection of poems, *Triptych*, published by the Russian press OGI in 2011, features three baroque arabesque panels with grotesque figures artfully intertwined.

42. R. Astruc, *Le Renouveau du grotesque dans le roman du XXe siècle* (Paris: Classiques Garnier, 2010).

43. Lipovetsky, *Russian Postmodernist Fiction*, 22.

44. John Ruskin, *Modern Painters* (Boston: Dana Estes, 1955), 132.

45. John Ruskin, "The Grotesque in Literature," in *Ruskin as Literary Critic: Selections*, ed. A. H. R. Ball (Cambridge: Cambridge University Press, 2013), 143.

46. Justin D. Edwards and Rune Graulund, *Grotesque* (London: Routledge, 2013), 17.

47. The piece is referred to as an "essay" in the few scholarly mentions it has received, and it is indeed about an actual person (the blind composer Mikhail Stepanovich Stepanov); however, since it is clearly a work of "creative nonfiction," it could perhaps be better designated a "story-essay."

48. Sasha Sokolov, "Vse tsveta radugi," *Zhizn' slepykh*, no. 9 (1968): 11.

49. The particular hand absent here is curious. It is in fact possible to sustain the career of pianist while missing a right hand. Many dazzling piano pieces have been written for the left hand alone, but hardly any solely for the right. Paradoxically, then, it is the left hand, typically considered the lesser of the two, that is most necessary for a pianist. Melody is usually placed in the right hand; writing a piece for the left hand alone, bass and melody in one hand, thus presents a challenge for composers. As the left hand is usually (and proverbially) less dexterous, moreover, performing such a piece enables a show of virtuosity on the part of the pianist. The right hand, being the more skilled, is uninspiring.

50. Vladimir Nabokov, "A Guide to Berlin," in *The Stories of Vladimir Nabokov* (New York: Alfred A. Knopf, 1995), 160.

51. Sasha Sokolov, *Shkola dlia durakov. Mezhdu sobakoi i volkom. Palisandriia. Esse* (St. Petersburg: Azbuka, 2011), 193. The English "cripple" and Russian *kaleka* are suitable equivalents in their modern offensiveness; language's ability to either stigmatize, normalize, or emphasize disability will be addressed in this book's conclusion.

52. Kravchenko, *Prose of Sasha Sokolov*, 52.

53. Interestingly, an English idiom for the relationship of cruelty and fierce competition features dogs—"dog-eat-dog world"—while an analogous Russian idiom, derived, like Sokolov's title, from a Latin expression (*Homo homini lupus*), features wolves: *chelovek cheloveku volk* ("A man is a wolf to another man").

54. Sokolov, *Shkola dlia durakov. Mezhdu sobakoi i volkom. Palisandriia. Esse*, 193.

55. Kahn et al., *History of Russian Literature*, 699.

56. Kahn et al., *History of Russian Literature*, 699.

57. They are akin even in their botanical nicknames: So-and-So's alter ego is *Nymphaea alba*, while the palisander is a type of rosewood, whose genus is *Dalbergia*.

58. Kravchenko, *Prose of Sasha Sokolov*, 105, 129.

59. Boris Groys, *The Total Art of Stalinism: Avant-Garde, Aesthetic Dictatorship, and Beyond*, trans. Charles Rougle (London: Verso, 2011), 105.

60. Kahn et al., *History of Russian Literature*, 699.

61. Not to mention that, at least in literature and popular culture, the delusion of grandeur is often a marker of a schizophrenia.

62. Cited from Reich, *State of Madness*, 63.

63. Reich, *State of Madness*, 63.

64. Reich, *State of Madness*, 63.

CHAPTER SIX

1. According to von Hirsch, "For more than half a century, Bitov has been composing a single indivisible, ongoing project to which he, on his own admission, constantly returns, furnishing it with properties that allow it to remain unending and open and thus be continued ad infinitum" ("The Illusion of Infinity: Andrei Bitov's Innovative Poetics of Commentary," *Russian Studies in Literature* 44, no. 2 [2008]: 79). Hirsch argues that the device of commentary creates an illusion of authorial presence—that is, the text's existence in the present moment, the present continuous tense.

2. Andrei Bitov, *Life in Windy Weather*, trans. Carol G. Luplow et al., ed. Priscilla Meyer (Ann Arbor, MI: Ardis, 1986), 59.

3. Andrei Bitov, *Sobranie sochinenii* (Moscow: Molodaia gvardiia, 1991), 1:45.

4. Bitov, *Sobranie sochinenii*, 1:47.

5. Bitov, *Sobranie sochinenii*, 1:148.

6. Bitov, *Sobranie sochinenii*, 1:45.

7. In *Pushkin House*, the "author" confesses, "Light at the end—we promised, we hoped. . . . But we have a premonition. We won't be able to get to that end now. Just between us, there is no end" (Andrei Bitov, *Pushkin House*, trans. Susan Brownsberger [Normal, IL: Dalkey Archive Press, 1987], 246).

8. Bitov, *Life in Windy Weather*, 153. Interestingly, Irina Surat sees the same combination of weariness and compulsion in relation to writing in Bitov's much later text, *The Teacher of Symmetry* (*Prepodavatel' simmetrii*), published in 1987. Surat writes: "In Bitov we encounter no apologia for creativity, only a sense of doom, of being condemned to the word, to the reflection of all and everything in oneself" ("Dreams Too Real: For Andrei Bitov's Birthday," *Russian Studies in Literature* 44, no. 2 [2008]: 68).

9. Bitov, *Life in Windy Weather*, 153; I have adjusted the translation slightly to maintain what was, in the original, one long sentence.

10. Bitov, *Life in Windy Weather*, 173.

11. On "the aesthetics of graphomania" as a phenomenon in late Soviet writing, see Richard Borden's insightful book *The Art of Writing Badly: Valentin Kataev's Mauvism and the Rebirth of Russian Modernism* (Evanston, IL: Northwestern University Press, 1999). Borden reads this "bad" writing as a reaction against the official injunction to produce "socially useful" literature, and he devotes a whole chapter to Andrei Bitov's prose ("The Elusive Self: Andrei Bitov," 283–310), which he sees as "littered with the playful signatures of graphomania" (284). According to Borden, Bitov ascribed an "intrinsic, significant vitality" to the act of writing itself, and thus dedicated himself unapologetically to solipsistic metaexploration of this act (309). I will engage with Borden's reading and will propose a counterargument later in this chapter.

12. Wai Chee Dimock, *Weak Planet: Literature and Assisted Survival* (Chicago: University of Chicago Press, 2020), 6.

13. Particularly apt is Olga Hassanoff Bakich's description of Bitov's portrayal of his characters as "often sketchy and incomplete, as if slightly out of focus" ("A New Type of Character in the Soviet Literature of the 1960s: The Early Works of Andrei Bitov," *Canadian Slavonic Papers* 23, no. 2 [1981]: 126).

14. Bitov, *Life in Windy Weather*, 344.

15. Cited in Bitov's commentary in *Sobranie sochinenii*, 1:566.

16. Cited in M. D. Andrianova, *Avtorskie strategii v romannoi proze Andreia Bitova* (St. Petersburg: BAN, 2011), 9.

17. Andrianova remarks (*Avtorskie strategii*) that "critics have repeatedly made the mistake of identifying the author with his characters, reproaching Bitov for seemingly attempting to justify his constant reflection ('self-absorption') and inability to act." As if in response to Bitov's rattling on about historical catastrophes, one Soviet critic complained that the real catastrophe is his character's self-absorption: "He is too—catastrophically!—self-involved" (cited by Andrianova, *Avtorskie strategii*).

18. O. V. Bogdanova, *Roman A. Bitova "Pushkinskii Dom": "Versiia i variant" russkogo postmoderna* (St. Petersburg: Filologicheskii fakul'tet Sankt-Peterburgskogo gosudarstvennogo universiteta, 2002), 39.

19. Komaromi, *Uncensored*, 81.

20. Komaromi, *Uncensored*, 82.

21. Komaromi, *Uncensored*, 79.

22. Bitov, *Pushkin House*, 345.

23. Pekka Pesonen, *Teksty zhizni i iskusstva: Stat'i po russkoi literature* (Helsinki: Helsinki University Press, 1997), 182.

24. Cited from T. G. Shemetova, *Poetika prozy A. G. Bitova* (Ulan-Ude, Russia: Izd-to Buriatskogo universiteta, 2001), 89.

25. Ellen B. Chances, *Andrei Bitov: The Ecology of Inspiration* (Cambridge: Cambridge University Press, 1993), 142.

26. Komaromi, *Uncensored*, 93.

27. Andrianova, *Avtorskie strategii*, 75.

28. In fact, in *The Brothers Karamazov*, it is precisely the abstention from dueling that characterizes Father Zosima's originality and courage.

29. Bitov, *Pushkin House*, 308; Andrei Bitov, *Pushkinskii dom* (Ann Arbor, MI: Ardis, 1978), 360.

30. Bitov, *Pushkin House*, 308; Andrei Bitov, *Pushkinskii dom*, 360.

31. Bitov, *Pushkin House*, 224.

32. Bitov, *Pushkin House*, 205; Bitov, *Pushkinskii dom*, 244.

33. Bitov, *Pushkinskii dom*, 305.

34. Bitov, *Pushkin House*, 184; Bitov, *Pushkinskii dom*, 218.

35. Bitov, *Pushkin House*, 98; Bitov, *Pushkinskii dom*, 119.

36. Bitov, *Sobranie sochinenii*, 1:538.

37. Cited from Daniel Grausam, *On Endings: American Postmodern Fiction and the Cold War* (Charlottesville: University of Virginia Press, 2011), 8.

38. Fredric Jameson, *Postmodernism, or, The Cultural Logic of Late Capitalism* (Durham, NC: Duke University Press, 1991), 6. For her part, the prominent theoretician of postmodernism Linda Hutcheon countered that the ability to document and bear witness to one's own epoch represents a historiographic element (and merit) of postmodernist fiction. *A Poetics of Postmodernism: History, Theory, Fiction* (New York: Routledge, 1988).

39. Cited from Grausam, *On Endings*, 1.

40. Chances, *Andrei Bitov*, 158.

41. On Stalinist repressions and the return of the repressed, the historical trauma and its acting out in *Pushkin House*, see Slobodanka Vladiv-Glover's illuminating "The 1960s and the Rediscovery of the Other in Russian Culture: Andrei Bitov," in Mikhail Epstein, Alexander Genis, and Slobodanka Vladiv-Glover, *Russian Postmodernism: New Perspectives on Post-Soviet Literature* (New York: Berghahn, 2016), 95–150.

42. Bitov, *Monkey Link*, 71.

43. Sven Spieker in fact asserts that "in the writings of urban authors such as Andrej Bitov and Jurii Trifonov, the problem of communication between different isolated organisms and their (social, historical) environment is perhaps the most central concern" (*Figures of Memory and Forgetting in Andrej Bitov's Prose: Postmodernism and the Quest for History* [Frankfurt, Germany: Peter Lang, 1996], 118). The terms used here—"organisms," "environment"— are indicative of Spieker's (like Chances's) ecological approach to Bitov and his concerns.

44. Bitov, *Life in Windy Weather*, 55; trans. adjusted slightly by me.

45. Bitov, *Life in Windy Weather*, 55–56; trans. adjusted slightly by me.

46. Bitov, *Life in Windy Weather*, 56.

47. Bitov, *Life in Windy Weather*, 93.

48. Joseph Meeker, *The Comedy of Survival* (Tucson: University of Arizona Press, 1997), 158.

49. Meeker, *The Comedy of Survival*, 158–59, 160.

50. Bitov, *Life in Windy Weather*, 128.

51. In this translation, the main character is named Alexei. The discrepancy appears to be owed to Bitov himself, to yet another instantiation of Bitovian weakness and vacillation—in this case, eschewing to hold firm with characters' names across various editions.

52. Bitov, *Life in Windy Weather*, 129.

53. Bitov, *Life in Windy Weather*, 131.

54. Chances, *Andrei Bitov*, 10.

55. Bitov, *Life in Windy Weather*, 120.

56. Bitov, *Life in Windy Weather*, 121.

57. Bitov, *Life in Windy Weather*, 122

58. Bitov, *Life in Windy Weather*, 121.

59. In "Days of Leavetaking" ("Proshchal'nye den'ki"), the protagonist clothes the same dilemma in the search for a balance between remembering and forgetting: "You see, I am not living, because I'm remembering yesterday, not living today and getting ready to live in my memory tomorrow as well. That means you have to forget in order to be alive and real now. But the world perished because they forgot. Doesn't that mean we must remember? . . . But in remembering I don't live, I perish in everything, with everything. In forgetting, the last one who remembers leaves the world. In forgetting, I perish completely for everything. Not to remember, so as to *live* without noticing death? Or to remember, so as to fear death and not live in general? To leave the world, forgetting about it, in order to live for oneself, or to remain in it, so as not to be in it ever, not to be in it *now*?" (trans. Kevin Klose, in *Metropol: Literary Almanac*, ed. Vasily Aksenov et al., [New York: W. W. Norton, 1982], 350). Here, Bitov rethinks Sartrean categories of being-in-itself, being-for-itself, and being-for-others through the prism of forgetting and remembrance. Were one able to abandon consciousness, and be like infants and plants, one would live fully in the moment, but that would mean "to perish for everything," not be for others. To embrace consciousness and remembrance would entail a different form of perishing, "perishing in everything," being removed from one's in-itself-ness. Either choice results in perishing, and the only solution lies in a continuous oscillation between remembering and forgetting.

60. Bitov, *Life in Windy Weather*, 134.

61. Bitov, *Life in Windy Weather*, 136.

62. Bitov, *Life in Windy Weather*, 134.

63. Bitov, *Life in Windy Weather*, 137; one word adjusted by me: "legato," which matches the cupola-like musical notation of that name.

64. This explosive dispersal of the self can only be uplifting under one condition: the survival of others who make your transcendence possible, who ensure

that you do not end, but continue in others. In "A View of the Trojan Sky" ("Vid neba Troi"), for example, a lonely writer, sick of life and of his own helpless ineptitude at living it, conceives of a novel entitled *The Life of a Dead Man*, which tells of a lonely man who hatches a plan to perform one potent act of defiance—the spectacular destruction of himself and everyone around him in a suicide bombing. Crucially, however, at the last minute, the man-bomb changes his mind. The writer's explanation for this seemingly anticlimactic ending is the absence of continuity. According to the writer, the human mind must associate any action with continuity, but the failed suicide bomber could not see his act as anything but final: "My hero didn't blow himself up—and for a good reason. Because there wasn't one. Every goal exists for the sake of continuity, to justify its own sequel; and there was no possible sequel here" (Andrei Bitov, *The Symmetry Teacher: A Novel-Echo*, trans. Polly Gannon [New York: Farrar, Straus and Giroux, 2014], 43). The anticipation of continuation is an essential element of Bitov's ecological thinking, as defined by Chances, since it presupposes the interdependence of oneself with the world. In "The Forest" ("Les"), the main character's father, who like all of Bitov's main characters' fathers is an avid consumer of popular science, has stumbled on a mind-blowing discovery about the relational and preservational aspects of the organic world: "A forest, it turns out, isn't simply a lot of trees, but . . . an association. . . . They're all connected by their roots, which are entangled, and they comprise a single system. . . . For example, a tree can be dying slowly, but as soon as it dies, it dries out the next day. Scientists think it's a riddle. But it turns out that as soon as it dies the forest immediately withdraws all its juices into its system. . . . It turns out . . . that a forest is not a multitude of trees, but a collective, a society, and each tree doesn't stand independently, but only together with all the others, and needs them all" (Bitov, *Life in Windy Weather*, 274–75). The son, as Bitovian sons usually do, dismisses the father's theory as "non-scientific," but later keeps thinking about it, finding this idea of continuity as a dispersal sustaining. By the end of the story, the son, worried about the father's frailty, suddenly feels a deep sense of love and concern for him; the son senses that he has finally truly understood the point the father was trying to make with the story about the forest. He does not, that is, just comprehend the idea of interdependence rationally; he experiences it psychically and emotionally, with the sensation described as a radical, sublime expansion ("And if the forest is one, then he and his father are simply one tree. . . . The stream of life had flowed for the last time from his father to him, almost with the same force with which it had flowed when this instant was beginning. Monakhov experienced a headlong expansion of his being—it opened—it was as though he were hanging in air over the bed. This live flow of his powerless father's last strength washed son-Monakhov's calcified [*obyzvestvlennuiu*] soul, and, transparent again, let into itself all the pain around it" Bitov, *Life in Windy Weather*, 333; one word here adjusted by me for the sake of accuracy).

65. Bitov, *Life in Windy Weather*, 136.

66. Bitov, *Life in Windy Weather*, 136.

67. Immanuel Kant, *The Critique of Judgement*, trans. James Creed Meredith (Oxford: Oxford University Press, 2008), 137.

68. Cited from Michael Haworth, "Genius Is What Happens: Derrida and Kant on Genius, Rule-Following and the Event," *British Journal of Aesthetics* 54, no. 3 (2014): 327.

69. Arthur Schopenhauer, *The World as Will and Representation*, trans. E. F. J. Payne (New York: Dover Publications, 1966), 2:390–91. The loquacious painter in "Man in a Landscape" sounds Schopenhauerian when he remarks, "The genius moves with the cosmic speed in his understanding, and he tears a hole in the image" (Bitov, *Monkey Link*, 109).

70. In claiming that Pushkin must have earned this resentment by offending Tiutchev somehow, Leva's article seems to build on Iurii Tynianov's assertion (in "Pushkin i Tiutchev," in *Pushkin i ego sovremenniki* [Moscow: Nauka, 1969]: 166–91.) that Pushkin did not recognize Tiutchev's gift, in effect snubbing him. The authorial narrator would have us know (in a footnote) that Leva had not yet had a chance to read Tynianov's article before writing his own (*Pushkin House*, 278).

71. Bitov, *Pushkin House*, 230. Leva draws a parallel with Pushkin's poem, in which the poetic persona allegedly possesses a preternatural ability to hear "convulsions in the sky, / And flights of angel hosts on high, / And beasts that move beneath the sea."

72. Bitov, *Pushkin House*, 232.

73. Bitov, *Monkey Link*, 133.

74. Bitov, *Monkey Link*, 133.

75. Bitov, *Monkey Link*, 83.

76. Schopenhauer, *World as Will and Representation*, 185–86.

77. Bitov, *Life in Windy Weather*, 137–38.

78. Boris Averin connects this contradictory drive toward being humanly singular and being divinely expansive with Bitov's fission of his self into multiple characters, in some way finding points of connectedness with all of them: "Divided, bifurcated, crucified. He wants to be himself and everyone and everything [*vsem*]" ("Ispoved' A. G. Bitova v trekh chastiakh," in A. Bitov, *Oglashennye: Roman-stranstvie* [St. Petersburg: Izdatel'stvo Ivana Limbakha, 1995], 513).

79. Bitov, *Oglashennye*, 153.

80. Bitov, *Life in Windy Weather*, 146.

81. Here again, the author wishes to both participate in and bear witness to an event—an impossibility, insofar as the event terminates the participant while the witness must go on.

82. Bitov, *Life in Windy Weather*, 154.

83. Bitov, *Life in Windy Weather*, 184.

84. Bitov, *Life in Windy Weather*, 184.

85. Bitov, *Life in Windy Weather*, 155.

86. Bitov, *Life in Windy Weather*, 156.

87. Bitov, *Oglashennye*, 162.

88. Bitov, *Life in Windy Weather*, 158.

89. Bitov, *Life in Windy Weather*, 147.

90. Bitov, *Life in Windy Weather*, 158.

91. Bitov, *Life in Windy Weather*, 147.

92. These attempts at recollection in the full awareness that, in the end, we end up where we have started in fact demonstrate the mechanism of memory in general. On this subject, see Sven Spieker's remarkable study *Figures of Memory and Forgetting in Andrej Bitov's Prose: Postmodernism and the Quest for History*. Spieker encapsulates Bitov's approach to memory thus: "Only that kind of remembering which remains mindful of its inadequacy vis-à-vis that which forever eludes representation may hope to preserve the traces of the past" (33). In Bitov's whole oeuvre, the most conspicuous and (in this regard) edifying movement backward—a kind of "rewind," accompanied by the restoration of the effects of centuries of destruction—takes place in "A Photograph of Pushkin" ("Fotografiia Pushkina"). This is accomplished by Leva Odoevtsev's distant descendant, who is, like Leva, a literary scholar, and who, after the discovery of time travel, goes back in time to take a snapshot of Pushkin (only to realize in the end that Pushkin is uncapturable). Here time travel appears like a movie run backward: "Igor flew, and beneath him the times rustled past, mushroom clouds withdrew as if into a funnel, and bombs flew backward; the Earth's scar tissue healed, was covered with megalopolises and inhabited by people; it broke down into cities, towns, and villages, was overgrown with grass and forest, came alive with bird and beast" (Andrei Bitov, "Fotografiia Pushkina (1799–2099)," https://royallib.com/read/bitov_andrey/fotografiya_pushkina_17992099_povest .html#0.

93. Lipovetsky, *Russian Postmodernist Fiction*, 43–45.

94. Bitov, *Pushkin House*, 64; Bitov, *Pushkinskii dom*, 80.

95. Maria Savel'eva, *Tvorchestvo Andreia Bitova v traktovkakh rossiiskoi i zarubezhnoi literaturnoi kritiki* (Moscow: MGIMO Universitet, 2016), 138–39.

96. In fact, my interpretation is closer to the one developed by V. Kuritsyn, according to which the openness of Bitov's novel *Pushkin House* stands as a counterpoint to the closure implicit in the actual Pushkin House, as an instantiation of the Soviet approach to culture. Savel'eva sums up Kuritsyn's reading thus: "Developing the theory of the 'museum concept'—everything that is nonvital, predetermined, and limited by the framework imposed in this 'museum-novel' (the author's genre designation)—the critic argues that Bitov 'succeeded, more than did his main character,' in turning a dead museum into a living one: 'The structure of the novel is fundamentally open in different directions'; even the first and second parts . . . practically do not intersect" (Savel'eva, *Tvorchestvo Andreia Bitova*, 142–43).

97. Ludwig von Bertalanffy, *General Systems Theory: Foundations, Development, Applications* (London: Penguin Press, 1971), 76–77.

98. Anthony Wilden, *System and Structure: Essays in Communication and Exchange* (London: Tavistock, 1972), 35.

99. Christopher Johnson, *System and Writing in the Philosophy of Jacques Derrida* (Cambridge: Cambridge University Press, 1993), 147–48.

100. Mark Lipovetsky in a way seems to discuss the same principle of overdetermination and redundancy when he writes about "the merger of the axiological contexts of the Author, the Novelist, and the Hero" that allows the hero to escape any permanent ends, to exist in a continuous present: "As a result of this merger, it is the values context of the literary hero (an open fiction, living only in the novel's present) that takes on the outsidedness that originally belonged to the author-creator. Bitov's hero can therefore go through the same situation again and again, returning to the key points of his plot. Paradoxically, this weak, unfree character, whose being is restricted by the novel's present, proves to be freer than the all-powerful author-creator, who is dependent on extratextual reality" (Lipovetsky, *Russian Postmodernist Fiction*, 62). In Shemetova's opinion, the principle I refer to here as overdetermination, which we perceive in the versions and variations of Leva's plotline, extends also to the author himself, which enables him to carry on: "The author splits himself into many characters that help him to exist in this reality, to follow an invisible path to an unprecedented truth" (*Poetika prozy A. G. Bitova*, 103–4).

101. Bitov, *Pushkin House*, 240.

102. Bitov, *Pushkin House*, 343.

103. Bitov, *Pushkin House*, 226.

104. Bitov, *Pushkin House*, 233; Bitov, *Pushkinskii dom*, 275.

105. Bitov, *Pushkin House*, 240.

106. Bitov, *Pushkin House*, 354.

107. For example, Monakhov thinks of himself: "His life was, in effect, lived out, and in no way ahead of him. He had lived it, then, either the wrong way, or lived past it [*mimo*], or in the wrong sense." Andrei Bitov, *Aptekarskii ostrov: Imperiia v chetyrekh izmereniiakh. Izmerenie pervoe* (Moscow: AST, 2013), 388.

108. Bitov, *Pushkin House*, 353.

109. Bitov, *Aptekarskii ostrov*, 320. This "multiplicity of being," the thought of which plagues Monakhov as much as Odoevtsvev and other Bitov's characters, recalls the Kantian mathematical sublime, which Neil Hertz describes as "a sense . . . arising out of sheer cognitive exhaustion, the mind blocked not by the threat of an overwhelming force, but by the fear of losing count or of being reduced to nothing but counting—this, and this, and this—with no hope of bringing a long series or a vast scattering under some sort of conceptual unity" ("The Notion of Blockage in the Literature of the Sublime," in *The End of the Line: Essays on Psychoanalysis and the Sublime* [New York: Columbia University Press, 1985], 40). Notably, Hertz uses this notion to explain why, in con-

temporary postmodern writing, as well as in Romantic poetry, the point of blockage (the sense of exhaustion in the face of sheer multiplicity) is followed by logorrhea. This might explain the mechanism by which Bitov's constant complaints about writing (that writing is impossible) proliferate and lead to more writing, such that writer's block looks suspiciously like graphomania. Positing blockage, articulating the impossibility of expression, paradoxically releases a stream of writing, makes writing possible. In support of his point, Hertz adduces Hume: "Difficulty . . . instead of extinguishing the mind's vigor and alacrity, has the contrary effect, of sustaining and increasing it" ("Notion of Blockage," 45). Hertz observes that the metaphor of blockage "draws its power from the literature of religious conversion, that is, from a literature that describes major experiential transformation" ("Notion of Blockage," 47). This notion might be helpful in understanding the vacillation between "blockage and release" in Bitov's text, in which difficulty, once posited, is approached as a challenge that necessitates effortful response.

110. Bitov, *Pushkin House*, 341; Bitov, *Pushkinskii dom*, 398.

111. Bitov's apprehension, discussed earlier, of the ultimate extinction of everything, from the individual human life to the solar system, which renders any activity meaningless, and necessitates a theoretical pivot that would validate life's efforts despite this final end, is akin to the contemporary school of philosophy known as "speculative materialism," which attempts to formulate philosophical thought in light of the fact that extinction is a condition of life. In *Nihil Unbound: Enlightenment and Extinction*, Ray Brassier maintains that Nietzsche's transcendental nihilism is ultimately life-affirming, and in the process expresses a thought that seems to me to encapsulate Bitov's approach to time: "The transitoriness of the instant which was considered worthless in the old mode of valuation, where becoming was deemed deficient with regard to the transcendent value of eternal being, becomes the focus of ultimate worth in the new one—transcendence is revoked and with it the possibility of appraising the worth or worthlessness of existence from some external vantage point. Accordingly, nihilism is overcome through a transvaluation whereby the pointlessness of becoming is embraced beyond its opposition to the supposed purposefulness of true being—aimlessness is affirmed in and for itself, without appeal to extrinsic justification" (*Nihil Unbound: Enlightenment and Extinction* [Basingstoke, UK: Palgrave Macmillan, 2007], 208).

112. Andrianova insightfully pairs Tiutchev's sense of life's aimlessness with his genius: "If we clarify Leva's reasoning in other words, it turns out that Pushkin sees in the world the possibility of divine insights that bring us closer to harmony, while Tiutchev is a *genius* at perceiving chaos and entropy. . . . If nothing human in this world is eternal, and culture is not tantamount to truth, then human life and the creation of culture are, according to Tiutchev, 'a useless feat,' alien to indifferent nature" (*Avtorskie strategii*, 103).

113. Bitov, *Pushkin House*, 247; Bitov, *Pushkinskii dom*, 289.

114. Bitov, *Pushkin House*, 341; Bitov, *Pushkinskii dom*, 398.

115. Bitov, *Pushkin House*, 344; Bitov, *Pushkinskii dom*, 401.

116. Bitov, "Puteshestvie k drugu detstva." http://loveread.me/read_book .php?id=36332&p=1; 101. (Further citations in the text are from this edition.) Compare this Bitovian assertion of the purposeless heroism of the living with Tiutchev's "useless feat" mentioned in note 112.

117. Bitov, "Puteshestvie k drugu detstva," 115.

118. Bitov, "Puteshestvie k drugu detstva," 115.

119. Bitov, "Puteshestvie k drugu detstva," 115.

120. Bitov, "Puteshestvie k drugu detstva," 116.

121. This first appeared under a different title: "The Birds, or, New Information on Man" ("Ptitsy, ili Novye svedeniia o cheloveke"). *Oglashenie* is a curious, polysemantic word that, aside from the religiously tinged "catechizing," could also be translated as "announcement" or "disclosure."

122. In his ecological concerns, Bitov was very much a product of his times; many Soviet scientists were becoming vocal about the need to establish a legal framework to protect the environment from the excesses of technological progress. Khrushchev's environmental policies were inconsistent: on the one hand, the Thaw enabled scientists to publicly share their concerns; on the other, keen to quicken the Soviet Union's pace on the path to communism, Khrushchev looked askance at checks on industrial development and initiated the closure of multiple nature preserves (*zapovedniki*), not unlike the Curonian Spit that Bitov liked to frequent. (See Paul Josephson et al., *An Environmental History of Russia* [Cambridge: Cambridge University Press, 2013], 173–74). In the Brezhnev years, environmental preservation became one of the markers in the ideological competition between the Soviet Union and the West. The early 1970s saw a number of environmental laws adopted, in the USSR as elsewhere. The ninth five-year plan (1971–75) was the first to include spending on environmental protection, and in 1972 the party issued a resolution "On Intensifying the Conservation of Nature and Improving the Utilization of Natural Resources" (Josephson et al., *Environmental History*, 190). Scientists and environmentalists in the Soviet Union had long sought to draw attention to the imperative of avoiding environmental degradation in the course of building state socialism—the All-Union Society for the Conservation of Nature was established all the way back in 1924 and remained active even through the Great Terror—but in the early 1970s, for the first time, these conversations became a larger cultural phenomenon, involving both governmental agencies and the public at large. Furthermore, this rethinking of the relationship between Soviet citizens and their natural habitat went hand in hand with the deepening of ties with the rest of humanity, beyond the country's borders. For instance, among the US-USSR cooperative agreements signed at the 1972 summit in Moscow was the creation of the Joint Committee on Environmental Protection (Josephson et al., *Environmental History*, 195).

123. Bitov, *Monkey Link*, 5.

124. Bitov, *Monkey Link*, 5.

125. On this central element of Bitov's ethics, see Komaromi's brilliant discussion of Leva Odoevtsev's recognition of his beloved Faina's autonomous existence and of "the irreducible otherness of fellow human beings" (*Uncensored*, 93).

126. Bitov, *Monkey Link*, 18–19. Having closely analyzed references in Bitov's writings to faulty photography, José Vergara draws the highly cogent conclusion that "the ability to recognize one's limitations, rather than to impose one's values and delusions upon the world (an inner drive that motivates many Bitovian characters), should be the driving force of knowledge, as in scientific inquiry, according to Bitov" ("The Distorted Images and Realities of Andrei Bitov's Literary Photographs," *Russian Review* 77, no. 2 [2018]: 274).

127. Borden, *Art of Writing Badly*, 304.

128. Lyotard, *Postmodern Condition*, 81. Lyotard writes, "The postmodern would be that which, in the modern, puts forward the unpresentable in presentation itself, that which denies itself the solace of good forms, the consensus of a taste which would make it possible to share collectively the nostalgia for the unattainable; that which searches for new presentations, not in order to enjoy them but in order to impart the stronger sense of the unpresentable."

129. Andrei Bitov, *A Captive of the Caucasus: Journeys in Armenia and Georgia*, trans. Susan Brownsberger (New York: Farrar, Straus and Giroux, 1992), 42.

130. Bitov, *Monkey Link*, 57–58.

131. Bitov, *Monkey Link*, 59.

132. Bitov, *Monkey Link*, 61.

133. Bitov, *Monkey Link*, 65.

134. Bitov, *Monkey Link*, 64.

135. Bitov, *Monkey Link*, 64–65.

136. Bitov, *Monkey Link*, 65. This is a curious moment: we arrive at a paradox in which thought and reality exceed each other. What is essential, however, is that they cannot fully coincide or overlap, and this impossibility bodes well for the endurance of both.

137. Bitov, *Monkey Link*, 18.

138. Bitov, *Monkey Link*, 17.

CONCLUSION

1. Dimitris Dalakoglou, "Failure and Fragility: Towards a Material Culture of the End of the World as We Know It," in *The Material Culture of Failure: When Things Do Wrong*, ed. David Jeevendrampillai et al. (London: Routledge, 2017), 3.

2. Giorgio Agamben, "On What We Can Not Do," in *Nudities*, trans. David Kishik and Stefan Pedatella (Stanford, CA: Stanford University Press, 2011), 44.

3. "Both travesty and transvestite go back to Latin *trans* 'across' and *vestire* 'to clothe,' and in the theatre a travesty role is still one designated to be played by a cross-dressing performer. The earliest use of travesty which came through French travesty 'disguised' was 'dressed to appear ridiculous.' The usual modern sense, 'a false or absurd representation of something,' developed from the word's application in parodies and burlesques. Academic interest in sexuality developed in Germany and Austria in the late 19th and early 20th centuries, and the immediate source of transvestite, recorded from the 1920s, was German *transvestit*." (Julia Cresswell, ed., *Oxford Dictionary of Word Origins* [Oxford: Oxford University Press, 2010], 455.). The word is also etymologically related to "invest"—that is, meaningfully for this discussion, to the conferring of value.

4. A term currently promoted by some organizations in the interest of creating a more inclusive social framework for people with disabilities. For example, see Melwood's abilIT program: https://www.arlnow.com/2020/06/08/melwoods-free-it-and-life-skills-training-program-for-people-of-differing-abilities-is-looking-for-candidates/.

5. Lennard Davis, *Enforcing Normalcy: Disability, Deafness, and the Body* (London: Verso, 1995), xii.

6. Davis, *Enforcing Normalcy*, xv.

7. Susan Wendell, "Toward a Feminist Theory of Disability," *Hypatia* 4 no. 2 (1989): 104–24.

8. Davis, *Enforcing Normalcy*, xix.

Works Cited

Adamovich, Ales', and Vasil' Bykov. "Dialog v pis'makh." *Sibirskie ogni*, no. 11 (2013): 138–52.

Agamben, Giorgio. "On What We Can Not Do." In *Nudities*, translated by David Kishik and Stefan Pedatella, 43–46. Stanford, CA: Stanford University Press, 2011.

Aitmatov, Chingiz, and Kurt Vonnegut. "Vstrecha nad planetoi Zemlia: Dialog sovetskogo i amerikanskogo pisatelei." *Literaturnaia gazeta*, no. 30 (July 23, 1975): 2.

Aksenov, Vasilii. "E. Kharitonov—podpol'nyi zhitel' Moskvy." *Glagol* 10, no. 2 (1993): 93–101.

Andrianova, M. D. *Avtorskie strategii v romannoi proze Andreia Bitova*. St. Petersburg: Biblioteka Akademii Nauk, 2011.

Andronov, Iona. "Shedevry absurda i neugodnye muzy." *Literaturnaia gazeta*, no. 4 (January 24, 1979): 15.

Annenkov, Pavel. "The Literary Type of the Weak Man (Apropos of Turgenev's Story 'Asya')." Translated by Tatiana Goerner. *Ulbandus Review* 1, no. 2 (1978): 74–85.

Annenkov, Pavel. "Literaturnyi tip slabogo cheloveka. Po povodu turgenevskoi 'Asi'." *Atenei* 32 (1858): 322–50.

Aristotle. *The Poetics of Aristotle*. Translated by S. H. Butcher. New York: Cosimo Classics, 2008.

Arkhangel'skii, Aleksandr, ed. *Svobodnye liudi: Dissidentskoe dvizhenie v rasskazakh uchastnikov*. Moscow: Vremia, 2018.

Astruc, R. *Le Renouveau du grotesque dans le roman du XXe siècle*. Paris: Classiques Garnier, 2010.

Averin, Boris. "Ispoved' A. G. Bitova v trekh chastiakh." In *Oglashennye: Roman-stranstvie*, 62–71. St. Petersburg: Izdatel'stvo Ivana Limbakha, 1995.

Bakhtin, Mikhail. *Rabelais and His World*. Translated by Hélène Iswolsky. Bloomington: Indiana University Press, 1984.

Bakich, Olga Hassanoff. "A New Type of Character in the Soviet Literature of the 1960s: The Early Works of Andrei Bitov." *Canadian Slavonic Papers* 23, no. 2 (1981): 125–33.

Bal'mont, Konstantin. *Poeziia kak volshebstvo*. Moscow: Skorpion, 1915.

Barth, John. *The Friday Book: Essays and Other Nonfiction*. New York: Putnam, 1984.

Baslyk, Valentina. "Venichka's Divided Self: The Sacred and the Monstrous." In Ryan-Hayes, *Venedikt Erofeev's "Moscow–Petushki": Critical Perspectives*, 53–78.

Bateson, Gregory. "Minimal Requirements for a Theory of Schizophrenia." *AMA Archives of General Psychiatry* 2, no. 5 (1960): 477–91.

Belyi, Andrei. "Liniia, krug, spiral'—simvolizma." *Trudy i dni*, no. 4–5 (1912): 13–22.

Benjamin, Walter. *The Origin of German Tragic Drama*. Translated by John Osborne. London: Verso, 1998.

Benjamin, Walter. "Theses on the Philosophy of History." In *Illuminations: Essays and Reflections*, 253–64. Translated by Harry Zohn. New York: Schocken Books, 1968.

Benjamin, Walter. *Understanding Brecht*. Translated by Anna Bostock. London: Verso, 1998.

Beraha, Laura. "Out of and into the Void: Picaresque Absence and Annihilation." In Ryan-Hayes, *Venedikt Erofeev's "Moscow–Petushki": Critical Perspectives*, 19–52.

Bernini, Lorenzo. *Queer Apocalypses: Elements of Antisocial Theory*. London: Palgrave Macmillan, 2017.

Bershtein, Evgenii. "Anglichanin v russkoi bane: K postroeniiu istoricheskoi poetiki russkoi gei-literatury." *Novoe literaturnoe obozrenie*, no. 111 (2011): 148–61.

Bershtein, Evgenii. "'Next to Christ': Oscar Wilde in Russian Modernism." In *The Reception of Oscar Wilde in Europe*, edited by Stefano Evangelista, 285–300. New York: Continuum, 2010.

Bezrukov, A. N. *Retseptsiia khudozhestvennogo teksta: Funktsional'nyi podkhod*. St. Petersburg: Giperion, 2015.

Bitov, Andrei. *Aptekarskii ostrov: Imperiia v chetyrekh izmereniiakh. Izmerenie pervoe*. Moscow: AST, 2013.

Bitov, Andrei. *A Captive of the Caucasus: Journeys in Armenia and Georgia*. Translated by Susan Brownsberger. New York: Farrar, Straus and Giroux, 1992.

Bitov, Andrei. "Days of Leavetaking." Translated by Kevin Klose. In *Metropol: Literary Almanac*, edited by Vasily Aksenov, Viktor Erofeev, Fazil Iskander, Andrei Bitov, and Evgenii Popov, 273–315. New York: W. W. Norton, 1982.

Bitov, Andrei. "Fotografiia Pushkina (1799–2099)." Moscow: Panorama, 1998. https://royallib.com/read/bitov_andrey/fotografiya_pushkina_17992099_povest.html#0.

Bitov, Andrei. *Life in Windy Weather*. Translated by Carol G. Luplow, Richard

Luplow, Jascha Stewart, Helena Goscilo, et al. Edited by Priscilla Meyer. Ann Arbor, MI: Ardis, 1986.

Bitov, Andrei. *The Monkey Link: A Pilgrimage Novel*. Translated by Susan Brownsberger. New York: Farrar, Straus and Giroux, 1995.

Bitov, Andrei. *Oglashennye: Roman-stranstvie*. St. Petersburg: Izdatel'stvo Ivana Limbakha, 1995.

Bitov, Andrei. *Pushkin House*. Translated by Susan Brownsberger. Normal, IL: Dalkey Archive Press, 1987.

Bitov, Andrei. *Pushkinskii dom*. Ann Arbor, MI: Ardis, 1978.

Bitov, Andrei. "Puteshestvie k drugu detstva." In Andrei Bitov, *Nulevoi Tom*, Moscow: AST, 2014. http://loveread.me/read_book.php?id=36332&p=1.

Bitov, Andrei. *Sobranie sochinenii v trekh tomakh*. 3 vols. Moscow: Molodaia gvardiia, 1991.

Bitov, Andrei. *The Symmetry Teacher: A Novel-Echo*. Translated by Polly Gannon. New York: Farrar, Straus and Giroux, 2014.

Bitov, Andrei. *Uletaiushchii Monakhov: Roman-punktir*. Moscow: Molodaia gvardiia, 1990.

Bogdanova, O. V. *"Moskva–Petushki" Venedikta Erofeeva kak pratekst russkogo postmodernizma*. St. Petersburg: Filologicheskii fakul'tet Sankt-Peterburgskogo gosudarstvennogo universiteta, 2002.

Bogdanova, O. V. *Roman A. Bitova "Pushkinskii Dom": "Versiia i variant" russkogo postmoderna*. St. Petersburg: Filologicheskii fakul'tet Sankt-Peterburgskogo gosudarstvennogo universiteta, 2002.

Borenstein, Eliot. *Men without Women: Masculinity and Revolution in Russian Fiction, 1917–1929*. Durham, NC: Duke University Press, 2000.

Borden, Richard. *The Art of Writing Badly: Valentin Kataev's Mauvism and the Rebirth of Russian Modernism*. Evanston, IL: Northwestern University Press, 1999.

Boym, Svetlana. *Death in Quotation Marks: Cultural Myths of the Modern Poet*. Cambridge, MA: Harvard University Press, 1991.

Brassier, Ray. *Nihil Unbound: Enlightenment and Extinction*. Basingstoke, UK: Palgrave Macmillan, 2007.

Bulgakov, Mikhail. *Master i Margarita*. Moscow: Eksmo, 2010.

Bukovskii, V., and S. Gluzman. "Posobie po psikhiatrii dlia inakomysliashchikh." In *Antologiia samizdata. Nepodtsenzurnaia literatura v SSSR (1950-e–1980-e)*. Vol. 3, *Posle 1973*, edited by V. V. Igrunov, 147–59. Moscow: Mezhdunarodnyi institut gumanitarno-politicheskikh issledovanii, 2005.

Bykov, Dmitrii. *Vremia izoliatsii: 1951–2000 g: Sto lektsii o russkoi literature XX veka*. Moscow: Eksmo, 2018. https://ru-bykov.livejournal.com/2865531.html.

Chaadaev, Petr. *Filosofskie pis'ma*. Moscow: AST, 2022.

Chances, Ellen B. *Andrei Bitov: The Ecology of Inspiration*. Cambridge: Cambridge University Press, 1993.

Chances, Ellen B. *Conformity's Children: An Approach to the Superfluous Man in Russian Literature*. Columbus, OH: Slavica, 1978.

Chekhov, Anton. "Palata n. 6." In *Polnoe sobranie sochinennii i pisem v 30ti tomakh*. Vol. 8, 72–126. Moscow: Nauka, 1986.

Chu, Jinyi. "The Aphoristic Way: Lev Tolstoy's Translations of the *Dao de Jing*," *Comparative Literature Studies* 51, no. 1 (2021): 146–75.

Ciullo, Valentina, Gianfranco Spalletta, Carlo Caltagirone, Ricardo E. Jorge, and Federica Piras. "Explicit Time Deficit in Schizophrenia: Systematic Review and Meta-Analysis Indicate It Is Primary and Not Domain Specific." In *Schizophrenia Bulletin*. 42, n. 2 (2016): 505–18.

Clardy, Jesse V., and Betty S. Clardy. *The Superfluous Man in Russian Letters*. Washington, DC: University Press of America, 1980.

Clark, Katerina. *Moscow, The Fourth Rome: Stalinism, Cosmopolitanism, and the Evolution of Soviet Culture, 1931–1941*. Cambridge, MA: Harvard University Press, 2011.

Cresswell, Julia, ed. *Oxford Dictionary of Word Origins*. Oxford: Oxford University Press, 2010.

Dalakoglou, Dimitris. "Failure and Fragility: Towards a Material Culture of the End of the World as We Know It." In *The Material Culture of Failure: When Things Do Wrong*, edited by David Jeevendrampillai, Aaron Parkhurst, Timothy Carroll, and Julie Shackelford, xii–xv. London: Routledge, 2017.

Davis, Lennard. *Enforcing Normalcy: Disability, Deafness, and the Body*. London: Verso, 1995.

Deleuze, Gilles. *Essays Critical and Clinical*. New York: Verso, 1998.

Denner, Michael. "Tolstoyan Nonaction: The Advantage of Doing Nothing." *Tolstoy Studies Journal* 13 (2001): 8–22.

Dimock, Wai Chee. *Weak Planet: Literature and Assisted Survival*. Chicago: University of Chicago Press, 2020.

Dobrolyubov, Nikolai. "What Is Oblomovism?" In *Readings in Russian Civilization*, ed. Thomas Riha, 2:332–43. Chicago: University of Chicago Press, 2009.

Dolinin, V. E., B. I. Ivanov, et al., eds. *Samizdat Leningrada, 1950e–1980e*. Moscow: Novoe literaturnoe obozrenie, 2003.

Dostoevskii, F. M. *Pis'ma*. Moscow: DirectMedia, 2015.

Dostoevsky, Fyodor. *The Brothers Karamazov*. Translated by Richard Pevear and Larissa Volokhonsky. New York: Farrar, Straus and Giroux, 1992.

Dostoevsky, Fyodor. *Notes from Underground*. Translated by Richard Pevear and Larissa Volokhonsky. New York: Vintage Books, 1994.

Dostoevsky, Fyodor. *Poor People*. Translated by Hugh Aplin, London: Hesperus Press, 2002.

Dostoevsky, Fyodor. *White Nights*. Translated by Constance Garnett. New York: HarperPerennial Classics, 2015.

Dovlatov, Sergei. *Sobranie prozy v trekh tomakh*. 3 vols. St. Petersburg: Litmus Press, 1995.

Dumančić, Marko. *Men out of Focus: The Soviet Masculinity Crisis in the Long Sixties*. Toronto: University of Toronto Press, 2021.

Dyer, Geoff. *Zona: A Book about a Film about a Journey to a Room*. New York: Pantheon Books, 2012.

Edwards, Justin D., and Rune Graulund. *Grotesque*. London: Routledge, 2013.

Eikhenbaum, Boris. *Molodoi Tolstoi*. Petrograd, Russia: Izd. Z. I. Grezhbina, 1922.

Epstein, Mikhail. "Malen'kii chelovek v futliare: Sindrom Bashmachkina-Belikova." *Voprosy literatury*, no. 6 (2005): 193–203.

Epstein, Mikhail. "Posle karnavala, ili vechnyi Venichka." In *Ostav'te moiu dushu v pokoe: Pochti vse*, by V. Erofeev, 3–30. Moscow: Kh. G. S., 1995.

Epstein, Mikhail. *Postmodern v Rossii: Literatura i teoriia*. Moscow: Izdaniie R. Elinina, 2000.

Erofeev, Venedikt. *Moscow to the End of the Line*. Translated by H. William Tjalsma. Evanston, IL: Northwestern University Press, 1994.

Erofeev, Venedikt. *Moscow Stations*. Translated by Stephen Mulrine. London: Gardners Books, 1998.

Erofeev, Venedikt. *Moskva–Petushki*. Paris: YMCA Press, 1981.

Erofeev, Venedikt. *Zapiski psikhopata*. Moscow: Vagrius, 2000.

Erofeev, Venedikt. *Zapisnye knizhki*. 2 vols. Moscow: Zakharov, 2005.

Esenin-Vol'pin, A. S. *Filosofia. Logika. Poeziia. Zashchita prav cheloveka: Izbrannoe*. Moscow: Rossiiskii gosudarstvennyi gumanitarnyi universitet, 1999.

Essing, Laurie. *Queer in Russia: A Story of Sex, Self, and the Other*. Durham, NC: Duke University Press, 1999.

Fainberg, Dina, and Artemy M. Kalinovsky. "Stagnation and Its Discontents: The Creation of a Political and Historical Paradigm." In *Reconsidering Stagnation in the Brezhnev Era*, edited by Dina Fainberg and Artemy M. Kalinovsky, vii–xx. London: Lexington Books, 2016.

Faustov, A. A., and S. V. Savinkov. *Universal'nye kharaktery russkoi literatury*. Voronezh, Russia: Izdatel'skii dom VGU, 2015.

Foucault, Michel. *The Essential Works of Foucault*. Vol. 1, *Ethics. Subjectivity and Truth*. Edited by Paul Rabinow. Translated by Robert Hurley et al. New York: New Press, 1994.

Foucault, Michel. *The History of Sexuality*. Vol. 3, *The Care of the Self*. Translated by Robert Hurley. New York: Pantheon Books, 1986.

Franklin, Daria. "Soviet Journals Content and Authors, 1956–1990." https://github.com/dariafrank/Soviet-journals, data released May 7, 2024.

Fredrickson, George. *The Inner Civil War: Northern Intellectuals and the Crisis of the Union*. Urbana: University of Illinois Press, 1993.

Frenkel, Sheera, and Alan Feuer, "A Total Failure: The Proud Boys Now Mock Trump." *New York Times*, January 20, 2021.

Fürst, Juliane. *Flowers through Concrete: Explorations in Soviet Hippieland.* Oxford: Oxford University Press, 2021.

Fürst, Juliane, and Josie McLellan, eds., *Dropping out of Socialism: The Creation of Alternative Spheres in the Soviet Bloc*, Lanham, MD: Lexington Books, 2017.

Gaiser-Shnitman, Svetlana. *Venedikt Erofeev: "Moskva–Petushki" ili "The Rest is Silence."* Bern, Switzerland: Peter Lang, 1989.

Gertsen, A. I. "Lishnie liudi i zhelcheviki." In *Sochineniia A. I. Gertsena*. Vol. 19. Geneva: H. Georg, Libraire-Editeur, 1879.

Ginzburg, Lydia. *On Psychological Prose.* Edited and translated by Judson Rosengrant. Princeton, NJ: Princeton University Press, 1991.

Ginzburg, Lidiia. *O psikhologicheskoi proze.* Leningrad: Khudozhestvennaia literatura, 1977.

Gnedov, Vasilisk. "Poema kontsa." *Daugava* 160, no. 10 (1990): 105.

Gnedov, Vasilisk. *Smert' iskusstvu. Piatnadtsat' poem.* St. Petersburg: Peterburgskii glashatai, 1913.

Gogol, Nikolai. *Peterburgskie povesti.* St. Peterburg: Nauka, 1995.

Golubev, Alexey. *The Things of Life: Materiality in Late Soviet Russia.* Ithaca, NY: Cornell University Press, 2020.

Grausam, Daniel. *On Endings: American Postmodern Fiction and the Cold War.* Charlottesville: University of Virginia Press, 2011.

Green, Michael. *Russian Symbolist Theater: An Anthology of Plays and Critical Texts.* New York: Abrams, 2013.

Griboedov, Aleksandr. *Gore ot uma.* Moscow: Folio, 2009.

Grimm, Wilhelm, and Jacob Grimm. *The Complete Grimm's Fairy Tales.* New York: Random House, 1972.

Groys, Boris. *The Total Art of Stalinism: Avant-Garde, Aesthetic Dictatorship, and Beyond.* Translated by Charles Rougle. London: Verso, 2011.

Gulin, Igor'. "Korit—znachit liubit." *Kommersant*, March 6, 2020. https://www.kommersant.ru/doc/4268824.

Halberstam, Jack. *The Queer Art of Failure.* Durham, NC: Duke University Press, 2011.

Haworth, Michael. "Genius Is What Happens: Derrida and Kant on Genius, Rule-Following and the Event." *British Journal of Aesthetics* 54, no. 3 (2014): 323–37.

Healey, Dan. *Homosexual Desire in Revolutionary Russia: The Regulation of Sexual and Gender Dissent.* Chicago: University of Chicago Press, 2001.

Hertz, Neil. "The Notion of Blockage in the Literature of the Sublime." In *The End of the Line: Essays on Psychoanalysis and the Sublime*, 40–60. New York: Columbia University Press, 1985.

Herzen, Alexander. *My Past and Thoughts: The Memoirs of Alexander Her-*

zen. Translated by Constance Garnett and Humphrey Higgins. Edited by Dwight Macdonald. Berkeley: University of California Press, 1982.

Higham, John. "The Reorientation of American Culture in the 1890s." In *Writing American History: Essays on Modern Scholarship*, edited by John Higham, 73–110. Bloomington: Indiana University Press, 1970.

Hokkaido Global Campus Initiative Report. "Introduction: The Era of Soft Matter." *Tackling Global Issues: Soft Matter, Material of the Future*, vol. 1 (2018): 5–6.

Holland, Peter. "The Play of Eros: The Paradoxes of Gender in English Pantomime." *New Theatre Quarterly* 13, no. 51 (1997): 195–204.

Hunt, Priscilla. "Holy Foolishness as a Key to Russian Culture." In Hunt and Kobets, *Holy Foolishness in Russia: New Perspectives*, 1–14.

Hunt, Priscilla, and Svitlana Kobets, eds. *Holy Foolishness in Russia: New Perspectives*. Bloomington, IN: Slavica, 2011.

Hutcheon, Linda. *A Poetics of Postmodernism: History, Theory, Fiction*. New York: Routledge, 1988.

Ilf, Ilya, and Evgeny Petrov. *The Little Golden Calf*. Translated by Anne O. Fisher. Montpelier, VT: Russian Life Books, 2009.

Ivanov, Sergey A. *Holy Fools in Byzantium and Beyond*. Translated by Simon Franklin. Oxford: Oxford University Press, 2006.

Jakobson, Roman. "Two Types of Language and Two Types of Aphasic Disturbances." In *Language in Literature*, 95–114. Cambridge, MA: Harvard University Press, 1987.

Jameson, Fredric. *Brecht and Method*. London: Verso, 2011.

Jameson, Fredric. *Postmodernism, or The Cultural Logic of Late Capitalism*. Durham, NC: Duke University Press, 1991.

Johnson, Christopher. *System and Writing in the Philosophy of Jacques Derrida*. Cambridge: Cambridge University Press, 1993.

Johnson, D. Barton. "Sasha Sokolov: A Literary Biography." *Canadian-American Slavic Studies* 21, nos. 3–4 (1987): 203–30.

Jones, Polly. *Revolution Rekindled: The Writers and Readers of Late Soviet Biography*. Oxford: Oxford University Press, 2019.

Josephson, Paul, Nicolai Dronin, Aleh Cherp, Ruben Mnatsakanian, Dmitry Efremenko, and Vladislav Larin. *An Environmental History of Russia*. Cambridge: Cambridge University Press, 2013.

Kaganovsky, Lilya. *How the Soviet Man Was Unmade: Cultural Fantasy and Male Subjectivity under Stalin*. Pittsburgh, PA: University of Pittsburgh Press, 2008.

Kaganovsky, Lilya."Ways of Seeing: On Kira Muratova's *Brief Encounters* and Larisa Shepit'ko's *Wings*." *Russian Review* 71, no. 3 (2012), 482–99.

Kahn, Andrew, Mark Lipovetsky, Irina Reyfman, and Stephanie Sandler. *A History of Russian Literature*. Oxford: Oxford University Press, 2018.

Kahn, Madeleine. *Narrative Transvestism: Rhetoric and Gender in the*

Eighteenth-Century English Novel. Ithaca, NY: Cornell University Press, 1991.

Kamenskii, Vasilii. *Ego-moia biografiia velikogo futurista*. Moscow: Kitovras, 1918. https://ruslit.traumlibrary.net/page/kamenskiy-biografia.html.

Kammer, Ann E., Cherlyn S. Granrose, and Jan B. Sloan. *Science, Sex, and Society*. Women's Educational Equity Act Program, US Department of Health, Education, and Welfare, 1979.

Kant, Immanuel. *The Critique of Judgement*. Translated by James Creed Meredith. Oxford: Oxford University Press, 2008.

Karriker, Alexandra Heidi. "Double Vision: Sasha Sokolov's *School for Fools*." *World Literature Today* 53, no. 4 (1979): 610–14.

Kayiatos, Anastasia. "Silent Plasticity: Reenchanting Soviet Stagnation." *WSQ: Women's Studies Quarterly* 40, nos. 3–4 (2012): 105–25.

Kelly, Catriona. "The Education of the Will: Advice Literature, *Zakal*, and Manliness in Early Twentieth-Century Russia." In *Russian Masculinities in History and Culture*, edited by Barbara Evans Clements, Rebecca Friedman, and Dan Healey, 131–51. New York: Palgrave Macmillan, 2002.

Kharitonov, Evgenii. *Pod domashnim arestom*. Moscow: Glagol, 2005.

Kharitonov, Yevgeny. *Under House Arrest*. Translated by A. L. Tait. London: Serpent's Tail, 1998.

Khazanov, Pavel. "Honest Jacobins: High Stalinism and the Socialist Subjectivity of Mikhail Lifshitz and Andrei Platonov." *Russian Review* 77, no. 4 (2018): 576–601.

Kim, Iulii. *Antologiia satiry i iumora Rossii XX veka*. Vol. 38. Moscow: Eksmo, 2005.

Kim, Iulii. *Odnazhdy Mikhailov*. Moscow: Vremia, 2004.

Kim, Iulii. "Zolushka v kontslagere." In *Stikhi i pesni*, 493–525. Moscow: Vremia, 2007.

Kizirian, Shari. "*The Ascent* (1977): Larisa Shepitko's Final Word." *Senses of Cinema*, no. 90 (2019). https://www.sensesofcinema.com/2019/cteq/the-ascent-1977-larisa-shepitkos-final-word/.

Knapp, Liza. *Dostoevsky's "The Idiot": A Critical Companion*. Evanston, IL: Northwestern University Press, 1998.

Kochetkova, Natal'ia. "'Ia vsegda znal, chto uedu iz Sovetskogo Soiuza': Sasha Sokolov o roditeliakh-razvedchikakh, psikhbol'nitsakh i Kanade." *Lenta.ru*, February 11, 2017. https://lenta.ru/articles/2017/02/11/sokolovfilm/.

Kolymagin, Boris. "Kitaiskie motivy v poezii andergraunda." *Novoe literaturnoe obozrenie* 135, no. 5 (2015). https://www.nlobooks.ru/magazines/novoe_literaturnoe_obozrenie/135_nlo_5_2015/article/11629/.

Komaromi, Ann. *Uncensored: Samizdat Novels and the Quest for Autonomy in Soviet Dissidence*. Evanston, IL: Northwestern University Press, 2015.

Kozitskaia, E. A. "Put' k smerti i ee smysl v poeme Ven. Erofeeva 'Moskva–

Petushki.'" In *Analiz odnogo proizvedeniia: "Moskva–Petushki" Venedikta Erofeeva: Sbornik nauchnykh trudov*, edited by I. V. Fomenko, 17–22. Tver, Russia: Tverskoi gosudarstvennyi universitet, 2001.

Kravchenko, Elena. *The Prose of Sasha Sokolov: Reflections on/of the Real*. MHRA Texts and Dissertations, 86. London: Modern Humanities Research Association, 2013.

Kustanovich, Konstantin. "Venichka Erofeev's Grief and Solitude: Existentialist Motifs in the Poema." In Ryan-Hayes, *Venedikt Erofeev's "Moscow–Petushki": Critical Perspectives*, 123–51.

Kuzmin, Mikhail. *Wings*. Translated by Hugh Aplin. London: Hesperus, 2007.

Lacan, Jacques. "On a Question Prior to Any Possible Treatment of Psychosis." In *Écrits*, edited by J. Lacan and J. A. Miller, translated by Bruce Fink, 445–88. New York: W. W. Norton, 2004.

Lacan, Jacques. *The Sinthome: The Seminar of Jacques Lacan, Book XXIII*. Translated by A. R. Price. Cambridge: Polity Press, 2016.

Lao Tzu. *The Sayings of Lao Tzu*. Translated by Lionel Giles. London: John Murray, 1905.

Lawrence, John Shelton, and Robert Jewett, *The Myth of the American Superhero*. Grand Rapids, MI: Wm. B. Eerdmans, 2002.

Leah, Robert. *Russian Futurist Theatre: Theory and Practice*. Edinburgh, UK: Edinburgh University Press, 2018.

Leeds, Marc. *The Vonnegut Encyclopedia*. New York: Delacorte, 2016.

Lekmanov, Oleg, Mikhail Sverdlov, and Il'ia Simanovskii. *Venedikt Erofeev: Postoronnii*. Moscow: AST, 2019.

Lermontov, Mikhail. "Skazka dlia detei." In *Poemy*. St. Petersburg: Azbuka-klassika, 2008.

Leskov, Nikolai. "Pamphalon the Entertainer." In *Lady Macbeth of Mtsensk and Other Stories*, translated by David McDuff. London: Penguin, 2015.

Lesskis, Natal'ia. "Fil'm *Ironiia sud'by* . . . : Ot ritualov solidarnosti k poetike izmenennogo soznaniia." *Novoe literaturnoe obozreniie* 76, no. 6 (2005): 314–27. https://magazines.gorky.media/nlo/2005/6/film-ironiya-sudby-ot-ritualov-solidarnosti-k-poetike-izmenennogo-soznaniya.html.

Levin, Iurii. *Kommentarii k poeme "Moskva–Petushki" Venedikta Erofeeva*. Graz, Austria: Grazer Gesellschaft zur Förderung Slawischer Kulturstudien, 1996.

Levitin, Mikhail. *Menia ne bylo*. Moscow: Izdanie teatra "Ermitazh," 2005.

Lipovetsky, Mark. *Charms of the Cynical Reason: The Trickster's Transformations in Soviet and Post-Soviet Culture*. Boston: Academic Studies Press, 2010.

Lipovetsky, Mark. *Russian Postmodernist Fiction: Dialogue with Chaos*. London: Routledge, 1999.

Lipovetsky, Mark, Maria Engström, Tomáš Glanc, Ilja Kukuj, and Klavdia Smola, eds. *The Oxford Handbook of Soviet Underground Culture*. Oxford: Oxford University Press, 2024.

Lipovetsky, Mark, and Ilya Kukulin. "'The Art of Penultimate Truth': Dmitrii Prigov's Aesthetic Principles." *Russian Review* 75, no. 2 (April 2016): 186–208.

Lyotard, Jean-François. *The Postmodern Condition: A Report on Knowledge*. Translated by Brian Massumi and Geoffrey Bennington. Minneapolis: University of Minnesota Press, 1984.

Malmstad, John, and Nikolai Bogomolov. *Mikhail Kuzmin: A Life in Art*. Cambridge, MA: Harvard University Press, 1999.

Matich, Olga. *Erotic Utopia: The Decadent Imagination in Russia's Fin de Siècle*. Madison: University of Wisconsin Press, 2005.

Medovoi, Leerom. *Rebels: Youth and the Cold War Origins of Identity*. Durham, NC: Duke University Press, 2005.

Medvedev Zhores, and Roy Medvedev. *Kto sumasshedshii?* London: Macmillan, 1971.

Meeker, Joseph. *The Comedy of Survival*. Tucson: University of Arizona Press, 1997.

Mineeva, Inna. "Neizvestnye fakty iz istorii sozdaniia povesti I. S. Leskova "Skomorokh Pamfalon (Starinnoe skazanie)." *Uchennye zapiski petrozavodskogo gosudarstvennogo universiteta*, no. 7 (2015): 74–80.

Mirchev, A. "Interv'iu s Kurtom Vonnegutom." *Kontinent*, no. 51 (1987): 437–46.

Mogutin, Iaroslav. "Katorzhnik na nive bukvy." *Glagol* 10, no. 1 (1993): 5–18.

Murav, Harriet. *Holy Foolishness: Dostoevsky's Novels and the Poetics of Cultural Critique*. Stanford, CA: Stanford University Press, 1993.

Nabokov, Vladimir. "A Guide to Berlin." In *The Stories of Vladimir Nabokov*. New York: Alfred A. Knopf, 1995.

Nancy, Jean-Luc. Introduction to *Who Comes after the Subject?*, edited by Eduardo Cadava, Peter Connor, and Jean-Luc Nancy, 1–8. New York: Routledge, 1991.

Naylor, Brian. "Read Trump's Jan. 6 Speech, a Key Part of Impeachment Trial." *NPR*, February 10, 2021.

Ngai, Sianne. *Ugly Feelings*. Cambridge, MA: Harvard University Press, 2005.

Nicolosi, Riccardo. "Paranoia, Resentment, and Reenactment: The Russian Political Discourse on the War in Ukraine." *Ab Imperio*, no. 3 (2022): 247–61.

Nietzsche, Friedrich. *The Antichrist*. Translated by H. L. Mencken. New York: Alfred A. Knopf, 1931.

Nissinen, Martti. *Homoeroticism in the Biblical World: A Historical Perspective*. Minneapolis: Augsburg Fortress Press, 1998.

Olssen, Mark. *Constructing Foucault's Ethics*. Manchester, UK: Manchester University Press, 2021.

Ostrovsky, Nikolai. *Kak zakalialas' stal'*. Moscow: Detskaia literatura, 1979.

O'Sullivan, Michael. *Weakness: A Literary and Philosophical History*. London: Continuum, 2012.

Panchenko, A. M. "Laughter as Spectacle." Translated by P. Hunt, S. Kobets, and B. Braley. In Hunt and Kobets, *Holy Foolishness in Russia: New Perspectives*, 41–147.

Paperno, Irina, and Boris Gasparov. "Vstan' i idi." *Slavica Hierosolymitana*, no. 5–6 (1981): 389–400.

Pesonen, Pekka. *Teksty zhizni i iskusstva: Stat'i po russkoi literature*. Helsinki: Helsinki University Press, 1997.

Phillips, Adam, and Barbara Taylor. *On Kindness*. New York: Farrar, Straus and Giroux, 2010.

Platonov, Andrei. *Chevengur*. Moscow: Vysshaia shkola, 1991.

Platonov, Andrey. "On the First Socialist Tragedy." In *Happy Moscow*. Translated by Robert and Elizabeth Chandler, 153–59. New York: NYRB, 2012.

Platt, Jonathan Brooks. "Postsocialist Platonov: The Question of Humanism and the New Russian Left." In *The Human Reimagined: Posthumanism in Russia*, edited by Colleen McQuillen and Julia Vaingurt, 218–43. Boston: Academic Studies Press, 2018.

Platt, Kevin M. F. *Terror and Greatness: Ivan and Peter as Russian Myths*. Ithaca, NY: Cornell University Press, 2011.

Popov, Evgenii. "Kus ne po zubam: Rassuzhdeniia o knige Evg. Kharitonova *Pod domashnim arestom*." *Glagol* 10, no. 2 (1993): 102–5.

Popov, I. A. *Pravoslavie sviatykh i inkvizitorov*. Moscow: Obshchina Pravoslavnoi Tserkvi Bozhiei Materi Derzhavnaia, 2003.

Pushkin, Aleksandr. "Mednyi vsadnik. Peterburgskaia povest'." Polnoe sobranie sochinenii v 16ti tomakh. Vol. 5, 131–50. Leningrad: Izd-vo AN SSSR, 1937–59.

Ready, Oliver. "In Praise of Booze: *Moskva–Petushki* and Erasmian Irony." *Slavonic and East European Review* 88, no. 3 (2010): 437–67.

Reich, Rebecca. *State of Madness: Psychiatry, Literature, and Dissent after Stalin*. DeKalb: Northern Illinois University Press, 2018.

Ribolsi, Michele, Jasper Feyaerts, and Stijn Vanheule. "Metaphor in Psychosis: On the Possible Convergence of Lacanian Theory and Neuro-Scientific Research." *Frontiers in Psychology* 6, article 664 (2015): 1–12.

Richards, Jeffrey. "E. L. Blanchard and 'The Golden Age of Pantomime.'" In *Victorian Pantomime: A Collection of Critical Essays*, edited by Jim Davis, 21–41. London: Palgrave Macmillan, 2010.

Rorty, Richard. Foreword to Vattimo, *Nihilism and Emancipation*, ix–xx.

Rozanov, Vasilii. *Liudi lunnogo sveta. Metafizika khristianstva*. St. Petersburg, 1913.

Rozanov, Vasilii. *Opavshie list'ia*. Moscow: Iurait, 2018.

Rudova, Larissa. "Embracing Eccentricity: Zolushka and the Avant-Garde Imagination." In *A Companion to Soviet Children's Literature and Film*, edited by Olga Voronina, 417–30. Leiden, the Netherlands: Brill, 2019.

Ruskin, John. "The Grotesque in Literature." In *Ruskin as Literary Critic: Selections*, edited by A. H. R. Ball, 135–45. Cambridge: Cambridge University Press, 2013.

Ruskin, John. *Modern Painters*. Boston: Dana Estes, 1955.

Ryan-Hayes, Karen L. "Erofeev's Grief: Inconsolable and Otherwise." In Ryan-Hayes, *Venedikt Erofeev's "Moscow–Petushki": Critical Perspectives*, 101–22.

Ryan-Hayes, Karen L., ed. *Venedikt Erofeev's "Moscow–Petushki": Critical Perspectives*. Bern, Switzerland: Peter Lang, 1997.

Sakharov, Andrei. *Progress, Coexistence, and Intellectual Freedom*. New York: W. W. Norton, 1970.

Salinger, J. D. *The Catcher in the Rye*. New York: Bantam Books, 1964.

Savel'eva, Maria. *Tvorchestvo Andreia Bitova v traktovkakh rossiiskoi i zarubezhnoi literaturnoi kritiki*. Moscow: MGIMO Universitet, 2016.

Savitskii, Stanislav. *Andergraund: Istoriia i mify leningradskoi neofitsial'noi literatury*. Moscow: Novoe literaturnoe obozrenie, 2002.

Schopenhauer, Arthur. *The World as Will and Representation*. Translated by E. F. J. Payne. New York: Dover Publications, 1966.

Shemetova, T. G. *Poetika prozy A. G. Bitova*. Ulan-Ude, Russia: Izd-to Buriatskogo universiteta, 2001.

Shepit'ko, Larisa. "Voskhozhdenie k pravde." *Sovetskii ekran*, no. 1 (1978). https://chapaev.media/articles/8936.

Shtyrkov, Sergei. "The Unmerry Widow: The Blessed Kseniia of Petersburg in Hagiography and Hymnography." In Hunt and Kobets, *Holy Foolishness in Russia: New Perspectives*, 281–304.

Simmons, Cynthia. *Their Father's Voice: Vasily Aksyonov, Venedikt Erofeev, Eduard Limonov, and Sasha Sokolov*. New York: Peter Lang, 1993.

Simmons, David. *The Anti-Hero in the American Novel: From Joseph Heller to Kurt Vonnegut*. New York: Palgrave Macmillan, 2008.

Skoropanova, Irina. *Russkaia postmodernistskaia literatura*. Moscow: Flinta, 1999.

Smirnitskii, Ian. "Fotosimfoniia odnoi zhizni: 75 let kompozitoru Vladimiru Dashkevichu." *Moskovskii komsomolets RU*, January 19, 2009. https://www.mk.ru/culture/cinema/article/2009/01/19/3928-fotosimfoniya-odnoy-zhizni.html.

Smith, Theresa C., and Thomas A. Oleszczuk, *No Asylum: State Psychiatric Repression in the Former USSR*. New York: New York University Press, 1996.

Smola, Klavdia. "Community as Device: Metonymic Art of the Late Soviet Underground," *Russian Literature* 96–98 (2018): 13–50.

Sokolov, Sasha. *In the House of the Hanged: Essays and Vers Libres*. Translated by Alexander Boguslawski. Toronto: University of Toronto Press, 2012.

Sokolov, Sasha. *A School for Fools*. Translated by Carl R. Proffer. New York: Four Walls Eight Windows, 1988.

Sokolov, Sasha. *Shkola dlia durakov*. Ann Arbor, MI: Ardis, 1983.

Sokolov, Sasha. *Shkola dlia durakov. Mezhdu sobakoi i volkom. Palisandriia. Esse*. St. Petersburg: Azbuka, 2011.

Sokolov, Sasha. *Triptikh*. Moscow: OGI, 2012.

Sokolov, Sasha. "Vse tsveta radugi." *Zhizn' slepykh*, no. 9 (1968): 9–11.

Spieker, Sven. *Figures of Memory and Forgetting in Andrej Bitov's Prose: Postmodernism and the Quest for History*. Frankfurt, Germany: Peter Lang, 1996.

Steiner, Lina. *For Humanity's Sake: The Bildungsroman in Russian Culture*. Toronto: University of Toronto Press, 2011.

Steiner, Peter. "Tropos Kynikos: Jaroslav Hašek's *The Good Soldier Švejk*." *Poetics Today* 19, no. 4 (1998): 25–68.

Sullivan, Jill A. *The Politics of the Pantomime: Regional Identity in the Theatre, 1860–1900*. Hatfield, UK: University of Hertfordshire Press, 2011.

Surat, Irina. "Dreams Too Real: For Andrei Bitov's Birthday." *Russian Studies in Literature* 44, no. 2 (2008): 62–76.

Taylor, Millie. *British Pantomime Performance*. Bristol, UK: Intellect Books, 2007.

Terent'ev, Igor'. *Rekord nezhnosti: Zhizn' Il'i Zdanevicha*. Tiflis, Georgia: Izdatel'stvo 41, 1919.

Threadgold, Steven. *Youth, Class, and Everyday Struggles*. London: Routledge, 2018.

Tolstoi, Lev. *Polnoe sobranie sochinenii*. 90 vols. Moscow: Khudozhestvennaia literatura, 1937.

Tolstoy, Leo. *War and Peace*. Translated by Louise and Aylmer Maude. London: Collector's Library, 2004.

Trifonov, Iurii. *Dom na naberezhnoi*. Ann Arbor, MI: Ardis, 1983.

Turgenev, Ivan. "Hamlet and Don Quixote." Translated by Elizabeth Cheresh Allen. In *The Essential Turgenev*. Edited by Elizabeth Cheresh Allen, 547–64. Evanston, IL: Northwestern University Press, 1995.

Turovsky, V. "Liudi i teni," *Komsomol'skaia Pravda*, no. 30 (June 2, 1976): 2.

Tynianov, Iurii. "Pushkin and Tiutchev." *Pushkin i ego sovremenniki*. Moscow: Nauka, 1969: 166–91.

Ushakin, Sergei. "'Chelovek roda on': Znaki otsutstviia." In *O Muzhe(N)stvennosti*, edited by Sergei Ushakin, 7–40. Moscow: Novoe literaturnoe obozrenie, 2002.

Vail', Petr, and Aleksandr Genis. *Shestidesiatye: Mir sovetskogo cheloveka*. Ekaterinburg, Russia: U-Faktoriia, 2004.

Vaingurt, Julia. *Wonderlands of the Avant-Garde: Technology and the Arts in Russia of the 1920s*. Evanston, IL: Northwestern University Press, 2013.

Valentino, Russell Scott. *The Woman in the Window: Commerce, Consensual Fantasy, and the Quest for Masculine Virtue in the Russian Novel*. Columbus: Ohio State University Press, 2014.

Vampilov, Aleksandr. *Utinaia okhota: P'esy*. Ekaterinburg, Russia: U-Faktoriia, 2004.

Vattimo, Gianni. "Conclusion: Metaphysics and Violence." In *Weakening Philosophy: Essays in Honor of Gianni Vattimo*, edited by Santiago Zabala, 400–421. Montreal: McGill-Queen's University Press, 2007.

Vattimo, Gianni. "Dialectics, Difference, Weak Thought." In *Weak Thought*, edited by Gianni Vattimo and Pier Aldo Rovatti, 39–52. Translated by Peter Carravetta. Albany: SUNY Press, 2012.

Vattimo, Gianni. *Nihilism and Emancipation: Ethics, Politics, and Law*. Translated by William McCuaig. New York: Columbia University Press, 2004.

Vergara, José. "The Distorted Images and Realities of Andrei Bitov's Literary Photographs." *Russian Review* 77, no. 2 (2018): 259–78.

Vinogradov, Viktor. *Istoriia slov*. Moscow: RAN, 1999.

Vladiv-Glover, Slobodanka. "The 1960s and the Rediscovery of the Other in Russian Culture: Andrei Bitov." In Mikhail Epstein, Alexander Genis, and Slobodanka Vladiv-Glover, *Russian Postmodernism: New Perspectives on Post-Soviet Literature*, 95–150. New York: Berghahn, 2016.

Vlasov, E. "Bessmertnaia poema Venedikta Erofeeva *Moskva–Petushki*. Sputnik pisatelia." In V. Erofeev, *Moskva–Petushki*, 121–574. Moscow: Vagrius, 2001.

von Bertalanffy, Ludwig. *General Systems Theory: Foundations, Development, Applications*. London: Penguin Press, 1971.

von Hirsch, Marina. "The Illusion of Infinity: Andrei Bitov's Innovative Poetics of Commentary." *Russian Studies in Literature* 44, no. 2 (2008): 77–89.

Vonnegut, Kurt. *Boinia nomer piat', ili krestovyi pokhod detei*. Translated by Rita Rait-Kovaleva. Moscow: Khudozhestvennaia literatura, 1978.

Vonnegut, Kurt. *Letters*. Edited and with an introduction by Dan Wakefield. New York: Delacorte, 2012.

Vonnegut, Kurt. *Slaughterhouse-Five*. New York: Random House, 1991.

Wendell, Susan. "Toward a Feminist Theory of Disability." *Hypatia* 4, no. 2 (1989): 104–24. doi:10.1111/j.1527–2001.1989.tb00576.x.

Wilden, Anthony. *System and Structure: Essays in Communication and Exchange*. London: Tavistock, 1972.

Yurchak, Alexei. *Everything Was Forever, Until It Was No More: The Last Soviet Generation*. Princeton, NJ: Princeton University Press, 2006.

Zdravomyslova, Elena, and Anna Temkina. "Krizis maskulinnosti v pozdnesovetskom diskurse." In *O Muzhe(N)stvennosti*, edited by Sergei Ushakin, 432–51. Moscow: Novoe literaturnoe obozrenie, 2002.

Zeitlin, Froma I. "Playing the Other: Theater, Theatricality, and the Feminine in Greek Drama." *Representations*, no. 11 (1985): 63–94.

Žižek, Slavoj. *Looking Awry: An Introduction to Jacque Lacan through Popular Culture*. Cambridge, MA: MIT Press, 1991.

Žižek, Slavoj. *The Parallax View*. Cambridge, MA: MIT Press, 2016.

Žižek, Slavoj. *The Sublime Object of Ideology*. London: Verso, 1989.

Žižek, Slavoj. *Tarrying with the Negative: Kant, Hegel, and the Critique of Ideology*. Durham, NC: Duke University Press, 1993.

Zverev, A. "Signal predosterezheniia." In *Boinia nomer piat', ili krestovyi pokhod detei* by Kurt Vonnegut, translated by Rita Rait-Kovaleva, 3–18. Moscow: Khudozhestvennaia literatura, 1978.

Index

Index

Index

discourse, 123–26; metaphorical, as symptom of madness, 118, 120, 123–24, 132–33, 139; psychoanalytic (*see* Freud, Sigmund; Lacan, Jacques); subjectivity and, 23, 75–76, 84, 171–73, 195–96n27; in translation, 93, 209n10

Lao Tzu. *See* Taoism

Lawrence, John Shelton, 41–42

"Leaflet, A" ("Listovka"). *See under* Kharitonov, Evgeny

Leninism, 95–96, 217n45. *See also* collectivism; Marxism; socialism; Soviet Union

Lermontov, Mikhail: "A Fairy Tale for Children" ("Skazka dlia detei"), 112–13; *A Hero of Our Time*, 18–19, 22; individualism of, 154, 173–76; "The Prophet" ("Prorok"), 173–74

Leskov, Nikolai: "The Buffoon Pamphalon" ("Skomorokh Pamfalon"), 4–5, 31–32; Origen of Alexandria, allusions to, 4–5, 32; religious censorship of, 31–32; *Tao Te Ching*, connections to, 4–5, 30–32, 193n2, 194n6, 202n46; Tolstoy, correspondence with (*see under* Tolstoy, Leo); weakness, in works of, 4–5, 10, 31–32, 193n2, 194n7

Lesskis, Natal'ia, 37–38

Lessons of Armenia (*Uroki Armeni*). *See under* Bitov, Andrei

Levin, Yuri (Iurii), 104–5, 204–5n83, 214n4

Levitin, Mikhail. See *The Wanderings of Billy Pilgrim* (*Stranstviia Billi Piligrima*, Kim and Rozovsky, dir. Levitin)

"Life in Windy Weather" ("Zhizn' v vetrennuiu pogodu). *See under* Bitov, Andrei

liminality, 121, 128–30, 138–39, 170, 198n22

Lipovetsky, Mark: on Bitov's *Pushkin House*, 169, 232n100; on Erofeev's *Moscow–Petushki*, 96–97, 134–35, 139–40, 215n7, 215n11; on Russian postmodernism, 12–13, 96–97, 134–35, 198n22, 210–11n38; on Sokolov's *A School for Fools*, 134–35, 139–40; on Soviet subjectivity, 38–39, 43

literature: avant-garde, 10, 59–61, 186, 203n61, 208n33; decadent or symbolist, 73–75, 83–86, 122; dissident, 12–13, 48–49, 71–75, 87, 122; experimental, 10–13, 26, 59–60, 186–87, 194n13; futurist, 113–16; gay aestheticism in, 38, 71–79, 83–94; hagiographic, 4–5, 23–24, 31–32; of madness, 117–43; modernist (Russian), 10, 24–28, 85–90, 169, 210–11n38; postmodern (*see under* postmodernism); Romantic, 22, 117, 122, 232–33n109; Russian (canonical), 4–9, 17–24, 39–40, 71–75, 111–15; socialist realist (*see* socialist realism); Soviet era (late), 6–17, 24–26, 50–72, 117–18, 144–50; Stalinist era, 25–26, 33–35, 188, 207n22, 208n33; underground, 6–13, 24–25, 71–72, 87–99, 117–22. *See also* films

— genres of: detective story, 108, 138–39; diaries, 29, 87–88, 160, 165–66, 200n39; epic poetry (*poemy*), 95–116; fairy tales, 46, 54, 57, 60, 183; pantomime, 46–47, 53–54, 59–70, 76, 80–83; poetry, 35, 47, 73–78, 111–17, 122–25; romance, 37, 218n57; theater (*see* theater). *See also* comedy; tragedy

"Literature of Exhaustion, The" (Barth), 9, 49–50

Little Golden Calf, The (*Zolotoi telenok*, Ilf and Petrov), 221n6, 222n14

little men, 10, 15, 21–24, 118, 198n22

little men, examples of. *See* Chekhov, Anton: "The Man in a Case"; Dostoevsky, Fyodor: *Poor People*; Gogol, Nikolai: "The Overcoat" ("Shinel'"); *The Good Soldier Švejk* (Hašek); *I Served the King of England* (Hrabal)

Lot's wife (biblical character), 52–53, 55–56, 66–67. See also *Slaughterhouse-Five* (Vonnegut)

love: ascetic or asexual, 76, 87–89, 212n52; Christian, 23–24, 83–85, 87–89, 110; familial, 106–7, 159, 170; gerontophilic *vs.* pedophilic, 140–41; between men, 76–78, 82–83, 85–88, 94; of nation or state, 86–90, 100–101; of self (*see* egoism; Narcissus; selfishness *vs.* selflessness); as self-annihilation, 153, 170; of women, 35–36, 110–11, 114–16, 140–41, 185

Lyotard, Jean-François, 25, 181, 195n20, 235n128

261

machismo. *See* hypermasculinity; masculinity; strongmen

madness: as artistic sensibility, 117–18, 121–24, 126–28; counterdiscourses of, 117–24; dissidence pathologized as, 15, 117–21, 127, 142–43; genius presenting as, 118, 134–36; institutionalization based on, 117–21, 123–24, 125; metaphorical language, as symptom of, 118, 120, 123–24, 132–33, 139; as self-bifurcation or -fracturing, 121, 125–26, 128–34; stigmatization of, 23–24, 117–24; as strategy under oppression, 117, 120–22; in weak characters, 53–54, 75–79. *See also* disability; fear: phobic; melancholy; paranoia; psychoses; schizophrenia

malleability. *See* flexibility

Malmstad, John, 211–12n48

"Man in a Landscape" ("Chelovek v peizazhe," Bitov). *See under* Bitov, Andrei

"Man in the Case, The" (Chekhov). *See under* Chekhov, Anton

"Manual on Psychiatry for Nonconformists, A" ("Posobie po psikhiatrii dlia inakomysliashchikh," Bukovsky and Gluzman), 120–22, 221n3

marginalization, 71–75, 86, 92–93, 132–34. *See also* Jews; queerness; outsiderhood

"Mark of Illumination, A" ("Znak ozaren'ia). *See under* Sokolov, Sasha

Marxism, 34, 59–62, 72, 95–96. *See also* collectivism; Leninism; socialism; Soviet Union

masculinity: class dynamics of, 40–43, 49–54, 61–70, 78–79, 97; crisis perceived in, 7–9, 17–19, 35–38; critique of as critique of power, 8–9, 34–35; demystification of, 49–54, 61–70; as dissimulation or performance, 35–36, 43, 53–54; femininity, as complement to, 115, 189; hegemonic, 8–9, 14, 33–35, 195n14, 199n29; Hellenistic, 23–30, 84–87, 89, 204n81, 212n49; as heroic or romantic, 8, 22, 50–51, 64–65, 221n2; homosocial, 7, 14, 33–34, 86–91; of the intelligentsia, 7, 27–28, 38–42, 50, 215n16; Nazi models of, 47, 101, 188; nonconformity in, 8–9, 38, 49–50, 103, 129; as phallic or non-

phallic, 63–66, 71, 89, 114–16; queering of (*see* gender subversion; queerness; transvestism); resentment and, 14, 36, 177–78; sacrificial, 35, 41–43, 53; Soviet models of, 8–11, 34–40, 188, 194n11; as totalizing, 47–50, 53–54, 101, 188; U.S. model of, 7–8, 15, 41–42, 48–53, 199n29; war or post-war models of, 40, 54–55, 188–89, 199n23; weak/strong binary of, 8, 14, 40–45, 48–53, 204n81. *See also* femininity; hypermasculinity; strongmen; women

medical discourse. *See under* language

Medvedev, Roy and Zhores, 119, 221n4, 221n7

Meeker, Joseph, 157–58

melancholy, 19, 32–33, 96, 139, 219n64

memory: in confronting the past, 11, 55–59, 155, 168–70, 173; representation of, 56–57, 60–61, 139, 181–82

messianism, 10, 55–56, 77, 204n77

metanarratives. *See* grand narratives; masculinity: as totalizing

Miagkov, Andrei, 37–38

Mikhailov, Yuly (pseudonym). *See* Kim, Yuly

militancy. *See* hypermasculinity; strongmen

mimicry, 130, 136–40, 148, 151–52, 186–87. *See also* pantomime

Mineeva, I. N. (Inna), 31–32

modernism, 10, 24–28, 85–90, 169, 210–11n38

Monakhov (character). *See* Bitov, Andrei: *Flying Away Monakhov* (*Uletaiushchii Monakhov*)

monasticism, 32, 74–75, 86–88, 93, 213n64

Monkey Link, The. See Bitov, Andrei: *The Catechized* (*Oglashennye, The Monkey Link*)

monstrosity, 106, 132–36, 140–42. *See also* abjection; the grotesque; horror; otherness

moral disquietude. *See under* ethics

Moscow–Petushki (*Moscow to the End of the Line*, Erofeev): alcohol consumption in, 38, 95–99, 102–4, 217–18n49; cruelty or vengeance in, 96, 106, 108–10, 219n74; as epic poetry (*poemy*), 95–96; grief in, 106–10, 218–19n59, 219n64; guilt or shame in, 103, 105–

9; individuality in, 98, 101–2, 215n7,
215n11; *IO*, significance of letter in,
109–16, 220n76; sacrificial interpretation of, 96–97, 110–11, 219n74; salvation *vs.* solitude in, 98–99, 105–6,
216n11, 216n23, 219n64; tragic ending
and hero of, 97–98, 100–101, 215n7,
215n16, 219n64; weak subjectivity in,
15, 71, 97–103, 215n7, 217–18n49.
See also Erofeev, Venedikt
Murav, Harriet, 23–24
mutability, 5, 16, 82, 140–41, 168–69. *See
also* flexibility; fluidity; transformation;
weakness
Myshkin (character). *See* Dostoevsky,
Fyodor: *The Idiot*

Nabokov, Vladimir, 138–40
Nagasaki, Japan, 52, 66–68
Napoleon, 28, 31, 64–65, 103
Narcissus, 84–85, 133–34, 141–42. *See also*
egoism; selfishness *vs.* selflessness
national character, 41, 48–49, 75, 89–90,
92–94. *See also* love: of nation or state
nationalism. *See* love: of nation or state
Nazis. *See* fascism
negation, 91–94, 99, 174, 190–91, 217n35
Ngai, Sianne, 36–37
Nietzsche, Friedrich, 11, 85–86, 210n22,
233n111
nihilism, 11–12, 35–36, 103–4, 167,
233n111
N. N. (character). *See* Turgenev, Ivan:
"Asya"
nonbelonging. *See* alienation; otherness
nonconformity: in artists and writers, 72–
75, 100, 120–23, 196n29, 215n16; in
asceticism, 87–88; *vs.* conformity in
characters, 20–24, 129–30, 140, 150,
169; to gender norms, 8–9, 38, 49–50,
103, 129; mental illness, diagnosed
as, 117–23, 127, 129–31; as outside
ideology, 37–38, 98–104; as political
critique, 21, 46–55, 66; Russian masculinity as, 35, 71–76. *See also* dissidence; normativity; pathologization;
queerness
normativity, 23–24, 76–80, 118–32, 142–
43, 190–91. *See also* nonconformity;
pathologization

"Notes from the Corner" ("Zapiski iz-za
ugla"). *See under* Bitov, Andrei
Notes from Underground. See under Dostoevsky, Fyodor
"Notes of a Madman" ("Zapiski sumasshedshego"). *See under* Gogol, Nikolai
nuclear war, 49, 146, 152–59, 180–81

objectification: instrumentality as, 34–35;
of the self, 84–85, 133–34, 141–42; of
weak men or women (*see under* the
gaze)
Oblomov (Goncharov), 19–20
Odoevtsev, Lev (Leva, character). See
Pushkin House (*Pushkinskii dom*,
Bitov)
Onegin, Eugene (character). *See* Pushkin,
Aleksandr: *Eugene Onegin* (*Evgenii
Onegin*)
Ordeal, The (*Sotnikov*, Bykov), 40–45
Origen of Alexandria, 4–5, 32
otherness: abjection of, 41–42, 83, 93–94,
135–36, 142 (*see also* negation); in
antisemitic discourses (*see* antisemitism; judeophobia); coexistence with
or cultivation of, 63, 81–83, 92–94,
115–16, 191–92; internalization of, 23,
36, 111, 151–53, 165; isolation sought
from, 98–99, 103–4, 109–10, 159–60;
openness to (*see* futurity; responsiveness); orientation of subject to, 27–32,
39–42, 139, 160–61, 179–80; perspective of, 66, 179; in psychoanalysis (*see*
Lacan, Jacques); self-estrangement
as, 23–24, 51, 138, 144, 148; uncan-
niness of, 55–56, 135–36, 144; value
measured by, 28–29, 34, 162; of world
outside Soviet bloc, 72–74, 86, 93–94,
138, 169. *See also* alienation; self-other
relation
outsiderhood, 11–12, 24–25, 71–75, 90–94,
190. *See also* alienation
"Overcoat, The" ("Shinel'"). *See under*
Gogol, Nikolai

Palisandriia (*Astrophobia*). *See under*
Sokolov, Sasha
Pamphalon (character). *See* Leskov,
Nikolai: "The Buffoon Pamphalon"
("Skomorokh Pamfalon")

Index

in, 152–54, 162–63, 173–75, 177, 184.
    See also Bitov, Andrei
Putin, Vladimir, 13–14, 221n3

queerness: affirmation of, 81–82, 88; as art
    of failure, 10, 38, 78–80, 94, 134; au-
    thors of (*see* Kharitonov, Evgeny; Kuz-
    min, Mikhail; Rozanov, Vasily; Wilde,
    Oscar); bodily semiotics of, 76; as can-
    onized or sacred, 35, 71–76, 86–90,
    92–93, 213–14n73; in Christianity, 71–
    72, 76–78, 82–89, 211n41; feminin-
    ity as, 52–53, 76–78, 82–85, 188–89;
    of gay aestheticism, 38, 71–78, 83–94,
    122; in holy fool figure, 15, 71–94;
    masculinity as, 8–9, 38, 50, 103, 129;
    of Russian masculinity or sexuality,
    71–76, 86; sexual aesthetics of, 71–72,
    76–79, 82–91, 210–11n38, 210n16;
    as weakness, 78–79, 188–89. *See also*
    gender subversion; transgenderism
quietism. *See* complacency; isolationism

Rait-Kovaleva, Rita, 46, 51–52, 205n5,
    205n6
Ready, Oliver, 217–18n49
Record of Tenderness, The (*Rekord nezh-
    nosti*). *See* Terentev, Igor
redemption, 54–56, 79, 84
reflection: introspective, 13, 42, 47–48; on
    the self, 27–29, 32–33, 42, 99–100,
    173–74 (*see also* ethics: of doubt or
    self-doubt). *See also* truth: questioning
    of; weak subjectivity
Reich, Rebecca, 117, 142–43, 221n4
relationality, 14, 26, 32, 185, 218–19n64.
    See also collectivism; weakness
renunciation, 31–32, 71, 96, 105–6, 184.
    See also asceticism; isolationism; solip-
    sism; weakness
resilience. *See* survival; weakness: resil-
    ience, as source of
responsiveness, 11–12, 15–16, 29–31, 99,
    185–91
retrospection. *See under* the gaze
Reyfman, Irina, 18, 139–41
ritualism, 29, 38, 61, 86, 141
romance (genre), 37, 218n57. *See also* mas-
    culinity: as heroic or romantic

Romantic literature, 22, 117, 122, 232–
    33n109
Rorty, Richard, 11–12
Rozanov, Vasily, 87–92, 97–101, 212n52,
    216n18, 217n35
Rozovsky, Mark. See *The Wanderings of
    Billy Pilgrim* (*Stranstviia Billi Pili-
    grima*, Kim and Rozovsky, dir. Levitin)
Ruskin, John, 134–35
Russia: Crimea and Ukraine, invasion of,
    13–14; film or literature of (*see under*
    films; literature); prerevolutionary,
    17–19, 118, 169; revolution in, 34–35,
    155, 207n26. *See also* Soviet Union;
    Stalinism
Russian Orthodoxy, 23, 73–79, 93–94,
    193n5. *See also* Christianity
Russian Revolution, 34–35, 155, 207n26

sacrifice, 35–36, 40–45, 85–93, 110, 186
Saint John the Evangelist. *See* John, Saint
    (apostle)
Saint Paul. *See* Paul, Saint
Salinger, J. D., 199n29
samizdat (underground publishing net-
    work), 49, 99, 120, 194n13, 207n26.
    See also censorship; dissidence
Sandler, Stephanie, 18, 139–41
Savinkov, S. V, 22, 26, 28
schizophrenia, 52, 56, 118–30, 135, 142–43
School for Fools, A (*Shkola dlia durakov*,
    Sokolov): associative texture of, 120–
    21, 123–24, 128; fantastic elements
    of, 118–19, 132–36; father figures in,
    123–25, 127–30, 132, 139–40; flower/
    river symbolism in, 124, 127–34, 139–
    42, 189, 225n57; grotesque excess and
    hybridity in, 124–25, 127, 132–34,
    139–43; language and subjectivity in,
    132–36, 138–39; Narcissus myth, re-
    prisal of, 133–35, 141; non-linearity or
    prolepsis of, 118–19, 132–33, 135–36,
    140; schizophrenic sensibility of, 118–
    19, 121, 123–28, 135–36, 142; school-
    ing, interpretation of, 121–23; So-
    and-So as narrator or protagonist of,
    118–19, 123–24, 139–40; suppletion
    principle in, 124–26. *See also* Sokolov,
    Sasha

265

Index